HIEROGLYPHIC TEXTS FROM EGYPTIAN STELAE

ETC.

THE BRITISH MUSEUM

HIEROGLYPHIC TEXTS FROM EGYPTIAN STELAE ETC.

PART 10

EDITED BY

M. L. BIERBRIER

ASSISTANT KEEPER IN THE DEPARTMENT OF EGYPTIAN ANTIQUITIES

PUBLISHED FOR
THE TRUSTEES OF THE BRITISH MUSEUM
BY BRITISH MUSEUM PUBLICATIONS LIMITED
LONDON
1982

Published by British Museum Publications Ltd,
46 Bloomsbury Street, London WC1B 3QQ

British Library Cataloguing in Publication Data
Hieroglyphic texts from Egyptian stelae etc.
Part 10
1. British Museum
2. Stele (Archaeology)—Egypt
3. Egyptian Language—Writing, Hieroglyphic
I. Bierbrier, M.L. II. British Museum
493'.1 PJ1097

ISBN 0 – 7141 – 0926 – 6

Composition in Photina by Filmtype Services Limited,
Scarborough, N. Yorkshire, and printed in Great Britain
at the University Press, Oxford by Eric Buckley,
Printer to the University.

Preface

The texts published in this volume belong mostly to the period of the Nineteenth and Twentieth Dynasties. The majority are found on funerary stelae and fragments of tomb decoration, many deriving from Deir el-Medina, the settlement inhabited by the workmen and artists engaged on the preparation of royal tombs. This volume, unlike others in the series, contains some texts found on small objects.

Dr. Morris Bierbrier, Assistant Keeper in the Department, has prepared the textual copies which accompany the photographic plates, and has written the descriptions and commentaries. He wishes to express his gratitude for help received from Dr. Jaromír Málek of the *Topographical Bibliography* in the Griffith Institute, Oxford; also to Professor Silvio Curto of the Egyptian Museum, Turin, for assisting with comparative material, and to Mr. W. V. Davies of this Department who has made many helpful suggestions.

Department of Egyptian Antiquities
18 August 1981

T. G. H. JAMES

Abbreviations

Ann. Serv.	*Annales du Service des Antiquités de l'Égypte.*
Arundale and Bonomi, *Gallery*	F. Arundale and J. Bonomi, *Gallery of Egyptian Antiquities selected from the British Museum.* London, n.d.
Belmore Collection	*Tablets and other Egyptian Monuments from the Collection of the Earl of Belmore, now deposited in the British Museum,* 1843.
Bierbrier, *Late New Kingdom*	M. L. Bierbrier, *The Late New Kingdom in Egypt.* Warminster, 1975.
BIFAO	*Bulletin de l'Institut français d'archéologie orientale.*
Bi. Or.	*Bibliotheca Orientalia.*
BMQ	*British Museum Quarterly.*
Bruyère, *Deir el Médineh*	B. Bruyère, *Rapport sur les fouilles de Deir el Médineh.* Cairo, 1924–53.
BSFE	*Bulletin de la Société française d'Égyptologie.*
Černý, *Community*	J. Černý, *A Community of Workmen at Thebes in the Ramesside Period.* Cairo, 1973.
Černý, *Répertoire*	J. Černý, B. Bruyère, and J.J. Clère, *Répertoire onomastique de Deir el-Médineh.* Cairo, 1949.
Chron. d'Ég.	*Chronique d'Égypte.*
Gauthier, *LdR* III	H. Gauthier, *Le Livre des Rois d'Égypte.* III. Cairo, 1914.
Guide (1922)	*British Museum. A Guide to the Fourth, Fifth and Sixth Egyptian Rooms, and the Coptic Room.* London, 1922.
Helck, *Materialien*	W. Helck, *Materialien zur Wirtschaftgeschichte des Neuen Reiches.* Wiesbaden, 1961–69.
Helck, *Verwaltung*	W. Helck, *Zur Verwaltung des Mittleren und Neuen Reichs.* Leiden, 1958.
Hier. Ostr.	J. Černý and A. H. Gardiner, *Hieratic Ostraca.* Oxford, 1957.
JARCE	*Journal of the American Research Center in Egypt.*
JEA	*Journal of Egyptian Archaeology.*
JNES	*Journal of Near Eastern Studies.*
Kees, *Priestertum*	H. Kees, *Das Priestertum im ägyptischen Staat vom Neuen Reich bis zur Spätzeit.* Leiden, 1953.
KRI	K. A. Kitchen, *Ramesside Inscriptions.* 7 vols. Oxford, 1968 ff.
Lepsius, *Denkmäler* Text	R. Lepsius, *Denkmäler aus Aegypten und Aethiopien.* Text. 5 vols. Leipzig, 1897–1913.
Lieblein, *Dictionnaire*	J. Lieblein, *Dictionnaire de noms hiéroglyphiques en ordre généalogique et alphabétique.* Leipzig, 1871–92.
MDAIK	*Mitteilungen des Deutschen archäologischen Instituts Abteilung Kairo.*
MMA Bulletin	*The Metropolitan Museum of Art Bulletin.*
O. Cairo	J. Daressy, *Ostraca* (Catalogue géneral des Antiquités égyptiennes du Musée du Caire). Cairo, 1901. Nos. 25001–25385.
	J. Černý, *Ostraca hiératiques* (Catalogue général des Antiquités égyptiennes du Musée du Caire). Cairo, 1935. Nos. 25501–25832.
O. DeM.	J. Černý, *Catalogue des ostraca hiératiques non litteraires de Deir el Médineh.* Cairo, 1937 ff. Nos. 1–456, 624–705.
	S. Sauneron, *Catalogue des ostraca hiératiques non litteraires de Deir el Médineh.* Cairo, 1959. Nos. 550–623.
Porter and Moss, *Top. Bibl.*	B. Porter and R.L.B. Moss, *Topographical Bibliography of Ancient Egyptian Hieroglyphic Texts, Reliefs and Paintings.* 7 vols. Oxford, 1927–51. Vols. I-III revised 1960 ff.
Ranke, *Personennamen*	H. Ranke, *Die ägyptischen Personennamen.* 2 vols. Glückstadt, 1935–52.
Rec. trav.	*Recueil de travaux relatifs à la philologie et à l'archéologie égyptiennes et assyriennes.*
Rev. d'Ég.	*Revue d'Égyptologie.*
SAK	*Studien zur altägyptischen Kultur.*
Sculpture Guide (1909)	*British Museum. A Guide to the Egyptian Galleries (Sculpture).* London, 1909.
Sharpe, *Eg. Inscr.*	S. Sharpe, *Egyptian Inscriptions from the British Museum and other sources.* London, 1837–55.
Synopsis (1848)	*British Museum. Synopsis of the Contents of the British Museum.* London, 1848.
Tosi and Roccati, *Stele*	M. Tosi and A. Roccati, *Stele e altre Epigrafi di Deir el Medina.* Turin, 1972.
ZÄS	*Zeitschrift für ägyptische Sprache und Altertumskunde.*

Description of the Plates

Plate 1

Fragments with the name and titulary of Horemheb — 58468a, 58468c, 58469

Date: Late Eighteenth Dynasty
Provenance: El-Amarna
Date of acquisition: 1927[1]
Material: Limestone
Dimensions: 10 cm *h.*, 13.8 cm *l.* (58468a); 10 cm *h.*, 10.6 cm *l.* (58468c); 5.2 cm *h.*, 10.5 cm *l.* (58469)

Three fragments of coarse limestone are incised with parts of the name and titulary of Horemheb and epithets. Fragment 58468a reads ... *Ḥr-m-ḥb mry-ʾImn dỉ ʿnḫ* [*mỉ*] *Rʿ*... The stone is slightly circular and may be part of a pillar base. Fragment 58468c reads *nṯr nfr tỉt Rʿ sw*... Fragment 58469 reads *wr bỉ3wt m*... part of the *nebty* name of Horemheb. Two other fragments, BM 58468b reading *wr bỉ3wt* and BM 58468d reading *mr.f*... *Ḥr-m-ḥb mry-ʾImn*, appear in the register but cannot at present be traced. Together with BM 58468 they are listed in Pendlebury, *City of Akhenaten* III, 12, nos. 26/s 24, 30, 114–17 as belonging to the same monument. However, these fragments are quite distinct in style and material from BM 58468. They may all belong to one monument or several.

Preservation and colour: These pieces are worn in places and heavily pitted. There are no traces of colour.

Bibliography: J. Pendlebury, *City of Akhenaten* III (London, 1951), 12, nos. 26/s 30, 114-17.

1. Presented by the Egypt Exploration Society.

Plates 2–3

1. Statue of Tutankhamun usurped by Horemheb — 37639

Date: Eighteenth Dynasty
Provenance: Not recorded
Date of acquisition: 1903[1]
Material: Schist
Dimensions: 30 cm *h.*, 12 cm *w.* at the shoulders

This fine statue of a king in the Amarna style bears the prenomen of Tutankhamun incised at the centre of the belt of the royal kilt (A). He carries a standard in his left hand on which are the remains of an incised text (B). This text begins with the Horus name of Tutankhamun and also contains a cartouche which has been erased. The back pillar was presumably inscribed at first with the name and epithets of Tutankhamun, but his cartouche has been erased and replaced by the prenomen of Horemheb which has been only partially written and faces the wrong way (C).[2] The inscriptions which replace the original text are exceedingly crude. There is a further erasure at the bottom of the surviving part of the inscription where the nomen should have been, but there does not appear to have been any attempt to replace it.

Preservation and colour: Only the torso and the upper part of the left leg remain and the surviving part has been badly chipped. Most of the standard has been lost.

Bibliography: *Guide* (1922), 126 (no. 58); H. R. H. Hall, *JEA* 14 (1928), 75–6; R. Hari, *Horemheb et Moutnedjmet* (Geneva, 1965), 278–9.

1. Presented by W. McOran Campbell.
2. It is possible that these additions were made in modern times.

2. Base of Horemheb — 58468

Date: Late Eighteenth Dynasty
Provenance: El-Amarna
Date of acquisition: 1927[1]
Material: Limestone
Dimensions: 10 cm *h.*, 55 cm *l.*

This fragment of a statue base is deeply incised along its surviving side with the prenomen of Horemheb with epithets.

Preservation and colour: The left edge of this piece is lost, and the surface of the stone is worn in several places. There are no traces of colour.

Bibliography: H. Frankfort, *JEA* 13 (1927), 210; J. S. Pendlebury, *City of Akhenaten* III (London, 1951), 12, no. 26/s 24 and pl. LX, no. 3; R. Hari, *Horemheb et Moutnedjmet* (Geneva, 1964), 284, no. 33 and pl. L.

1. Presented by the Egypt Exploration Society.

Plates 4–5

Relief of *Ptḥ-ms* (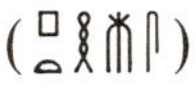) — 160

Date: Late Eighteenth Dynasty
Provenance: Uncertain[1]
Date of acquisition: 1835 (Salt collection)[2]
Material: Limestone
Dimensions: 14.75 cm *h.*, 52 cm *w.*

This relief is divided into two registers with figures in sunk relief and incised texts. In the upper register the royal scribe and overseer of the royal harem, Ptahmose, stands with his arms raised in adoration. Eight lines of text contain a prayer to Reʿ-Harakhty on his behalf. The upper part of this register has been lost.

In the lower scene the god Anubis stands on the left holding the mummy of the lady *Ry* (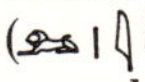). A male figure on the right is pouring a libation over the mummy and behind him stands a lector-priest holding a papyrus roll from which he is doubtless reading the opening-of-the-mouth ritual which is incised above the figures.

Ptahmose is cited on several other monuments. A stela in the Vatican discloses that Roy was the mother of Ptahmose (G. Botti and P. Romanelli, *Le Sculture del Museo Gregoriano Egizio* (Vatican, 1951), 77 and pl. LX). Another stela now in the Metropolitan Museum of Art, New York, gives the name of his father as the military scribe of the lord of the two lands, Iuny (MMA 67.3, see

A. Kamal, *Rec. trav.* 27 (1905), 29–31; S. B. Mercer, *Rec. trav.* 36 (1914), 176–8; Porter and Moss, *Top. Bibl.* I,^{2} ii, 812; *MMA Bulletin* N.S. 26 (October 1967), 62–3). There is also an unpublished relief in the Cairo Museum, JE 90221. The style of the carving dates BM 160 to the late Eighteenth Dynasty. For Ptahmose's title, *ỉmy-r ỉpt nsw*, see D. B. Redford, *The Akhenaten Temple Project* (Warminster, 1976), 107–8.

Preservation and colour: The surviving portion of the relief has been broken in two and repaired in modern times with the loss of a small part of the upper scene. The surface is badly worn especially at the top and bottom edges. There are traces of green or blue paint in some of the hieroglyphs.

Bibliography: *Sculpture Guide* (1909), 178 (no. 642); Porter and Moss, *Top. Bibl.* III^{2}, i, 308; C. Zivie, *Giza au Deuxième Millénaire* (Cairo, 1976), 217, no. 67.

1. The sale catalogue suggests that this piece was acquired near the pyramids, but this provenance is not reliable. There is no evidence that it comes from a New Kingdom cemetery at Giza as postulated by Zivie in *BIFAO* 75 (1975), 285 ff. and *BIFAO* 76 (1976), 17 ff. It may have come from Saqqara which was the main cemetery for Memphis.
2. Lot 1265 in the sale catalogue (Sotheby, 29 June 1835).

Plate 6

Relief of *N3ẖy* ( ) 281

Date: Late Eighteenth Dynasty
Provenance: Thebes[1]
Date of acquisition: 1843 (Belmore collection)
Material: Limestone
Dimensions: 26 cm *h.*, 84 cm *w.*

This relief, possibly a lintel from a tomb, is divided into two scenes. All figures are sunk in relief and the texts are incised in columns above the figures. In the scene on the left side the god Reʿ-Harakhty is seated upon a throne before an altar heaped with offerings. The workman Nakhy and his wife *Nfrt-ỉry* ( ) stand before him with their arms raised in adoration. On the right side Nakhy and his wife appear in an identical scene of worship before the seated figure of Osiris.

The workman Nakhy and his wife are also known from stela no. 50010 in the Turin Museum (Tosi and Roccati, *Stele*, 43–4) and from funerary cones discovered in pit 1138 at Deir el-Medina (Bruyère, *Deir el Médineh (1928)*, 12–16). The relief may have come from that same pit. This workman Nakhy is not to be confused with the workman Nakhy, son of Bukentef, who flourished at the end of the Nineteenth Dynasty or indeed the latter's grandfather, the chief craftsman Nakhy, who comes from a different family; for these individuals see below, BM 1629, pl. 63.

Preservation and colour: Apart from a large gap at the top right of the relief and damage along the edges, the slab is well preserved. There are no traces of colour.

Bibliography: *Belmore Collection*, pl. 4; G. Maspero, *Rec. trav.* 2 (1880), 180; *Sculpture Guide* (1909), 233 (no. 841); Bruyère, *Deir el Médineh (1928)*, 18; Porter and Moss, *Top. Bibl.* I^{2}, ii, 726.

1. Undoubtedly Deir el-Medina on internal evidence.

Plate 7

Stela of *N3ẖy* ( ) 360

Date: Late Eighteenth Dynasty
Provenance: Not recorded[1]
Date of acquisition: 1834 (Sams collection)
Material: Limestone
Dimensions: 23.7 cm *h.*, 16 cm *w.*

This round-topped stela consists of one scene with figures in shallow sunk relief and incised texts. On the left a figure, with a sidelock of youth and a cone upon his head, wearing a broad collar and kilt, is seated on a chair with animal legs. He is holding a lotus-bud in one hand and is stretching the other over a table piled with offerings which stands before him. He is identified as *S3t-p3-ỉr* ( ) by the text which is inscribed above him. A figure stands on the right holding two bouquets before Sitpair, and a line of text at the bottom of the stela indicates that it was made by or for the workman Nakhy who must be the standing figure.

The context of this stela is quite clear but has been badly misinterpreted in the past. Sitpair is in fact the deified Prince Ahmose Sipair who was the subject of a funerary cult after his death (A. Rowe, *Ann. Serv.* 40 (1940), 39–40; M. Gitton, *L'Épouse du Dieu Ahmes Néfertary* (Paris, 1975), 10–11, C. Vandersleyen, *Chron. d'Ég.* 52 (1977), 239–41; F. J. Schmitz, *Amenophis* I (Hildesheim, 1978), 46–9). The spelling Sitpair with the otiose *t* is attested at Deir el-Medina at the end of the Eighteenth Dynasty (see Tosi and Roccati, *Stele*, 50010–11). Several workmen named Nakhy are known (see above BM 281, pl. 6 and below BM 1629, pl. 63), but, as this stela can be attributed on stylistic grounds to the late Eighteenth Dynasty, Nakhy can be identified with Nakhy, the husband of Nefertari, of BM 281, one of whose sons was named Sitpair (Tosi and Roccati, *Stele*, 50010).

Preservation and colour: This stela is well preserved with much colour still remaining. Red paint appears on the bodies of the figures and in the dividing lines between the columns of hieroglyphs. Traces of black paint can be seen in the hieroglyphs and on the chair. There is a touch of blue paint on the collar below Sitpair's right shoulder. The pupils of the eye-sign ( ) are painted in black and not incised.

Bibliography: *Sculpture Guide* (1909), 150 (no. 539); *Hieroglyphic Texts*, VII, pl. 14; Porter and Moss, *Top. Bibl.* I^{2}, ii, 734.

1. Undoubtedly Deir el-Medina on internal evidence.

Plate 8

Stela of *Ty* ( ) 972

Date: Late Eighteenth Dynasty
Provenance: Saqqara[1]
Date of acquisition: 1875 (Harris collection)
Material: Limestone
Dimensions: 73.3 cm *h.*, 46.5 cm *w.*

This round-topped stela bears a scene in sunk relief with incised texts. The High Priest of Ptah, Ty, is seated on the left behind an altar of offerings. On the right stands his son, the lector-priest of Bast, *S3y* ( ), with one arm raised and holding an incense-burner in the other. Beneath this scene there were four horizontal lines of text, of which only two are now partially preserved, containing a prayer to Ptah and Osiris on behalf of the High Priest of Ptah, Ty, son of the God's Father of Ptah, Ḥr (𓅃). The lower part of this stela was already lost when it entered this collection in 1875, but, fortunately, Sir John Gardner Wilkinson made two copies of the text when it was still intact and in the possession of A. C. Harris. A copy based on Wilkinson MSS, xviii, 72, is reproduced with some alternate readings from ix, 140, with the kind permission of the Committee of Management of the Griffith Institute, Oxford, where these manuscripts are now housed.

The High Priest of Ptah, Ty, also called Ptahemhat, is known from several other monuments, all probably from his unlocated tomb at Saqqara (J. Málek, *Göttinger Miszellen* 22 (1976), 43; C. Maystre, *Rev. d'Ég.* 27 (1975), 175–9). A companion stela of almost identical dimensions, once in the Amherst collection, had a similar text with a dedication to Reʿ-Harakhty and Atum (Málek, op. cit., 43–6). The tomb of Ty is usually dated to the reign of Tutankhamun or Ay (A. Schulman, *JARCE* 4 (1965), 55–68; Maystre in *Ägypten und Kusch*, 303). This dating can be reconciled with the Berlin genealogy of the High Priests of Ptah where Ty is said to have flourished in the reign of Horemheb if the suppression of the Amarna pharaohs is taken into account (L. Borchardt, *Die Mittel zur zeitlichen Festlegung von Punkten der ägyptischen Geschichte und ihre Anwendung* (Cairo, 1935), 99 and 104). However, the accuracy of this later account for the Eighteenth Dynasty is questionable since Ty is there described as a son of the God's Father of Amun, Sokaremsaf, whereas the contemporary stelae name his father as the God's Father of Ptah, Hori, unless these references are to one and the same man with two names (as Ty/Ptahemhat had) and two titles.

Preservation and colour: This stela is in a poor state of preservation. The upper part is badly worn and much of the surface of the lower part of the stela is lost. There are no traces of colour.

Bibliography: *Sculpture Guide* (1909), 241(no. 876); Maystre in E. Endesfelder *et al*, *Ägypten und Kusch* (Berlin, 1977), 303–7; Porter and Moss, *Top. Bibl.* III^{2}, 711.

1. Wilkinson MSS, xviii, 72.

Plate 9

Stela of Sethos I — 1665

Date: Nineteenth Dynasty
Provenance: Not recorded
Date of acquisition: 1930
Material: Sandstone
Dimensions: 67 cm *h.*, 55.5 cm *w.*

This piece is the lower right-hand portion of a stela of Sethos I. An unidentifiable part of a scene in sunk relief is at the top of this fragment, and underneath are nine horizontal lines of incised text, part of which concerns the renewal of a religious festival at Thebes.

Preservation and colour: The left edge of this piece is worn and pitted in places, and there is also some loss in the lower right-hand corner. The uneven bottom edge has been restored in modern times. There are no traces of colour.

Bibliography: *BMQ* 5 (1930–1), 19; A. W. Shorter, *JEA* 19 (1933), 60–1 with translation; *KRI* I, 231 (no. 99).

Plates 10–11

Stela of Sethos I — 1189

Date: Nineteenth Dynasty
Provenance: Wadi Halfa[1]
Date of acquisition: 1887[2]
Material: Sandstone
Dimensions: 126.5 cm *h.*, 83 cm *w.*

This fragmentary round-topped stela consists of twelve horizontal lines of text below a main scene. All texts are incised and all figures are in sunk relief. Sethos I is shown on the right of the scene with one arm raised and the other holding an incense-burner. In front of him are two altars on which rest water-pots cooled by lotus-flowers. Facing him are Amen-Reʿ, Min and Isis. The text is dated to Year 1 of Sethos I and commemorates temple endowments. For a closely related text see Louvre C57 in *KRI* I, 2–3.

Preservation and colour: This stela has been broken into several fragments and has been restored in modern times. The surviving portions are worn and chipped in places. There are no traces of colour.

Bibliography: *Sculpture Guide* (1909), 159 (no. 574); Porter and Moss, *Top. Bibl.* VII, 129; *KRI* I, 37–8 (no. 18); H. Smith, *The Fortress of Buhen, The Inscriptions* (London, 1976), 148 and 211.

1. Undoubtedly from Buhen on internal evidence, and, according to Budge, from the South Temple; see E. A. W. Budge, *The Egyptian Sudan* (London, 1907), I, 578 and *By Nile and Tigris* (London, 1920), I, 101–2. However, it is more likely that it comes from Forecourt G of the North Temple where a companion stela of Ramesses I was found; see D. Randall-MacIver and C. Woolley, *Buhen* (Philadelphia, 1911), 86, 96.
2. Presented by Sir Charles Holled Smith.

Plate 12

Inscription of Sethos I — 1103

Date: Nineteenth Dynasty
Provenance: Bubastis
Date of acquisition: 1891[1]
Material: Red granite
Dimensions: 91.5 cm *h.*, 200 cm *w.*

This relief bears a renewal inscription of Sethos I incised in two columns in the centre. On either side of the inscription appears a scene in which Amenophis II is depicted making an offering to Amen-Reʿ who is seated on a throne before two altars on each of which is a water-pot cooled by a lotus-blossom. In the scene on the left the figure of the king and the altars have largely been lost.

Preservation and colour: The relief is well preserved apart from extensive loss on the left side and slight damage to the right edge. There are no traces of colour.

Bibliography: E. Naville, *Bubastis* (London, 1891), 30–1, pl. XXXV(D); *Sculpture Guide* (1909), 214 (no. 773); Porter and Moss, *Top. Bibl.* IV, 30; *KRI* I, 227, no. 98(a).

1. Presented by the Egypt Exploration Fund.

Plate 13

1. Relief of Sethos I — 609

Date: Nineteenth Dynasty
Provenance: Abydos
Date of acquisition: 1902[1]
Material: Limestone
Dimensions: 49 cm *h.*, 64.5 cm *w.*

This finely carved piece in raised relief has a *kheker*-frieze decoration at the top and below the remains of a scene with several columns of text also in raised relief. The protective figure of Nekhbet is preserved almost entirely. At the bottom there are part of the *atef*-crown of the king and part of the double crown of Egypt surmounting the lost figure of *Ḥr-nḏ-ỉt.f*. On the extreme right is part of a standard surmounted by a figure of Wepwawet.

Preservation and colour: Only a fragment of the original scene is preserved, and this is damaged along the edges and badly cracked in places on the surface. There appear to be no traces of colour.

Bibliography: *Sculpture Guide* (1909), 159 (no. 571).

1. Presented by the Egypt Exploration Fund.

2 Fragment with the name of Ramesses II 1102

Date: Nineteenth Dynasty
Provenance: Bubastis
Date of acquisition: 1891[1]
Material: Red granite
Dimensions: 97.5 cm *h*., 100 cm *w*.

This block originally bore the incised prenomen of Sesostris III, but this has been partially erased and replaced by the nomen of Ramesses II which is only partly preserved.

Preservation and colour: The right side of the block has been lost. There are no traces of colour.

Bibliography: E. Naville, *Bubastis* (London, 1891), 9, pls. XXVI(C) and XXXIII(E) where the image is reversed; *Sculpture Guide* (1909), 48–9 (no. 167); Porter and Moss, *Top. Bibl.* IV, 30.

1. Presented by the Egypt Exploration Fund.

3. Relief of Ramesses II 1104

Date: Nineteenth Dynasty
Provenance: Bubastis
Date of acquisition: 1891[1]
Material: Red granite
Dimensions: 100.5 cm *h*., 55.5 cm *w*.

On the upper part of this fragment are incised the prenomen and nomen of Ramesses II. Below this are carved three name-rings of conquered peoples – *'Itr* (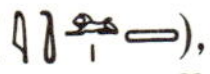), *Mšwš* (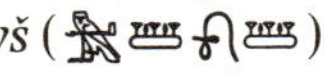) and *Kškš* (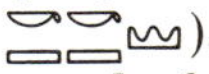). This piece suffered extensive loss both before and after its discovery. A comparison with the photograph of the newly discovered object (Naville, *Bubastis*, pl. XVII) shows that another name-ring – *Sngr* (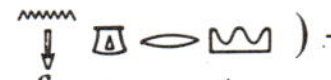) – was preserved on the left of the existing fragment, and traces of another were visible on the right side as well as more of the royal cartouches. The crack on the left, along which the piece later shattered, can be clearly seen. There is no indication that the missing fragments ever reached the British Museum, and they were probably lost prior to transit from Bubastis.

Preservation and colour: The surviving fragment is chipped on the right and left edges where the recent breaks have occurred. There are no traces of colour.

Bibliography: E. Naville, *Bubastis* (London, 1891), 40, pls. XVII, XXXVI (B); *Sculpture Guide* (1909), 162 (no. 586); Porter and Moss, *Top. Bibl.* IV, 31; J. Simons, *Handbook for the Study of Egyptian Topographical Lists relating to Western Asia* (Leiden, 1937), 77 and 163; *KRI* II, 194 (no. 35).

1. Presented by the Egypt Exploration Fund.

Plates 14–15

Stela of Ramesses II 1630

Date: Nineteenth Dynasty
Provenance: Not recorded[1]
Date of acquisition: 1913
Material: Limestone
Dimensions: 61 cm *h*., 48 cm *w*.

This stela consists of six horizontal lines of incised text surmounted by a scene of which the lower parts of three figures in sunk relief remain. The figure of the king on the left stands with raised arms offering wine before Amen-Re' in the centre. Behind the god on the right stands a goddess who clasps the god with one hand. The text outlines certain endowments which the king made for the gods which favoured him.

Preservation and colour: The stela is broken at the top and along the right side with loss to the scene and the main text. There is also a large gouge through the first three lines of text. The left edge has been restored in modern times. There are no traces of colour.

Bibliography: None.

1. Said to come from Thebes.

Plate 16

Offering-table of Ramesses II 1355

Date: Nineteenth Dynasty
Provenance: Not recorded[1]
Date of acquisition: 1901
Material: Black granite
Dimensions: 14.5 cm *h*., 87.6 cm *l*., 46.8 cm *w*. (table); 21.5 cm *l*., 20 cm *w*. (spout)

In the centre of this offering-table is carved in raised relief an altar (*ḥtp*) on which are depicted various food offerings. A channel runs around this centre to carry off liquids by means of the spout at the top of the offering-table. Along the top and side edges of the table are incised once on each side the Horus name and prenomen of Ramesses II (A and B).

Preservation and colour: The offering-table is well preserved apart from a slight break at the left side of the top edge near the spout and some unevenness along the bottom edge. No colour is preserved.

Bibliography: *Sculpture Guide* (1909) 165 (no. 600); Porter and Moss, *Top. Bibl.* II², 443.

1. In *Sculpture Guide* (1909), 165 (no. 600) Budge gives the provenance of this piece as the Ramesseum but elsewhere names Karnak as the find-spot. As the object was acquired through purchase, no firm provenance can be given.

Plate 17

Monument of Ramesses II and Queen Merytamun (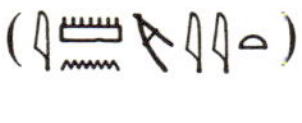) 1662

Date: Nineteenth Dynasty
Provenance: Not recorded
Date of acquisition: 1929
Material: Black granite
Dimensions: 27 cm *h*., 52.7 cm *w*., 90.8 cm *l*.

This rectangular block is incised on one side with the Horus name, prenomen and nomen of Ramesses II and the name of Queen Merytamun (A). Along the other three sides are two inscriptions giving the titles of Merytamun (B and C). The shallow depression at the top of the monument indicates that it was probably the plinth of a statue.

Princess Merytamun is named in the inscriptions of Ramesses II as his fourth daughter, and it is known from Abu Simbel that she was the eldest daughter of Queen Nefertari (Gauthier, *LdR* III, 104–5; C. Desroches-Noblecourt and C. Kuentz, *Le petit temple d'Abou Simbel* (Cairo, 1968), 22–5). She was raised to the rank of queen probably after the death of her mother, although it is not certain whether the marriage to her father was nominal or not. (W. Helck, *Chron. d'Ég.* 44 (1969),22–4). For her monuments see Gauthier, *LdR* III, 104–5, and L. Habachi in Berlin Museum, *Festschrift zum 150jährigen Bestehen des Berliner Ägyptischen Museums* (Berlin, 1974), 103–12. She was buried in Tomb 68 in the Valley of the Queens (Porter and Moss, *Top. Bibl.* 1^2, ii, 765–6).

Preservation and colour: This piece is extremely well preserved apart from some wear to the bottom. There are no traces of colour.

Bibliography: *BMQ* 4 (1929–30), 3; *KRI* II, 925, no. 392(A).

Plate 18

Monument of Ramesses II — 681

Date: Nineteenth Dynasty
Provenance: Not recorded
Date of acquisition: 1905
Material: Alabaster
Dimensions: 12 cm *h*., 38 cm *w*., 65.5 cm *l*.; 3.5 cm *h*., 17 cm *w*., 25.8 cm *l*. (plinth)

This rectangular block on a plinth has been hollowed out in the centre to a depth of 10.5 cm. The Horus name, prenomen and nomen of Ramesses II are twice incised along the sides of the piece together with epithets naming Atum (A) and possibly Horus (B). This block may originally have been the base of a statue or a libation trough.

Preservation and colour: This piece is cracked and broken in several places with severe loss to one side and damage to two corners. It has been restored in modern times. There are no traces of colour.

Bibliography: *Sculpture Guide* (1909), 163 (no. 590).

Plate 19

1. Recumbent lion of Ramesses II — 857

Date: Nineteenth Dynasty
Provenance: Benha (Athribis)[1]
Date of acquisition: 1857[2]
Material: Red granite
Dimensions: 85 cm *h*., 178 cm *l*., 62 cm *w*.

The prenomen and nomen of Ramesses II with the epithet 'beloved like Horus' are incised on the back of this recumbent lion (A). An incised inscription, originally written twice around the base, gives the Horus name, *nebty* name, prenomen and nomen of Ramesses II with the same epithet (B and C). A portion of the left side of the surviving part of the inscription at the corner, which was seen by Lepsius at Athribis on 26 September 1845, is now lost (Lepsius, *Denkmäler* Text I, 221).

For similar inscriptions of Ramesses II from Athribis see P. Vernus, *Athribis* (Cairo, 1978), nos. 39–42. For the use of the epithet *mrwt mỉ Ḥr* and the same epithet with other gods see Vernus, 46 and note 2 for bibliography, with the addition of G. Brunton, *Matmar* (London, 1948), pl. XLIX, no. 16 and pl. LI, no. 18, for a comparable epithet of Ramesses II with Seth.

Preservation and colour: This statue has suffered badly from damp and erosion. The entire front of the lion has been worn away leaving only the back in a good state of preservation. The lower left side of the base on the back has been slightly chipped with loss to the inscription probably during transport from Athribis.

Bibliography: Lepsius, *Denkmäler* Text I, 221; H. Brugsch, *Thesaurus Inscriptionum Aegyptiacarum* (Leipzig, 1883–4), 1223; Brugsch, *Recueil de monuments égyptiens* (Leipzig, 1862–3), pl. X(2); *Sculpture Guide* (1909), 163–4 (no. 593); Gauthier, *LdR* III, 62 (no. CV); Porter and Moss, *Top. Bibl.* IV, 66; *KRI* II, 467, no. 171(e); P. Vernus, *Athribis* (Cairo, 1978), 41 (no. 41).

1. Moved to Cairo in 1851.
2. Presented by the Hon. (later Sir) Charles Augustus Murray.

2. Foundation Deposit Plaque of Ramesses II — 36859

Date: Nineteenth Dynasty
Provenance: Not recorded
Date of acquisition: Not recorded
Material: Basalt
Dimensions: 10.3 cm *l*., 5.7 cm *w*.

This oval- shaped plaque bears the incised prenomen of Ramesses II with the same epithet as BM 857 above.

Preservation and colour: The top left edge of the inscribed surface has been badly chipped. There are no traces of colour.

Bibliography: None.

Plate 20

Part of a monument with the name of Ramesses II[1] — 40966

Date: Nineteenth Dynasty
Provenance: Thebes, Deir el-Bahri
Date of acquisition: 1904[2]
Material: Black granite
Dimensions: 7.5 cm *h*., 19.5 cm *w*., 17.5 cm *deep*

At the top of this fragment are the remains of probably three figures, and below them are incised the names of Ramesses II and Queen Nefertari. There are the remains of four vertical columns of incised hieroglyphs on the front of the piece (A) and three horizontal lines of text on the curved right shoulder (B).

Preservation and colour: The original monument has been badly broken, and only this fragment of the front and right side survives. There are traces of yellow paint in the hieroglyphs on the side.

Bibliography: E. Naville, *The XIth Dynasty Temple at Deir el-Bahari*, III (London, 1913), 6–7, pls. XIC and XVI2; Porter and Moss, *Top. Bibl.* II^2, 395 without BM number; *KRI* II, 849, no. 303(A).

1. Fragments of this monument have been discovered by the Polish expedition to Deir el-Bahri, to be published by Dr. J. Lipińska in the Deir el-Bahri series.
2. Presented by the Egypt Exploration Fund.

Plate 21

1. Falcon with cartouche of Ramesses II 1006

Date: Nineteenth Dynasty
Provenance: Tell el-Maskhuta
Date of acquisition: 1883[1]
Material: Black granite
Dimensions: 95 cm *h.*, 35.5 cm *w.*

A seated falcon on a pedestal behind a deeply incised cartouche containing the nomen of Ramesses II. An incised inscription on the front of the pedestal names the god Re‘-Harakhty. The sides and back of the pedestal are uninscribed.

Preservation and colour: The state of preservation is good apart from the beak which has been broken away. There are no traces of colour.

Bibliography: E. Naville, *The Store-City of Pithom and the Route of the Exodus* (London, 1885), 4, pl. 12; *Sculpture Guide* (1909), 164 (no. 596); Porter and Moss, *Top. Bibl.* IV, 53; *KRI* II, 404, no. 151(B).

1. Presented by the Egypt Exploration Fund.

2. Statue of Queen Nefertari ( ) 1133

Date: Nineteenth Dynasty
Provenance: Not recorded
Date of acquisition: 1893
Material: Black granite
Dimensions: 27 cm *h.*

This fine female head has an incised text on the back pillar which gives the name and titles of Queen Nerfertari, wife of Ramesses II. The queen is wearing a tripartite wig surmounted by double uraei. This piece appears to be part of a group statue, probably a dyad.

For the monuments of Queen Nefertari see Gauthier, *LdR* III, 75–7; G. Thausing and H. Goedicke, *Nefertari* (Graz, 1971); and C. Desroches-Noblecourt and C. Kuentz, *Le Petit Temple d'Abou Simbel* (Cairo, 1968).

Preservation and colour: Only the upper part of the statue is preserved. The top of the crown and the left edge of the back pillar are lost. There are no traces of colour.

Bibliography: *Sculpture Guide* (1909), 99 (no. 344); Porter and Moss, *Top. Bibl.* I², ii, 788.

3. Block with names of Ramesses II 442

Date: Nineteenth Dynasty
Provenance: Giza[1]
Date of acquisition: 1818[2]
Material: Limestone
Dimensions: 47 cm *h.*, 47.5 cm *w.*

Parts of the prenomen and nomen of Ramesses II are deeply incised on this piece of stone. The writing of the nomen can be compared to BM 440 (*Hieroglyphic Texts* 9, pl. 7, and Zivie, *Giza au Deuxième Millénaire* (Cairo, 1976), 194, where the figure of Amun is mistakenly represented by that of a king) and Louvre B 18–19 (Zivie, op. cit., 198, pl. 14), both of which come from Giza.

Preservation and colour: The surface of the stone is worn in parts. Traces of red paint are visible on the stone.

Bibliography: Howard Vyse, *Operations carried on at the Pyramids of Gizeh* (London, 1842), III, 109, pl. A, fig. 5; *Sculpture Guide* (1909), 198 (no. 718); Porter and Moss, *Top. Bibl.* III², i, 37 and 310; C. Zivie, *Giza au Deuxième Millénaire* (Cairo, 1976), 199, note 2 (no. 1).

1. The piece appears twice in Porter and Moss, *Top. Bibl.* III², i – once under Caviglia's finds as that of Ramesses II (p. 37) and once under miscellaneous finds as that of Ramesses III (p. 310).
2. Presented by Capt. G. B. Caviglia. The attribution to Salt in *Sculpture Guide* (1909), 198, is erroneous, the confusion undoubtedly arising as this piece and others were forwarded by Salt on Caviglia's behalf. Howard Vyse, op. cit., 107, mistakenly dates Caviglia's excavations to 1818, whereas the work took place at Giza between March and June 1817 (*The Quarterly Review* 19 (1818), 391–418). The pieces from this excavation arrived at the British Museum in the spring of 1818.

Plate 22

1. Foundation Deposit Block of Ramesses II 49235

Date: Nineteenth Dynasty
Provenance: Not recorded[1]
Date of acquisition: 1910
Material: Faience, blue
Dimensions: 4.8 cm *h.*, 3.1 cm *w.*, 1.8 cm *thick*

The prenomen and nomen of Ramesses II are painted on the upper face of this block (A), while the name of the *sem*-priest, Prince *Ḫ‘-m-w3st* ( ), appears on each side (B,C). The lower face is worn away and may not have been inscribed. The two ends are blank. This piece was purchased in Cairo, and there is no doubt that it forms part of a foundation deposit from Memphis (compare W. M. F. Petrie, *Memphis* I (London, 1909), pl. 19, lower left).

Preservation and colour: The block is chipped on the edges, and the surface is heavily worn in places.

Bibliography: F. Gomaà, *Chaemwese* (Wiesbaden, 1973), 83; J. Weinstein, *Foundation Deposits in ancient Egypt*, 258 (unpublished thesis, 1973).

1. Undoubtedly Memphis on internal evidence.

2. Foundation Deposit Block of Ramesses II 48664

Date: Nineteenth Dynasty
Provenance: Not recorded[1]
Date of acquisition: 1909
Material: Sandstone
Dimensions: 12.5 cm *h.*, 8.6 cm *w.*, 4.1 cm *thick*

The prenomen and nomen of Ramesses II are incised on one side of this block (A) and the name of the *sem*-priest of Ptah, Prince *Ḫ‘-m-W3st* ( ), on the other (B). The edges are uninscribed. This piece was purchased in Cairo in 1909, and there is no doubt that it originates from Memphis (compare W. M. F. Petrie, *Memphis* I (London, 1909, pl. 19, lower left).

Preservation and colour: The block is in good condition. There are no traces of colour.

Bibliography: A. W. Shorter in *Studies to F. Ll. Griffith* (London, 1932), 132; *Guide* (1922), 292 (no. 61); F. Gomaà, *Chaemwese* (Wiesbaden, 1973), 83; J. Weinstein, *Foundation Deposits in Ancient Egypt*, 258 (unpublished thesis 1973); *KRI* II, 897, no. 354(A).

1. Undoubtedly Memphis on internal evidence.

Plate 23

Door jamb of Merenptah 1469

Date: Nineteenth Dynasty
Provenance: Memphis
Date of acquisition: 1908[1]
Material: Limestone
Dimensions: 206.5 cm *h.*, 83 cm *w.*, 40.5 cm *deep* (unrestored)

This massive door jamb is deeply incised on two sides with the names of Merenptah. The outer face (A) bears two vertical columns with only the nomen and epithets of the king now preserved. The columns are divided by a *was*-sceptre, below which are several signs now largely illegible. At the bottom of the jamb is a scene in sunk relief depicting the union of the two lands by two Nile gods. The inner face of the jamb (B) contains one column of text with part of the prenomen, the nomen and epithets of the king. This jamb comes from the western side of the door of the temple of Merenptah at Memphis.

Preservation and colour: Only the lower part of the original jamb is preserved. The middle part of the outer face has suffered badly from erosion. At the time of its discovery the piece appears to have been cut into three sections for transport and later restored with some loss to the inner face. There are no traces of colour.

Bibliography: W. M. F. Petrie, *Memphis* I (London, 1909), 11, pl. 29; *Sculpture Guide* (1909), 303 (no. 1169); Porter and Moss, *Top. Bibl.* III[1], 223.

1. Presented by the Egyptian Research Account.

Plate 24

1. Fragment with cartouches of Merenptah 1826

Date: Nineteenth Dynasty
Provenance: Not recorded
Date of acquisition: 1888[1]
Material: Limestone
Dimensions: 26 cm *h.*, 20 cm *w.*

This fragment bears part of the prenomen and most of the nomen of Merenptah (deeply incised). It possibly originates from Nabesha where Griffith records a limestone block with the name of Merenptah built into a tomb (W. M. F. Petrie, *Nabesheh* (London, 1888), 31 in *Tanis* II).

Preservation and colour: The fragment is well preserved apart from the left edge which is much worn near the break. There are no traces of colour.

Bibliography: None.

1. Presented by the Egypt Exploration Fund.

2. Fragment with the name of Merenptah 36863

Date: Nineteenth Dynasty
Provenance: Serabit el-Khadim
Date of acquisition: 1849[1]
Material: Pink alabaster
Dimensions: 6.9 cm *h.*, 7 cm *w.*

A fragment with part of the prenomen of Merenptah. For BM 14382, another fragment from the same site, see no. 3.

Preservation and colour: The surviving fragment is worn in places. There are traces of blue inlay in the hieroglyphs.

Bibliography: J. D. Cooney, *JEA* 58 (1972), 284.

1. Presented by Major C. K. Macdonald.

3. Fragment with the name of Merenptah 14382

Date: Nineteenth Dynasty
Provenance: Serabit el-Khadim
Date of acquisition: 1849[1]
Material: Pink limestone
Dimensions: 8.7 cm *h.*, 15 cm *l.*, 3 cm *w.*

A fragment composed of two sides of an original block with the nomen of Merenptah on one side (A) and the name of Hathor on the other (B), possibly the remains of a pedestal. For BM 36863 from the same site see no. 2. Several faience fragments with the name of Merenptah were acquired at the same time as the above piece (R. Weill, *Recueil des Inscriptions égyptiennes du Sinai* (Paris, 1904), 220–1).

Preservation and colour: This fragment consists of two pieces broken in antiquity and rejoined in modern times. The fragments are chipped along the edges. Both parts exhibit possible traces of burning. There are no traces of colour.

Bibliography: J. D. Cooney, *JEA* 58 (1972), 284.

1. Presented by Major C. K. Macdonald.

Plate 25

Pillar base of Ramesses III 634

Date: Twentieth Dynasty
Provenance: Not recorded
Date of acquisition: 1904
Material: Alabaster[1]
Dimensions: 12 cm *h.*, 32.5 cm *diam.*

On the front of this circular base are incised the prenomen and nomen of Ramesses III. Two inscriptions around the base (A and B) repeat these names with epithets. For the use of the epithet *ʿn ẖr nḥḥ* under Ramesses IV see L. Christophe, *Ann. Serv.* 52 (1952), 201–14.

Budge supposed that this object came from the temple of Karnak at Thebes, naming alternatively the temple of Ramesses III in Karnak (*Sculpture Guide* (1909), 198 (no. 716)) or the temple of Khons (BM MS Report) as its original location, but its exact provenance remains unknown.

Preservation and colour: The base is well preserved apart from some minor abrasions. There are no traces of colour.

Bibliography: *Sculpture Guide* (1909), 198 (no. 716); Porter and Moss, *Top. Bibl.* II[2], 297.

1. Erroneously described as limestone in *Sculpture Guide* (1909), 198 (no. 716).

Plates 26–27

Statue of Ramesses III 1821

Date: Twentieth Dynasty
Provenance: Tanis
Date of acquisition: 1960[1]
Material: Sandstone
Dimensions: 94 cm *h*., 50 cm *w*. (max.), 62 cm *deep*

The lower part of a kneeling figure of Ramesses III holding before him an offering-table of food and drink. The table is supported by a stand on which the prenomen of the king is deeply incised (A). Two inscriptions ran around the three visible edges of the table, giving the prenomen, nomen and epithets of the king (B and C). The Horus name, prenomen and nomen are incised around the base in two inscriptions (D and E). A single line of vertical hieroglyphs is also cut on the back pillar (F).

Preservation and colour: Only the lower portion of the statue is preserved. The right side of the offering-table and the right-hand of the figure has been lost. The inscriptions along the sides of the offering-table and the base are very worn. There are no traces of colour.

Bibliography: W. M. F. Petrie, *Tanis* II (London, 1888), 29, pl. VII (no. 142); Porter and Moss, *Top. Bibl.* IV, 17.

1. Formerly in Zetland House, Zetland Road, Wallasey, Cheshire.

Plate 28

1. Lintel of Ramesses III 1344

Date: Twentieth Dynasty
Provenance: Not recorded[1]
Date of acquisition: 1901
Material: Limestone
Dimensions: 65.5 cm *h*., 139.5 cm *w*.

At the top of this lintel is a winged sun-disk with two uraei carved in low relief. Underneath are two lines of incised hieroglyphs which repeat the prenomen and nomen of Ramesses III with titles.

Preservation and colour: The lintel has been broken in two and repaired in modern times. The edges and parts of the surface have been damaged and recently restored. There are traces of brown or red paint on the feathers of the winged sun-disk.

Bibliography: *Sculpture Guide* (1909), 198 (no. 717).

1. In *Sculpture Guide* (1909), 198 (no. 717), Saqqara is said to be the provenance of this piece, but there appears to be no definite evidence for this conjecture.

2. Fragment with the names of Ramesses III 38277

Date: Twentieth Dynasty
Provenance: Tell el-Yahudiya
Date of acquisition: 1871
Material: Alabaster
Dimensions: 24.5 cm *h*., 15 cm *w*., 6.5 cm *deep*

This slightly curved piece of alabaster is incised with the prenomen and nomen of Ramesses III and the edge of the *serekh*. It may have come from the side of a basin or altar.

Preservation and colour: The piece is broken with the loss of half the nomen, most of the prenomen and the entire Horus name. The surface is damaged on the right side and bottom. There are no traces of colour.

Bibliography: None.

3. Fragment with the names of Ramesses III 38279

Date: Twentieth Dynasty
Provenance: Tell el-Yahudiya
Date of acquisition: 1871
Material: Alabaster
Dimensions: 14 cm *h*., 19 cm *w*., 7 cm *deep*

This thick curved fragment is incised with parts of the Horus name, prenomen and nomen of Ramesses III. It may have come from the side of a basin or altar.

Preservation and colour: Only the upper portion of this piece has been preserved with losses on both sides. The back surface is rough and broken. There are no traces of colour.

Bibliography: None.

4. Cartouches of Ramesses III 11753

Date: Twentieth Dynasty
Provenance: Tell el-Yahudiya
Date of acquisition: 1876 and 1880
Material: Limestone
Dimensions: 9.8 cm *diam*.

This fragment in the shape of a rounded knob has the prenomen and nomen of Ramesses III deeply incised on its face.

Preservation and colour: This piece is composed of two separate fragments which entered the collection at different times and have been joined together. Part of the left edge is still lacking. The polished surface has worn thin on the base of the object and on the right edge of the face. Traces of inlay whose colour has now faded can be seen in certain hieroglyphs.

Bibliography: *Guide* (1922), 271 (no. 122).

Plate 29

Statue of Ramesses IV 1816

Date: Twentieth Dynasty
Provenance: Not recorded
Date of acquisition: 1958 (Chute collection)[1]
Material: Schist
Dimensions: 68.3 cm *h*., 25.5 cm *w*., 20 cm *deep* (unrestored)

A kneeling figure of Ramesses IV wearing the *nemes* head-dress and *shendyt* kilt. On his right shoulder is incised his prenomen (A1), and his nomen is carved on his left shoulder (A2). His prenomen is also incised in an oval in the centre of the girdle of his kilt (A3). The back pillar bears two columns of incised hieroglyphs giving the king's names with epithets (B). Fragments of the king's name and titles remain on the right (C) and left (D) sides of the base. At the top of the base there are the remains of inscriptions on the right and left sides (E and F).

Preservation and colour: The front part of the statue including the front of the base, knees and hands of the figure are lost and have been restored in recent times with a *nw*-bowl in each hand. The rear of the base and the bottom of the back pillar have also been lost and recently restored. The nose and uraeus of the figure have been damaged. The surviving portion of the back pillar is worn in places. There are no traces of colour.

Bibliography: C. W. Chute, *A History of the Vyne in Hampshire* (Winchester, 1888), 160; *BMQ* 22 (1960), 75–7.

1. The statue entered the Chute collection prior to 1754 when it is mentioned in an inventory, and it may have been acquired in Italy in the early eighteenth century.

Plates 30–31

1. Pyramidion of the God's Adorer 3st (𓊨𓏏𓆇)　　1742

Date: Twentieth Dynasty
Provenance: Not recorded
Date of acquisition: 1930[1]
Material: Limestone
Dimensions: 382 cm *h.*, 43 cm *w.*, 7.5 cm *deep*

The pyramidion bears on its principal surviving face three columns of incised text of which the middle column names the God's Wife of Amun, the King's Daughter, the God's Adorer Isis (A). On either side of the royal cartouche the princess, carved in sunk relief, is shown kneeling with her arms raised in adoration. The preserved portions of the other two sides each bear similar representations of the princess and the remains of a column of text (B and C).

The God's Adorer Isis, daughter of Ramesses VI and Queen Nubkhesbed, is known from a stela (now Manchester 781) found at Coptos (W. M. F. Petrie, *Koptos* (London, 1896), pl. XIX) and an inscription, now lost, from Deir el-Bakhît which recorded her installation as God's Wife under Ramesses VI (Lepsius, *Denkmäler* Text III, 101; J. Černý, *JEA* 44 (1958), 31–2; K. Seele, *JNES* 19 (1960), 192–7; J. Monnet, *BIFAO* 63 (1965), 214–16; K. A. Kitchen, *JEA* 58 (1972), 189–91).[2] Since Isis is not recorded as having married and was installed in office in the lifetime of her father, she may have been one of the first God's Wives to remain a celibate priestess (C. Sander-Hansen, *Das Gottesweib des Amun* (Copenhagen, 1940); J. Yoyotte, *BSFE* 64 (1972), 42–3). The tomb from which this piece presumably derived has not been located but probably lies in the Theban area. An alabaster cup inscribed for the God's Adorer Isis may also have come from the same location (H. W. Muller, *Ägyptische Kunstwerke, Kleinfunde und Glas in der Sammlung E. und M. Kofler-Truniger, Luzern* (Berlin/Munich, 1964), no. A143).

Preservation and colour: This piece consists of the lower portion of the pyramidion. Only one side has been preserved entirely in width, while the two adjoining sides are fragmentary. The preserved portion is pitted in places. There are no traces of colour, but the plaster covering the hard stone has gone yellow.

Bibliography: None.

1. Presented by Sir Robert Mond.
2. B. Schmitz, *Untersuchungen zum Titel S3-Njswt 'Königssohn'* (Bonn, 1976), 314, 322, note 4, differentiates between Isis, daughter of Ramesses IV, and Isis, daughter of Ramesses VI, whereas present research has shown that the existence of the former is unlikely (Monnet, *BIFAO* 63 (1965), 215–26; Kitchen, *JEA* 58 (1972), 190–91).

2. Fragment with the name of the God's Adorer 3st (𓊨𓏏𓆇)　　481

Date: Twentieth Dynasty
Provenance: Not recorded
Date of acquisition: Not recorded
Material: Limestone
Dimensions: 12 cm *h.*, 13.5 cm *w.*

The cartouche of the God's Adorer Isis flanked by uraei appears in raised relief on the left side of this fragment. On either side of the name is a design consisting of an *udjat*-eye above a basket. The remains of a figure wearing a wig and double crown can be seen on the right.

For the God's Adorer Isis, daughter of Ramesses VI, see BM 1742, no. 1 (above).

Preservation and colour: Only a fragment of the original piece survives. It is heavily blackened, possibly through fire.

Bibliography: *Synopsis* (1848), 184, (no. 481).

3. Relief of Ramesses VI　　1711

Date: Twentieth Dynasty
Provenance: Armant
Date of acquisition: 1929[1]
Material: Limestone
Dimensions: 49 cm *h.*, 36.5 cm *w.*

This fragment of a scene depicts the head and shoulders of Ramesses VI in raised relief. The king, who wears the Blue Crown, faces right and raises one arm in adoration. The other hand is lost. At the extreme right the upper part of a *was*-sceptre is shown in the lower corner. Above the king a sun-disk with two uraei is carved in sunk relief. Three vertical lines of hieroglyphs name Behdet, the great god, and the prenomen and nomen of the king.

Preservation and colour: Only a fragment of the original scene is preserved. The top, bottom and right edges are broken and uneven. Traces of red paint remain on the face of the king and certain hieroglyphs and areas of the relief still preserve a coating of white plaster.

Bibliography: R. Mond and O. H. Myers, *The Bucheum* (London, 1934), II, 51, and III, pl. LV (no. 52); Porter and Moss, *Top. Bibl.* V, 159.

1. Presented by the Egypt Exploration Society.

Plate 32

Monument of P3-sr (𓏤𓈖𓊪𓋴𓂋)　　35628

Date: Nineteenth Dynasty
Provenance: Not recorded
Date of acquisition: Not recorded
Material: Glazed composition, grey
Dimensions: 9.3 cm *h.*, 15.5 cm *w.*

The figures and text which appear on both sides of this plaque (?) are deeply cut and inlaid with white glaze. The feet and lower part of a *was*-sceptre of a standing god are preserved on the left of one side facing the lower part of a standing figure in a long kilt, probably the god Amun being adored by Paser. Below the figures is a text which gives the name and titles of Paser (A). On the other side of this piece the figure of an official, doubtless Paser, appears on the left, and three columns of text on the right contain the name and titles of Paser, as does a horizontal line of text at the bottom (B).

The vizier Paser, son of the High Priest of Amun, Nebnetjeru, entered office under Sethos I and was still functioning as vizier in Year 21 of Ramesses II. Between Years 21 and 30 he was appointed to his father's office (E. Edel, *SAK* 1 (1974), 131–2; Helck, *Verwaltung*, 311–15). He was the owner of Tomb 106 in the Theban necropolis (*KRI* I, 285–301). A list of his monuments can be conveniently consulted in Helck, *Verwaltung*,

447–51; J. Černý, *Bi. Or.* 19 (1962), 142; and *KRI* III, 1–36. See also BM nos. 687, 510 and 954 in *Hieroglyphic Texts*, 9, pls. 10–11.

Preservation and colour: Only the lower portion of this piece is intact, and parts of the surface and inlaid glaze have been lost. The white inlay that remains has gone brown in places.

Bibliography: None.

Plates 33–35

Statue of *Ḫ‘-m-W3st* ( ) 947

Date: Nineteenth Dynasty
Provenance: Asyut
Date of acquisition: 1866[1]
Material: Breccia
Dimensions: 138 cm *h.*, 43.1 cm *w.*, 55 cm *deep*

This fine statue of Prince Kha‘emwese, son of Ramesses II, depicts him as a standing figure in a short wig, with vertical striations, which covers the ears and a kilt, holding a standard in each hand. The one in his right hand, which is damaged, probably was surmounted by the Osirian triad, while that in his left is surmounted by the fetish of Abydos. The standard in the right hand is incised with the prenomen of Ramesses II and epithets (A1), while that in the left hand bears his nomen with epithets (A2). The inscription around the base contains a prayer to Atum on behalf of Prince Kha‘emwese (B). There is also an inscription in five columns on the top of the base describing the setting up of this monument in *Ta-wer*, probably at Abydos (C). There are two vertical lines of text on the back pillar containing prayers to Osiris, one of which continues on the left side of the statue (D) and the other on the right side (E). From internal evidence it appears that this statue was originally erected at Abydos. For Prince Kha‘emwese and his monuments see F. Gomaà, *Chaemwese* (Wiesbaden, 1973), and *KRI* II, 871–99.

Preservation and colour: The top of the standard in the right hand and the prince's beard have been broken off. There are several holes in the body caused by the falling out of small pebbles from the agglomerate stone. The top of the left front of the base and the lower rear corners of the base are damaged, and the bottom of the base is uneven. A section of the right side and back of the statue has been cut away and lost. A similar cut was made on the left side and back, but the piece which was removed has been restored with slight loss to the inscriptions. There are no traces of colour.

Bibliography: F. Teynard, *Égypte et Nubie* (Paris, 1858), I, pl. 18; *Sculpture Guide* (1909), 170 (no. 615); E. A. W. Budge (ed.), *Egyptian Sculptures in the British Museum* (London, 1914), 18, pl. 36; Shorter in *Studies Presented to F. Ll. Griffith* (London, 1932), 128–32; Porter and Moss, *Top. Bibl.* IV, 268; F. Gomaà, *Chaemwese* (Wiesbaden, 1973), 86, no. 60; J. Vandier, *Manuel d'Archéologie égyptienne* III (Paris, 1958), 474, pl. clxviii, 1. 4; *KRI* II, 889–90 (no. 343).

1. Presented by Samuel Sharpe. In 1850 this statue was in the possession of Dr. Charles Cuny of Asyut (1811–58) (F. Teynard, *Égypte et Nubie* (Paris, 1858), I, 7). In 1862 it was owned by E. A. Diamandidi, a former business associate of Cuny, from whom it was purchased by Sharpe in order to present it to the British Museum.

Plates 36–39

1. Statue of *Ḥri* ( ) 845

Date: Nineteenth Dynasty
Provenance: Not recorded
Date of acquisition: 1859[1]
Material: Limestone
Dimensions: 33 cm *h.*, 17 cm *w.*, 31.5 cm *deep*

The lower part of a kneeling statue holding before it a naos in which is a figure of the god Ptah. Two dedications to Ptah on behalf of the High Priest of Ptah, Hori, are lightly incised around the front of the naos (A and B). His name and titles appear again on the front base of the naos (C) and on the top of the naos (D). On the right side of the naos is incised an invocation to Hathor (E) on behalf of the High Priest of Ptah, Hori, son of the High Priest of Ptah, *Ḫ‘-m-W3st* ( ), made by his son the *w‘b*-priest and lector-priest of Ptah, *Wr-ḫrp-ḥmww* or *Ḥmww-wr-sḫm* ( ).[2] A standing figure of this son with arms raised in adoration is carved in sunk relief on the left side of the naos with an incised text giving his name and titles (F).[3] The name and titles of Hori can be seen on the back pillar (G).

The High Priest of Ptah, Hori, son of Prince Kha‘emwese and grandson of Ramesses II, is known from several scattered monuments, possibly from his tomb at Saqqara (J. Quibell, *Excavations at Saqqara (1908–9, 1909–10)* (Cairo, 1912), pl. LXX, 1–3; G. Roeder, *Aegyptische Inscriften aus der Staatlichen Museen zu Berlin* II (Leipzig, 1924), 361–7; Maystre, *Ann. Serv.* 48 (1948), 449–55; H. de Meulenaere, *Annuaire de l'Institut de Philologie et d'Histoire orientales et slaves*, 20 (1968–72), 191–8; Porter and Moss, *Top. Bibl.* III², 703–4; *KRI* III, 414–15). These include two canopic jars (BM 36530 and BM 36535). It is not known when Hori was in office, but he probably succeeded his father at the end of the reign of Ramesses II. His son, Hori the younger, is attested as a vizier under Sethos II and was still in office under Ramesses III (Helck, *Verwaltung*, 328–30, 460–3, corrected by De Meulenaere, op. cit. 191–8). His wife Setka, his son Hori the younger, another son Kem and three daughters are named on a stela (Maystre, *Ann. Serv.* 48 (1948), 450–1), but Werkherphemu appears to be otherwise unknown.

Preservation and colour: The upper part of the statue comprising the head and torso is lost. The surviving portion is badly worn in places and heavily pitted. There are no traces of colour.

Bibliography: *Sculpture Guide* (1909), 240 (no. 879); De Meulenaere, op. cit., 196.

1. Purchased from T. O. Feetham.
2. For the alternative reading of the title from which the name derives see De Meulenaere in Berlin Museum, *Festschrift zum 150jährigen Bestehen des Berliner Ägyptischen Museums* (Berlin, 1974), 183–4 and, opposed to his interpretation, H. G. Fisher, *Egyptian Studies* I: *Varia* (New York, 1976), 66–7.
3. For the use of the sign to write *n* before Ptah see Kees, *ZÄS* 74 (1938), 109–13; *ZÄS* 77 (1942), 55–6.

Plates 38–39

2. Bust of a royal prince 68682

Date: Nineteenth Dynasty
Provenance: Not recorded
Date of acquisition: 1976
Material: Black granite
Dimensions: 26.5 cm *h.*, 21 cm *w.*

The upper part of a naophorous or theophorous statue of a Ramesside prince wearing a short round wig with a sidelock. The back pillar is incised with the titles *[rp]ʿ ḥry-tp t3wy sš-nsw ỉmy-r mšʿ [wr ...*]. Only two royal princes are so far known with this exact style of titulary: Merenptah, son of Ramesses II (Gauthier, *LdR* III, 96 (no. Hb)) and Merenptah's son, the future Sethos II (Gauthier, *LdR* III, 126 (no. B) corrected by Christophe, *Ann. Serv.* 51 (1951), 340).

Preservation and colour: The head, shoulders and part of the upper arms are preserved. The beard is broken and the nose and upper part of the back pillar are damaged.

Bibliography: V. Davies in *The British Museum Society Bulletin* 23 (Nov. 1976), 21–2; J. Bourriau, *JEA* 64 (1978), 125 (no. 65).

3. Foundation Deposit of *Nb-wnn-f* — 57690

Date: Nineteenth Dynasty
Provenance: Not recorded[1]
Date of acquisition: 1924[2]
Material: Limestone
Dimensions: 11.2 cm *h.*, 6.7 cm *w.*, 4.5 cm *thick*

On the face of this block are incised the name and titles of the High Priest of Amun, Nebwenenef. The block originally formed part of the foundation deposit of the mortuary temple of Nebwenenef at Thebes (W. M. F. Petrie, *Qurneh* (London, 1909), 14–15 and pl. XXXIII; Porter and Moss, *Top. Bibl.* II^2, 421; H. Stewart, *Egyptian Stelae, Reliefs and Paintings from the Petrie Collection* (Warminster, 1976), 58; *KRI* III, 291 (no. 2).

For Nebwenenef see BM 1820 below, pl. 40.

Preservation and colour: The block is slightly cracked and chipped about the edges.

Bibliography: None

1. Undoubtedly Thebes on internal evidence.
2. Presented by Professor P. E. Newberry.

4. Plaque of *P3-ḥm-nṯr* — 59259

Date: Nineteenth Dynasty
Provenance: Not recorded
Date of acquisition: 1929
Material: Alabaster
Dimensions: 8 cm *h.*, 4 cm *w.*

This plaque is incised on one side with the name and titles of the High Priest of Ptah, Pahemnetjer. Several high priests of this name are known at this period (Kees, *Priestertum*, 111–13; B. Peterson, *Medelhavsmuseet Bulletin* 5 (1969), 13–14; *Hieroglyphic Texts*, 9, pl. 15; *KRI* III, 411–14). This piece was acquired in Luxor, but its exact provenance remains unknown.

Preservation and colour: The plaque is badly chipped along the edges. There are no traces of colour.

Bibliography: None.

Plate 40

Relief of *Nb-wnn·f* — 1820

Date: Nineteenth Dynasty
Provenance: Thebes
Date of acquisition: 1959 (Nash collection)
Material: Limestone
Dimensions: 69 cm *h.*, 35 cm *w.*

This fine relief depicts the overseer of the prophets of all the gods and High Priest of Amun, Nebwenenef, in an attitude of adoration. The figure of the High Priest is cut in raised relief and the hieroglyphs are incised. The High Priest of Amun, Nebwenenef, was appointed in Year 1 of Ramesses II and was the owner of Tomb 157 in Dra Abu el-Naga on the western bank of the Nile (G. Lefebvre, *Histoire des grands prêtres d'Amon* (Paris, 1929), 117–23, 248–9; K. Sethe, *ZÄS* 44 (1907), 30–5; *KRI* III, 282–91). This relief originates from this tomb, and from a copy taken prior to its removal it can be seen that Nebwenenef was worshipping the Djed-pillar in a scene in the entrance hall (Lepsius MSS, 226–7 cited by Porter and Moss, *Top. Bibl.* I^2, 267).

It is unlikely that the royal scribe and general Nebwenenef of BM 357 can be identified with the High Priest Nebwenenef who possessed neither of these titles, the latter of which has been erroneously assigned to him in the past (Sethe, *ZÄS* 44 (1907), 22; *Hieroglyphic Texts* 9, 57, pl. 44; Yoyotte and J. López, *Bi. Or.* 26 (1969), 13 (no. 348c)).

Preservation and colour: The relief has been broken in two and repaired. The right side has also been damaged probably on removal from the tomb. Traces of red, blue and green paint survive on the hieroglyphs and dashes of red paint on the skirt of Nebwenenef.

Bibliography: I. E. S. Edwards, *BMQ* 23 (1960–1), 10–11 and pl. V; Porter and Moss, *Top. Bibl.* I^2, ii, xxi; *KRI* III, 291, no. 1(j).

Plate 41

Stela of *St3w* — 556

Date: Nineteenth Dynasty
Provenance: Not recorded
Date of acquisition: 1839 (Anastasi collection)[1]
Material: Sandstone
Dimensions: 76 cm *h.*, 58.5 cm *w.*

This stela is in the form of a doorway with a cavetto-cornice, on which are incised the name and titles of Setau, and a torus moulding at the top. Standard offering-texts to Reʿ-Harakhty, Hathor, Wepwawet-Thoth and Anubis on behalf of Setau are incised on the lintel and jambs. Two scenes appear on the body of the stela with figures in sunk relief and incised texts. In the upper scene the festival-leader of Amun, Setau, stands on the right with his arms raised in adoration. On the left Reʿ-Harakhty is seated on a throne behind which stands the goddess Hathor. A table piled with offerings is placed between Setau and the seated god. In the lower scene Setau, on the right, is offering incense and pouring a libation over an altar piled with offerings. Osiris is enthroned on the left, and in front of him stand a lotus-flower on which are the four sons of Horus and a feather fan on a small table. For this Setau who later became viceroy of Nubia see BM 78, pls. 42–3.

Preservation and colour: The top right corner of the stela has been broken off and restored in modern times. The bottom is damaged and there are several breaks on its surface. There are no traces of colour.

Bibliography: *Sculpture Guide* (1909), 189 (no. 679); *KRI* III, 80, no. 42(1).

1. The attribution to the Salt collection in *Sculpture Guide* (1909), 189 (no. 679) is erroneous.

Plates 42–43

Sarcophagus Lid of St3w (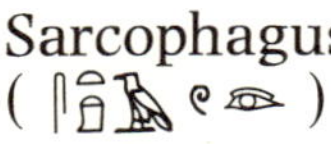) 78

Date: Nineteenth Dynasty
Provenance: Thebes[1]
Date of acquisition: 1823 (Salt collection)
Material: Red granite
Dimensions: 232 cm *h.*, 83 cm *w.*

A massive anthropoid sarcophagus lid inscribed with texts for the viceroy of Kush, Setau. On the lid, beneath the head, is a seated figure of Nut, who is named (A), and beneath this a single column of text with a prayer to Nut on behalf of Setau (B). A line of text runs around the edge of the lid below the shoulders, interrupted at intervals by short lines of text inscribed at right angles to the main line, creating six panels on the lower half of the lid. The main text consists of two balancing inscriptions which begin at each shoulder, both containing standard sarcophagus texts addressed to Geb (C) and Nut (D). The transverse bands of text, five on each side, presumably continued from the lid down the sides of the sarcophagus which is now lost. In the four upper texts on each side Setau, whose name is lost, is described as a person revered before various funerary and canopic deities: on one side [name lost] either Hapy or Amsety (E), Anubis (F), Duamutef (G) and Geb (H); and on the other side [name lost] either Hapy or Amsety (J), Anubis (K), Qebhsenuef (L) and Dunanwy (M). The fifth transverse line on each side contains the name and titles of Setau (I and N).

The six panels on the lower part of the sarcophagus contain figures in sunk relief and incised texts. In the upper four panels Setau is shown adoring various deities before each of whom is an altar with offerings: Osiris in the upper two scenes (O and P); Anubis (Q) and Hapy (R) in the lower scenes. The two panels at the foot of the coffin depict, in opposite order to the rest of the scenes and inscriptions, the goddesses Isis (S) and Nephthys (T) in an attitude of mourning.

The viceroy of Kush, Setau, son of Siwadjyt and An, is attested on many monuments (G. Reisner, *JEA* 6 (1920), 41–4; H. Gauthier, *Rec. trav.* 39 (1921), 209–13; L. Habachi in *Cahier d'histoire égyptienne* x (1966), 53 ff.; K. A. Kitchen in *Orientalia Lovaniensia Periodica* 6/7 (1975–6), 295–302; W. Helck, *SAK* 3 (1975), 85–112, with a list of monuments on 111–12 of which nos. 3 and 4 = BM 78 (the reference to a pyramidion results from a misreading of Lepsius, *Denkmäler* Text v, 391 where this inaccurate description refers to BM 61); Habachi, *JARCE* 13 (1976), 113–14; Schulman, *The SSEA Journal* 8 (1978), 42–5; *KRI* III, 80–111). Setau appears to have been of Theban origin and, prior to his viceregal appointment, held the rank of chief steward of Amun at Thebes. He held office in Kush at least from Years 38 to 44 of Ramesses II. He was buried in Tomb 289 of the Theban necropolis together with his wife Nefretmut who may have originated from El-Kâb (Porter and Moss, *Top. Bibl.* I², I, 369–72; R. Drenkhahn, *SAK* 3 (1975), 43–8). The BM collection possesses a *shabti* of Setau, BM 33921.

Preservation and colour: The lid has been broken in two and rejoined in modern times. The foot of the lid is damaged and the foot-end is lost. There are no traces of colour.

Bibliography: *Sculpture Guide* (1909), 199 (no. 720); Reisner, *JEA* 6 (1920), 43; Gauthier, *Rec. trav.* 39 (1921), 211; *KRI* III, 81, no. 42 (3); Porter and Moss, *Top. Bibl.* I², ii, xxii.

1. Undoubtedly from Tomb 289 at Dra Abu el-Naga. The lid was discovered by Drovetti in a tomb at Qurna and examined by Belzoni in 1816 and was removed by him from Thebes in 1817 (G. Belzoni, *Narrative of the Operations and Recent Discoveries in Egypt and Nubia*, 3rd edn. (London, 1822), I, 46–7, 80–5, 287). The shattered sarcophagus was presumably left in the tomb.

Plates 44–45

1. Relief of *St3w* (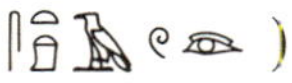) 1055

Date: Nineteenth Dynasty
Provenance: Wadi Halfa[1]
Date of acquisition: 1887[2]
Material: Sandstone
Dimensions: 47.5 cm *h.*, 41.5 cm *w.*

This rock relief in the form of a round-topped stela depicts the viceroy of Kush, Setau, on the right pouring a libation over an altar and offering incense to the goddess Renenutet who in the form of a serpent is seated upon a *neb*-basket on a pedestal. Behind her on the extreme left is a cartouche with the prenomen of Ramesses II. All figures are in sunk relief and the texts are deeply incised.

For Setau see above BM 78, pls. 42–3. For Renenutet see J. Broekhuis, *De Godin Renenwetet* (1971).

Preservation and colour: The relief is well preserved and there are no traces of colour.

Bibliography: *Sculpture Guide* (1909), 168 (no. 608); Porter and Moss, *Top. Bibl.* VII, 141; W. Helck, *SAK* 3 (1975), 112 (no. 38); J. Broekhuis, *De Godin Renenwetet* (1971), 24–5 (no. 31); *KRI* III, 109, no. 55 (56).

1. According to Budge, *The Egyptian Sudan* (London, 1907) I, 578, and *By Nile and Tigris* (London, 1920) I, 101–2, from the Temple of Tuthmosis III at Buhen, but his other attributions to this temple are possibly erroneous and thus this provenance is uncertain; see above, BM 1189, pls. 10–11.
2. Presented by General Sir C. Holled Smith.

2. Stela of *Wn-t3-w3t* (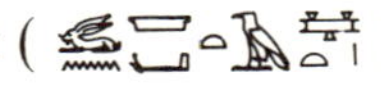) 792

Date: Twentieth Dynasty
Provenance: Not recorded
Date of acquisition: 1858[1]
Material: Limestone
Dimensions: 58 cm *h.*, 43 cm *w.*

This round-topped stela with slightly sloping sides is divided into two registers of scenes carved in sunk relief accompanied by incised texts and below them four horizontal lines of text. In the upper register Osiris is depicted in the centre seated on a throne, and behind him stand *Ḥr-nḏ-ỉt.f*, whose name is strangely written, and Isis, each with one arm raised. In front of Osiris are two altars, each bearing a water-pot cooled by a lotus-flower. On the right stands the first prophet of Amun of Ramesses and viceroy of Kush, Wentawat, with his arms raised in adoration.

The second register shows six people, five adults and one child, in an attitude of worship: the lady of the house and chantress of Wepwawet, *T3-wsr(t)* (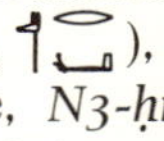), her [son],[2] the stable-master of the Residence, *N3-ḥr-ḥr* (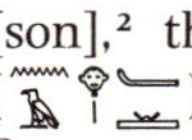),[3] his brother, the first prophet of Amun of Ramesses, *ʾImn-w3ḥ-sw* (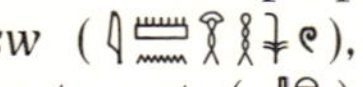), his sister, the chantress of Wepwawet, *3st* (), his sister the chantress of Wepwawet, *T3-ʿḳy* (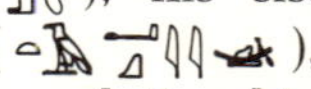), and a child, *T3-wsr(t)* (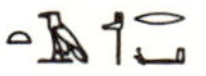), whose relationship to the others is lost. At the bottom of the stela the incised text contains a prayer to Osiris, Isis and Horus on behalf of the stable-master of the Residence, Naherher, and his father, the first prophet of Amun of Ramesses, Wentawat.

The viceroy of Kush, Wentawat, is known from several other monuments (Reisner, *JEA* 6 (1920), 50–1; H. Gauthier, *Rec. trav.* 39 (1921), 218–19; J. Černý, *Kush* 7 (1959), 71–5). Excavations at Amara West have revealed that he was the son of the viceroy of Kush, Naherher, and flourished under Ramesses IX (H. W. Fairman, *JEA* 25 (1939), 143). It would appear that his priestly title was connected with the mortuary temple of Ramesses II at Thebes (Helck, *Materialien*, 80 and 105). With regard to the relatives on the stela, Tewosret is obviously Wentawat's wife, and the text establishes that the stable-master Naherher was his son, named after his paternal grandfather. His title was previously held by Wentawat (H. Smith, *The Fortress of Buhen: The Inscriptions* (London, 1976), pl. 81, no. 5). Amenwahsu, Isis and Taaky are either the brother and sisters of Wentawat or possibly those of Naherher and so children of Wentawat. In that case Wentawat would have passed one title to Naherher and another to Amenwahsu, and it is possible that a third son, Ramessesnakht, not on this stela, succeeded to the office of viceroy of Kush (Gauthier, *Ann. Serv.* 28 (1928), 135; Černý, *Kush* 7 (1959), 71–5).

Preservation and colour: This stela is in a poor state of preservation and much worn. Part of the last line has been lost subsequent to the taking of the photograph used here. There are traces of red paint on the hands and face of the lady Tewosret.

Bibliography: Lieblein, *Dictionnaire*, no. 1002; *Sculpture Guide* (1909), 202–3 (no. 736), pl. 25; G. Lefebvre, *Histoire des grands prêtres d'Amon* (Paris, 1929), 160–1; Kees, *Priestertum*, 144.

1. Lot 119 of an unidentified sale at Stevens.
2. Lost but can be restored from bottom text.
3. For the reading of this name see J. Černý, *Kush* 7 (1959), 75. A possible feminine form of the name can be seen on BM 1188 (see below, pls. 54–5).

Plates 46–47

Statue of *P3-sr* (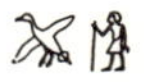) 1376

Date: Nineteenth Dynasty
Provenance: Abu Simbel[1]
Date of acquisition: 1835 (Belzoni collection)[2]
Material: Sandstone
Dimensions: 74 cm *h.*, 29 cm *w.*, 51 cm *deep*

A kneeling figure of the viceroy of Kush, Paser, holding an altar on the top of which rests a ram's head. An inscription incised down the front of the altar consists of an invocation to Amen-Reʿ resident in *Pr-Rʿmss-mry-ʾImn p3 dmỉ* (A). Prayers to Min (B) and Isis (C) are incised along the base. The back pillar bears two columns of text containing prayers to Horus, lord of Nubia, and Amen-Reʿ on behalf of the viceroy of Kush, Paser (D).

The viceroy Paser, son of Minmose, is known only from a series of monuments at Abu Simbel and a statue of his cousin now at Naples (Reisner, *JEA* 6 (1920), 41, 45–6; H. Gauthier, *Ann. Serv.* 36 (1936), 49–71; *KRI* III, 74–6). He apparently flourished in the middle of Ramesses II's reign. The reference to *Pr-Rʿmss-mry-ʾImn p3 dmỉ* may possibly indicate Amara West where there certainly was a temple to Amen-Reʿ (Fairman, *JEA* 25 (1939), pl. 16 (no. 2); Helck, *Materialien*, 208).

Preservation and colour: The back pillar and edges of the base have suffered much wear on the surface. The statue was broken in two when found and has since been repaired. The flesh of the statue is coloured red, the wig black and the gown white with red stripes, but these colours may have been added in modern times. There are traces of blue paint in many of the hieroglyphs.

Bibliography: Arundale and Bonomi, *Gallery*, 119, pl. 51; *Sculpture Guide* (1909), 166–7 (no. 604); H. Gauthier, *Rec. trav.* 39 (1921), 208–9; Porter and Moss, *Top. Bibl.* VII, 110; *KRI* III, 74, no. 37 (2).

1. The statue was discovered on Friday 1 August 1817 (C. L. Irby and J. Mangles, *Travels in Egypt and Nubia, Syria and Asia Minor during the years 1817 and 1818* (London, 1823), 76; G. Belzoni, *Narrative of the Operations and Recent Discoveries in Egypt and Nubia*, 3rd edn (London, 1822), I, 333.
2. Lot 1275 in the sale catalogue of the Salt collection (Sotheby, 29 June 1835), described as the property of G. Belzoni.

Plate 48

Stela of P3-sr (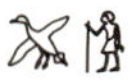) 1214

Date: Twentieth Dynasty
Provenance: Not recorded
Date of acquisition: 1897
Material: Limestone
Dimensions: 42.2 cm *h.*, 25.5 cm *w.*

This round-topped stela is divided into two registers with all figures carved in raised relief and all texts incised. In the upper register Amen-Reʿ is seated on a throne in the centre and behind him stand Mut and Khons-Neferhotep. The Theban triad is being worshipped by the god's father of Amun,[1] fan-bearer and mayor of Thebes, Paser, who kneels on the right with one arm raised and the other holding a fan. In the lower scene the guardian of the treasury of Upper and Lower Egypt(?), ʾImn ⟨. . .⟩ (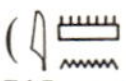),[2] kneels on the right in adoration of the goddess Waset, a personification of Thebes, who holds a bow and staff in one hand and an *ankh*-sign in the other.

Three mayors of Thebes named Paser are attested, one under Ramesses II, a second under Ramesses III and a third in Years 16–19 of Ramesses IX (Helck, *Verwaltung*, 425–8, 527–9, 531). In view of the crudeness of the carving and poor quality of the inscriptions, it seems likely that this piece should be ascribed to the last-named Paser (as in Helck, *Verwaltung*, 531, no. 20a, erroneously given as BM 1241). The name of the worshipper in the lower scene is obviously incomplete, and the carver probably omitted the latter part of his name in error. It may be speculated that it should be completed as Amenmose, a name otherwise attested in the family of mayors of Thebes in the Twentieth Dynasty (Bierbrier, *JEA* 58 (1972), 195–7). From its subject-matter there seems little doubt that this stela originates from Thebes.

Preservation and colour: The stela is well preserved apart from the top right corner which has been broken off. There are traces of green paint on the gown of the kneeling figure in the lower scene and black paint smudges on the bow and knees of the goddess.

Bibliography: *Sculpture Guide* (1909), 185 (no. 662); Helck, *Verwaltung*, 531.

1. The carver appears to have omitted the phrase 'of Amun' after the god's father and then to have squeezed it in after fan-bearer.
2. There is definitely no sign after Amen and before the male determinative.

Plates 49–51

Statue of *P3-nḥsy* (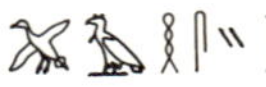) 1377

Date: Nineteenth Dynasty
Provenance: Not recorded[1]
Date of acquisition: 1833 (Barker collection)[2]
Material: Limestone
Dimensions : 107 cm *h.*, 52 cm *w.*, 60.5 cm *deep* (max.)

A kneeling statue of the overseer of the treasury, Panehsy, who holds between his hands a naos containing the figures of Horus, Osiris and Isis and surmounted by a winged sun-disk. The prenomen of Ramesses II is incised on the right shoulder of the statue (A1), and his nomen appears on the left shoulder (A2). Along the front edges of the naos are incised two prayers on behalf of Panehsy (B and C). On the lap of the figure are carved two horizontal lines of text which name Ramesses II and Panehsy, son of *Rʿ-ms* (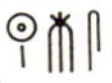) (D), and below these on the top of the shrine are five columns of text with invocations to Osiris, Isis, Horus, Wepwawet and Anubis (E). These prayers continue on the right side of the naos in one horizontal and three vertical lines (F) and on the left side of the naos in a similar fashion (G). A line of text containing two prayers runs along the base (H and I). Two columns of text are also incised down the back pillar (J).

The overseer of the treasury, Panehsy, is known from several other monuments, but this statue is the only one to name his father and the king under whom he served (Helck, *Verwaltung*, 515; *KRI* III, 136-40). The invocation of the Osiride triad together with Wepwawet and Anubis might tend to suggest that this statue came from Abydos, but no other monuments of Panehsy are known from this site.

Preservation and colour: The statue has suffered much surface damage with resultant cracks and flaking. The bottom of the base has been lost, and parts of the top and sides of the naos and the front of the base were lost prior to its acquisition. A small fragment from the front of the naos and the rear two corners of the base appear to have been lost since its acquisition. There are no traces of colour.

Bibliography: Arundale and Bonomi, *Gallery*, pl. 56, fig. 189; Sharpe, *Eg. Inscr.* I, pl. 54; *Sculpture Guide* (1909), 165–6 (no. 603); E. A. W. Budge (ed.), *Egyptian Sculptures in the British Museum* (London, 1914), pl. 37; J. Vandier, *Manuel d'archéologie egyptienne* III, (Paris, 1958)) 469; Helck, *Verwaltung*, 515; Porter and Moss, *Top. Bibl.* I², ii, 790; *KRI* III, 136–7, no. 87(1).

1. The provenance of Thebes given in *Sculpture Guide* (1909), 165–5, appears to be based on no firm evidence and can be regarded as conjectural.
2. Lot 245 in the sale catalogue (Sotheby, 15 and 16 March 1833).

Plates 52–53

Stela of *Ršpw* (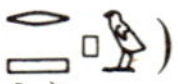) and *'Imn-ms* (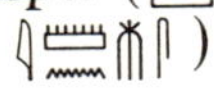) 161

Date: Nineteenth Dynasty
Provenance: Uncertain[1]
Date of acquisition: 1835 (Salt collection)[2]
Material: Limestone
Dimensions: 132.5 cm *h.*, 90 cm *w.*

This large round-topped stela is divided into four registers with figures in sunk relief and incised texts. In the centre of the upper register stands the standard of Osiris flanked on either side by ram standards. Isis stands with one arm raised on the left of the standards and Horus appears in a similar position on the right. On the far left of the register the royal scribe and chief steward Reshpu stands with his arms raised in adoration, while the royal scribe and chief steward Amenmose is shown in a similar posture on the far right.

The remaining three registers depict a series of standing male and female figures with their arms raised in an attitude of worship. The stela is divided vertically in the middle, and in each register the figures on one half face those on the other. On the left of the stela in the second register the first individual is identified as the royal scribe and chief steward Reshpu who is followed by his brother,[3] the deputy and overseer of cattle, *Nfr-rnpt* (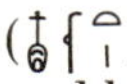), his brother *Nb-ms* (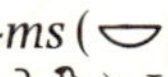), of the estate of Amun, and his son *Ḥnsw* (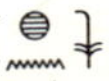). In the third register appear his father, the deputy and overseer of cattle, *Nb-ms* (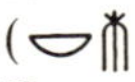), his brother, the deputy and overseer of cattle, *'Imn-ms* (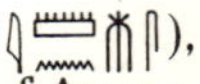), his paternal grandmother, the chantress of Amun, *'Ipt-nfrt* (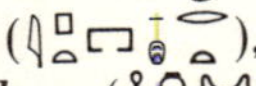), his mother, the chantress of Amun, *Ḥnwt-ḏww* (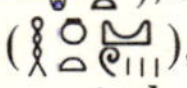), and a female relative of his mother whose name is broken but may begin with *Mwt* ... (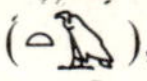), unless that phrase is part of the relationship. In the fourth register appear his maternal grandmother, the chantress of Amun, *Nšʿ* (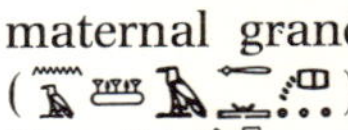), his sister of one mother and one father, *'Ipt-nfrt* (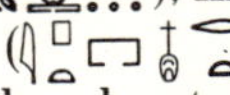), his sister of one mother and one father, the chantress of Amun, *T3-wr(t)* (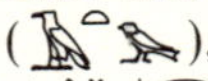), his wife, the chantress of Amun, *'Iy-nfr.tỉ* (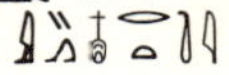), and a female ancestor whose name is lost.

On the right side of the stela in the second register there appear the stable-master of the great stable of Ramesses-miamun, *Wp-w3wt-ms* (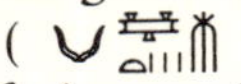), the overseer of cattle of the estate of Amun, *'Imn-ms* (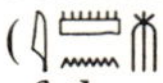), his paternal grandfather, the overseer of cattle of the estate of Amun, *'Imn-w3ḥ-sw* (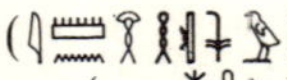), and his brother, the overseer of cattle, *Nb-ms* (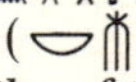). In the third register are named his son, the scribe of the estate of Amun, *P3-Wp-w3wt-ms* (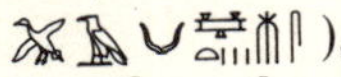), his son, the scribe *Ns-'Imn* (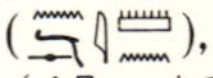), his mother, the chantress of Amun, *'Ipt-nfrt* (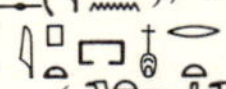), his mother, the chantress of Amun, *T3-ʿḳ3y* (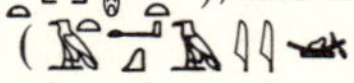). In the last register appear his mother, the chantress of Amun, *3st* (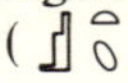), his mother or maternal grandmother, the chantress of Amun, *Ḥnwt-ḏww* (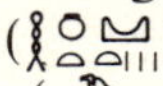),[4] his sister, the chantress of Amun, *Mwt-m-wỉ3* (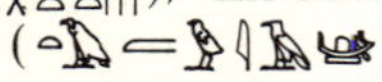), and her mother, the chantress of Amun, *T3-n-shrry* (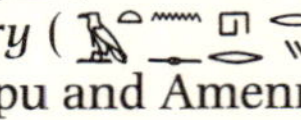).

The relationship between Reshpu and Amenmose the joint owners of this stela, is not stated explicitly. Reshpu is clearly the son of Nebmose and Henutdjuu. He had a brother Nebmose, and a brother Amenmose, the deputy overseer of cattle, who may be identical with Amenmose, the overseer of cattle, who appears on the right of the stela and who also had a brother Nebmose. This Amenmose may in turn be identified with the chief steward Amenmose who appears at the top of the stela. If Reshpu and Amenmose were brothers, they were not necessarily full brothers since Reshpu's relatives include two sisters of one mother and one father implying that he had some half-sisters and conceivably half-brothers as well. Thus the stable-master Wepwawetmose who precedes Amenmose could be his father after whom he named a son. Unfortunately, Amenmose's maternal relationships are not precise enough to settle the question, since several women are named as his mothers. Thus the exact relationship of Reshpu and Amenmose remains in doubt since they may have been uncle and nephew or even cousins. The lady Mutemwia who is named at the end of Amenmose's relations is probably his wife.

Another joint monument of Reshpu and Amenmose is known but gives no information on relationships, namely a kneeling statue, Inv. n. B 1821, in Bologna (G. Kminek-Szedlo, *Museo Civico di Bologna: Catalogo di Antichità Egizie* (Turin, 1895), 155–6; K. Piehl, *Inscriptions hiéroglyphiques recueillies en Europe et en Egypte*, 1e ser. (Leipzig, 1886–8), I, pl. XXXVB; II, 43; S. Curto, *L'Egitto antico* (Bologna, 1961), 74–5, pl. 21; S. Pernigotti, *La Statuaria egiziana nel Museo Civico Archeologico di Bologna* (Bologna, 1980), 49–51 (no. 17), pls. XIII, LXII-LXIV). Although no provenance is known for this statue, it is probable that it came from Abydos. The title, chief steward of Amun, found on the base shows clearly that Reshpu and Amenmose were officials of the temple of Amun and not the civil administration. None of the other relatives can be identified with certainty from other sources. The overseer of cattle Amenmose cannot be identified with the overseer of cattle Amenmose of Louvre stela C286, as the latter flourished in the Eighteenth Dynasty (F. Chabas, *Revue archéologique* 14 (1857), 65–81, 193–212). The overseer of cattle Neferrenpet cited in Helck, *Materialen*, 31, may or may not be the same man as the deputy and overseer of cattle Neferrenpet of this stela.

Preservation and colour: The top right corner of the stela is lost and the left side and bottom of the stela are damaged and uneven. Several small breaks appear on the face of the stela, and the lower left side is badly worn.

Bibliography: *Sculpture Guide* (1909), 205 (no. 748); Porter and Moss, *Top. Bibl.* v, 96 (erroneously called stela of Wer-reshpu in both).

1. Said to come from Abydos.
2. Lot 984 in the sale catalogue (Sotheby, 29 June 1835).
3. The word for brother is written throughout this stela with an otiose *t*.
4. The second *mwt.f* which appears in the middle of her title may either be an outright error or accidentally displaced from the description of her relationship.

Plates 54–55

Stela of *Mr-nḏm* (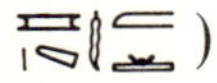) 1188

Date: Nineteenth Dynasty
Provenance: Wadi Halfa[1]
Date of acquisition: 1887[2]
Material: Sandstone
Dimensions: 182 cm *h.*, 93 cm *w.*

This stela is composed of two sections – a pyramidion containing two registers and below it a round-topped stela consisting of three registers and a short text of four horizontal lines. All figures are in sunk relief and all texts are incised. In the upper register of the pyramidion is the sun-disk in the solar bark, being worshipped on either side by a baboon whose arms are raised in adoration. In the lower register the overseer of prophets, Mernedjem, is shown kneeling in worship before Anubis in two parallel scenes separated by a vertical band of text. Between the pyramidion and the main stela there is an *udjat*-eye on the left, and there was presumably a similar on the right now lost.

In the first register of the main stela, on the right the overseer of prophets and overseer of craftsmen Mernedjem, son of *Ḫnm-ms* (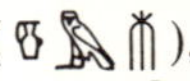), is offering incense and pouring a libation before an altar heaped with food offerings. On the left of the altar sit Osiris, Isis, Nephthys and Horus residing in Buhen. The second register depicts on the right his (Mernedjem's) son, the first prophet, divine scribe and mayor, *Ḥrw-nfr* (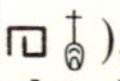), pouring a libation over an altar of food offerings. Behind him stands his second son, the second prophet *Ḥr-m-ḥb* (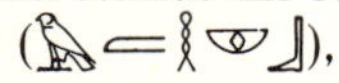), with arms raised. He is followed by three male adults with two children whose names are not inscribed in the five columns above them. On the left of the altar is a file of five women and four children (?), some of whom carry sistra. They are named as the lady *T-di.s(?)* (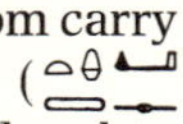), her daughter *T3-n. . . (?)* (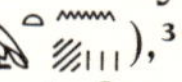),[3] and her daughter *Mrỉt-nbw* (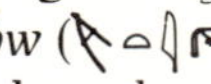). The remainder of the names appear not to have been inscribed.

In the third register an altar covered with food offerings lies in the centre. On its right stands his father, the overseer of gold-workers, Khnummose, his wife, the lady of the house, *S3ḥtỉ* (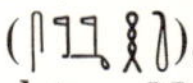), her daughter *T3-ḥr-ḥr* (), her daughter *N3-ỉb-ʿ3* (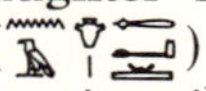) and a fourth woman whose name has not been inscribed. Six vertical lines of text on the left contain a prayer to Osiris, Anubis, Isis and Nephthys. The text at the bottom of the stela consists of a prayer on behalf of Mernedjem and names his sons, the first prophet of Horus, lord of Buhen, Herunufer and the second prophet Horemheb.

The overseer of the prophets of all the gods, Mernedjem is known from several other monuments found recently at Buhen (H. S. Smith, *The Fortress of Buhen: The Inscriptions* (London, 1976), nos. 1113, 1536 and 1537, 1568, 1713, 1737) and from a stela found at Wadi es-Sebua where he is associated with the viceroy of Kush, Setau, for whom see above BM 78, pls. 42–3 (H. Gauthier, *Ann. Serv.* 11 (1911), 81–2; *Rec. trav.* 39 (1921), 234–5). Thus he flourished at the end of the reign of Ramesses II. There appears to be some question as to the reading of his name. Smith reads the name as *T3-nḏm* (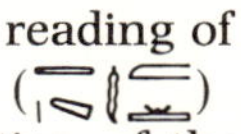) rather than *Mr-nḏm* (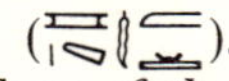). Examination of the stela shows that the edges of the crucial sign appear more straight than rounded, but sandstone is not the best medium for epigraphic precision. However, in line 1 of the main text of four lines at the bottom of the stela the appearance of an undoubted *t3* sign differs markedly in size from the disputed sign used in the owner's name which appears in the same line, so the reading of *t3* is probably excluded. A similar difference in size can be observed in Smith, op. cit., nos. 1536 and 1537 and in two other writings of *t3* on BM 1188, one of which in the upper register has three distinctive strokes beneath it. It is possible that such strokes may also have occurred below the *t3* in the first line of the text at the bottom of the stela, but it is now impossible to determine whether the mark now preserved represents the remains of these strokes, two of which may have worn away, or is simply a scratch on the surface of the stone.The reading of *mr* has been adopted here, but it is also possible that the name could be read as *Š-nḏm* (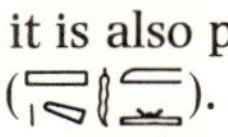). The son Horemheb is mentioned on other monuments at Buhen as well as a daughter Tay . . . who is perhaps to be identified with the daughter Taen . . . of this stela or perhaps Taherher as Smith suggests (Smith, op. cit., nos. 1713 and 1737). The female figures in the lower register are the wife and daughters of Mernedjem, as confirmed by Smith, op. cit. no. 1737 where the name of Sahte can be restored from traces.

Preservation and colour: The stela has been broken into several pieces in antiquity with much loss and restored in modern times. The surface is worn and pitted in several places. There are no traces of colour.

Bibliography: E. A. W. Budge, *The Egyptian Sudan* (London, 1907), i, 576; *Sculpture Guide* (1909), 179 (no. 645); Porter and Moss, *Top. Bibl.* VII, 141; *KRI* III, 132–4, no. 84(1).

1. Undoubtedly from Buhen on internal evidence. According to Budge, *By Nile and Tigris* (London, 1920), I, 101–2, from the South Temple of Tuthmosis III, but see D. Randall-MacIver and C. Woolley, *Buhen* (Philadelphia, 1911), 96, who suggest the North Temple.
2. Presented by General Sir Charles Holled Smith.
3. The bird-sign would appear to be a *t3* rather than a *mwt*. The plural strokes are not spaced evenly under the *n* but crowded to one side, so there must have been a long vertical sign on the right which has now worn beyond recognition.

Plate 56

Stela of *’Iw.w-n-’Imn* ( ) and *‘ḥ3wty-nfr* ( ) 794

Date: Nineteenth Dynasty
Provenance: Not recorded
Date of acquisition: 1858[1]
Material: Limestone
Dimensions: 48 cm *h.*, 32.5 cm *w.*

This round-topped stela is divided into two registers with representations in sunk relief and texts deeply incised. In the upper register Osiris is seated on a throne on the left of the scene, and before him stands a lotus-flower on which are the four sons of Horus. He is being worshipped by the scribe Iuuenamun who kneels on the right. The lower register depicts the table-scribe of the lord of the two lands, Ahautinefer, kneeling on the right in adoration of the ram-headed god Harsaphes, resident in Abydos, who is enthroned on the left.

Both Iuuenamun and Ahautinefer are known from monuments at Abydos, and it is most likely that this stela came from there as well. A stela of the overseer of the cities of Kush and royal table-scribe of the lord of the two lands Iuuenamun (now Cairo Museum, TN 15/12/24/2), and one of the royal table-scribe Iuy, both from Abydos, probably belong to the same man as BM 794 (A. Mariette, *Catalogue général des monuments d'Abydos* (Paris, 1880), nos. 1169 and 1223, 438 and 461; Mariette, *Abydos* (Paris, 1880), pl. 57a). A stela in the Leicester City Museum dedicated to Osiris and Harsaphes names the table-scribe of the lord of the two lands Iuuenamun and various individuals (K. A. Kitchen, *Orientalia* 29 (1960), 81–7, who originally read the name as Iauenamun but now agrees that Iuuenamun is more probable).

Ahautinefer is known as the son of the fan-bearer Huy from a lintel found at Abydos (Mariette, *Catalogue*, no. 1165,437). This piece or part of it is presumably the one recorded by De Rougé, *Inscriptions hiéroglyphiques copiées en Egypte* (Paris, 1877 ff.), pl. xliv, as in the Cairo Museum.[2] Ahautinefer also appears on a stela of unknown provenance together with his wife, parents and relations worshipping the triad of Abydos (E. von Bergmann, *Rec. trav.* 12 (1892), 17–18). Two of the women's names match those on the Leicester stela, but they are both too common to be certain of identity. Most important of all there is a block statue of the table-scribe of the lord of the two lands Ahautinefer in Bologna (Inv. n. B 1810) which is dedicated to Osiris, Harsaphes and Wepwawet, and dated by the cartouches of Merenptah (G. Kminek-Szedlo, *Museo Civico di Bologna: Catalogo di Antichità Egizie* (Turin, 1895), 148–9; K. Piehl, *Inscriptions hiéroglyphiques recueillies en Europe et en Égypte*, 1e ser. (Leipzig, 1886–8), I, pls. XXXVC-XXXVI, II, 43; S. Curto, *L'Egitto antico* (Bologna, 1961), 34, pl. 23; *La Statuaria egiziana nel Museo Civico Archeologico di Bologna* (Bologna, 1980), 47–9 (no. 16), pls. XI-XII, LVIII-LXI). It is probable that both these monuments also came from Abydos. No relationship is indicated between Iuuenamun and Ahautinefer, and they may have been only colleagues in office.

Preservation and colour: Apart from some damage to the top centre edge and the lower right corner, the stela is well preserved. There are no traces of colour.

Bibliography: *Sculpture Guide* (1909), 203 (no. 737).

1. Lot 115 of a sale at Stevens.
2. There are two different entries in Porter and Moss, *Top. Bibl.* V, 90, 95.

Plate 57

Stela of *Ḥri* ( ) 588

Date: Twentieth Dynasty
Provenance: Thebes[1]
Date of acquisition: 1843 (Belmore collection)
Material: Limestone
Dimensions: 69 cm *h.*, 53 cm *w.* (unrestored)

A round-topped stela, the surface of which is divided into two registers containing representations carved in sunk relief and finely incised texts. In the upper register on the right King Ramesses IV is depicted seated on a throne and protected by the wings of the goddess Ma‘et who stands behind him. It would appear that he originally wore the Blue Crown, and the one shown now is the result of a misguided restoration of the last century (J. Janssen, *JEA* 49 (1963), 65). Before the king stands the royal scribe and royal butler Hori, son of *Ptḥ-m-wỉ3* ( ), and the lady *Ḥwt-Ḥr* ( ), holding a feathered fan. Between Hori and the king the remains of an altar can be seen.

The lower register is separated from the upper by a blank horizontal strip and consists of thirteen vertical columns of text enumerating the goods given by Hori on behalf of the king to the necropolis-foreman *’In-ḥr(t)-ḫ‘w* ( ). On the left of the scene there is the figure of a man possibly in an attitude of worship.

The royal butler Hori, son of Ptahemwia, is known from several other monuments from Deir el-Medina and was in office in Year 2 of Ramesses IV (Janssen, *JEA* 49 (1963), 66). The chief workman Anherkh‘au, son of the chief workman Hay, succeeded his father in Year 21 or 22 of Ramesses III and held office until at least Year 1 of Ramesses VI (Janssen, *JEA* 49 (1963), 70; Černý, *Community*, 306–8; Bierbrier, *Late New Kingdom*, 37–8). He was the owner of Tomb 359 at Deir el-Medina from which this stela may have come (Porter and Moss, *Top. Bibl.* I^2, i, 421–4; ii, xxiii). Several wall paintings from this tomb are also in this collection (BM 1291, 1329, 1373, 5612).

Preservation and colour: This stela has been badly damaged and heavily restored along the edges. The royal crown and most of the body of the figure in the lower register are not original. The first seven columns of text in the lower register are badly worn in parts. Traces of red paint remain on the bodies of the figures.

Bibliography: *Belmore Collection*, pl. 15; Maspero, *Rec. trav.* 2 (1880); 170; Bruyère, *Deir el Médineh (1930)*, 111; Porter and Moss, *Top. Bibl.* 1², ii, 721; *Sculpture Guide* (1909), 198 (no. 719); Janssen, *JEA* 49 (1963), 64–70; M. Valloggia, *Recherche sur les 'Messagers' (Wpwtyw) dans les sources égyptiennes profanes* (Geneva, 1976), 169–70 (no. 129) – wrongly dated to Ramesses III.

1. Undoubtedly from Deir el-Medina on internal evidence.

Plates 58–60

Naos of *R-k3* (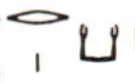) 476

Date: Nineteenth Dynasty
Provenance: Not recorded[1]
Date of acquisition: 1845 (d'Athanasi collection)[2]
Material: Limestone
Dimensions: 68.5 cm *h.*, 56 cm *w.*, 41 cm *deep*

The two jambs and lintel on the front of this shrine as well as the two sides and the back are covered with scenes in sunk relief and incised texts. The interior of the shrine is uninscribed. The jambs bear representations of the overseer of craftsmen, Raka, standing with his arms raised in worship and texts of a prayer to Osiris, while on the lintel a conventional group of symbols in the centre is flanked on either side by a figure of Anubis and a *ba*-bird (A). The name of the lady *Sn-snb* (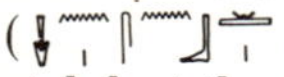) is incised on the top right corner of the lintel, but the left corner is broken off. On the right (B) and left (C) sides of the naos Raka is depicted worshipping a standing figure of Osiris, in mummiform guise, at whose feet are shown Isis and Nephthys in the form of serpents.

On the rear of the shrine there are two registers which cover only the upper part of the surface (D). The lower half of the back is uninscribed and probably unfinished. In the upper register the overseer of craftsmen Raka is shown seated with the lady *Ḥnwt-'Iwnw* (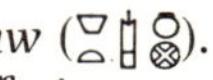). Before them is an altar on which are piled offerings and over which his son, the chief goldsmith, *B3k-n-wrnr* (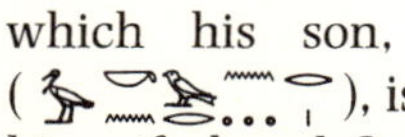), is pouring a libation. Behind Raka and his wife kneel five figures holding lotus-blossoms: his daughter, the chantress of Amun, *Mrwt-t3-dy* (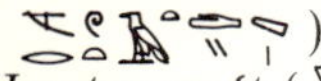), his daughter, the chantress of Amun, *Ḥnwt-n-m3ʿt* (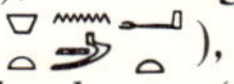), his son [*sic*], the chantress of Amun, *Ḥnwt-bw-ḥmt.s* (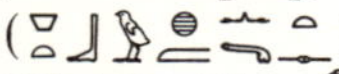), his daughter, the chantress of Amun, *Ḥ3t-šps(t)* (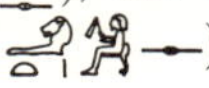), and his son *P(3)-n-ʿnḳt* (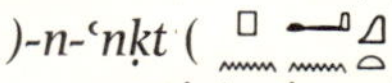).

The lower register is unfinished as the figures have not been carved and only the text remains. It names Raka, his wife, the lady Seniseneb, his son, the *wʿb*-priest of Amun, Raka, his daughter, the chantress of Amun, *'Iy-m-wnwt* (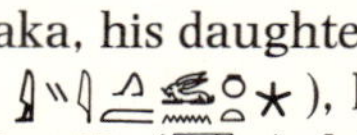), his daughter, the chantress of Amun, *Ḥwt-Ḥr* (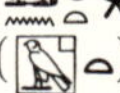), his daughter *Twl3* (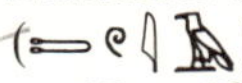), and his son, the *wʿb*-priest of Amun, *'Inw-šfw* (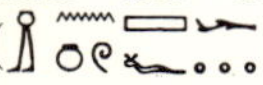).[3] In view of the fact that Seniseneb's name appears on the front of the shrine, there can be little doubt that she was the wife of the overseer of craftsmen, Raka, who thus would have been married twice.

The joint grave of the overseer of craftsmen Raka and the overseer of craftsmen Bakenwerner (SA 31) has been found at Aniba (G. Steindorff, *Aniba* II (Glückstadt, 1937), 83, 232–3). Thus Bakenwerner was undoubtedly the eldest son who inherited his father's position. The overseer of craftsmen Raka also appears with a group of officials adoring Ramesses II in the rock shrine of the viceroy of Nubia, Setau, at Ibrim (R. Caminos, *The Shrines and Rock-Inscriptions of Ibrim* (London, 1968), 46 and pl. 14; for Setau see above BM 78, pls. 42–3). Dewachter identifies the *wʿb*-priest Huy, son of the overseer of craftsmen Raka, son of the temple-scribe Ahmose, known from a graffito at Ellesiya as another son of Raka of Aniba, especially as a graffito of Bakenwerner is also known from this site (M. Dewachter, *BIFAO* 70 (1971), 91–3; Porter and Moss, *Top. Bibl.* VII, 91). Dewachter further suggests that the temple-scribe Ahmose may be identical with a temple-scribe Ahmose known from a graffito at Abu Simbel and points out the existence of a scribe Ahmose, son of User, known from the tomb of the latter at Aniba (Steindorff, op. cit., 59) and possibly an inscription at Toshka (Porter and Moss, *Top. Bibl.* VII, 95), but full publication of the Abu Simbel and Ellesiya graffiti shows that the father of temple-scribe Ahmose was named Hatia (*KRI* III, 129). With regard to the other children of Raka, Penanuket may be the scribe Pen ... who follows Raka in the shrine of Setau at Ibrim, while the younger Raka might be the owner of grave S49 at Aniba where *shabtis* of that name without titles were found (Steindorff, op. cit., 77, 178).

Preservation and colour: The naos is well preserved apart from some loss to the top-left corner and along the edges and bottom, especially at the rear where it has been repaired in modern times. The top and interior of the shrine are rough and unsmoothed. There are no traces of colour.

Bibliography: Sharpe, *Eg. Inscr.* 2nd ser., pl. 82; Lieblein, *Dictionnaire*, no. 944; *Sculpture Guide* (1909), 196 (no. 714); Porter and Moss, *Top. Bibl.* VII, 274, *KRI* III, 126–8, no. 79(1).

1. Undoubtedly Aniba on internal evidence.
2. Lot 153,1 in the sale catalogue (Sotheby, 17 July 1845). The small shrine, BM 472, which was sold with it is completely unrelated to it.
3. For the use of 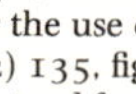 as a sportive writing of 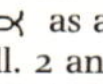 see Gaballa, *BIFAO* 71 (1972) 135, fig. 5, ll. 2 and 4, and p. 136, note (b), who suggests that it may there stand for *m*. It is to be noted that this writing is used in these cases after three water signs where confusion might result if a fourth was written. The name is garbled in Ranke, *Personennamen*, 26 (no. 23), but see 35 (no. 24), for a comparable name.

Plate 61

Stela of *Ḥr-Mnw* (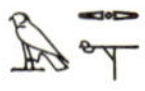) 64641

Date: Nineteenth Dynasty
Provenance: Not recorded
Date of acquisition: 1946 (Acworth collection)
Material: Limestone
Dimensions: 18 cm *h.*, 14.3 cm *w.*

This small round-topped stela consists of two registers with incised texts and figures in sunk relief. In the upper register Thoth, lord of Hermopolis, stands on the right before an altar on which rests a water-pot cooled by a lotus-flower. Amen-Reʿ, lord of the thrones of the two lands and foremost of Ipet-Sut, is seated on a throne in the centre and behind him stand Mut and Khons. In the lower register the *wʿb*-priest and temple-scribe Harmin is kneeling on the right in adoration before a statue of Ramesses II, named Reʿ-of-the-rulers.

Several statues of Ramesses II named Reʿ-of the-rulers are known from Abu Simbel, Luxor, the Ramesseum at Thebes and Bubastis (Habachi, *Ann. Serv.* 52 (1952), 553; Habachi, *Features of the Deification of Ramesses* II (Gluckstadt, 1969) 8–10, 18–20, 25–6, 38–9). A statue of this name is also mentioned in Papyrus Anastasi VIII, I, 7 (A. H. Gardiner, *The Inscription of Mes* (Leipzig, 1905), 16–17). Moulds with the name of Reʿ-of-the-rulers were found at Qantir (M. Hamza, *Ann. Serv.* 30 (1930), 59–61). Habachi has published a collection of stelae, now in Hildesheim, which he argues come from Qantir and not Horbeit as formerly believed and which depict the worship of various statues of Ramesses II including two (nos. 374 and 1085) which name Reʿ-of-the-rulers (Habachi, *Ann. Serv.* 52 (1952), 527–59; *Features of the Deification of Ramesses* II, 28–30).

BM 64641 differs from the previously published stelae as Thoth, Mut and Khons are not attested on those pieces. The statue on BM 64641 wears the *nemes* head-dress alone and not the double crown as on the other two depictions of this statue. Furthermore, the name of the statue on BM 64641 is compounded with the prenomen and not the nomen of the king as on the Hildesheim stelae, although examples of the use of the prenomen are known from Luxor and the Ramesseum. The reference to Karnak in the epithet of Amen-Reʿ and the appearance of the Theban triad might tend to suggest that this stela came from Thebes, although it is conceivable that it could have come from the temple to Amen-Reʿ at Qantir (Piramesse).

The scribe Harmin is not otherwise known. He is unlikely to be the same man as the scribe Harmin who was involved in Year 55 of Ramesses II in the collection of grain, belonging to another statue of Ramesses II, named Beloved-of-Atum (Gardiner, *JEA* 27 (1941), 58–60).

Preservation and colour: The lower right-hand corner of the stela has been broken off but later rejoined with slight loss. Otherwise the stela is well preserved, apart from a chip near the top and some wear in the centre. Traces of red paint remain on the body and legs of Thoth and the body of Harmin, and some black paint is visible on the face and beard of Khons and on some of the hieroglyphs.

Bibliography: *KRI* III, 499 (no. 227).

Plate 62

Statue of *Mry-Ptḥ* ([hieroglyphs]) 2291

Date: Nineteenth Dynasty
Provenance: Not recorded
Date of acquisition: 1839 (Sallier collection)
Material: Steatite
Dimensions: 14 cm *h.*, 3.8 cm *w.*, 6.4 cm *deep*

This small kneeling figure holds before him a plaque on which is incised the prenomen of Ramesses II (A). The edge of a cartouche is visible below the right shoulder. The name and title of the royal table-scribe of all the gods, Meryptah, appear on the back pillar (B).

He is possibly identical with the royal table-scribe of the lord of the two lands in Karnak, Meryptah, owner of Theban Tomb 387 (Porter and Moss, *Top. Bibl.* I², i, 439; *KRI* III, 319–20).

Preservation and colour: The top of the plaque containing the cartouche has been broken off. The two arms of the statue have been worn or cut smooth resulting in the loss of the cartouche on the right side. There are traces of white paint in the hieroglyphs and on the wig and gown.

Bibliography: Arundale and Bonomi, *Gallery*, 120–1, pl. 54; *Guide* (1922), 129 (no. 75); *KRI* III, 497 (no. 224).

Plate 63

Stela of *Dydy* ([hieroglyphs]) 1629

Date: Nineteenth Dynasty
Provenance: Not recorded[1]
Date of acquisition: 1926
Material: Limestone
Dimensions: 36.5 cm *h.*, 45 cm *w.*

This fragment of a large stela is divided into two registers, both of which are incomplete. The scene in the upper register is carved in slightly raised relief with deeply incised texts. In the centre of the scene as preserved are two standing figures facing right and with arms raised. They are named as his son *B3k-n-3⟨n⟩y* ([hieroglyphs]) and his son *N3ḫy* ([hieroglyphs]). On the right are two kneeling and apparently one standing figure, all facing left. The texts name *Nfr(t)-ỉry* ([hieroglyphs]), whose titles if any are lost, and the lady of the house, *Mwtwy* ([hieroglyphs]). On the extreme right is a pile of offerings.

The lower scene is carved in sunk relief with twelve columns of text consisting of a funerary invocation to Osiris, Anubis, Hathor and the gods and goddesses of the necropolis on behalf of the chief craftsman Didi. The pyramidion of a tomb is depicted on the left of the scene, and on the right are the upper parts of four standing mummiform figures. An opening-of-the-mouth adze and the top of an incense-burner, both of which must have been held by an individual now lost, appear on the extreme right. The name of the lady *Ḥmt-nṯr* ([hieroglyphs]) and that of her daughter, which is now lost, were incised on the right side of the bottom edge.

The chief craftsman Didi is known from the fragments of a large stela found at Deir el-Medina (Bruyère, *Deir el Médineh (1933–1934)*, 120, fig. 51; Porter and Moss, *Top. Bibl.* I², ii, 708, where read 'chief craftsman' and not 'foreman'; *KRI* I, 402, no. 170 (1)), a *shabti* in Turin (*KRI* I, 403, no. 170 (5a)), and an unpublished stela in the Fitzwilliam Museum (E.191.1932). He is also named on the statue of his son, the chief craftsman Pendua, who flourished in the reign of Ramesses II (J. Vandier, *Manuel d'archéologie égyptienne* III (Paris, 1958), pl. CLX, no. 5; O. Cairo, 25573, l. 12, where the filiation has been omitted). He is presumably the same man as the workman Didi attested on a fragment of a stela and a *shabti* (*KRI* I, 402, no. 170 (2); D. Valbelle, *Ouchebtis de Deir el-Médineh* (Cairo, 1972),79) and the Didi without title who appears on other monuments (*KRI* I, 402–3, no. 170 (3–4,5b)). He is cited as the father of the workman Amennakhte on a stela in Turin and appears together with him on an offering-table (Tosi and Roccati, *Stele*, 50059; Bruyère, *Deir el Médineh (1935–1940)*, ii, 128, no. 306 see now *KRI* III, 712–4 (no. 269)).

It is quite probable that BM stela 1629 forms part of the large stela of Didi from Deir el-Medina (Bruyère, *Deir el Médineh (1933–1934)*, 120, fig. 51). BM 1629 could be the left-hand portion of registers one and two, as the lower part of register two includes the lower part of a tomb and the feet of several standing mummiform figures to match exactly the scene on the lower register of BM 1629. The *udjat*-eye which Bruyère has placed in the upper left-hand corner of the second register would then belong elsewhere, possibly to the upper left-hand corner of register one of the stela. Unfortunately, apart from part of the cornice (Bruyère, op.cit., fig. 38), the fragments of the stela have not been reproduced in photograph so that it is impossible to compare the style of carving with BM 1629. The fact that BM 1629 has a straight left edge without a jamb text is not necessarily significant as that side has been sawn straight in modern times.

The ladies Nefertari and Mutuy are otherwise unknown but are presumably relations of Didi, perhaps his daughter and his wife. Bakenany and Nakhy are presumably his sons. The former is not known from other sources, although the name is attested in the contemporary tomb of Khabekhnet (Černý, *Répertoire*, p.16). The position of the latter raises an interesting genealogical question. In a long genealogy of the deputy Hay of the Twentieth Dynasty on BM ostracon 8494 he names among his ancestors the deputy Didi, his son, the deputy ... and his grandson Bukentef (Hay's grandfather) (Černý, *Community*, 139–40; D. Valbelle, *BIFAO* 75 (1975), 134–8). The titles assigned to the ancestors are dubious, and, as Hay's own father was a chief craftsman, it is probable that the 'deputy' Didi is in fact the chief craftsman Didi, especially as the *floruits* of both Didis coincide. The name of Didi's son is lost on BM ostracon 8494, and Černý has conjectured that he was Amennakhte, known to have been a son of Didi. The grandson Bukentef would have flourished under Ramesses II, and indeed one or more Bukentefs are so attested. A Bukentef is attested in Year 40 of Ramesses II and on another ostracon of that reign (BM ostracon 5634, see *Hier. Ostr.* pl. 83, l. 17;o. Cairo, 25573, col. II, l. 12).[2] A Bukentef, his wife Iy and his son Khaemopet appear in Tomb 219 which was painted in the reign of Ramesses II prior to Year 38 due to the presence of the scribe Ra'mose (Bruyère, *Deir el Médineh (1927)*, 70–4; Černý, *Community*, 317–27 for Ra'mose). The same man is attested with his wife Iy, daughter of the chief craftsman Amennakhte, on an offering-table in the Louvre (D. Valbelle, *La Tombe de Hay à Deir el-Médineh* (Cairo, 1975),39). Finally, the workman Bukentef, son of the chief craftsman Nakhy and father of Kenna and Nakhy, who appear under Amenmesse, is named on a stela in Stockholm (S. Wångstedt, *Medelhavsmuseet Bulletin* 4 (1964), 10–11;o. Cairo 25779–80). It is conceivable that all these references are to one and the same man whose father, the chief craftsman Nakhy, is to be identified with Nakhy, son of the chief craftsman Didi. The lacuna on BM 8494 tends to suggest a smaller name than Amennakhte as the father of Bukentef. If this is accepted, then Bukentef's father-in-law, the chief craftsman Amennakhte, who flourished early in the reign of Ramesses II (BM 265 in *Hieroglyphic Texts*, 9, pl. 35), could well be his uncle, Amennakhte, son of Didi. The fact that three sons – Pendua, Amennakhte and Nakhy – inherited their father's position need occasion no surprise and they may have held this title concurrently.

The lady Hemetnetjer and her daughter who are named at the edge of this fragment can be identified with Hemetnetjer and her daughter Iy who appear regularly together or separately as professional mourners in the reign of Ramesses II. They are cited in Tombs 2,218,219, 250, and 335 and on stelae in Turin and in this collection (Bruyère, *Deir el Médineh (1926)*, 65–6; Tosi and Roccati, *Stele*, 50053; *Hieroglyphic Texts*, 9, pl. 30). Presumably the two women were depicted kneeling at the feet of the mummiform figures in the original stela.

Preservation and colour: The left edge of this fragment is sawn straight, but the other edges are rough and damaged. The surface of the stone is pitted in several places, and some of the text in the lower register is almost worn away. There are no traces of colour.

1 Undoubtedly Deir el-Medina on internal evidence.
2 The workman Bukentef under Sethos II and Siptah is probably a different man unless he was very old at the time (O. Cairo, 25510; O. Cairo, 25521; *Hier. Ostr.*, pl. 51, no. 1).

Bibliography: None.

Plate 64

Stela of *Nfr-ḥtp* (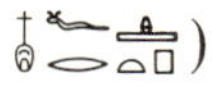) 1516

Date: Nineteenth Dynasty
Provenance: Thebes[1]
Date of acquisition: 1911
Material: Limestone
Dimensions: 46 cm *h.*, 30.5 cm *w.*

There are two registers on the face of this round-topped stela. In the upper register Amenophis I and Queen Ahmes-Nefertari are seated on thrones facing an altar on which rests a water-pot and a floral bouquet. The figures and the accompanying text are all carved in raised relief. In the lower register the foreman Neferhotep, son of the foreman *Nb-nfr* (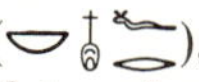), is shown on the left kneeling with arms raised in adoration. His figure is carved in sunk relief and the text in the lower register, consisting of a prayer to Amenophis I and Queen Ahmes-Nefertari, is incised.

The career of the foreman Neferhotep, son of Nebnufer and owner of Tomb 216 at Deir el-Medina, is well documented. He succeeded his father as foreman about Year 38 of Ramesses II and is last attested in Year 1 of Sethos II. By Year 5 of Sethos II he had been replaced by Paneb, for whom see below, BM 272 and BM 273 (pls. 70–1). He apparently died a violent death in some civil disturbance (Černý, *Community*, 288–90; Bierbrier, *Late New Kingdom*, 21–3; Bierbrier, *JEA* 63 (1977), 188; M. Green, *Orientalia* 45 (1976),399). For a stela of his father in this collection see BM 267 in *Hieroglyphic Texts*, 9, pl. 38.

Preservation and colour: The stela is broken along the right and bottom edges with some loss. There are two gouges in the upper register and the surface is cracked in places. There are traces of red paint on the bodies of the figures, the bouquet and the lines between the hieroglyphs.

Bibliography: Porter and Moss, *Top. Bibl.* II², 279; M. Gitton, *L'Épouse du Dieu Ahmes Néfertary* (Paris, 1975), 46 (19).

1 Undoubtedly Deir el-Medina on internal evidence. The attribution of its provenance to a supposititious chapel of Hatshepsut in Karnak is erroneous (T. G. H. James, *BSFE* 75 (1976),7–30).

Plate 65

Stela of *Ḳ3ḥ3* (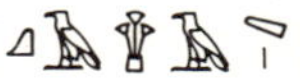) 291

Date: Nineteenth Dynasty
Provenance: Not recorded[1]
Date of acquisition: Not recorded
Material: Limestone
Dimensions: 52 cm *h.*,35 cm *w.*

The round-topped stela is divided into two registers with figures in sunk relief and incised texts. In the upper register the chief workman Qaha stands on the right with one arm raised and the other holding an incense-burner over an altar heaped with offerings. He is worshipping the figure of Amen-Re' in the form of a ram.

In the lower register Hathor, Amenophis I and Queen Ahmes-Nefertari are seated on the left and are being worshipped by Qaha's father, the chief craftsman *Ḥwy* (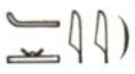), and the workman *Mr(.ỉ)-W3st* (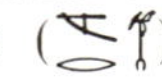) who are standing on the right.

The chief workman Qaha, son of the chief craftsman Huy, is well-known as the owner of Tomb 360 and many stelae. He is attested in office in Year 38 of Ramesses II (Porter and Moss, *Top. Bibl.* I², i, 424–4; ii, 722–3; *Hieroglyphic Texts*, 9, pl. 39; Černý, *Community*, 294–5; Bierbrier, *Late New Kingdom*, 36–7; *KRI* III, 598–609). He had at least two sons, Anherkha'u (for whom see below, BM 597, pls. 66–7, no. 2) and Meriwese (for whom see below, BM 444, pl. 69).

Preservation and colour: This stela is in a poor state of preservation. It is badly worn and chipped, and the top, left and bottom edges are almost completely lost. There are no traces of colour.

Bibliography: *Sculpture Guide* (1909), 136 (no. 483); *Hieroglyphic Texts*, VI, pl. 32; Porter and Moss, *Top. Bibl.* I², ii, 723; M. Gitton, *L'Épouse du Dieu Ahmes Néfertary* (Paris, 1975), 45 (7); *KRI* III, 604, no. 242(5).

I Undoubtedly Deir el-Medina on internal evidence.

Plates 66–67

1. Stela of *Ḳ3ḥ3* (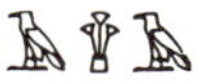) 274

Date: Nineteenth Dynasty
Provenance: Thebes[1]
Date of acquisition: 1843 (Belmore collection)
Material: Limestone
Dimensions: 17 cm *h.*, 11.5 cm *w.*

This round-topped stela bears a scene in sunk relief with incised texts. The workman Qaha, standing on the left, is making an offering before the deified Amenophis I who stands on the right.

The workman Qaha might be identified with the future chief workman Qaha (for whom see above, BM 291 pl. 65), although other workmen of this name are known.

Preservation and colour: The top right corner of this stela is broken away and the edges are chipped in places. There are no traces of colour.

Bibliography: *Belmore Collection*, pl. 7; Maspero, *Rec. trav.* 2 (1880), 192–3; *Sculpture Guide* (1909), 104 (no. 358); Porter and Moss, *Top. Bibl.* I², ii, 722–3. *Hieroglyphic Texts*, VI, pl. 41.

1. Undoubtedly Deir el-Medina on internal evidence.

2. Naos of *'In-ḥr(t)-ḫ'w* (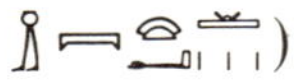) 597

Date: Nineteenth Dynasty
Provenance: Thebes, Deir el-Medina
Date of acquisition: 1843 (Belmore collection)
Material: Limestone
Dimensions: 37 cm *h.*, 25.1 cm *w.*

Only the lintel and right jamb of this naos are preserved in this collection. The left jamb was excavated at Deir el-Medina by Schiaparelli and is now in Turin (Tosi and Roccati, *Stele*, 50220).[1] All figures are in sunk relief and the texts are incised. On the left side of the lintel the workman Anherkha'u kneels facing right in worship of the goddess Renenutet in the form of a serpent. On the right side of the lintel Anherkha'u is depicted facing left in worship of Ptah and Sobek who are seated on thrones. The right jamb contains a prayer to Ptah on behalf of Anherkha'u and below it the lady of the house, *Ḥnwt-ḏww* (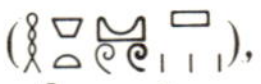), kneels in worship. On the left jamb in Turin there is a prayer to Renenutet on behalf of Hentdjuu who kneels in adoration at the base of the jamb.

The workman Anherkha'u can probably be identified with the later chief workman Anherkha'u, son of the chief workman Qaha (for whom see above, BM stela 291, pl. 65) and owner of Theban Tomb 299 (Černý, *Community*, 296–9). His wife Hentdjuu is likely to be identified with Hentdjuu, daughter of Kar and Takh'at, sister of Qaha and hence a first cousin of her husband (BM stela 818 in *Hieroglyphic Texts*, 9, pl. 40). With regard to the sisters of Hentdjuu who are named on stela 818, Pashed married the draughtsman Nebre' (for whom see below, BM stela 276, pl. 79); Meresger was the wife of the workman Nebenma'et, owner of Theban Tomb 219 (Maystre, *Le Tombe de Nebenmât* (Cairo, 1936); and Nefertari married Pendua, probably son of the chief workman Pashed (Bruyère, *Deir el Médineh (1930)*, 114, citing Turin statue N. Suppl. 8127). The last two appear with their parents, husbands and children in a scene in Tomb 219 (Maystre, op. cit., pl. IV, scenes 25–6). For another monument of (Anher)Kh'au and Hentdjuu in this collection see BM stela 1515 in *Hieroglyphic Texts*, VIII, pl. 45.

Preservation and colour: The preserved portion of this piece is cracked on the surface and chipped along the edges. There are traces of black and white paint in some of the hieroglyphs.

Bibliography: *Belmore Collection*, pl. 12; Maspero, *Rec. trav.* 2 (1880), 169; *Sculpture Guide* (1909), 136 (no. 482); *Hieroglyphic Texts*, VII, pl. 28; Porter and Moss, *Top. Bibl.* I², ii, 721; *KRI* III, 610, no. 243 (2).

1. I wish to thank Professor Dr. S. Curto of the Egyptian Museum, Turin, for permission to reproduce the jamb in his collection.
2. Her son Wepwautmose is described as a *s3 n* ⟨*s3t.f*⟩ of Kar on a statue in the Metropolitan Museum of Art (MMA 65.114) where part of the relationship appears to have been accidentally omitted by the sculptor. Fischer restores *s3.f* (H. G. Fischer, *Egyptian Studies* III. *The Orientation of Hieroglyphs. Part* I. *Reversals* (New York, 1977), 138, fig. 125 (e) and 140 note (d)).

Plate 68

Lintel of *Ḥwy* (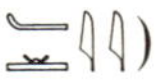) 448

Date: Nineteenth Dynasty
Provenance: Not recorded[1]
Date of acquisition: Not recorded[2]
Material: Limestone
Dimensions: 29.5 cm *h.*, 102 cm *w.*

The surface of this lintel bears two scenes with representations in sunk relief and incised texts. On the left the chief craftsman Huy stands with his arms raised in adoration before the seated figures of Amen-Re' and Mut. Between Huy and the deities stand one altar heaped with offerings and another altar on which rests a water-pot cooled by a lotus-blossom. On the right side of the lintel the workman *Mr(.ỉ)-W3st* (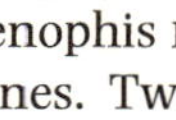) stands with arms raised in worship before Amenophis I and Ahmes-Nefertari who are seated on thrones. Two altars, one with offerings and another with a water-pot cooled by a lotus-flower, also stand before the deities.

The chief craftsman Huy, son of Hay and Takh'at, was the owner of Tomb 361 in the Theban necropolis, husband of Tanehesy and father of the future foreman Qaha (for whom see BM stela 291, pl. 65) and the workman Hay (for whom see BM 8495, pl. 82). For his monuments see *KRI* I, 397–402; Bierbrier *Late New Kingdom*, 36. The workman Meriwese, son of Qaha, appears with his grandfather and father on BM 291. See also BM 444, pl. 69, for further details on his career. This lintel may have come from Tomb 361.

Preservation and colour: The lintel is broken into three fragments, now joined, with some loss to the scene on the left side. The edges are worn and chipped. There are traces of red paint on the bodies, the dresses of the goddesses and parts of the thrones as well as on some of the offerings on the left side. There are traces of blue paint on the wig and crown of Amenophis I and parts of the thrones, and black paint on the wig of Huy.

Bibliography: *Sculpture Guide* (1909), 101 (no. 352); *Hieroglyphic Texts*, VI, pl. 38; Porter and Moss, *Top. Bibl.* I², ii, 738; *KRI* I, 401, no. 169 (10); M. Gitton, *L'Épouse du Dieu Ahmes Néfertary* (Paris, 1975) 51(2); K. Myśliwiec, *Le Portrait royal dans le bas-relief du Nouvel Empire* (Warsaw, 1976), 29.

1. Undoubtedly Dier el-Medina on internal evidence.
2. In the collection by 6 June 1826 see C. Yorke and W. M. Leake, *Remarks on some Egyptian Monuments in England*, pl. viii (22), originally published in the *Transactions of the Royal Society of Literature*, i, Part I, 1827.

Plate 69

Stela of *Mr(.ỉ)-W3st* ([hieroglyphs]) 444

Date: Nineteenth Dynasty
Provenance: Not recorded[1]
Date of acquisition: Not recorded
Material: Limestone
Dimensions: 31 cm *h.*, 56.5 cm *w.*

This piece appears to be the lower portion of a large stela carved in shallow sunk relief with incised texts. In the lower left-hand corner the workman Meriwese is kneeling with his arms raised in adoration. Five columns of text contain a prayer to Amen-Reʿ on his behalf. In the centre and right side of the piece the bark of Amen-Reʿ is being borne by three pairs of priests at the front and three pairs at the rear. A further pair wearing leopard skins on their shoulders walk by the side of the bark.

One each of the first three pairs is named: the *wʿb*-priest and outline-draughtsman *M33-n.ỉ-nḫt.f* ([hieroglyphs]), the *wʿb*-priest *P3y* ([hieroglyphs]) and the *wʿb*-priest *Ḥwy* ([hieroglyphs]). The two officiating priests are given as the prophet *ʾIpy* ([hieroglyphs]) and Meriwese. The fourth pair of bearers are identified as the *wʿb*-priest *Rʿ-ms* ([hieroglyphs]) and the *wʿb*-priest *B3k-n-ʾImn* ([hieroglyphs]). One of the fifth pair is called the *wʿb*-priest *Bw-nḫt.f* ([hieroglyphs]), but the remaining bearers are unidentified. The scene presumably commemorates an occasion when Meriwese presided at a religious ceremony.

The workman Meriwese can be identified with Meriwese, son of the chief workman Qaha (for whom see above, BM stela 291, pl. 65), as the only other Meriweses who are attested flourished in the Eighteenth Dynasty (Tosi and Roccati, *Stele*, 50009). Meriwese, son of Qaha, appears on several monuments with his father and his grandfather, the chief craftsman Huy (BM stela 291 and BM stela 448, pl. 68; BM stela 144 in *Hieroglyphic Texts*, 9, pl. 39; Tosi and Roccati, *Stele*, 50069). He is attested in Year 40 of Ramesses II (BM ostracon 5634, see *Hier. Ostr.*, pl. 84, l. 14).

The draughtsman Maaninakhtuf, son of Pashed, is well known from Tomb 323 of his father (*KRI* I,392–4), and he appears on many monuments (Porter and Moss, *Top. Bibl.* I², ii, 725; *Hieroglyphic Texts*, 9, pls. 30, 32, 37; Habachi, *Tavole d'offerta, are e bacili da libagione* (Turin, 1977), 22025; see now *KRI* III, 650–2). He is attested as a workman in Year 40 of Ramesses II (BM ostracon 5634, see *Hier. Ostr.*, pl. 83, l. 18). Pay could be identified with the well-known draughtsman Pay, son of Ipuy (for whom see BM 186, pl. 78) or his grandson Pay, son of Parahotep (Lieblein, *Dictionnaire*, no. 2234). Huy can be identified with the workman Huy mentioned in Year 40 of Ramesses II (BM ostracon 5634, see *Hier. Ostr.*, pl. 83, l. 19) and possibly the workman Huy, son of Qen, attested about this time (O. Cairo 25573), but the name of Huy is very common at this period; for example, Huy, son of Raweben (Černý, *Répertoire*, 84), and the scribe Huy, son of Djehuthermaktuf (Černý, *Community*, 215–16).

The prophet Ipy may be Ipy, otherwise Ipuy or Amenemopet, son of Piay and husband of Duaemmerset, daughter of Huy (Černý, *Répertoire*, 84; Bierbrier, *Late New Kingdom*, 24–5; Tosi and Roccati, *Stele*, 50031; see now *KRI* III, 660–6), or less likely Ipuy, son of Parahotep, and grandson of the draughtsman Pay (Lieblein, *Dictionnaire*, no. 2234; Habachi, op. cit., 22028). A workman Ipy is attested in the middle of the reign of Ramesses II (O. Cairo 25573, col. II, l. 8).

The *wʿb*-priest Ramose is undoubtedly Ramose, son of Raweben, for whom see BM 320 pl. 81, no. 2. He is attested in the work-force in Year 40 of Ramesses II (BM ostracon 5634, see *Hier. Ostr.*, pl. 84, l. 15). No workman by the name of Bakenamun appears to be attested at this time. Bunakhtuf might be identical with Bunakhtuf, son of Sennedjem, who must have flourished under Ramesses II (Černý, *Répertoire*, 22, 25–6).

Preservation and colour: The upper right-hand corner of the block is lost and the upper centre section has been badly damaged with loss of part of the scene. The edges of the piece are chipped apart from the upper edge which has been sawn clean. There are copious traces of red paint on the bodies of the figures and on the face and wig of Meriwese.

Bibliography: Lieblein, *Dictionnaire*, no. 942; *Sculpture Guide* (1909), 154 (no. 557); Maspero, *Rec. trav.* 2 (1880), 179.

1. Undoubtedly Deir el-Medina on internal evidence.

Plate 70

1. Stela of *Nfr-snt* ([hieroglyphs]) 316

Date: Nineteenth Dynasty
Provenance: Not recorded[1]
Date of acquisition: Not recorded
Material: Limestone
Dimensions: 42.5 cm *h.*, 28.3 cm *w.*

This round-topped stela, which has not been completely cut away from its rock face, is divided into two registers with figures in sunk relief and incised texts. In the upper register the goddess Hathor is seated on a throne on the left in front of an altar on which stands a water-pot cooled by a lotus-blossom. The workman Nefersenut kneels on the right with one arm raised in adoration and the other holding an offering of incense.

In the lower register three figures kneel facing left with their arms raised in worship. They are identified as his son, the workman *P3-nb* ([hieroglyphs]), his son *ʿ3-pḥty* ([hieroglyphs]) and the son of his daughter *P3-nb* ([hieroglyphs]).

The workman Nefersenut, son of Kasa and father of the future foreman Paneb, is well attested in the tombs of his father (no. 10) and his son (no. 211) and on several other monuments (Černý, *Répertoire*, 76, 88; Bruyère, *Deir el Medineh* (1934–5), 360, 362; *Hieroglyphic Texts*, 9, pl. 37). He is named as a member of the work-force in Year 40 of Ramesses II (BM ostracon 5634, see *Hier. Ostr.*, pl. 84, l. 8; *KRI* III, 780–1). For his son Paneb see below, no. 2. ʿApehti is elsewhere attested as the son of Paneb (see below, BM stela 35630, pl. 71, no. 2), and it is probable that he is so to be regarded on this stela. It is conceivable that there were two ʿApehtis, uncle and nephew, and that the elder ʿApehti was the father of the workman Kasa, son of ʿApehti, who flourished at the end of the Nineteenth Dynasty (O. Cairo 25510, O. Cairo 25517, O. Cairo 25521). The younger Paneb, a grandson of Nefersenut or his son Paneb, is not otherwise known.

Preservation and colour: The stela is well preserved apart from numerous small gouges on the surface. There appear to be no traces of colour.

Bibliography: *Sculpture Guide* (1909), 144 (no. 510); *Hieroglyphic Texts*, VII, pl. 30; Porter and Moss, *Top. Bibl.* I², ii, 729; *KRI* III, 780, no. 289(2).

1. Undoubtedly Deir el-Medina on internal evidence.

2. Stela of *P3-nb* ([hieroglyphs]) 272

Date: Nineteenth Dynasty
Provenance: Thebes[1]
Date of acquisition: 1843 (Belmore collection)
Material: Limestone
Dimensions: 19.3 cm *h.*, 17 cm *w.*

This small rectangular stela is divided into two registers. All figures are carved in sunk relief and all texts are incised. In the upper register on the left the foreman Paneb is kneeling with arms raised in adoration before a coiled serpent on the right, doubtless the goddess Meresger. In the lower his son, the workman *ʿ3-pḥty* ([hieroglyphs]), his son *P3-nb* ([hieroglyphs]) and his son *Nb-mḥy(t)* ([hieroglyphs])[2] are shown kneeling in a similar attitude of worship.

The chief workman Paneb, son of Nefersenut, is well known from several sources (J. Černý, *JEA* 15 (1929), 254; Černý, *Community*, 301–4; Bierbrier, *Late New Kingdom*, 22–3; R. Krauss, *SAK* 4 (1976), 173–4; Bierbrier, *The SSEA Journal* 8 (1978), 138–40). He is first attested as a workman in Year 66 of Ramesses II (O. Cairo 25237). He began to prepare Tomb 211 when still a workman (Černý, *Répertoire*, 87–90). He became chief workman between Years 1 and 5 of Sethos II and is last attested in office in Year 2, probably of Siptah. He was most likely disgraced and removed from office at the end of the Nineteenth Dynasty, although the exact date is uncertain. For his eldest son ʿApehti see below BM stela 35630, pl. 71, no. 2. No son of his named Paneb is elsewhere attested, and it is possible that this Paneb might be identified with the maternal grandson Paneb who appears on BM 316, above, no. 1, in which case the latter would be grandson of the foreman Paneb and not Nefersenut. Similarly, Nebmehyt is not otherwise known as a son of Paneb, but it appears from offering-table 22037 in Turin that ʿApehti had a son Nebmehyt and thus he too may be a grandson rather than a son of Paneb (Habachi, *Tavole d'offerta, are, e bacili da libagione*, 45–8).

Preservation and colour: The stela is in a good state of preservation apart from some scratches on the surface and chipping around the edges. There are no traces of colour.

Bibliography: *Belmore Collection*, pl. 7; Maspero, *Rec. trav.* 2 (1880), 174; *Sculpture Guide* (1909), 138 (no. 490); *Hieroglyphic Texts*, V, pl. 42; J. Černý, *JEA* 15 (1929), 254; Bruyère, *Meret Seger à Deir el Médineh* (Cairo, 1930), fig. 54; Bruyère, *Tombes thébaines à decoration monochrome* (Cairo, 1952), 86; Porter and Moss, *Top. Bibl.* I², ii, 730.

1. Undoubtedly Deir el-Medina on internal evidence.
2. The ([hieroglyph]) in the writing of the name of Nebmehyt may be due to an incorrect intrusion from the hieratic form of [hieroglyph].

Plate 71

1. Stela of *P3-nb* ([hieroglyphs]) 273

Date: Nineteenth Dynasty
Provenance: Thebes[1]
Date of acquisition: 1843 (Belmore collection)
Material: Limestone
Dimensions: 19.5 cm *h.*, 12.8 cm *w.*

This round-topped stela carries two registers with representations carved in shallow sunk relief accompanied by texts which are simply incised. In the upper register the chief workman Paneb kneels on the left in adoration of the goddess Meresger, who is depicted in human form with a serpent's head, seated on a throne on the right. In the lower register Paneb's sons, the workman *ʿ3-pḥty* ([hieroglyphs])[2] and *Ḥd-nḫt* ([hieroglyphs]) kneel with arms raised in worship.

For the chief workman Paneb see above, BM 272 pl. 70, no. 2, and for ʿApehti see below, no. 2. The other son Hednakht is otherwise unknown.

Preservation and colour: The top and bottom corners on the left side of the stela are chipped, but otherwise the stela is well preserved. There are no traces of colour.

Bibliography: *Belmore Collection*, pl. 7; Maspero, *Rec. trav.* 2 (1880), 174; *Sculpture Guide* (1909), 151 (no. 543); *Hieroglyphic Texts*, VII, pl. 28; J. Černý, *JEA* 15 (1929), 254; Bruyère, *Meret Seger à Deir el Médineh* (Cairo, 1930), fig. 52; Bruyère, *Tombes thébaines à décoration monochrome* (Cairo, 1952), 85; Porter and Moss, *Top. Bibl.* I², ii, 730.

1. Undoubtedly Deir el-Medina on internal evidence.
2. The [hieroglyph] in his name is strangely formed.

2. Stela of *ʿ3-pḥty* ([hieroglyphs]) 35630

Date: Nineteenth Dynasty
Provenance: Not recorded[1]
Date of acquisition: 1856 (Samuel Rogers collection)[2]
Material: Limestone
Dimensions: 21.2 cm *h.*, 14 cm *w.*

This round-topped stela depicts the god Seth who stands on the left, being worshipped by the deputy of the gang, ʿApehti, who is standing on the right with his arms raised. The figures are carved in sunk relief accompanied by incised texts. The writing of the text is erratic as can be seen in the word *ỉdnw* and the reversal of the *pḥty*-sign in the owner's name.

ʿApehti was the eldest son of the chief workman Paneb, for whom see above, BM stelae 272 and 273 pls. 70–1. He was presumably appointed deputy by his father some time after the latter became foreman in

Years 1–5 of Sethos II and possibly after Year 6 of Sethos II when other deputies are attested (Černý, *Community*, 135–6). ʿApehti appears as a deputy on one other monument, an offering-table seen and copied by Wilkinson at Thebes but since lost to view (Porter and Moss, *Top. Bibl.* I^2, ii, 743–4).[3] He is shown worshipping Meresger, while in a parallel scene his father, the chief workman Paneb, adores Amen-Reʿ. Inscribed on the offering-table are the prenomina of all the legitimately recognised rulers of the Eighteenth Dynasty, with the apparent omission of Tuthmosis II, and the Nineteenth Dynasty up to Sethos II, whose name appears on the sides of the spout of the table. Thus ʿApehti may have been named deputy prior to the death of Sethos II. He was presumably removed from office at the same time as his father. See also Bierbrier, *The SSEA Journal* 8 (1978) 138–40.

Preservation and colour: The stela is in a good state of preservation apart from a gouge in the centre, possibly repaired with plaster at one time, and slight damage along the bottom edge. There are traces of red paint on the body of the god and the face, body and skirt of ʿApehti as well as in the lines between the hieroglyphs. There are remnants of blue paint in the hieroglyphs, the sceptre and *ankh*-sign carried by Seth, and on the upper part of the god's costume. There are traces of black paint on the eye and the wig of the god and the wig of ʿApehti and in places on the surface of the stela.

Bibliography: J. Burton, *Excerpta Hieroglyphica* (Cairo, 1825); pl. xxxvii, no. 15; *Guide* (1922), 103 (no. 5) 114 (no. 52); Porter and Moss, *Top. Bibl.* I^2, ii, 717.

1. Undoubtedly Deir el-Medina on internal evidence. This stela was copied by Burton about 1825, but he gives no location.
2. Lot 77 in the sale catalogue of the collection (Christie, 28 April 1856).
3. Wilkinson MSS, xvii, F.d. 15. I wish to thank the Committee of Management of the Griffith Institute for permission to examine this manuscript.

Plate 72

Stela of *Pnbwy* (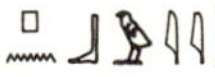) 65355

Date: Nineteenth Dynasty
Provenance: Not recorded[1]
Date of acquisition: 1939 (Mond collection)
Material: Limestone
Dimensions: 20 cm *h.*, 14.5 cm *w.*

This round-topped stela is divided into two registers with incised texts and representations in sunk relief. The upper register depicts the workman Penbuy kneeling on the right in worship of Ptah who is seated on a throne on the left. Between them lies an altar bearing a water-pot cooled by a lotus-flower. In the lower register his son *ʾImn-ms* (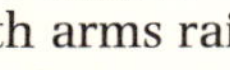) and his wife *ʾIrt-nfr(t)* () kneel with arms raised in adoration.

The workman and guardian of the tomb Penbuy, son of Iry, and his wife Irtnefret are well-known from other monuments from Deir el-Medina, notably Tomb 10, and flourished in the reign of Ramesses II (Černý, *Répertoire*, 75–84; B. Bruyère, *Tombes thébaines de Deir el Médineh à décoration monochrome* (Cairo, 1952), 57–65; Porter and Moss, *Top. Bibl.* I^2, ii, 712, 731–2; Černý, *Community*, 155; Habachi, *Tavole d'offerta, are e bacili da libagione*, 22026–27; *KRI* III, 737–44). In Tomb 10 he appears with another wife, Amentetwosret (Černý, *Répertoire*, 80). It has been suggested that he had yet a third wife, Iahati, who was the daughter of his brother Penmerneb (Bruyère, op. cit., 64). However, it is clear from Tomb 322 that the Iahati there depicted was not the daughter of Penmerneb and his known wife, and thus was probably not his daughter at all (Bruyère, *Deir el Médineh (1923–1924)*, 57). Moreover, it is not certain that Iahati was the wife of Penbuy since she is not so described on the stela on which they appear together and their relationship might be otherwise interpreted (Bruyère, *Deir el Médineh (1934–1935)*, 355, fig. 206). A stela in Turin, unfortunately broken, appears to indicate that a Iahati was the daughter of Irtnefret, but the name of the father is lost (Tosi and Roccati, *Stele*, 50075). Thus her relationship to Penbuy remains unclear. Penbuy's son Amenmose is known from another monument in Turin (Maspero, *Rec. trav.* 2 (1880), 177).

The relationship between Penbuy and Kasa, with whom he shared a tomb, is obscure. Kasa had a sister and a daughter Amentetwosret, either of whom could have been Penbuy's wife of that name (Černý, *Répertoire*, 77; BM 369 in *Hieroglyphic Texts*, 9, pl. 37). It has been suggested that Irtnefret was Kasa's daughter (Bruyère, op. cit., 63), but the inscriptions in Tomb 10 are too broken to be definite. Turin stela 50037 names Penbuy, Kasa and a lady, Ii, who may have been Kasa's wife or mother and sister of Penbuy, but again the context is not absolutely clear (Tosi and Roccati, *Stele*, 50037; Habachi, op. cit., 32).

Preservation and colour: This stela is in an excellent state of preservation with much of the colour still intact. The lower border of the stela is black, and there are traces of blue paint along the other edges. The hieroglyphs are painted black and the lines between the columns are red. The bodies of the human figures and the outlines and pleats of their costumes are red, while the wigs and the edges and pupils of their eyes are black. The lotus in Irtnefret's hair is blue. The throne of Ptah was painted red, yellow and blue. The body of the god is outlined in red and his hands in blue. His cap appears to have been blue or green, while his eye and beard are black. The altar is edged in red, the water-pot is yellow and red, while the stem of the lotus is red and the flower blue with black strokes. The background, body of the god and skirts of the human figures are left unpainted.

Bibliography: Porter and Moss, *Top. Bibl.* I^2, ii, 732; *KRI* III, 740, no. 277(4).

1. Undoubtedly Deir el-Medina on internal evidence.

Plate 73

Stela of *Pnbwy* (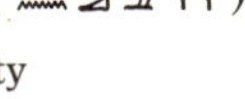) 1466

Date: Nineteenth Dynasty
Provenance: Not recorded[1]
Date of acquisition: 1908
Material: Limestone
Dimensions: 38.5 cm *h.*, 27 cm *w.*

This round-topped stela carries two registers with representations in shallow sunk relief accompanied by lightly incised texts. In the upper register Ptah is seated on a throne inside a shrine on the left, and on the right lies an altar heaped with food offerings. Behind the shrine are four ears and another three ears are shown above it. In the lower register the guardian of the tomb Penbuy kneels on the right with his arms raised in an attitude of worship. On the left a large *ka*-sign is depicted. A text of ten columns of varying length contains a prayer to the *ka* of Ptah by Penbuy.

For Penbuy see above, BM stela 65355, pl. 72.

Preservation and colour: This stela is extremely well preserved apart from some damage to the lower left edge, and most of the colour is intact. The background is yellow and the border shows traces of blue. The hieroglyphs are painted black and the lines between the columns are red. The hands and face of Ptah are green, his cap is blue, and his body is white. His beard and the outline of his eye are black, and his collars are yellow edged in red. The shrine is yellow edged in red with blue dots. The ears are black, blue and red. The food offerings are painted in a variety of colours. The human figure and the *ka*-sign are red, and Penbuy's wig and features are black. His collars are blue and green, while his skirt is white with red pleats.

Bibliography: *Sculpture Guide* (1909), 304 (no. 1173); Porter and Moss, *Top. Bibl.* I^2, ii, 731; *KRI* III, 740, no. 277(3).

1. Undoubtedly Deir el-Medina on internal evidence. Budge's attribution of this stela to Memphis is erroneous.

Plates 74–75

Stela of *P(3)-n-nbw* (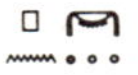) 8497

Date: Nineteenth Dynasty
Provenance: Not recorded[1]
Date of acquisition: 1834 (Sams collection)
Material: Limestone
Dimensions: 23 cm *h.*, 16.9 cm *w.*

This stela is in the form of a doorway with a cavetto-cornice and torus moulding at the top. The lintel, jambs and the central area are carved with representations in sunk relief and incised texts. The lintel bears the figure of a winged disk, while the jambs carry invocations to Reʿ-Harakhty and Ptah on behalf of the workman Pennub. In the doorway Ptah is depicted sitting on a throne before an altar on which rests a water-pot cooled by a lotus-blossom. Five columns of text containing a prayer to Ptah by Pennub are incised on the rear of the stela.

The workman Pennub is probably to be identified with the workman Pennub who is attested in Year 40 of Ramesses II (BM ostracon 5634, see *Hier. Ostr.*, pl. 83, l. 11). He is associated with several workmen of that period, in particular Khamy whose exact relationship to Pennub is unknown (Porter and Moss, *Top. Bibl.* I^2, ii, 724–5, 732; *Hieroglyphic Texts*, 9, pls. 34, 41; Tosi and Roccati, *Stele*, 50024). Green has suggested that Pennub might have been deputy of the gang, but this is not certain (*Orientalia* 45 (1976), 398). His ancestry is unclear, as two references to the father of a Pennub at this period are both broken and may not necessarily refer to him (Černý, *Répertoire*, 105; Tosi and Roccati, *Stele*, 50008). He left at least three sons, Pashed, Nebnufer and Nebnakht, who appear in ostraca during the reign of Amenmesse (O. Cairo 25779; O. Cairo 25782). A second Pennub appears briefly at the end of the Nineteenth Dynasty or the beginning of the Twentieth Dynasty (*Hier. Ostr.*, pl. 51, 1; O. Cairo 25793). He may be the same man as Pennub, son of Pashed, of Fitzwilliam Museum stela EGA. 3002. 1943 and hence a grandson of Pennub the elder (Janssen, *Chron. d'Ég* 25 (1950), 209–12).

Preservation and colour: The stela is in a good state of preservation apart from slight damage to the rear right edge. The hieroglyphs largely preserve their original colour of black, and the dividing lines between the columns are red. Parts of the throne of Ptah, his collars, the lotus stem and the edge of the altar are painted red, while the beard of the god and the lotus-flower are black. There are slight traces of blue paint on the head of the god but most of the colour on his body is lost. The sun-disk on the lintel is red, and the cornice is decorated alternately in red, white and blue edged in black, although most of the blue has faded.

Bibliography: *Guide* (1922), 103 (no. 4), 114 (no. 51); Porter and Moss, *Top. Bibl.* I^2, ii, 732.

1. Undoubtedly Deir el-Medina on internal evidence.

Plate 76

Stela of *ʾImn-ms* (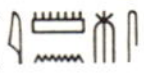) 1388

Date: Nineteenth Dynasty
Provenance: Uncertain[1]
Date of acquisition: 1845 (d'Athanasi collection)[2]
Material: Limestone
Dimensions: 56 cm *h.*, 38 cm *w.*

This round-topped stela is divided into two registers with figures in sunk relief and incised texts. In the upper register the workman Amenmose stands on the right with his arms raised in adoration of the goddesses Thoueris, Nekhbet and Hathor who are seated on thrones on the left. In front of them stands an altar on which rests a water-pot cooled by a lotus-flower.

In the lower register six female figures stand facing left with one arm raised in adoration and the other holding a lotus-blossum or other offering. They are named as the lady of the house, *Mḥ3y-[ib]* (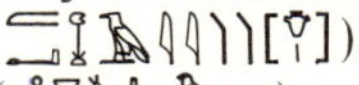), the lady of the house, *Ḥnwt-wḏbw* (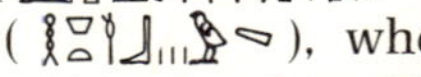), whose relationship to the preceding is lost, her daughter *Nfrt-Stt* (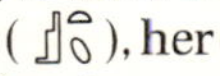), her daughter *3st* (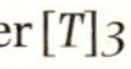), her daughter *[T]3-h3* ... (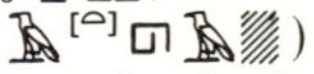) and a sixth whose name is lost.

The individuals named on this stela are members of the family of Pashed, son of Hehennekhu, owner of Theban Tomb 292 (Černý, *Community*, 111; Bierbrier, *Late New Kingdom*, 24–6, where for Makhy read Makhy-ib; *KRI* I, 404–9). The lady Makhy-ib and Amenmose are well attested as the wife and eldest son of Pashed. The lady Hentwedjebu is presumably to be identified with Hentwedjebu who is described as a daughter of Pashed on Turin stela 50076 (Tosi and Roccati, *Stele*, 113–15; *KRI* I, 407). However, in Tomb 250 of the scribe Raʿ-mose Amenmose and Hentwedjebu appear as husband and wife (Bruyère, *Deir el Médineh (1926)*, 63). This relationship would explain why she is described, apart from Amenmose's mother Makhy-ib, as lady of the house. Her appearance on Turin stela 50076 would be as the daughter-in-law and not the daughter of Pashed. She might be identified with Hentwedjebu, daughter of the workman Raʿweben, of Tomb 210 (Černý, *Répertoire*, 84).

The third lady, Nefertsatet, also appears as a daughter of Pashed on Turin stela 50076 where the editors have misread her name as Hentsatet (corrected in *KRI* I, 407). She can be identified with Nefert(em)satet who is attested at this time as the wife of the workman Khaʿemtri (Bruyère, *Deir el Médineh* (1924–5), 139; Porter and Moss, *Top. Bibl.* I^2, 711. Thus it is obvious that the description of the workman Khaʿemtri as a brother of Pashed's sons Amenmose and Hehennekhu on Turin stela 50076 can be explained as a reference to a brother-in-law. The fourth lady, Isis, is attested as a daughter of Pashed and Makhy-ib on Turin stela 50076. She can be identified with Isis, wife of the scribe Minmose, son of Amenemopet, who appears on the same stela with his brothers-in-law. For Minmose see Černý, *Community*, 210.

The last surviving name can possibly be restored as *T3-h3nw* (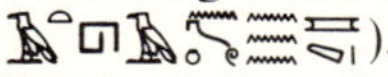), a name which is attested at Deir el-Medina but not so far as is known in the family of Pashed, son of Hehennekhu. One Tahenu was the daughter of Raʿweben and sister of Hentwedjebu, but she could hardly be described as a daughter of Makhy-ib (Černý, *Répertoire*, 84). It is conceivable that Nefertsatet, Isis and Tahenu on this stela were not daughters of Makhy-ib but of Hentwedjebu and Amenmose and named after their aunts, but such a younger generation is not attested elsewhere. It would seem that the lower register depicts Amenmose's mother, his wife and at least two of his sisters. Amenmose, together with his brothers Hehennekhu and Nefersenut and his sisters Makhy-ib, Isis (wife of Minmose) and Nebuemshaset (wife of Nakhtamun), are cited in a draft of their father's will under Sethos I and were presumably born in that reign or earlier (*KRI* I, 409). Thus this stela was probably set up in the reign of Sethos I or early in that of Ramesses II. Two other monuments of this family are in the collection: BM no. 262 (*Hieroglyphic Texts*, 9, pl. 35) and BM no. 598, see below pl. 77.

Preservation and colour: The stela is in a poor state of preservation. It is badly pitted and worn, and the plaster used to smooth the surface has gone yellow, cracked and flaked away in some places. There are no traces of colour.

Bibliography: Lieblein, *Dictionnaire*, no. 1000; Maspero, *Rec. trav.* 2 (1880), 169; *Sculpture Guide* (1909), 188 (no. 676); Porter and Moss, *Top. Bibl.* I², ii, 716.

1. Undoubtedly Thebes, Deir el-Medina on internal evidence. The sale catalogue erroneously gives Abydos as the provenance.
2. Lot 138 in the sale catalogue (Sotheby, 17 July 1845).

Plate 77

Lintel of *P3-šd* (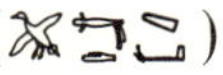) 598

Date: Nineteenth Dynasty
Provenance: Not recorded[1]
Date of acquisition: 1843 (Belmore collection)
Material: Limestone
Dimensions: 48 cm *h*., 81 cm *w*.

This lintel bears one scene and part of another. All representations are in sunk relief with incised texts in columns above them. On the left the workman Pashed stands with his arms raised in adoration, and behind him stands his wife *Mh3y-ib* (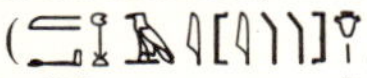) with one arm raised and the other holding a vessel. In front of them is an altar heaped with offerings which stands before the seated figures of Amenophis I and Queen Ahmes-Nefertari. A similar scene originally filled the right-hand section of the slab, but only the seated figures of the king and queen are preserved.

For Pashed and his wife see above, BM 1388 pl. 76. The lintel presumably comes from his tomb, no. 292 (Porter and Moss, *Top. Bibl.* I², i, 374–6).

Preservation and colour: The edges of this fragment are damaged especially in the lower left-hand corner. There are several gouges and cracks on the surface of the stone, some of which have been repaired in modern times. There are traces of red paint on the faces and bodies of the figures, on the disk of the crown of Amenophis I on the right-hand edge, and in some of the lines between the hieroglyphs.

Bibliography: *Sculpture Guide* (1909), 100–1 (no. 348); *Hieroglyphic Texts*, VI, pl. 37; Porter and Moss, *Top. Bibl.* I², ii, 740; M. Gitton, *L'Épouse du Dieu Ahmes Néfertary* (Paris, 1975), 51 (no. 3); K. Myśliwiec, *Le Portrait royal dans le bas-relief du Nouvel Empire* (Warsaw, 1976), 29; *KRI* I, 408, no. 172(5).

1. Undoubtedly Deir el-Medina on internal evidence.

Plate 78

Door jamb of *P3y* (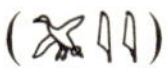) 186

Date: Nineteenth Dynasty
Provenance: Not recorded[1]
Date of acquisition: Not recorded[2]
Material: Limestone
Dimensions: 92 cm *h*., 37 cm *w*.

In the centre of this jamb is a groove in which a design of touching circles is painted. On either side of the groove is a column of incised hieroglyphs containing an invocation on behalf of the outline-draughtsman Pay. The names of his sons, the outline-draughtsman *Rʿ-ḥtp* (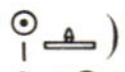) and the outline-draughtsman *P3-Rʿ-m-ḥb* (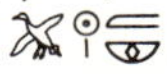), also appear.

The draughtsman Pay, son of Ipuy and Wadjrenpet, flourished in the early part of the Nineteenth Dynasty (*KRI* I, 390–1 no. 166; Roeder, *Aegyptische Inschriften aus den Staatlichen Museen zu Berlin* II (Leipzig, 1924), no. 6908, 58–9; Habachi, *Tavole d'offerta, are e bacili da libagione*, 22029). He appears in Tombs 4 and 218 (Černý, *Rèpertoire*, 50; Bruyère, *Deir el Médineh* (1927), 68) and is cited on several ostraca (*Hier. Ostr.*, pl. 54, no. 4; O. DeM. 233; O. DeM. 240). The collection also possesses two limestone model vases inscribed for Pay (BM 9526 and 9527). His monuments name his wife Meritreʿ and three sons Raʿhotpe, Paraʿemheb and Nebreʿ.

His son, the outline-draughtsman Raʿhotpe (often Paraʿhotpe), appears in Tombs 1, 4, 5, 218 and 335, all dating to the first half of the reign of Ramesses II (Bruyère, *La Tombe no. 1 de Sen-nedjem a Deir el Médineh* (Cairo, 1959), 10; Černý, *Répertoire*, 49, 52; Bruyère, *Deir el Médineh (1927)*, 64; *idem*, *Deir el Médineh (1924–1925)*, 139). He is undoubtedly the Raʿhotpe attested in Years 36 and 40 of Ramesses II (Janssen, *Commodity Prices from the Ramessid Period* (Leiden, 1975), 53; BM ostracon 5634, see *Hier. Ostr.*, pl. 84, l. 17). He also appears on BM 36861 for which see below, pl. 80. See also *KRI* III, 649-50 for other references. He married Taisennefret, probably daughter of the workman Neferrenpet, and had at least two sons, the draughtsmen Ipuy and Pay the younger.[3] His brother Paraʿemheb is cited on several ostraca (*Hier. Ostr.*, pl. 54, no. 4; O. DeM. 240). For the third brother Nebreʿ see BM stela 276, pl. 79.

Preservation and colour: The jamb is broken off at the top with the loss of the upper parts of both inscriptions. The lower left edge is chipped. The surface of the stone has been painted grey and traces of red, blue and grey paint remain in the hieroglyphs. The circles in the central design are red and black, but the centre section has been lost.

Bibliography: C. Yorke and W. M. Leake, *Transactions of the Royal Society of Literature*, i, Part I, 1827, pl. viii (21); Sharpe, *Eg. Inscr.* 2 ser., pl. 43; *Sculpture Guide* (1909), 101 (no. 351); *Hieroglyphic Texts*, VI, pl. 40; Porter and Moss, *Top. Bibl.* I^2, ii, 740; *KRI* I, 391, no. 166 (5).

1. Undoubtedly Deir el-Medina on internal evidence.
2. Already in the collection by 6 June 1826. Possibly from Salt collection, 1823.
3. Taisennefret appears as a daughter-in-law of Pay on Turin 22029, and it is known from Tomb 335 that the name of Ra'hotpe's wife began with Ta ..., while Nebre' 's wife was Pashed. In Tomb 5 Ra'hotpe is described as 'his brother' in a list of individuals headed by Neferrenpet and his son Nefer'abu. However, some of the pronouns in this list definitely refer to Nefer'abu and not Neferrenpet. Other indications suggest that Taisennefret was Nefer'abu's sister (Černý, *Répertoire*, 52–3; *Hieroglyphic Texts*, 9, pls. 30, 32).

Plate 79

1. Stela of *Nb-Rʿ* ( ) 276

Date: Nineteenth Dynasty
Provenance: Thebes[1]
Date of acquisition: 1843 (Belmore collection)
Material: Limestone
Dimensions: 26.5 cm *h.*, 17.2 cm *w.*

The representations on this round-topped stela are arranged in two registers; they are carved in sunk relief and accompanied by incised texts. In the upper register the god Haroeris is seated on a throne in the centre. Before him stands an altar on which rests a water-pot cooled by lotus-flowers. Behind him are carved four eyes and two ears. Four columns of text name the god and the outline-draughtsman Nebreʿ, son of the outline-draughtsman *P3y* ( ). In the lower register Nebreʿ kneels on the right with his arms raised in adoration. A prayer to Haroeris on his behalf is incised on the left.

The outline-draughtsman Nebreʿ, son of Pay (for whom see above, BM 186, pl. 78) is attested on several other monuments (Porter and Moss, *Top. Bibl.* I^2, ii, 683, 727, 729; Tosi and Roccati, *Stele*, 50036, 50056, 50063; Habachi, *Tavole d'offerta, are e bacili da libagione* 22029; see *KRI* III, pp. 652–659). He also appears in Tombs 2, 4, 218, 219 and 250, all dating to the first half of the reign of Ramesses II (Černý, *Répertoire*, 27, 49; Bruyère, *Deir el Médineh (1927)*, 64; C. Maystre, *La Tombe de Nebenmât* (Cairo, 1936), 9 and pl. IV, scene 26; Bruyère, *Deir el Médineh (1926)*, 72). He is also cited on several graffiti and ostraca including a model letter to the vizier Paser, for whom see above, BM 35628 (W. Spiegelberg, *Ägyptische und Andere Graffiti aus der thebanischen Nekropole* (Heidelberg, 1921), nos. 584, 849f, 1045a, 1050; O. Cairo 25573; A. Gardiner *et al.*, *Theban Ostraca* (Toronto, 1913), 16m-o; O. DeM. 558, 1153). He married Pashed, undoubtedly daughter of the workman Kar, and had at least four sons, Amenemopet, Paherpedjet, Khay and Nakhtamun whom Tosi and Roccati, *Stele*, 70 confuse with the carpenter Nakhtamun, son of Piay and owner of Tomb 335.

Preservation and colour: The stela is well preserved apart from some damage to the lower left corner. Traces of black paint remain in many hieroglyphs, on the outer border of the stela, on the wig of Nebreʿ, on the face of Haroeris, on part of the throne and the altar, and on the outer edge of the eyes. Traces of red paint can be seen on the face and body of Nebreʿ, the body and crown of Haroeris, the stem of the lotus, the pupils of the eyes and the edges of the ears in the upper register, and in the lines between the columns of text.

Bibliography: *Belmore Collection*, pl. 12; Maspero, *Rec. trav.* 2 (1880), 182; *Sculpture Guide* (1909), 132 (no. 467); *Hieroglyphic Texts*, v, pl. 43; Porter and Moss, *Top. Bibl.* I^2, ii, 727; *KRI* III, 655, no. 251(2), wrongly BM 275.

1. Undoubtedly Deir el-Medina on internal evidence.

2. Statuette of *Nb-Rʿ* ( ) 2292

Date: Nineteenth Dynasty
Provenance: Thebes[1]
Date of acquisition: 1835 (Salt collection)[2]
Material: Limestone
Dimensions: 25 cm *h.*

A statuette of a standing individual holding before him a figure of Osiris. The inscription, 'Osiris outline-draughtsman Nebreʿ justified', is painted in black on the rear of the statuette. On the right shoulder of the statuette appears the name of Thoth, lord of Hermopolis (A_1) painted in red. The name of [Thoth], lord of writing, is painted in red on the left shoulder, but the name of the god is no longer legible (A_2).

For Nebreʿ see above, no. 1.

Preservation and colour: The statuette is well preserved apart from a broken nose. The bodies of Nebreʿ and Osiris are painted white and their faces are red with details in black apart from the pupils of the eyes which are red. The crown of Osiris is white and the wig of Nebreʿ is black.

Bibliography: *Guide* (1922), 128 (no. 64).

1. Undoubtedly Deir el-Medina on internal evidence.
2. Lot 132 in the sale catalogue (Sotheby, 29 June 1835).

Plate 80

Block with the names of *Wn-nḫw* ( ), *Ḥr-Mnw* ( ) and others 36861

Date: Nineteenth Dynasty
Provenance: Not recorded[1]
Date of acquisition: 1868 (Hay collection)
Material: Limestone
Dimensions: 3.7 cm *h.*, 4.5 cm *w.*, 11.5 cm *l.*

This slightly irregular rectangular block is incised on all surfaces with hieroglyphic texts. Along the sides are two dedications to Ptah on behalf of the workman Wennekhu (A) and Harmin (B). On the upper surface there is a vertical line of text with the name of the workman *'Imn-m-wi3* ( ) (C), and on the lower surface is written the name of the outline-draughtsman *P3-Rʿ-ḥtp* ( ) (D).

The workman Wennekhu is known from several monuments (*Hieroglyphic texts*, VII, pl. 38; *Hieroglyphic Texts*, 9, pl. 30; J. J. Clère, *BIFAO* 28 (1929), 176–8; O. Koefed-Petersen, *Archiv Orientální* XX (1952), 431–2; Bruyère, *Deir el Médineh (1934–1935)*, III, 283; Bruyère and C. Kuentz, *La Tombe de Nakht-Min et la tombe d'Ari-Nefer* (Cairo, 1926), 96–7, 103–4; *KRI* III, 726–8). He flourished in the early part of the reign of Ramesses II and had at least one son called Penpakhenty. A fragment of a coffin from Tomb 290 lacks the name of its owner but mentions his wife Mutaat, his son Harmin, his son

Penpa . . . and his daughter Wadjyemheb (Bruyère and Kuentz, op. cit., 103). It has been suggested that Penpa . . . was Penpakhenty, son of Wennekhu, but in that case Mutaat must have been the wife and Harmin and Wadjyemheb the children of Wennekhu. Bruyère was misled by some fragments into believing that Wennekhu had a wife named Ii, but that woman, if she in fact existed, may have been Penpakhenty's wife. No other Harmin is known from Deir el-Medina at this period, and the linking of the names of Wennekhu and Harmin on BM 36861 strongly suggests that they were father and son. Mutaat is identified as the sister of Irinufer of Tomb 290, and this relationship would explain Wennekhu's burial in that tomb. See also E. Bogoslovsky, *Vestnik Drevnei Istorii*, no. 120 (1972), 69, who reaches the same conclusions. For a further monument of Wennekhu and Penpakhenty see below, BM stela 1248 pl. 81, no. 1.

The workman Amenemwia is probably to be identified with Amenemwia, son of ʿAmak, of Tomb 356 (Bruyère, *Deir el Médineh (1928)*, 77–93; Bruyère, *Deir el Médineh (1935–1940)*, II, 46, no. 175; *KRI* III, 702–6) and the workman Amenemwia attested in Year 40 of Ramesses II (BM ostracon 5634, see *Hier. Ostr.*, pl. 84, l. 2). For the outline-draughtsman Paraʿhotpe, son of the outline-draughtsman Pay, see BM no. 186, pl. 78.

Preservation and colour: The block is in good condition apart from slight damage to the bottom text. Considerable traces of red paint remain on the lines bordering the inscriptions. Traces of blue paint can be seen in some of the signs and white paint on the body of the block.

Bibliography: Maspero, *Rec. trav.* 2 (1880), 169, 172, 174; Porter and Moss, *Top. Bibl.* I², ii, 740; *KRI* III, 726, no. 273(1).

1. Undoubtedly Deir el-Medina on internal evidence.

Plate 81

1. Stela of *Wn-nḫw* (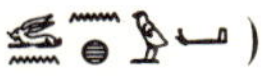) 1248

Date: Nineteenth Dynasty
Provenance: Not recorded[1]
Date of acquisition: 1898[2]
Material: Limestone
Dimensions: 35.3 cm *h.*, 23.5 cm *w.*

This round-topped stela is divided into two registers with figures carved in shallow sunk relief and incised texts. In the upper register the god Reʿ is depicted in the solar boat. In the lower register the workman Wennekhu and his son *P(3)-n-p3-ḫnty* (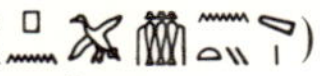) kneel facing left with their arms raised in adoration.

For Wennekhu and Penpakhenty see above, BM 36861 pl. 80.

Preservation and colour: The stela has a large crack in the lower right portion and is slightly chipped in places. There are traces of red paint on the body of Penpakhenty.

Bibliography: *Sculpture Guide* (1909), 143 (no. 507); *Hieroglyphic Texts*, VII, pl. 38; Porter and Moss, *Top. Bibl.* I², ii, 735–6; *KRI* III, 726, no. 273(4).

1. Undoubtedly Deir el-Medina on internal evidence.
2. Presented by Morgan Stuart Williams.

2. Stela of *Rʿ-wbn* (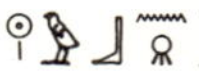) 320

Date: Nineteenth Dynasty
Provenance: Not recorded[1]
Date of acquisition: Not recorded
Material: Limestone
Dimensions: 33.5 cm *h.*, 23.5 cm *w.*

On the upper part of this round-topped stela appear representations in sunk relief accompanied by incised texts. Reʿ-Harakhty is seated on a throne on the left beneath a single-winged disk and before an altar on which rests a water-pot cooled by a lotus-flower. A figure on the right stands with raised arms in one of which he holds an offering. The text above him gives the name of *Ḳn-m-ḫps.f* (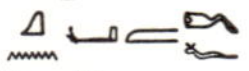), while two vertical lines on each side of the figures name Raʿweben and his son *Rʿ-ms* (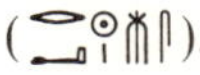). Three horizontal lines of text incised below the scene contain an invocation to Reʿ-Harakhty on behalf of the workman Raʿ-weben.

The workman Raʿweben, joint owner of tomb 210, is known as a contemporary of the carpenters Ipuy and Qen who flourished in the first half of the reign of Ramesses II (Černý, *Répertoire*, 50, 84–6; Bierbrier, *Late New Kingdom*, 24–5; *KRI* III, 782–5). His monuments include two offering-tables, BM 593 and BM 594 (*Hieroglyphic Texts*, VIII, pls. 47–8). Raʿweben is closely associated with the chiseller Ipuy, son of Piay, in tomb 210, but their relationship is never stated. Possibly Raʿ-weben might be identified with a brother of Ipuy named only as W who appears in tomb 335 (Bruyère, *Deir el Médineh (1924–1925)*, 167). On an offering-table in Turin he is described as a son of the draughtsman Pay, but this need not be taken literally (Habachi, *Tavole d'offerta, are e bacili da libagione*, 22029).

Raʿmose, son of Raʿweben, is attested in tomb 210 (Černý, *Répertoire*, 84). He appears as a workman in Year 40 of Ramesses II (BM ostracon 5634, see *Hier. Ostr.*, pl. 84, l. 15) and on other ostraca of that reign (O. Cairo 25573; O. DeM. 86). He is last attested in a Year 6 which must be that of Merenptah (D. Valbelle, *Catalogue des poids à inscriptions hiératiques de Deir el-Médineh* (Cairo, 1977), no. 5029). A Raʿweben, son of Raʿmose, and doubtless grandson of Raʿweben the elder, is attested at the end of the Nineteenth Dynasty (O. Cairo 25779, 25782–4, 25510, 25519–21). A daughter of Raʿweben the elder, Hentwedjebu, is probably to be identified with Hentwedjebu, wife of Amenmose, son of Pashed of BM stela 1388 (Černý, *Répertoire*, 84; Bierbrier, *Late New Kingdom*, 24–5, where her name is erroneously given as Henutist). Qenemkhepeshef is otherwise unknown.

It is possible that this stela has been repaired and reused, as the single-winged disk is attested almost entirely in the Eighteenth Dynasty.

Preservation and colour: A portion of the surface of the upper part of the stela is raised due to the unevenness of the stone. Traces of the original colour remain. The hieroglyphs were black with red lines between the columns. Traces of blue can be seen on the border of the stela. The bodies, pleats of the kilts and the sun-disk on the head of Reʿ-Horakhty are red, while the wig and individual features on the face of the standing figure are black. There are traces of blue and red on the throne, while the stem of the lotus is red and the altar edged in red.

Bibliography: Lieblein, *Dictionnaire*, no. 1001; Maspero, *Rec. trav.* 2 (1880), 184; *Sculpture Guide* (1909), 208 (no. 757); Porter and Moss, *Top. Bibl.* I^2, ii, 734; *KRI* III, 784, no. 291(2).

1. Undoubtedly Deir el-Medina on internal evidence.

Plate 82

Statuette Base of *Ḥ3y* (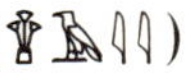) 8495

Date: Nineteenth Dynasty
Provenance: Not recorded[1]
Date of acquisition: 1834 (Sams collection)
Material: Limestone
Dimensions: 7.5 cm *h.*, 15 cm *w.*, 18.5 cm *deep*

On the top of this rectangular base are the remains of the two feet of a statuette. Two horizontal lines of incised hieroglyphs name the workman Hay and contain a dedication to Hathor (A). A band of incised text around the sides of the base consists of two prayers to Hathor on behalf of the workman *Nb-'Imntt* (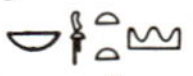) and the lady of the house, *Ḥwt-Ḥr* () (B), and on behalf of Nebamentet alone (C). On the bottom of the block a male head is carved in raised relief.[2]

The workman Nebamentet can be identified with Nebamentet, son of Kasa, who is known from several monuments (Bruyère, *Deir el Médineh (1927)*, 70; Bruyère, *Deir el Médineh (1934–1935)*, 361–2; J. Černý, *Egyptian Stelae in the Bankes Collection* (Oxford, 1958), no. 7; Černý, *Répertoire*, 75ff.; *Hieroglyphic Texts*, 9, pl. 37; D. Valbelle, *BIFAO* 72 (1972), 187; Bogoslovsky, *Vestnik Drevnei Istorii* no. 120 (1972), 74–80, 93 and pl. 5; *KRI* III, 755–7). He is attested as a workman in Year 40 of Ramesses II (BM ostracon 5634, see *Hier. Ostr.*, pl. 83, l. 8). The name of his wife is given as Hunero on his other monuments, but that is merely a pet form of Hathor, as in the cases of Hathor/Hunero, wife of Nebdjefau (*Hieroglyphic Texts*, 9, pl. 33–4) and Hathor, called Hunero, wife of the scribe Amenemopet (Berlin no. 6910 in *KRI* I, 386, l. 4). Thus it is clear that the lady Hathor of this monument is the same woman as Hunero, wife of Nebamentet.

No relationship between the workman Nebamentet and a workman Hay has hitherto been noted. The name Hay was not as common in Deir el-Medina in the early Nineteenth Dynasty as it was to become in the Twentieth Dynasty. The most prominent bearer of the name under Ramesses II was the workman Hay, son of Huy, brother of the foreman Qaha, for whom see above, BM 291, pl. 65. He was the owner of Tomb 328, married the lady Tatemhyt, and among his children had a daughter Hunero (Bruyère, *Deir el Médineh (1930)*, 29; Bruyère, *Deir el Médineh (1933–1934)*, 107; A. Moret, *Rec. trav.* 35 (1913), 49; Černý, *Répertoire*, 77; *Hieroglyphic Texts*, 9, pl. 39; Tosi and Roccati, *Stele*, 50069; *KRI* III, 787–9). This Hunero was undoubtedly the wife of Nebamentet since his daughter Nebuemirty (Bogoslovsky, op. cit., pl. 5) is elsewhere stated to be the daughter of Hay's daughter (Černý, *Répertoire*, 77, where the name is slightly damaged). Hunero and Nebuemirty, who is shown as a young girl beside her mother, also appear on a stela of Hay at Avignon, but no relationship is stated (Moret, *Rec. trav.* 35 (1913), 49, where the name of Nebuemirty is garbled). Moreover, Hay's son Seta is presumably the Nebseta who is stated to have been a brother (-in-law) of Nebamentet (Bruyère, *Deir el Médineh (1934–1935)*, 44). Thus BM 8495 names the workman Hay, son of Huy, his daughter Hathor (Hunero) and his son-in-law Nebamentet, son of Kasa.

Preservation and colour: Apart from chipped edges on the top and one of the sides, the base is well preserved. The lines which border the hieroglyphic texts are painted red, and traces of black paint remain in some of the hieroglyphs. White paint which was used for the background can be seen on the top and the front side. On the bottom the features and the stripes of the wig of the male face are black.

Bibliography: *Guide* (1922), 271 (no. 123); Porter and Moss, *Top. Bibl.* I^2, ii, 711; *KRI* III, 755, no. 284(3).

1. Undoubtedly Deir el-Medina on internal evidence.
2. Porter and Moss, *Top. Bibl.* I^2, ii, 711, erroneously report a Hathor head on the base.

Plate 83

Stela of *Nb-'Imn* (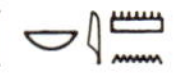) 8485

Date: Nineteenth Dynasty
Provenance: Not recorded[1]
Date of acquisition: Not recorded
Material: Wood
Dimensions: 33.8 cm *h.*, 21.5 cm *w.*

This round-topped stela is divided into two registers with painted representations and texts. In the upper register Amen-Re' in the form of a ram is sniffing a lotus-flower which is cooling a water-pot on top of an altar on the right of the scene. In the lower register the workman Nebamun kneels on the right with his arms raised in adoration. On the left, separated by two columns of text, his brother *'Iwy* (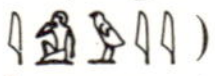) kneels in a similar posture.

These individuals cannot be identified precisely. The workman Nebamun might be Nebamun, son of Nebamentet, son of Kasa, who flourished under Ramesses II and presumably Amenmesse (Bruyère, *Deir el Médineh (1927)*, 70; Bogoslovsky, *Vestnik Drevnei Istorii*, no. 120 (1972), 76, pl. 5; O. Cairo 25779; O. Cairo 25782–4), but at least two Nebamuns, a son of Amenemonet and a son of Weskhet, are attested during the Twentieth Dynasty (O. Cairo 25737; J. Černý, *Egyptian Stelae in the Bankes Collection* (Oxford, 1958), no. 10; Bruyère, *Meret Seger à Deir el Médineh* (Cairo, 1930), 299). None of them is known to have had a brother Iuy, but the relationship need not be taken literally. Iuy is otherwise unknown.

Preservation and colour: The stela is badly cracked and worn away in the upper portion. Traces of the original white background remain, and traces of blue paint are visible on the border around the stela. The hieroglyphs are painted black and the lines between the columns are red. The human bodies are red, the eyes and wigs black, the skirts white outlined in red, and the collars blue. The ram is outlined in red with traces of white on its body and blue on its mantle. The altar and pot are outlined in red, while the lotus stem is red with traces of blue on the flower.

Bibliography: *Guide* (1922), 112 (no. 34); Porter and Moss, *Top. Bibl.* I^2, ii, 726.

1. Undoubtedly Deir el-Medina on internal evidence.

Plates 84–85

1. Stela of *Ḳn* ( ) 8493

Date: Nineteenth Dynasty
Provenance: Not recorded[1]
Date of acquisition: 1834 (Wilkinson collection)
Material: Limestone
Dimensions: 14.2 cm *h.*, 10.9 cm *w.*

There are two registers on this round-topped stela with lightly incised texts and figures in sunk relief. In the upper register Reʿ-Harakhty is seated on the left facing the goddess Meresger who is similarly seated on the right. In the lower register the chiseller of Amun, Qen, kneels on the right with his arms raised in adoration. On the left the lady of the house, *Nfrt-ỉry* ( ), is similarly depicted.

The chiseller of Amun, Qen, son of Tjanefer and Maʿetnefret, is a well-known member of the Deir el-Medina community and flourished in the first half of the reign of Ramesses II. His wife Nefertari and his other wife Henutmehyt are both depicted in his tomb, no. 4 in the Deir el-Medina necropolis (Černý, *Répertoire*, 44–50), and he is attested in tomb 335 (where his name is lost but that of his wife is preserved) and tomb 337 (Černý, *Répertoire*, 16; Bruyère, *Deir el Médineh (1924–1925)*, 122, 79). He is named on many monuments (Porter and Moss, *Top. Bibl.* I^{2}, ii, 694, 714, 723–4, 732, 739, 743; N. Scott, *MMA Bulletin* (Dec. 1962), 149–52; M.-L. Buhl, *A Hundred Masterpieces from The Ancient Near East* (Copenhagen, 1974), 27; Tosi and Roccati, *Stele*, 50040 and 50074; J. J. Clère, *Rev. d'Ég.* 27 (1975), 70–7; *KRI* III, 675–89).

Preservation and colour: The stela is not in a good state of preservation. It is badly worn with numerous small cracks. Traces of yellow paint can be seen on the hieroglyphs, the background and parts of the figures. There are the remains of red paint on the bodies of the figures in the lower register and on the body of the god and on his throne in the upper register. There are traces of blue paint on the serpent's head of Meresger. Spots of a black substance are found adhering to parts of the stela.

Bibliography: *Guide* (1922), 114 (no. 54); Porter and Moss, *Top. Bibl.* I^{2}, ii, 723–4.

1. Undoubtedly Deir el-Medina on internal evidence.

2. Stela of *Ḳn* ( ) 815

Date: Nineteenth Dynasty
Provenance: Not recorded[1]
Date of acquisition: 1854 (Valentia collection)[2]
Material: Limestone
Dimensions: 29 cm *h.*, 34.5 cm *w.*

This fragmentary round-topped stela bears a scene in raised relief with incised texts. Osiris stands in the centre facing right and behind him stands the deified Amenophis I with one arm raised. On the right the goddess Hathor was depicted as a cow emerging from the mountain, but most of this part of the scene has been lost. Below are four columns of text naming the chiseller Qen, son of *Ṯ3-nfr* ( ), and Maʿetnefret, whose name is lost, his wife *Nfrt-ỉry* ( ) and his son *Mry-mry* ( ).

For Qen see above, no. 1. His son Merymery appears frequently in Tomb 4 (Černý, *Répertoire*, 44–50).

Preservation and colour: Only two fragments of the original stela survive. They have been joined together in modern times, and the features of the gods have been restored. The surviving pieces are worn along the edges and chipped in places. There appear to be traces of red paint on the skirt of Amenophis I. The lower edge is blackened, possibly by fire.

Bibliography: *Sculpture Guide* (1909), 101 (no. 350); *Hieroglyphic Texts*, VI, pl. 31; Porter and Moss, *Top. Bibl.* I^{2}, ii, 723; *KRI* III, 687, no. 257(14).

1. Undoubtedly Deir el-Medina on internal evidence.
2. Presented by A. Lyttleton Annesley.

3. Statue of *Ḥwy* ( ) 942

Date: Nineteenth-Twentieth Dynasty
Provenance: Not recorded[1]
Date of acquisition: 1865[2]
Material: Limestone
Dimensions: 26 cm *h.*, 22 cm *w.*, 20.5 cm *deep*

This piece consists of the remains of a kneeling figure holding a stela in front of it. On the upper part of the stela the bark of Reʿ is depicted in sunk relief. Below it are six horizontal lines of incised text containing a prayer to Reʿ on behalf of the workman Huy.

The name of Huy is quite common in Deir el-Medina during the Ramesside period, and this workman cannot be identified with any certainty.

Preservation and colour: Only the lower part of the statue consisting of part of the torso and legs remains. The top of the stela is heavily damaged and the lowest line of text is preserved only in part. The sides of the stela are chipped and there are gouges and scratches on the face of the stela. Traces of red paint can be seen on the body and legs of the statue.

Bibliography: *Sculpture Guide* (1909), 148 (no. 530); Porter and Moss, *Top. Bibl.* I^{2}, ii, 711.

1. Undoubtedly Deir el-Medina on internal evidence.
2. Presented by the Trustees of the collection of Henry Christy.

Plate 86

Stela of *Ḳn-ḥr-ḫpš.f* ( ) 278

Date: Twentieth Dynasty
Provenance: Thebes[1]
Date of acquisition: 1843 (Belmore collection)
Material: Limestone
Dimensions: 33.5 cm *h.*, 23.5 cm *w.*

This round-topped stela is divided into two sections by a horizontal strip which is largely blank. The upper register bears a scene in sunk relief. The goddess Hathor is seated on a throne before an altar covered with offerings. Behind her stands a personified *ankh*-symbol holding up a fan. An invocation to Hathor, Amen-Reʿ and Mut is incised in six columns. In a further column on the right the name of the owner's mother, *Nỉwt-nḫt* ( ) is inscribed.[2] On the left side of the horizontal dividing strip the names of the owner's sons, *Nbt-st3* ( ) and *'Imn-(m)-ḥb* ( ), are incised.

The main body of the stela consists of a prayer to Hathor by the workman Qenhikhepeshef, son of the workman *Ḫʿ-(m)-nwn* ( ), in twelve columns of incised text. He names his wife, the lady of the house,[3] *T3-nfrt* ( ), and his sons *'Imn-nḫt* ( )

and *K3-(m)-pr-Ptḥ* (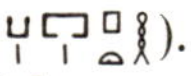). The figure of Qenhikhepeshef kneeling with arms raised in an attitude of worship is carved in raised relief at the bottom right of the stela. Part of his wig is depicted under his chin. On the left of the figure the name of his daughter *Nìwt-nḫt* (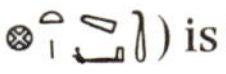) is incised. The text of this stela exhibits a number of errors in spelling and placement of signs.

The workman Qenhikhepeshef and his family are well-documented inhabitants of the Deir el-Medina community (J. Černý, *JEA* 31 (1945), 29–53; Bierbrier, *Late New Kingdom*, 28–9). He flourished during the reigns of Ramesses III to Ramesses V and was probably born about the beginning of the Twentieth Dynasty. His sons Amennakhte, Kaemperptah and Nebseta (written without the otiose *t*) are named in Theban graffiti together with another son, Ptahpahapi (omitted in Bierbrier, *Late New Kingdom*, Chart VII), unless he is to be identified with Amenemhab who is not otherwise attested (W. Spiegelberg, *Ägyptische und andere Graffiti aus der Thebanischen Nekropolis* (Heidelberg, 1921), nos. 803, 830, 868, 869b).

Preservation and colour: The stela is in a good state of preservation apart from some damage on the edges. There are no traces of colour.

Bibliography: *Belmore Collection*, pl. 6; Maspero, *Rec. trav.* 2 (1880), 189, 194–5; *Sculpture Guide* (1909), 175 (no. 632); Bruyère, *Mert Seger à Deir el Médineh* (Cairo, 1930), 23–8; J. Černý, *JEA* 31 (1945), 45–7; Porter and Moss, *Top. Bibl.* I², ii, 708–9.

1. Undoubtedly Deir el-Medina on internal evidence.
2. The reading is clearly *mwt.f*, but it appears that it was originally written *mwt.k* and then corrected.
3. Wrongly written *nbw* instead of *nb(t) pr*. Ranke, *Personennamen*, 187 (10) mistakenly transcribes it as *Nbw-t3-nfrt*.

Plate 87

1. Stela of *Kn-ʾImn* (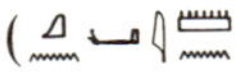)[1] 916

Date: Twentieth Dynasty
Provenance: Not recorded[2]
Date of acquisition: 1868 (Hay collection)
Material: Limestone
Dimensions: 21.5 cm *h.*, 16 cm *w.*

This small round-topped stela comprises one scene with two columns of text, all crudely incised. The deified Ahmes-Nefertari stands on the left and is being worshipped by the workman Qenamun who stands on the right. Between them lies an altar piled with offerings.

A workman Qenamun or Qeny, son of Amenemonet is attested on several monuments dated to the middle of the Twentieth Dynasty (J. Černý, *Egyptian Stelae in the Bankes Collection* (Oxford, 1958), no. 10; L. Speelers, *Recueil des Inscriptions égyptiennes des Musées Royaux du Cinquantenaire à Bruxelles* (Brussels, 1923), no. 257 and Bruyère, *Mert Seger à Deir el Médineh* (Cairo, 1930), fig. 83; Bruyère, op. cit., fig. 45; and probably Tosi and Roccati, *Stele*, 50032).

Preservation and colour: The stela is well preserved and there are no traces of colour.

Bibliography: *Sculpture Guide* (1909), 100 (no. 345); Porter and Moss, *Top. Bibl.* I², ii, 724; Gitton, *L'Épouse du Dieu Ahmes Néfertary* (Paris, 1975), 45–6 (13), 69.

1. The name appears to have been written *Pn-ʾImn* although there is a small scratch in the lower left corner of the  sign which may have been an attempt to correct it. There is no doubt that the name of *Kn-ʾImn* was intended from the determinative. The stela exhibits other spelling peculiarities in the titles of the workman and the queen.

2. Undoubtedly Deir el-Medina on internal evidence.

2. Fragment of a libation bowl 465

Date: Nineteenth-Twentieth Dynasty
Provenance: Not recorded
Date of acquisition: Not recorded
Material: Limestone
Dimensions: 57 cm *diam.*

This fragment of a libation bowl bears the remains of three figures at one end and an incised inscription along the rim consisting of a double dedication to Isis and T[houeris]. The son of the dedicant is named as *Ḥr-Mnw* (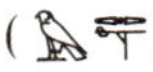). According to Birch, the end of the inscription on the right side, which is now broken away, read (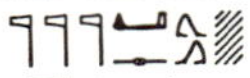).

This piece may possibly originate from Deir el-Medina where a Harmin, son of Wenenkhu, is attested in the Nineteenth Dynasty (see BM 36861, pl. 80), and a Harmin, son of Hori, is known in the Twentieth Dynasty (J. Černý, *Graffiti hiéroglyphiques et hiératiques de la Nécropole thébaine* 1082, 1323, 1338).

Preservation and colour: Only half of the bowl remains, and this section is broken and badly chipped. The three figures are cracked and chipped, and one is completely headless. There are no traces of colour.

Bibliography: *Sculpture Guide* (1909), 181 (no. 651); Porter and Moss, *Top. Bibl.* I², ii, 746.

Plate 88

1. Stela of *ʾIy-m-t3-pt* (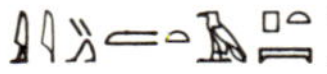) 8501

Date: Nineteenth-Twentieth Dynasty
Provenance: Not recorded
Date of acquisition: Not recorded
Material: Limestone
Dimensions: 15.4 cm *h.*, 10.8 cm *w.*

This small round-topped stela is divided into two registers with incised texts and figures in sunk relief. In the upper register the goddess Meresger is shown in the form of a coiled serpent with a plumed head-dress before an altar on which rests a water-pot cooled by a lotus-blossom. In the lower register the lady Iyemtapet kneels with her arms raised in adoration.

The lady Iyemtapet is otherwise unknown. It is possible that this stela comes from Deir el-Medina where the cult of Meresger was popular.

Preservation and colour: The stela is well preserved apart from some damage along the edges. Traces of blue paint remain on the altar, while some red paint is visible in the border between the two registers and on the disk in the head-dress of the goddess. There is black paint on the body of the serpent and on some hieroglyphs.

Bibliography: *Guide* (1922), 114 (no. 53); Porter and Moss, *Top. Bibl.* I², ii, 722.

2. Stela of *ʾIy* . . . (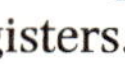) 810

Date: Nineteenth-Twentieth Dynasties
Provenance: Not recorded[1]
Date of acquisition: 1854 (Valentia collection)[2]
Material: Limestone
Dimensions: 26 cm *h.*, 24.8 cm *w.*

This fragmentary round-topped stela bears on its surface the remains of two registers. The figures are in sunk relief and the texts are incised. The goddess Sakhmet is seated on a throne on the left of the upper register. In front of her stands an altar on which sits a water-pot cooled by a lotus-blossom. A male figure, mostly obliterated, kneels on the right in adoration. He is identified as a workman from Deir el-Medina, but the name is damaged and only Iy ... can be read with certainty. The traces do not appear to suit any known name from Deir el-Medina.

Only the upper part of the lower register is preserved. The head of a figure, facing right and apparently kneeling in adoration, appears in the centre, but the object of his devotion on the right is not clearly preserved. Four short columns of text above the head apparently give the name of the father of the figure in the upper register.

Preservation and colour: The stela is in a poor state of preservation. Most of the lower portion is lost and the surface of the remainder is badly broken and worn away. The surface is discoloured by areas of black which may be traces of fire.

Bibliography: *Sculpture Guide* (1909), 185 (no. 663); Porter and Moss, *Top. Bibl.* I^2, ii, 722.

1. Undoubtedly Deir el-Medina on internal evidence.
2. Presented by A. Lyttleton Annesley.

Plate 89

Stela of *Nb-nfr* ( ) 65356

Date: Nineteenth-Twentieth Dynasty
Provenance: Not recorded[1]
Date of acquisition: 1939 (Mond collection)
Material: Limestone
Dimensions: 25.5 cm *h.*, 17 cm *w.*

This round-topped stela depicts Amen-Reʿ seated on a throne on the left being worshipped by the workman Nebnufer who stands on the right. It appears that Nebnufer originally held a brazier and a flower but these were later erased, possibly because the figure of the god and man were found to be too close together. Six columns of text appear at the top of the stela. Both figures and text are painted.

Nebnufer was a common name at Deir el-Medina during the Nineteenth and Twentieth Dynasties, and it is not therefore possible to identify this workman more precisely. See Tosi and Roccati, *Stele*, 50070, for another stela dedicated to Amen-Reʿ, *ṯhn nfr*, which also names a Nebnufer.

Preservation and colour: This stela is well preserved apart from some areas of the text which have worn away. There are slight cracks on the surface of the stone. Most of the colour has survived. The background of the stela is white with a black border at the bottom edge and a blue-green border along the sides and top edge. The hieroglyphs are black between red borders. The figure of Nebnufer is outlined in grey with a red body, black wig and facial features, blue jewellery and white kilt. Amen-Reʿ is painted dark green over a blue base with black facial features. He wears a white collar and white robe with red dots. His crown was reddish-brown, now mostly worn away, and his plumes were outlined in black and white and composed of red, blue and white blotches of colour. The throne is painted in sections of red, white and blue-green.

Bibliography: Porter and Moss, *Top. Bibl.* I^2, ii, 727.

1. Undoubtedly Deir el-Medina on internal evidence.

Plates 90–91

Pyramidion of *Ḥr-nfr* ( ) 479

Date: Nineteenth Dynasty
Provenance: Not recorded[1]
Date of acquisition: 1834[2]
Material: Sandstone
Dimensions: 40 cm *h.*, 33.5 cm *w.*

Each face of this pyramidion is divided into two sections by a horizontal line of text consisting of an invocation by the workman Harnufer to Reʿ and other gods. The lower parts of three sides (A, B, D) are further divided by a column of text in the middle of each containing a prayer by Harnufer. All representations are carved in sunk relief and all texts are incised.

On Face A the bark of Reʿ is depicted in the upper section, and at the top of the pyramidion is inscribed the name of Reʿ-Harakhty-Atum. Below, the *ʿ3 n ʿ m st m3ʿt* Harnufer and his 'son', the *ʿ3 n ʿ m st m3ʿt* Harnufer, stand facing each other with their arms raised in adoration. On the upper part of Face B the goddesses Isis and Nephthys kneel in adoration of the Amentet standard, the upper part of which is damaged. Below, Harnufer and his wife *Nfrt-ỉry* ( ) stand with arms raised in worship.

The upper part of Face C is heavily damaged and only the lower part of a figure holding a sceptre can be discerned. Below, the workman *ʿ3-ḥtp.f* ( ) stands in adoration together with his daughter (written *s3.f* but with female figure and female determinative) whose name is damaged but may end in *...dbt* ( ). On the upper part of Face D appears a winged scarab with sun-disk and, below, Harnufer and his wife *Wbḫt* ( ) stand in adoration.

Two distinct Harnufers appear on this pyramidion, one being described as the 'son' of the other, but it is probable that this expression is not to be taken literally and may only indicate a descendant. Each Harnufer is depicted with his wife on Faces B and D, although it is not clear which couple is the older and which represents the younger. Only the couple Harnufer-Nefertari is attested elsewhere (Bruyère, *Deir el Médineh (1933–1934)*, 140). An *ʿ3 n ʿ m st m3ʿt* Harnufer, son of Nebdjefau, who flourished in the reign of Ramesses II is well known from other monuments in this collection and elsewhere (*Hieroglyphic Texts*, 9, pls. 33–4; Tosi and Roccati, *Stele*, 50206; S. Bosticco, *Le Stele egiziane* II (Rome, 1965), no. 55; Bruyère, *Deir el Médineh (1926)*, 74; *KRI* III, 796–9). On BM 28 his wife's name is given as Hemetnetjer, but he also appears as a contemporary of the workman ʿAhotpef who is cited on BM 479. It would seem that he must be identical with one of the Harnufers on BM 479, probably the elder, and so had more than one wife. He is possibly the workman who is attested in Year 40 of Ramesses II (BM ostracon 5634, see *Hier. Ostr.*, pl. 83, l. 3), while the younger Harnufer may be the workman who appears under Sethos II (O. Cairo 25510) and Siptah (O. Cairo 25516; O. Cairo 25517; O. Cairo 25521).

The workman ʿAhotpef, who is twice associated with Harnufer, also appears on Stela Voronezh 157 where he is identified as a 'brother' of Nebamentet, son of Kasa

(E. Bogoslovsky, *Vestnik Drevnei Istorii* no. 120 (1972), pl. 5).

Preservation and colour: The pyramidion is severely damaged at the base and at the top resulting in loss to both scenes and text in varying degrees of severity. There are several large gouges on the surface. There are no traces of colour.

Bibliography: Maspero, *Rec. trav.* 2 (1880), 189; *Sculpture Guide* (1909), 192 (no. 699); Porter and Moss, *Top. Bibl.* I^2, ii, 744; *KRI* III, 798, no. 298(8).

1. Undoubtedly Deir el-Medina on internal evidence.
2. Presented by Sir J. Gardner Wilkinson.

Plate 92

Offering-table of *ʾI[m]n-...* (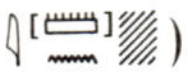) 424

Date: Nineteenth-Twentieth Dynasty
Provenance: Not recorded[1]
Date of acquisition: 1843 (Belmore collection)
Material: Limestone
Dimensions: 18.6 cm *l.*, 17.5 cm *w.*

The shape of this offering-table is based on the form of the sign the base of which represents the area for the reception of offerings, while the 'loaf' on top forms the spout. The offering area, which is depressed below the surface of the rim, is covered with representations of offerings carved in shallow sunk relief. The upper surface of the rim bears incised texts invoking funerary offerings on behalf of the workman A[me]n-... whose full name is lost; in the right-hand text Osiris is invoked and in the left-hand text Harakhty-Atum is named. To the right and left of the 'loaf' are cut the names of *Bw-ḳn t.f* (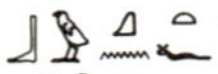) and the lady of the house, *Nbw-m-wsḫt* (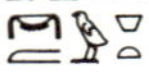), who are presumably husband and wife.

This couple is not attested elsewhere. At least two Bukentefs are known from Deir el-Medina: Bukentef, son of Nakhy, who is probably the same man as Bukentef, husband of Ii and father of Amennakhte, in the Nineteenth Dynasty (for whom see the discussion of BM 1629, pl. 63) and Bukentef, husband of Tarekhanu and father of Amennakhte, who flourished in the Twentieth Dynasty (Stato civile A, II, 1–2 cited by Černý, *Community*, 357).[2] Either Bukentef could have been the husband of Nubemweskhet if he married twice, but she would not have been the mother of Amennakhte if that is the name of the owner of this offering-table. It is possible that a third Bukentef might be considered or that the relationships of the three individuals on this table are otherwise than those initially proposed.

Preservation and colour: The lower left-hand edge and most of the bottom edge have been lost, and the right-hand edge is chipped in places. The losses have been restored in modern times. There are no traces of colour.

Bibliography: *Sculpture Guide* (1909), 173 (no. 627); Porter and Moss, *Top. Bibl.* I^2, ii, 743.

1. Undoubtedly Deir el-Medina on internal evidence.
2. I wish to thank the Committee of Management of the Griffith Institute for permission to consult the complete entry of this portion of the Stato civile as transcribed in *Černý Notebook* 15. 64.

Plate 93

Relief of *Nb-ms* (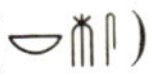) 1465

Date: Nineteenth-Twentieth Dynasties
Provenance: Not recorded
Date of acquisition: 1908
Material: Limestone
Dimensions: 75 cm *h.*, 215 cm *w.*

There are two almost identical scenes on each side of this relief with incised texts and figures and objects in sunk relief. The slab is divided in the centre by a vertical row of floral offerings and similar, although smaller, offerings occur on the left and right edges of the relief. On the left side of the relief the chantress of Isis, *B3k(t)-ʿnḫt* (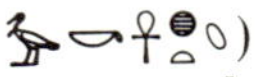) stands holding an offering before the fan-bearer on the right of the king, royal scribe, overseer of the treasury and first prophet of Isis, Mistress of Iseum, Nebmose, who is seated facing her and holding lotus-flowers in his hands. Between the two figures is an altar heaped with offerings. A similar scene occurs on the right side of the relief.

Nebmose appears to be otherwise unknown. It has been stated without any firm evidence that this relief comes from Memphis or Saqqara. As it was purchased in Cairo, the provenance of the New Kingdom cemetery at Saqqara seems possible. However, the relief may have come from a tomb at Iseum (Bahbit el-Higara).

Preservation and colour: The top left corner and most of the cornice (now restored) are lost. Several large cracks on the surface of the stone have been repaired in modern times. Traces of red paint remain on some of the flowers.

Bibliography: *Sculpture Guide* (1909), 176 (no. 635); Porter and Moss, *Top. Bibl.* III^2, 759.

Plate 94

Stela of *N3y3* (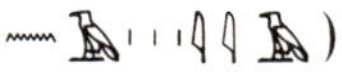)[1] 795

Date: Nineteenth Dynasty
Provenance: Not recorded
Date of acquisition: 1858[2]
Material: Limestone
Dimensions: 54.8 cm *h.*, 35.2 cm *w.*

This round-topped stela is divided into three registers. All figures are in sunk relief and all texts are incised. In the upper register the first stable-master of the lord of the two lands and royal messenger to every land, Naya, is kneeling on the right in adoration of Osiris who is seated in the centre and behind whom stand Isis, Horus and Khnum. In front of Osiris lies an altar on which rests a water-pot cooled by a lotus-blossom.

In the second register the stable-master Naya stands beside a heap of offerings and is pouring a libation and offering incense to six figures squatting on the ground: his father, the overseer of horses, *P3y* (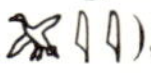), his mother, the lady of the house and chantress of Khnum, *ʿš3t-nbw* (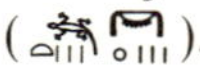), his sister, the lady of the house and chantress of Khnum, *Ty* (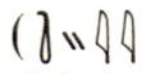), his son, the *wʿb*-priest of Khnum, *P(3)-n-T3-wr(t)* (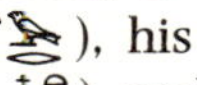), his sister, the chantress of Khnum, *Wrt-nfrt* (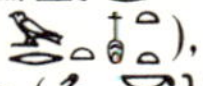), and his sister, the chantress of Khnum, *B3kti3* (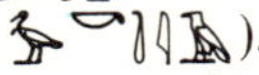).

In the third register Naya is shown making similar offerings before seven squatting individuals: his father (doubtless grandfather), the overseer of the cattle of

Amun, *N3y3* ([hieroglyphs]), his sister, the lady of the house and chantress of Khnum, *Wr(t)-nfrt* ([hieroglyphs]) (Naya the elder's wife and Naya the younger's grandmother), the chantress of Khnum, *Ḥry* ([hieroglyphs]), the chantress of Khnum, *Nbt-wnw* ([hieroglyphs])[3], his sister, the chantress of Khnum, *3st* ([hieroglyphs]), the *wʿb*-priest and temple-scribe of Khnum, *P3-sr* ([hieroglyphs]), and the porter of ... *P3-sr* ([hieroglyphs]), whose title is obscure but may refer to some type of shrine or ritual object.

This family does not appear to be otherwise attested apart from a *shabti* in Berlin of the overseer of cattle, Naya, who is possibly Naya the elder (G. Roeder, *Äegyptische Inschriften aus den Staatlichen Museen zu Berlin*, II (Leipzig, 1924), 592).

Preservation and colour: The stela is in a good state of preservation. In places the text and figures have been carved directly over the imperfections in the stone with no attempt being made to smooth the surface. There are no traces of colour.

Bibliography: Lieblein, *Dictionnaire*, no. 995; *Sculpture Guide* (1909), 183 (no. 656); M. Valloggia, *Recherche sur les 'Messagers' (WPWTYW) dans les sources égyptiennes profanes* (Paris, 1976), 162–4).

1. It would appear that some confusion has occurred among the records of the *Wörterbuch* since this stela is there stated to be in Turin, and this location is cited by both Ranke, *Personennamen*, and Valloggia who has seen a squeeze of this stela preserved in Berlin.
2. Lot 109 of an unknown sale at Stevens. Purchased by Sir Thomas Phillipps who presented it to the British Museum.
3. Wrongly read as *Nbt-wnšw* by Ranke, *Personennamen* I, 188.

Plate 95

Stela of *Nb-ḏf3w* ([hieroglyphs]) 793

Date: Nineteenth-Twentieth Dynasty
Provenance: Not recorded
Date of acquisition: 1858[1]
Material: Limestone
Dimensions: 57 cm *h*., 36 cm *w*.

The scene on this round-topped stela is carved in sunk relief. Osiris is depicted standing on the left. He is being worshipped by the royal scribe and overseer of the granaries of Upper and Lower Egypt, Nebdjefau, who stands on the right. Between them lies an altar on which rests a water-pot cooled by a lotus-flower. Four vertical columns of hieroglyphs incised above Nebdjefau contain a prayer to Osiris on his behalf, while a single horizontal line of text incised at the bottom of the stela gives his name and titles.

The overseer of the two granaries, Nebdjefau, appears not to be attested elsewhere (not in Helck, *Verwaltung*).

Preservation and colour: The stela is in an excellent state of preservation apart from a few scratches and a covering of small black smudges. There are no traces of colour.

Bibliography: *Sculpture Guide* (1909), 203 (no. 739).

1. Lot 106 of an unknown sale at Stevens.

Plates 96–97

Stela of *ʾIy-mỉ-sb3* ([hieroglyphs]) 1680

Date: Nineteenth-Twentieth Dynasty
Provenance: Not recorded
Date of acquisition: 1919
Material: Quartzite
Dimensions: 45 cm *h*., 25.5 cm *w*.

This round-topped stela is decorated on both sides with scenes in sunk relief and incised texts. Each side is divided into two registers. In the upper register of one side (A) Imiseba, the *wʿb*-priest before Thoth, god's father, and deputy in the temple of Thoth, is shown on the left offering incense and pouring a libation over an altar covered with offerings before Osiris who stands on the right. In the lower register there is a prayer to Osiris on behalf of Imiseba made by his son, the god's father of Thoth, *P(3)-n-Ḏḥwty* ([hieroglyphs]). A male figure, presumably this son, is depicted on the left kneeling with his arms raised in worship.

In the upper register on the other side (B) Imiseba stands on the right holding a censer and pouring a libation over an altar covered with offerings before Thoth who stands on the left. In the lower register there is a prayer to Thoth, lord of Hermopolis, on behalf of the chantress of Thoth, *Nfrt-ỉry* ([hieroglyphs]), made by her son, the god's father of Thoth and deputy in the temple of Thoth, Pendjehuty. The lady is depicted kneeling on the right with arms raised and a sistrum in one hand.

Imiseba, his wife, and his son are otherwise unknown. Although this stela was acquired in the Theban area, it is probable that it originates from Hermopolis.

Preservation and colour: The stela is in good condition apart from some wear to one surface which makes some signs difficult to distinguish. The surface is pitted with small holes. There are no traces of colour.

Bibliography: None.

Plate 98

Stela of *Smn-t3wy* ([hieroglyphs]) 312

Date: Nineteenth-Twentieth Dynasty
Provenance: Not recorded
Date of acquisition: Not recorded
Material: Limestone
Dimensions: 49.2 cm *h*., 35.5 cm *w*.

There are two registers with figures in sunk relief and incised texts on the face of this round-topped stela. In the upper register Osiris is seated on a throne on the left and Isis stands behind him with one arm upraised. Before him is an altar covered with a lotus-flower. The chief shield-bearer of His Majesty Smentawy stands on the right with his arms raised in worship. In the lower register stand four figures, one male, two females and another male, facing left with their arms raised in adoration. They are named as his father, the chief shield-bearer *Rʿỉ3* ([hieroglyphs]), [his] mother ... the chantress of [Ba]nebdjed, *ʾIs3y* or *Ḥn3y* ([hieroglyphs]), [the lady of] the house and chantress of Thoth, arbitrator of the two combatants, *T3-b3-s3* ([hieroglyphs]), and his son, the *wʿb*-priest of Banebdjed, *Ḥrỉ* ([hieroglyphs]).

For other shield-bearers see López and Yoyotte, *Bi. Or.* 26 (1969), 10–11, 17. The god Banebdjed was chiefly worshipped at Mendes, and Thoth was the main deity of near-by Hermopolis Parva, so it appears probable that this stela came from that vicinity as suggested to me by A. Zivie, whom I wish to thank for this and other comments regarding this stela.

Preservation and colour: The stela has been broken in two in the past and subsequently repaired with loss to part of the text at the top of the lower register. There are no traces of colour.

Bibliography: Lieblein, *Dictionnaire*, no. 948; *Sculpture Guide* (1909), 195 (no. 709).

Plate 99

Stela of *ʾImn-m-wỉ3* ([hieroglyphs]) 1183

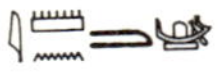

Date: Twentieth Dynasty
Provenance: Not recorded
Date of acquisition: 1894
Material: Limestone
Dimensions: 54.5 cm *h.*, 34 cm *w.*

This round-topped stela is divided into three registers with figures in sunk relief and incised texts. In the upper register the commander of the *mškbyw* of the ship's contingent Ramesses III, beloved of Sekhmet, Amenemwia, called *K3r* ([hieroglyphs]), kneels on the right in adoration of Osiris who is enthroned in the centre and behind whom stand Horus and Isis.

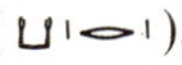

In the second register two women and one man kneel in an attitude of worship: the lady of the house and chantress of Preʿ, *T3-bw-b3* ([hieroglyphs]), his mother, the chantress of the lady of the sycamore, *Mwt-m-wỉ3* ([hieroglyphs]), and his paternal grandfather, the keeper of secrets of the temple of Reʿ, *ʾInḥr(t)–nḫt* ([hieroglyphs]). In the third register four men stand in adoration: his father, the *ỉt nṯr* priest and keeper of secrets of the temple of Merenptah in the temple of Reʿ, *Ḥwy* ([hieroglyphs]), his brother, the first charioteer of His Majesty, *P3-Rʿ-m-ḥb* ([hieroglyphs]), his brother, the King's Son (?), *My* ([hieroglyphs]), and his brother, the *wʿb*-priest of the temple of Reʿ-Harakhty, *P3-ỉwỉw* ([hieroglyphs]).

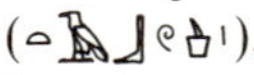

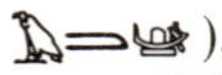

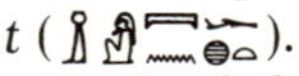

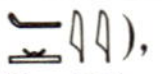

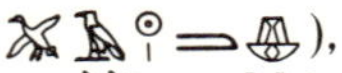

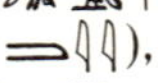

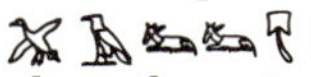

This family appears to be otherwise unknown. The titles of the father and grandfather indicate that they held office in Heliopolis, possibly the provenance of this stela. The temple of Merenptah in the temple of Reʿ is elsewhere attested only in the Wilbour papyrus of the time of Ramesses V (A. Gardiner, *The Wilbour Papyrus* (Oxford, 1948), A79). For a discussion of the meaning of the term *mškbyw* see J. Janssen, *Two Ancient Egyptian Ship's Logs* (Leiden, 1961), 34–5; A. R. Schulman, *ZÄS* 93 (1966), 129–32. Schulman's conjecture that they were connected with the chariotry is lessened by the clear connection with the navy in this stela. For the writing of *tpy* in the title of Pareemheb compare BM 154 in *Hieroglyphic Texts*, 9, pl. 2. Paiuiu, son of Kar, is presumably distinct from the stable-master Paiuiu, son of Karbu, who appears in the Wilbour papyrus A32 and A35.

The status of My is not clear. He does not occupy a prominent position on the stela, and yet his title indicates that he was a 'King's Son'. He is unlikely to have been a royal prince and no viceroy of Kush of this name is known, so it is probable that the title was of religious significance (B. Schmitz, *Untersuchungen zum Titel S3-Njswt 'Konigssohn'* (Bonn, 1976), 270–87).

Preservation and colour: Apart from the loss of the top right corner and several gouges and black blotches on the surface, the stela is well preserved. There are no traces of colour.

Bibliography: *Sculpture Guide* (1909), 193 (no. 701).

Plate 100

Stela of *Ḳry-Ḥrỉ* ([hieroglyphs]) or *Ḥrỉ* ([hieroglyphs]) 327

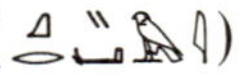

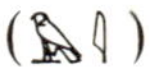

Date: Nineteenth Dynasty
Provenance: Not recorded
Date of acquisition: Not recorded
Material: Limestone
Dimensions: 37 cm *h.*, 25 cm *w.*

This round-topped stela in sunk relief with incised texts consists of three registers. In the upper register Isis stands on the left behind Osiris who is seated on a throne. Before him is an altar on which rests a lotus-flower. He is being worshipped by Qery-Hori or Hori who kneels with arms raised on the right.

The second register depicts one woman and two men in an attitude of adoration. They are named as the chantress of Amun, *T3-wr(t)* ([hieroglyphs]), the attendant *P(3)-n-T3-wrt* ([hieroglyphs]) and the attendant *B3k-n-ʾImn* ([hieroglyphs]). In the third register one woman, the chantress of Amun, *ʿn-t3-ḫytw* ([hieroglyphs]), and one man, the scribe *ʿn-ḥr-ỉ3wt.f* ([hieroglyphs]), are shown kneeling in worship.

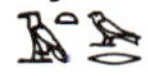

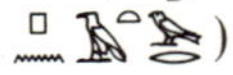

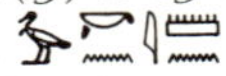

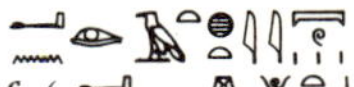

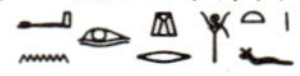

The word *ḳry* ([hieroglyphs]) is elsewhere only attested on a Dakhleh stela before the name of a *ỉt nṯr* priest and is taken by Gardiner and Ranke as part of his name, Qery-Sutekh (Gardiner, *JEA* 19 (1933), pl. VII.,l. 19 and Ranke, *Personennamen* I, 336). Ranke also regards this attestation on BM 327 as a name (Ranke, *Personennamen*, II, 320). However, *Wörterbuch* V, 57 regards *ḳry* as a title. It is unlikely to be a form of *ḳwr*, 'miner' (*Wörterbuch*, V, 21) or *ḳʿrw*, 'shield-bearer' (V, 59), in view of the fact that it once appears in connection with a god's father priest. For a detailed discussion of *ḳwr* see Y. Koenig, *Hommages à Serge Sauneron* I (Cairo, 1979), 212–15.

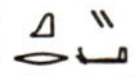

It is possible that the scribe Anheriautef is to be identified with a scribe of the lord of the two lands Anheriautef, whose statue, dated by the cartouche of Ramesses II, is in the Leiden collection (P. Boeser, *Beschreibung der Aegyptischen Sammlung in Leiden: Die Denkmäler des Neuens Reiches* II (The Hague, 1913), 7 (no. 17)).

Preservation and colour: The condition of the stela is good with only slight surface damage. There are no traces of colour.

Bibliography: Lieblein, *Dictionnaire*, no. 951; *Sculpture Guide* (1909), 184 (no. 660).

Index to Numbers

Indexes of Names and Titles

1 Royal Names

2 Private Names

Nfrt-ỉry f. 281 (pl. 6), 479 (pl. 90), 815 (pls. 84–5), 1629 (pl. 63), 1680 (pls. 96–7), 8493 (pls. 84–5)
Nfrt-stt f. 1388 (pl. 76)
Ns-'Imn m. 161 (pls. 52–3)
Nšʿ f. 161 (pls. 52–3)

R-k3 m. 476 (pls. 58–60)
Ry f. 160 (pls. 4–5)
Rʿ-wbn m. 320 (pl. 81)
Rʿ-ms m. 320 (pl. 81), 444 (pl. 69), 1377 (pl. 49)
Rʿ-ḥtp m. 186 (pl. 78)
Rʿỉ3 m. 312 (pl. 98)
Ršpw m. 161 (pls. 52–3)

Hrw-nfr m. 1188 (pls. 54–5)
Hd-nḫt m. 273 (pl. 71)

Ḥ3y m. 8495 (pl. 82)
Ḥ3t-šps(t) f. 476 (pl. 60)
Ḥwy m. 291 (pl. 65), 444 (pl. 69), 448 (pl. 68), 942 (pls. 84–5), 1183 (pl. 99)
Ḥwt-Ḥr f. 476 (pl. 60), 588 (pl. 57), 8495 (pl. 82)
Ḥmww-wr-sḫm m. 845 (pls. 36–7)
Ḥmt-nṯr f. 1629 (pl. 63)
Ḥn3y f. 312 (pl. 98)
Ḥnwt-'Iwnw f. 476 (pl. 60)
Ḥnwt-wḏbw f. 1388 (pl. 76)
Ḥnwt-bw-ḥmt.s f. 476 (pl. 60)
Ḥnwt-n-m3ʿt f. 476 (pl. 60)
Ḥnwt-ḏww f. 161 (pls. 52–3), 597 (pls. 66–7)
Ḥr-m-ḥb m. 1188 (pls. 54–5)
Ḥr-Mnw m. 465 (pl. 87), 36861 (pl. 80), 64641 (pl. 61)
Ḥr-nfr m. 479 (pls. 90–1)
Ḥrỉ m. 312 (pl. 98), 327 (pl. 100), 588 (pl. 57), 845 (pls. 36–9)
Ḥry f. 795 (pl. 94)

Ḫʿ-m-W3st m. 845 (pls. 36–7), 947 (pls. 33–5), 48664 (pl. 22), 49235 (pl. 22)
Ḫʿ-(m)-nn m. 278 (pl. 86)
Ḫnsw m. 161 (pls. 52–3)

H̱nm-ms m. 1188 (pls. 54–5)

S3y m. 972 (pl. 8)
S3ḥtỉ f. 1188 (pls. 54–5)
Smn-t3wy m. 312 (pl. 98)
Sn-snb f. 476 (pls. 58–60)
St3w m. 78 (pls. 42–3), 556 (pl. 41), 1055 (pls. 44–5)

Ḳ3ḥ3 m. 274 (pls. 66–7), 291 (pl. 65)
Ḳn m. 815 (pls. 84–5), 8493 (pls. 84–5)
Ḳn-'Imn m. 916 (pl. 87)
Ḳn-m-ḫps.f m. 320 (pl. 81)
Ḳn-ḥr-ḫps.f m. 278 (pl. 86)
Ḳry-Ḥrỉ m. 327 (pl. 100)

K3-(m)-pr-Ptḥ m. 278 (pl. 86)
K3r m. 1183 (pl. 99)

T-di.s (?) f. 1188 (pls. 54–5)
T3-ʿḳy f. 161 (pls. 52–3), 792 (pls. 44–5)
T3-wr(t) f. 161 (pls. 52–3), 327 (pl. 100)
T3-wsr(t) f. 792 (pls. 44–5)
T3-b3-s3 f. 312 (pl. 98)
T3-bw-b3 f. 1183 (pl. 99)
T3-nfrt f. 278 (pl. 86)
T3-n-... f. 1188 (pls. 54–5)
T3-n-shrry f. 161 (pls. 52–3)
T3-h3... f. 1388 (pl. 76)
T3-ḥr-ḥr f. 1188 (pls. 54–5)
Ty m. 972 (pl. 8)
Ty f. 795 (pl. 94)

Ṯ3-nfr m. 815 (pls. 84–5)
Ṯwỉ3 f. 476 (pl. 60)

Dydy m. 1629 (pl. 63)

...dbt f. 479 (pl. 91)

3 Titles

ỉmy ỉb n nṯr nfr 972 (pl. 8)
ỉmy-r ỉpt nsw 160 (pls. 4–5)
ỉmy-r iḥw 161 (pls. 52–3)
ỉmy-r iḥw n 'Imn 795 (pl. 94)
ỉmy-r iḥw n pr-'Imn 161 (pls. 52–3)
ỉmy-r wp(t) ḥtp n nṯr... 1377 (pl. 49)
ỉmy-r pr 556 (pl. 41)
ỉmy-r pr-wr 161 (pls. 52–3)
ỉmy-r pr-ḥḏ 1377 (pls. 49–51), 1465 (pl. 93)
ỉmy-r pr-ḥḏ n 'Imn 556 (pl. 41)
ỉmy-r pr-ḥḏ n nb t3wy 1377 (pls. 50–51)
ỉmy-r pr n nỉwt 78 (pls. 42–3), 556 (pl. 41)
ỉmy-r pr.wy n ḥḏ nbw 1377 (pls. 50–51)
ỉmy-r mšʿ... 68682 (pls. 38–9)
ỉmy-r nỉwt 35628 (pl. 32)
ỉmy-r ḥmw-nṯr 1188 (pls. 54–5)
ỉmy-r ḥmw-nṯr n nṯrw nbw 1188 (pls. 54–5), 1820 (pl. 40)
ỉmy-r ḥmw-nṯr (n) nṯrw nbw (n) T3-Šmʿw 1188 (pls. 54–5)
ỉmy-r ḥmwt 476 (pls. 58–60), 1188 (pls. 54–5)
ỉmy-r ḥmwt n pr-Ḥr nb Mỉʿm 476 (pls. 58–9)
ỉmy-r ḥmwt n nb t3wy 476 (pls. 58–59)
ỉmy-r ḫtmw rsyt mḥyt 1377 (pl. 49)
ỉmy-r ssmt 795 (pl. 94)
ỉmy-r šnwty n Šmʿw T3-mḥw 793 (pl. 95)
ỉm3t wrt 1662 (pl. 17)
ỉry-pʿt 845 (pls. 36–9), 972 (pl. 8), 1377 (pls. 50–1)
ỉry-pʿt ḥry-tp t3wy 68682 (pls. 38–9)
ỉry-pʿtt 1662 (pl. 17)
ỉrty n nsw 972 (pl. 8)
ỉt-nṯr 845 (pls. 36–9), 1183 (pl. 99), 1680 (pls. 96–7), 35628 (pl. 32)
ỉt-nṯr n 'Imn (?) 1214 (pl. 48)
ỉt nṯr n Ḏḥwty 1680 (pls. 96–7)
ỉdnw (n) ỉmy-r ỉḥw 161 (pls. 52–3)
ỉdnw (n) ỉmy-r ỉḥw n pr-'Imn 161 (pls. 52–3)
ỉdnw m pr-Ḏḥwty 1680 (pls. 96–7)
ỉdnw n t3 ỉswt 35630 (pl. 71)

ʿ3 n ỉswt m st m3ʿt 291 (pl. 65), 588 (pl. 57)
ʿ3 n ʿ m st m3ʿt 479 (pls. 90–1)
ʿnḫwy n bỉty 972 (pl. 8)
ʿḳ m Ḥwt-sr 476 (pls. 58–9)

wʿb 444 (pl. 69), 476 (pls. 58–9), 795 (pl. 94), 845 (pls. 36–7), 64641 (pl. 61)
wʿb n 'Imn 476 (pl. 60)
wʿb n B3-nb-ḏd 312 (pl. 98)
wʿb n pr-Rʿ-Ḥr-3ḫty 1183 (pl. 99)
wʿb n ḥ3t Ḏḥwty 1680 (pl. 96)
wʿb n H̱nm 795 (pl. 94)
wpty 588 (pl. 57)
wpty nsw r t3 nb 795 (pl. 94)
wr ḫrp ḥmww 845 (pls. 36–9), 972 (pl. 8), 59259 (pls. 38–9)
wr ḫrp hmww n pr-Ptḥ 845 (pl. 39)
wdpw nsw 588 (pl. 57)

mry nṯr 845 (pls. 36–9), 35628 (pl. 32)
mḥ-ỉb n nsw ... t3wy 1377 (pls. 50–1)
mḥt w3rḫy m sty ḏrt.s 1662 (pl. 17)

nbyw 1188 (pls. 54–5)
nbt-pr 278 (pl. 86), 281 (pl. 6), 312 (pl. 98), 424 (pl. 92), 476 (pls. 58–60), 479 (pls. 90–1), 597 (pls. 66–7), 598 (pl. 77), 792 (pls. 44–5), 795 (pl. 94), 815 (pls. 84–5), 1183 (pl. 99), 1188 (pls. 54–5), 1388 (pl. 76), 1465 (pl. 93), 1629 (pl. 63), 8493 (pls. 84–5), 8495 (pl. 82), 8501 (pl. 88), 65355 (pl. 72)
nbt mnỉwt 1662 (pl. 17)
nbt t3wy 1133 (pl. 21), 1662 (pl. 17)

ḥ3ty-ʿ 845 (pls. 36–39), 972 (pl. 8), 1188 (pls. 54–5), 1377 (pls.. 50–51), 35628 (pl. 32)

ḥ3ty-ʿ n W3st 121 (pl. 48)
ḥm-nṯr 444 (pl. 69)
ḥm-nṯr snw (n Ḥr nb Bhn) 1188 (pls. 54–5)
ḥm-nṯr tpy n 3st 1465 (pl. 93)
ḥm-nṯr tpy n ʾImn 1820 (pl. 40), 57690 (pls. 38–9)
ḥm-nṯr tpy n ʾImn (n) Rʿ-mss 792 (pls. 44–5)
ḥm-nṯr tpy n Ḥr nb Bhn 1188 (pls. 54–5)
ḥmt-nṯr (n) Ḥwt-Ḥr 1662 (pl. 17)
ḥmt nsw 1662 (pl. 17)
ḥmt nsw wrt 916 (pl. 87), 1133 (pl. 21), 1662 (pl. 17)
ḥmt nṯr 291 (pl. 65), 598 (pl. 77)
[ḥmt] nṯr n ʾImn 1742 (pls. 30–1)
ḥmww wr 1629 (pl. 63)
ḥmww wr m st m3ʿt 291 (pl. 65), 448 (pl. 68)
ḥnwt nsw wrt 1662 (pl. 17)
ḥnwt sššt 1662 (pl. 17)
ḥnwt Šmʿw T3-mḥw 1662 (pl. 17)
ḥry ỉḥw 795 (pl. 94)
ḥry ỉḥw n iḥw ʿ3 (n) Rʿ-ms-sw mry-ʾImn 161 (pls. 52–3)
ḥry ỉḥw n ḫnw 792 (pls. 44–5)
ḥry ỉḥw tpy n nb t3wy 795 (pl. 94)
ḥry ỉswt 1516 (pl. 64)
ḥry ỉswt n st m3ʿt 272 (pl. 70), 273 (pl. 71), 1516 (pl. 64)
ḥry mškbyw n ḫn Rʿ-mss ḥḳ3 ʾIwnw mry Sḫmt 1183 (pl. 99)
ḥry nbyw 476 (pl. 60), 1188 (pls. 54–5)
ḥry sšt3 m swt ʿḥ 1377 (pls. 50–1)
ḥry sšt3 n pr-Rʿ 1183 (pl. 99)
ḥry sšt3 (n) pt t3 dw3t(?) 845 (pls. 36–7)
ḥry sšt3 nt ḥwt-Mr-n-Ptḥ m pr-Rʿ 1183 (pl. 99)
ḥry-tp t3wy 68682 (pls. 38–9)
ḥry ḳʿr 312 (pl. 98)
ḥry ḳʿr n ḥm.f 312 (pl. 98)
ḥswt wrt 1662 (pl. 17)
ḥsb b3kw (n) t3w ḫ3swt 1377 (pl. 49)

ẖry-ḥb n Ptḥ 845 (36–7)
ẖry-ḥb m ḥwt-B3stt 972 (pl. 8)

s3 nsw 78 (pls. 42–3), 947 (pls. 33–5), 1183 (pl. 99), 48664 (pl. 22), 49235 (pl. 22)
s3 nsw n Kš 78 (pls. 42–3), 792 (pls. 44–5), 1055 (pls. 44–5), 1376 (pls. 46–7)
s3t nsw 1662 (pl. 17), 1742 (pls. 30–1)
s3wty (n) pr-ḥḏ m Šmʿw T3-mḥw(?) 1214 (pl. 48)
s3wty m st m3ʿt 1466 (pl. 73)
s3b 1377 (pl. 49), 35628 (pl. 32)
sm 845 (pls. 36–9), 947 (pls. 33–5), 972 (pl. 8), 49235 (pl. 22), 59259 (pls. 38–9)
sm n Ptḥ 48664 (pl. 22)
smr wʿ.tỉ 972 (pl. 8), 1377 (pls. 50–1)
sš 161 (pls. 52–3), 327 (pl. 100), 794 (pl. 56)
sš wḏḥw n nb t3wy 794 (pl. 56)
sš n pr-ʾImn 161 (pls. 52–3)
sš nsw 78 (pls. 42–3), 160 (pls. 4–5), 161 (pls. 52–3), 588 (pl. 57), 793 (pl. 95), 1377 (pls. 49–51), 1465 (pl. 93), 68682 (pls. 38–9)
sš nsw wḏḥw n nṯrw nbw 2291 (pl. 62)
sš nṯr 1188 (pls. 54–5)
sš ḥwt-nṯr 64641 (pl. 61)
sš ḥwt-nṯr n Ḫnm 795 (pl. 94)
sš ḳdwt 186 (pl. 78), 276 (pl. 79), 444 (pl. 69), 2292 (pl. 79), 36861 (pl. 80)
sš ḳdwt m st m3ʿt 186 (pl. 78), 276 (pl. 79)
sš ḳdwt n ʾImn 186 (pl. 78)
sš ḳdwt n ʾImn m st m3ʿt 276 (pl. 79)
sšm ḥb n ʾImn 556 (pl. 41)
sḏ3wty bỉty 972 (pl. 8), 1377 (pls. 50–51)
sḏm ʿš 8497 (pls. 74–5)
sḏm ʿš m st m3ʿt 273 (pl. 71), 274 (pls. 66–7), 278 (pl. 86), 281 (pl. 6), 291 (pl. 65), 316 (pl. 70), 320 (pl. 81), 424 (pl. 92), 444 (pl. 69), 479 (pls. 90–1), 597 (pls. 66–7), 598 (pl. 77), 810 (pl. 88), 916 (pl. 87), 942 (pls. 84–5), 1248 (pl. 81), 1388 (pl. 76), 8485 (pl. 83), 8495 (pl. 82), 36861 (pl. 80), 65355 (pl. 72)
sḏm ʿš m st m3ʿt ḥr ʾImntt W3st 448 (pl. 68), 810 (pl. 88), 8497 (pls. 74–5)
sḏm ʿš n ʾImntt 360 (pl. 7)
sḏm ʿš n nb t3wy m st m3ʿt 272 (pl. 70), 65356 (pl. 89)
sḏm ʿš n nb t3wy m st m3ʿt (ḥr) ʾImntt W3st 479 (pls. 90–1)
sdty Ḥr 1662 (pl. 17)

šmʿyt 1188 (pls. 54–5)
šmʿyt n(t) 3st 1465 (pl. 93)
šmʿyt n(t) ʾImn 161 (pls. 52–3), 278 (pl. 86), 327 (pl. 100), 476 (pl. 60)
šmʿyt n(t) Wp-w3wt 792 (pls. 44–5)
šmʿyt n(t) B3-nb-ḏd 312 (pl. 98)
šmʿyt (nt) p3-Rʿ 1183 (pl. 99)
šmʿyt n(t) nb(t) nht 1183 (pl. 99)
šmʿyt n(t) Ḫnm 795 (pl. 94)
šmʿyt n(t) Ḏḥwty wp ḥwy 312 (pl. 98)
šmʿyt n(t) Ḏḥwty nb Ḫmnw 1680 (pl. 96–7)
šmsw 327 (pl. 100)

ḳḏn tpy n ḥm.f 1183 (pl. 99)

t3yty 35628 (pl. 32)

ṯ3y . . . (?) 795 (pl. 94)
ṯ3y mḏ3t m st m3ʿt 815 (pls. 84–5)
ṯ3y mḏ3t n ʾImn 8493 (pls. 84–5)
ṯ3y ḫw 1214 (pl. 48)
ṯ3y ḫw ḥr wnm nsw 1377 (pls. 50–1), 1465 (pl. 93)
ṯ3ty 35628 (pl. 32)

dw3t nṯr 481 (pls. 30–1), 1742 (pls. 30–1)

. . . prt-ḫrw n 3ḫw 1377 (pl. 49)

Plates

PLATE 1

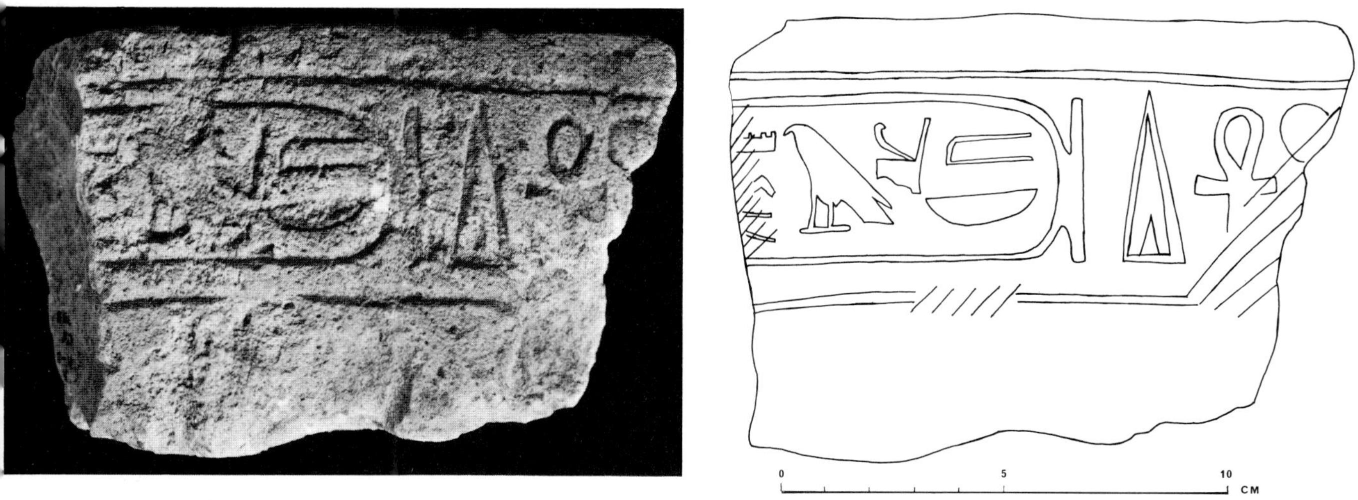

1. No. 58468a

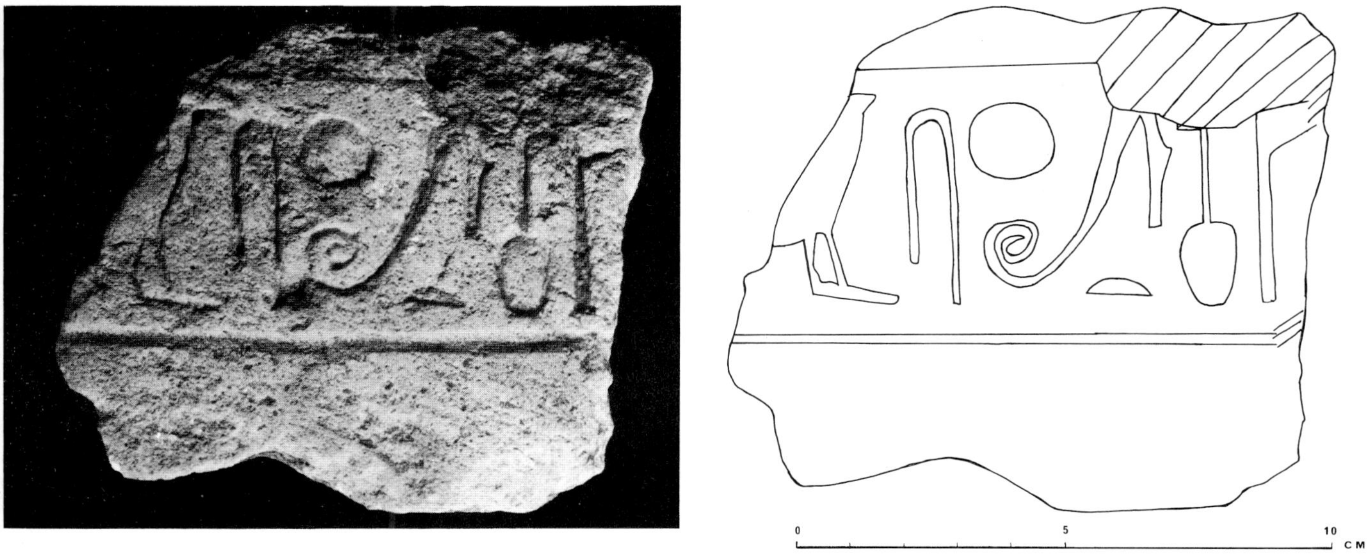

2. No. 58468c

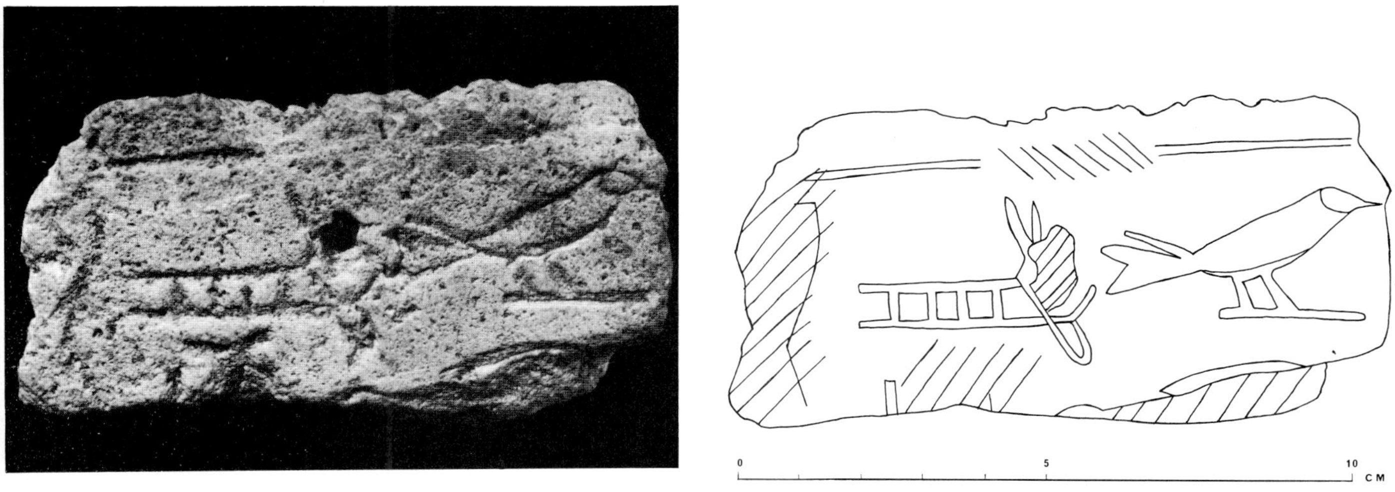

3. No. 58469

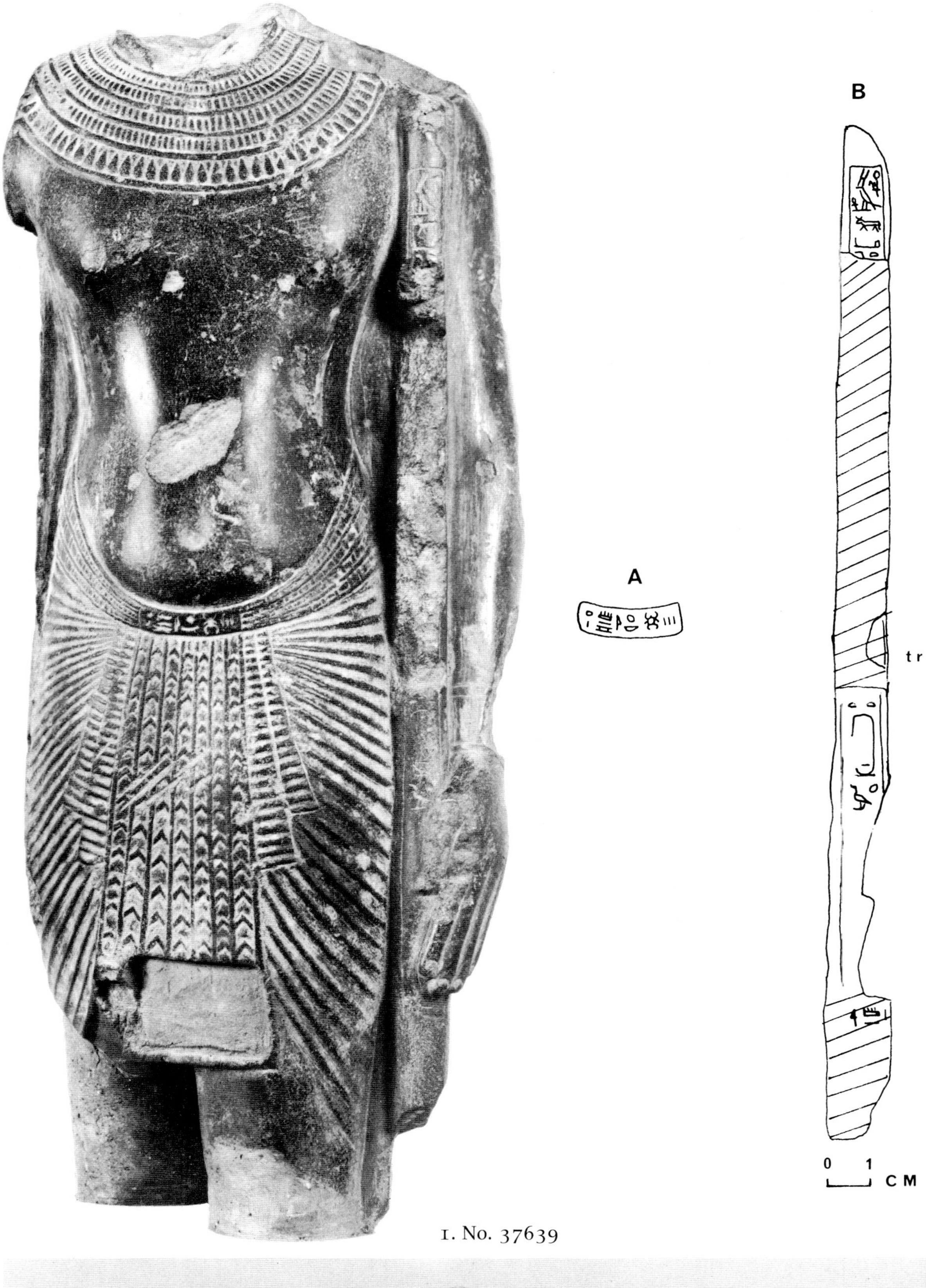

1. No. 37639

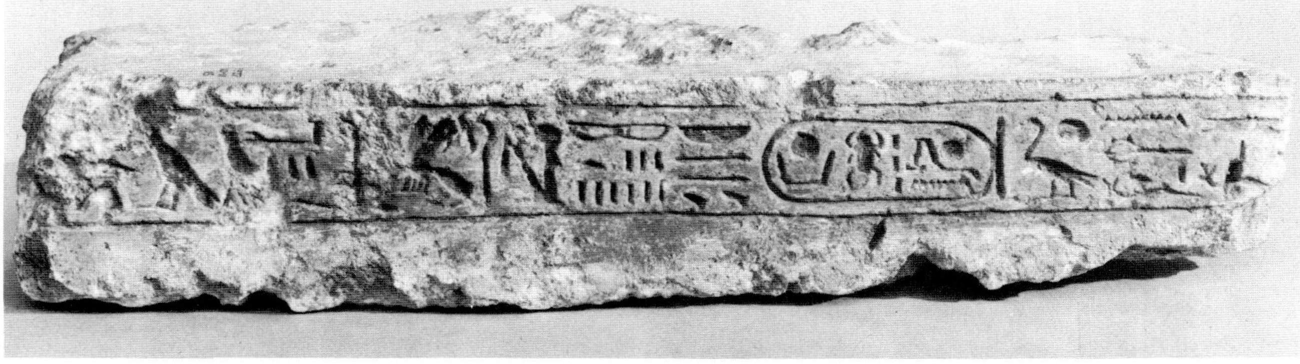

2. No. 58468

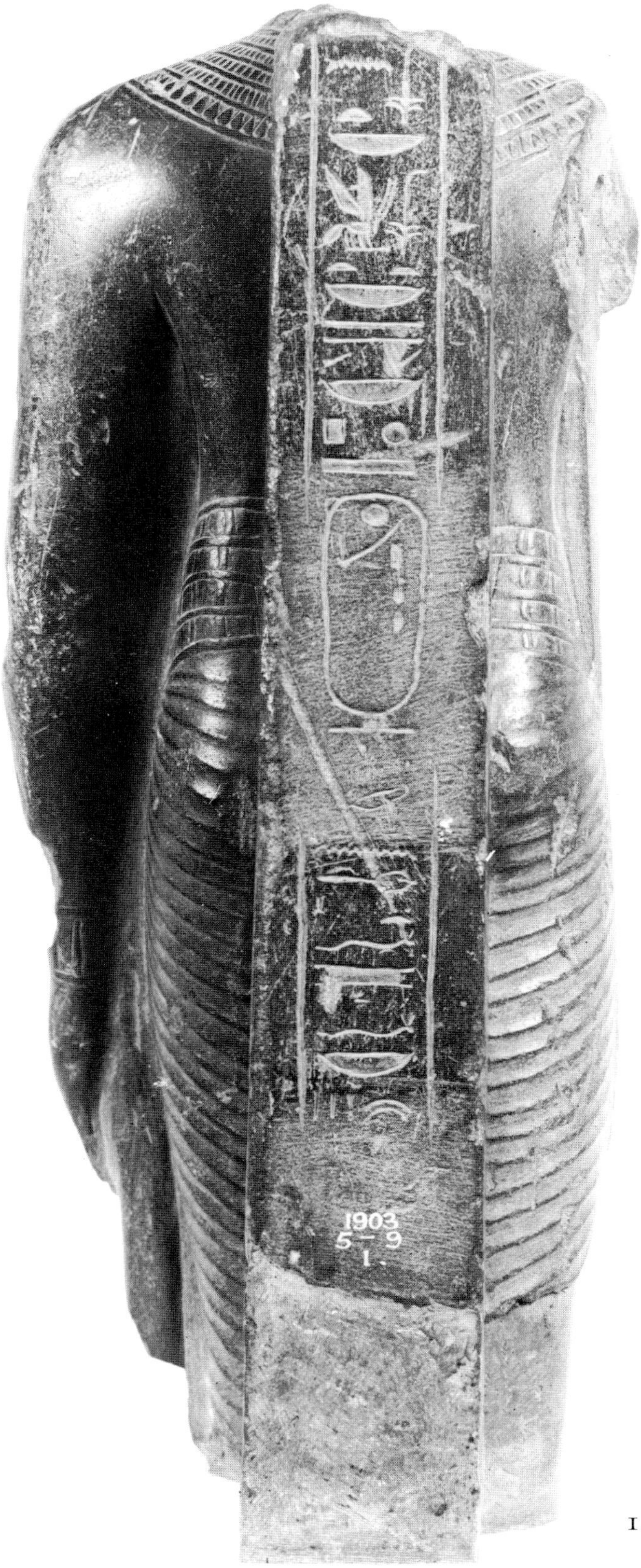

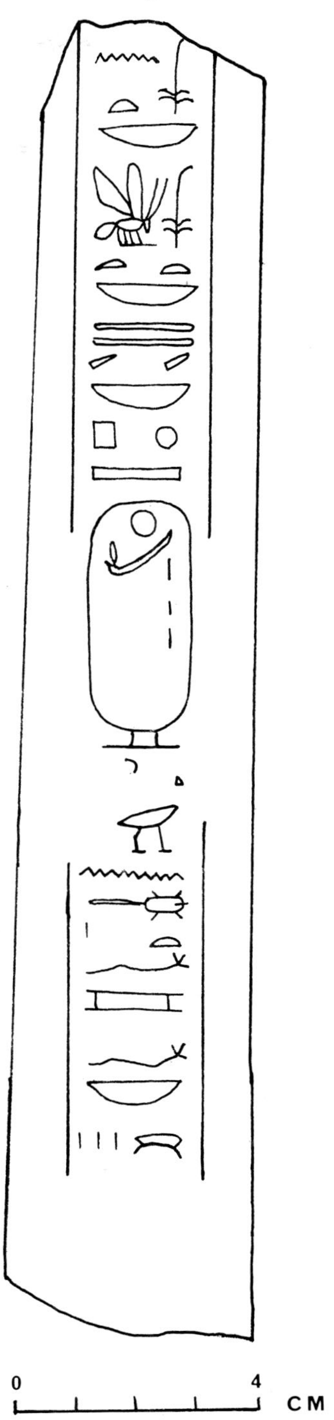

1. No. 37639

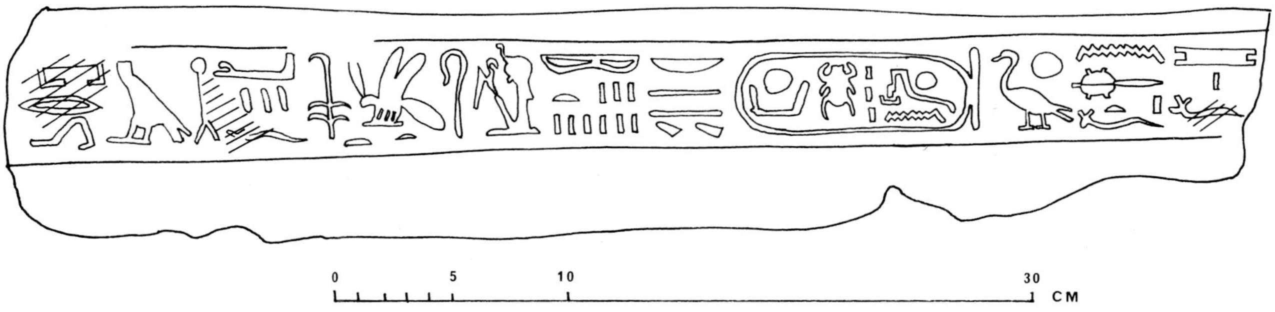

2. No. 58468

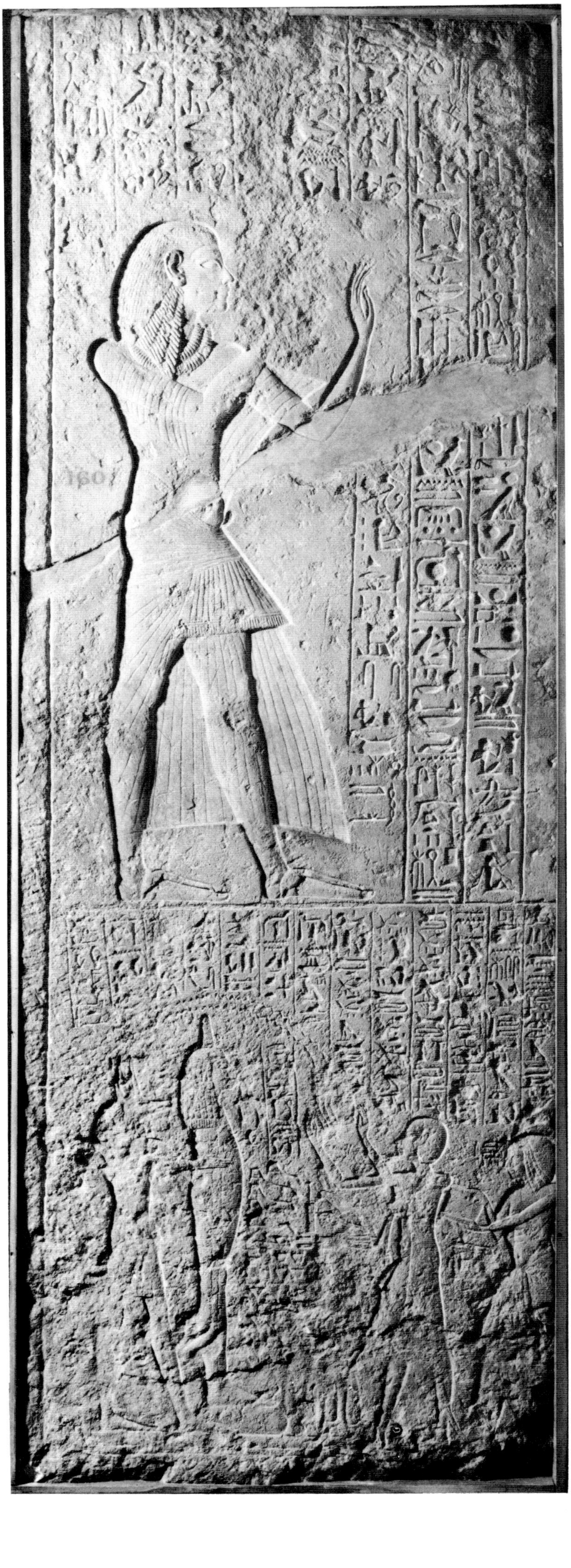

No. 160

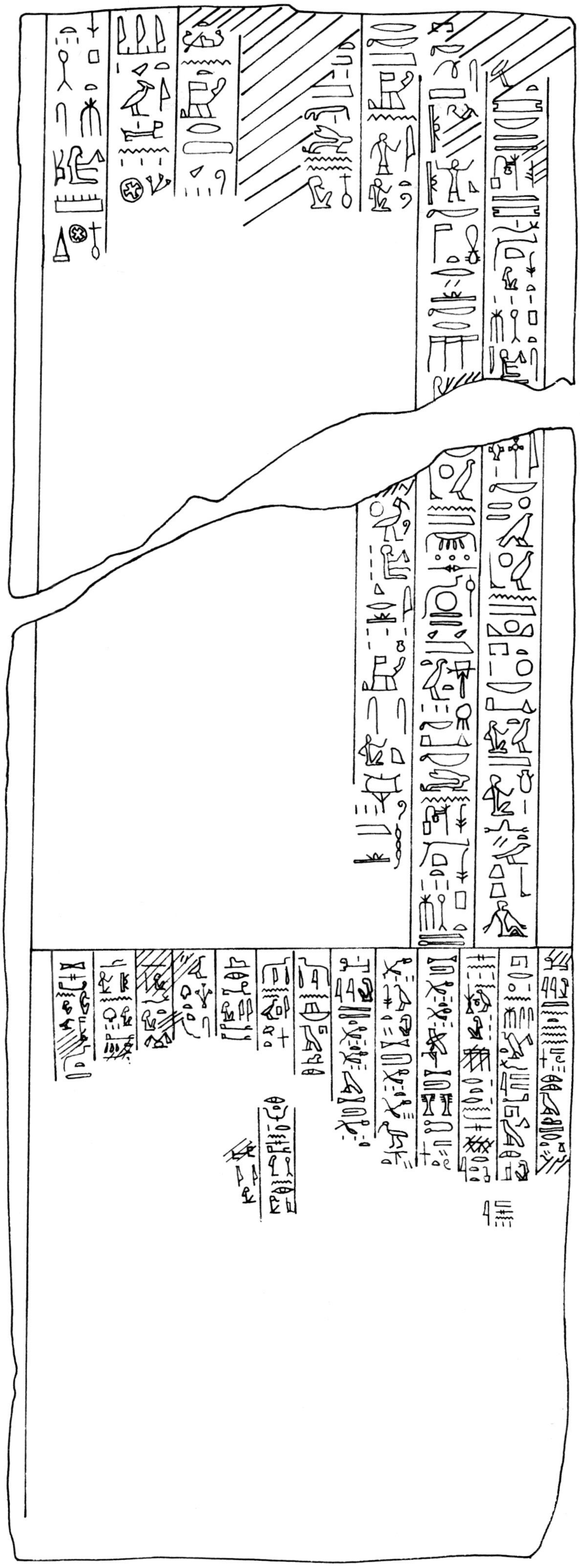

No. 160

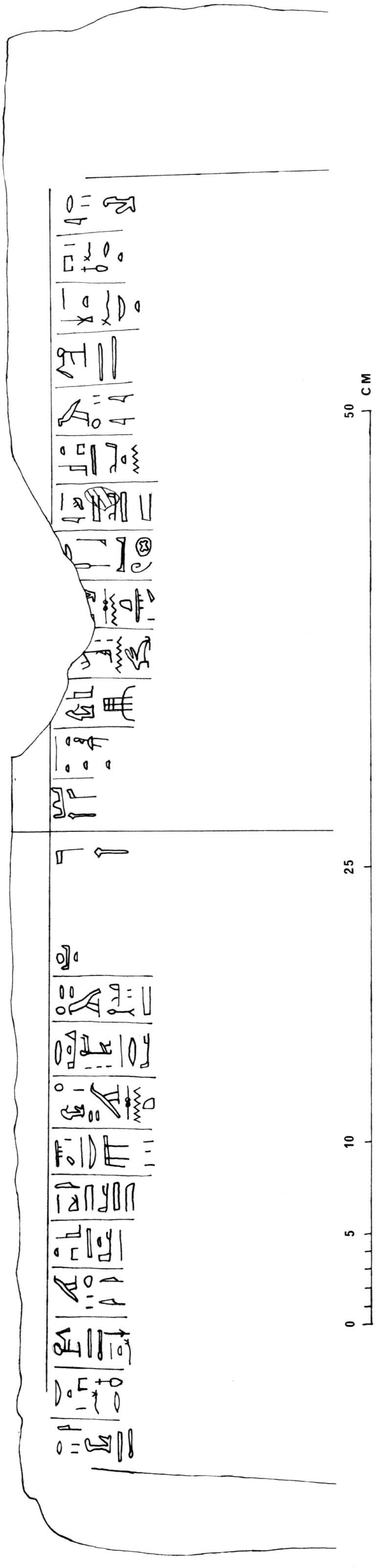

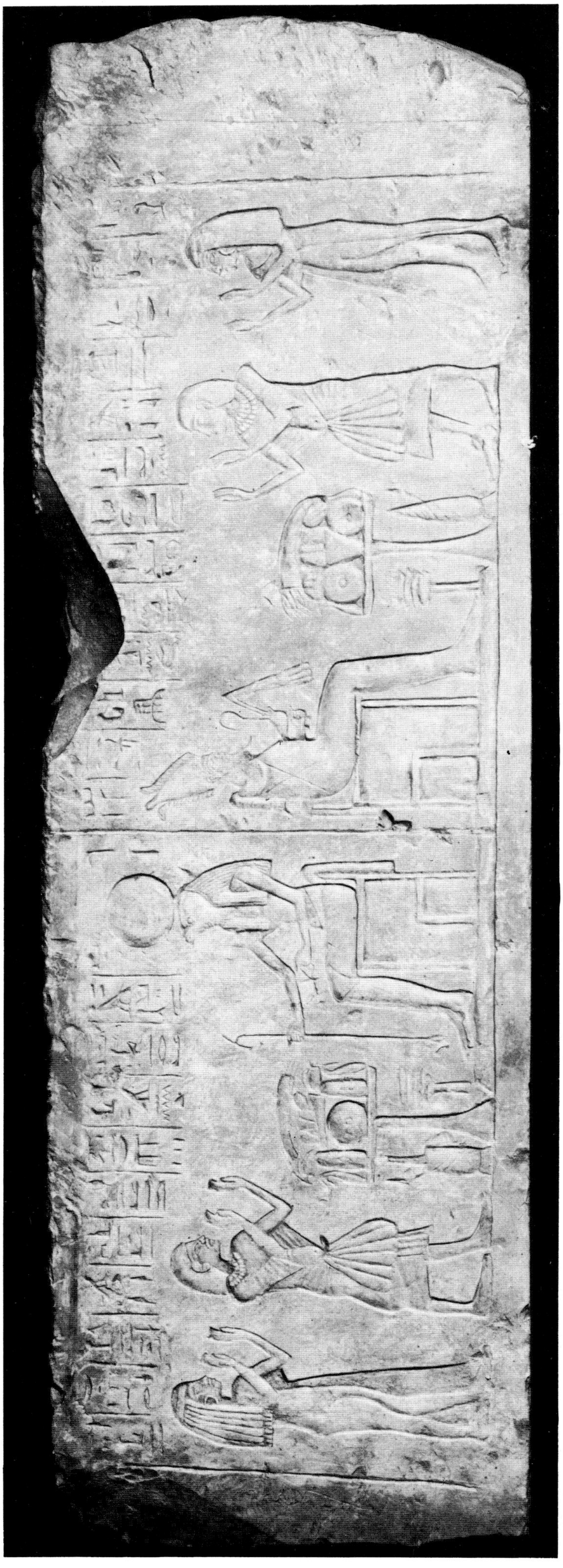

No. 281

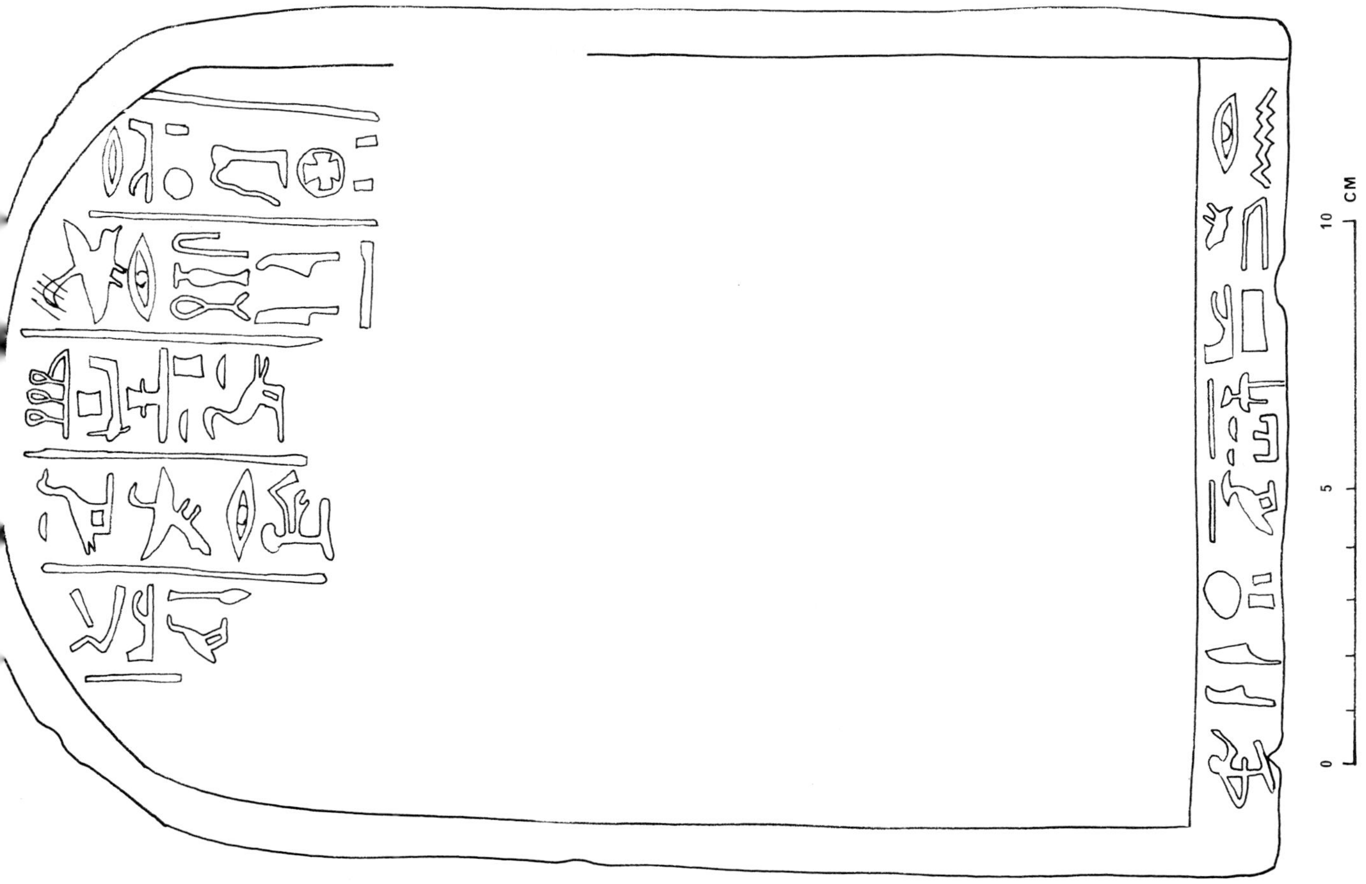

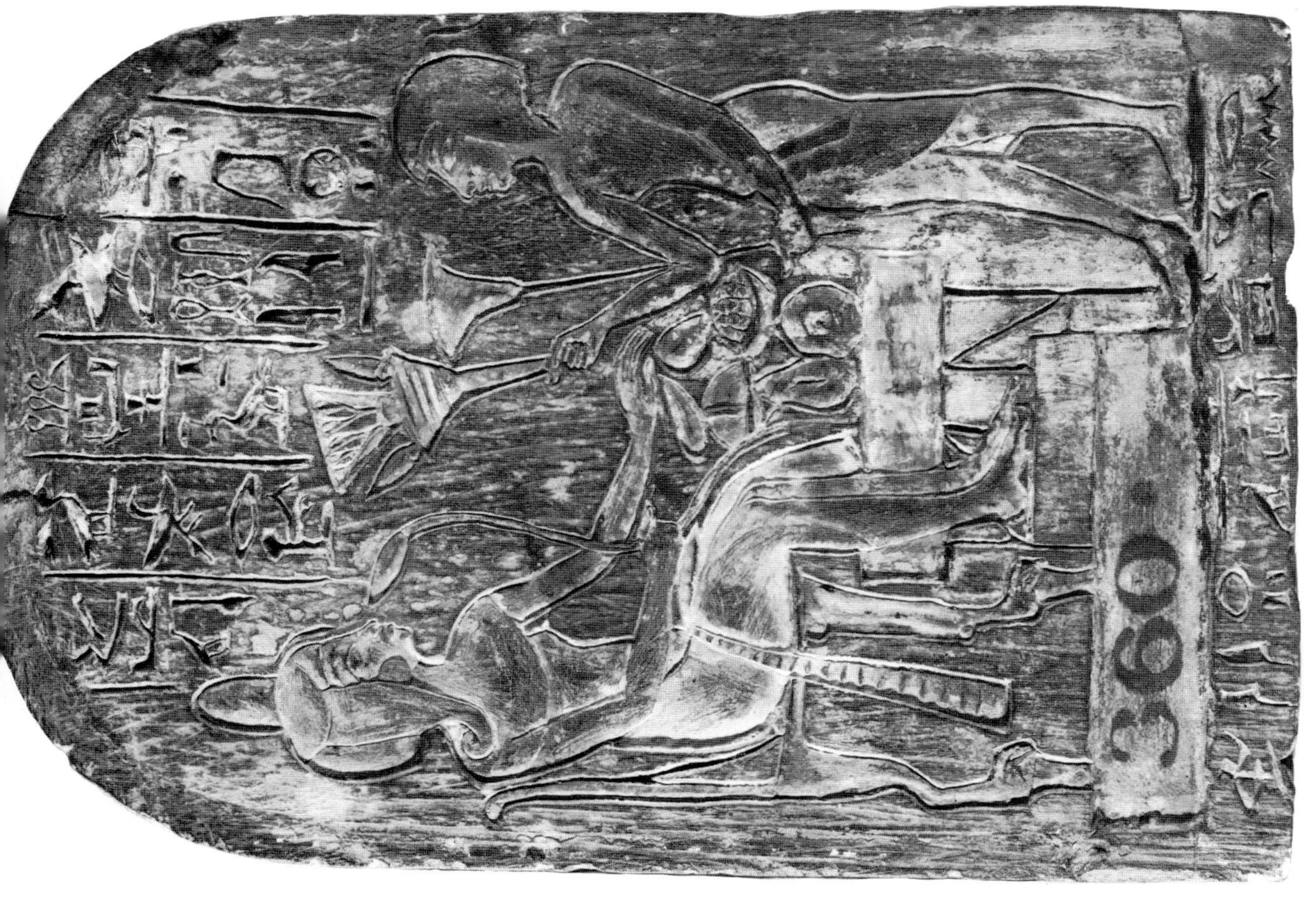

No. 360

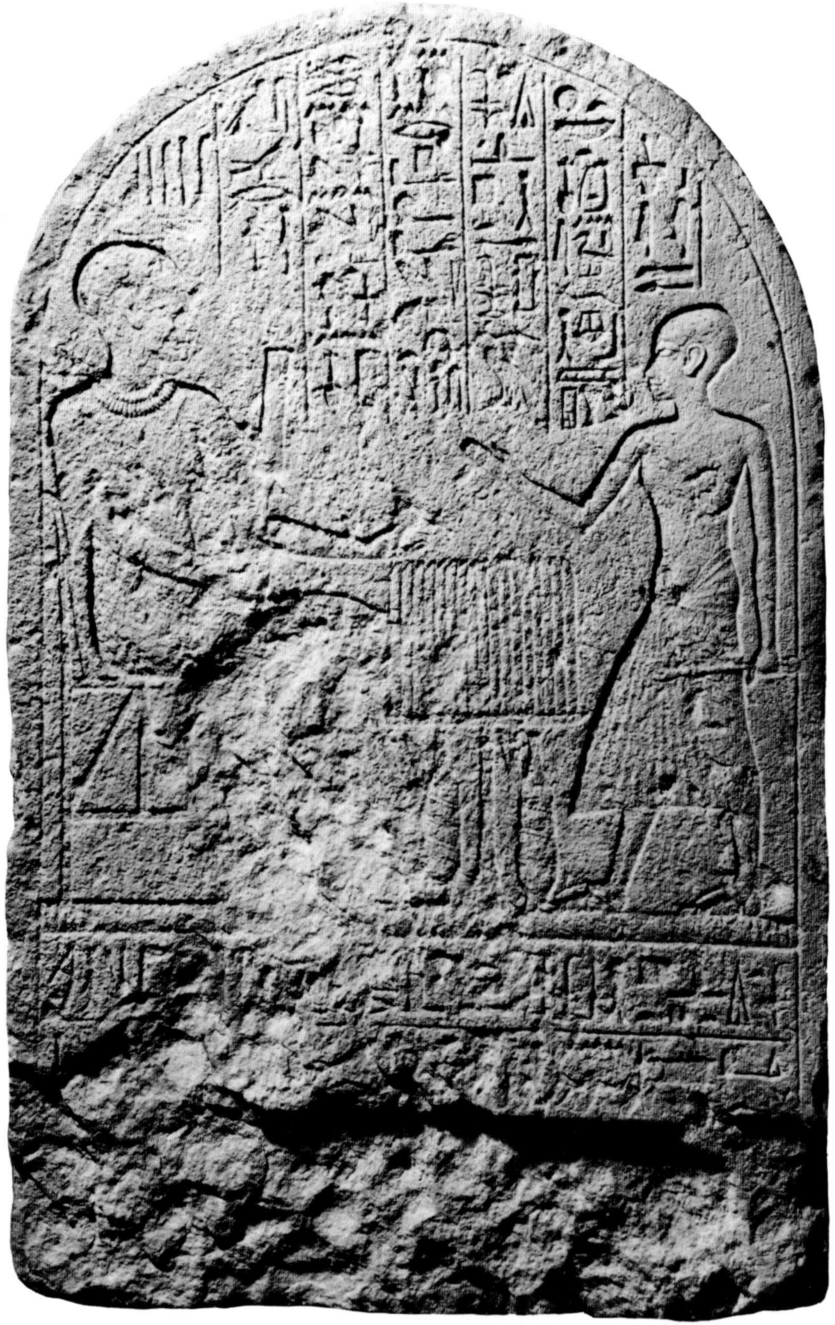

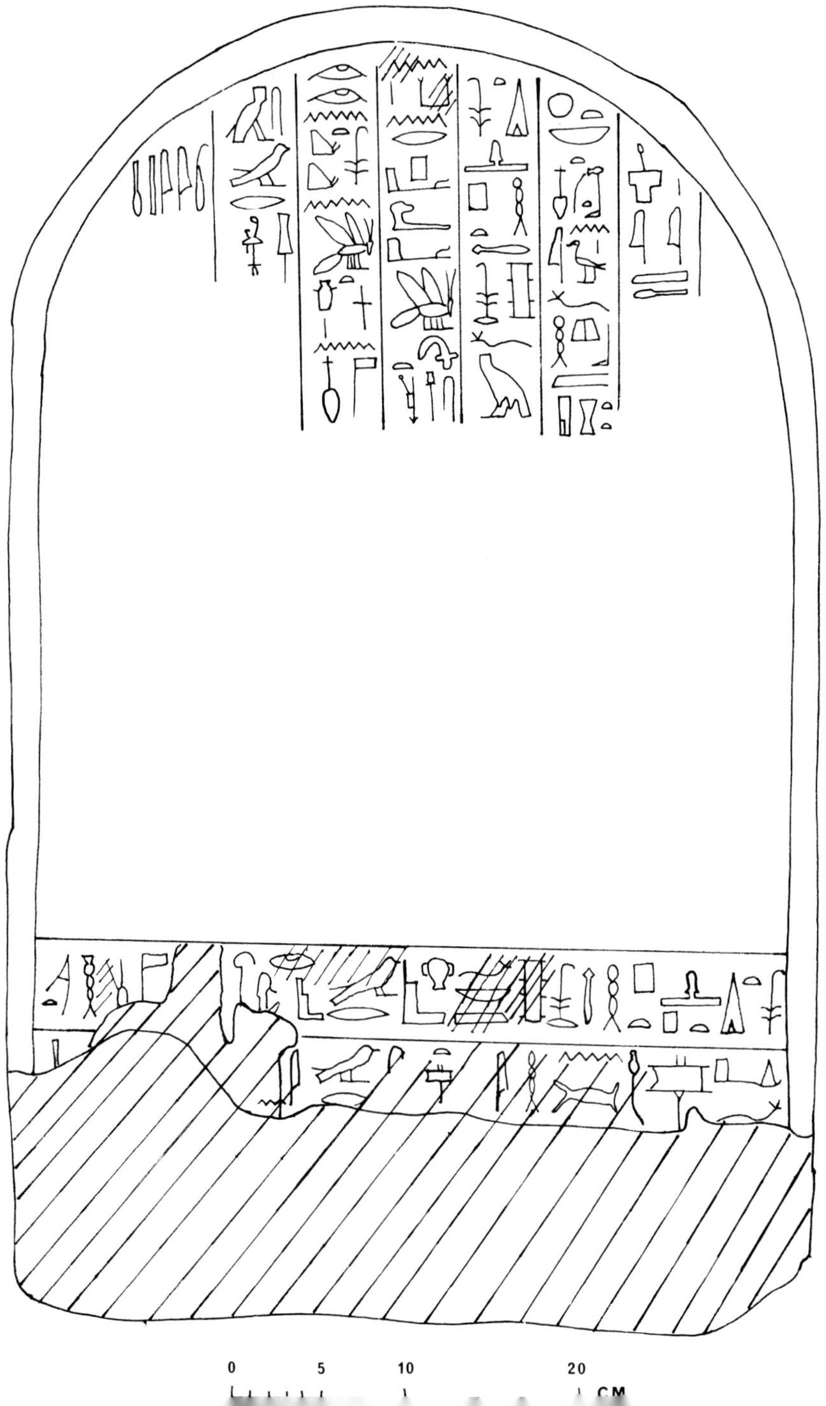

WILKINSON MSS xviii 72

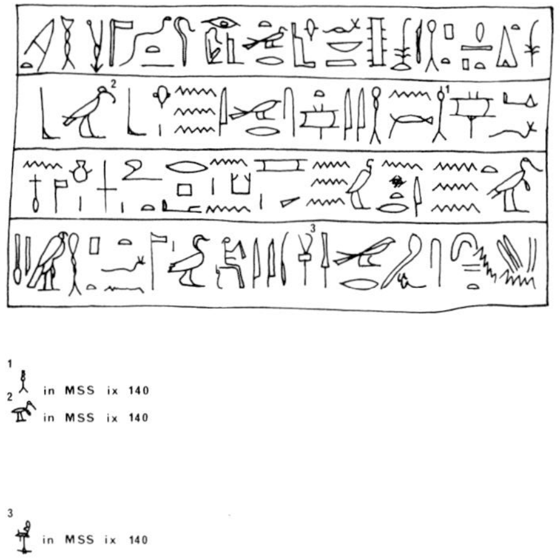

No. 972

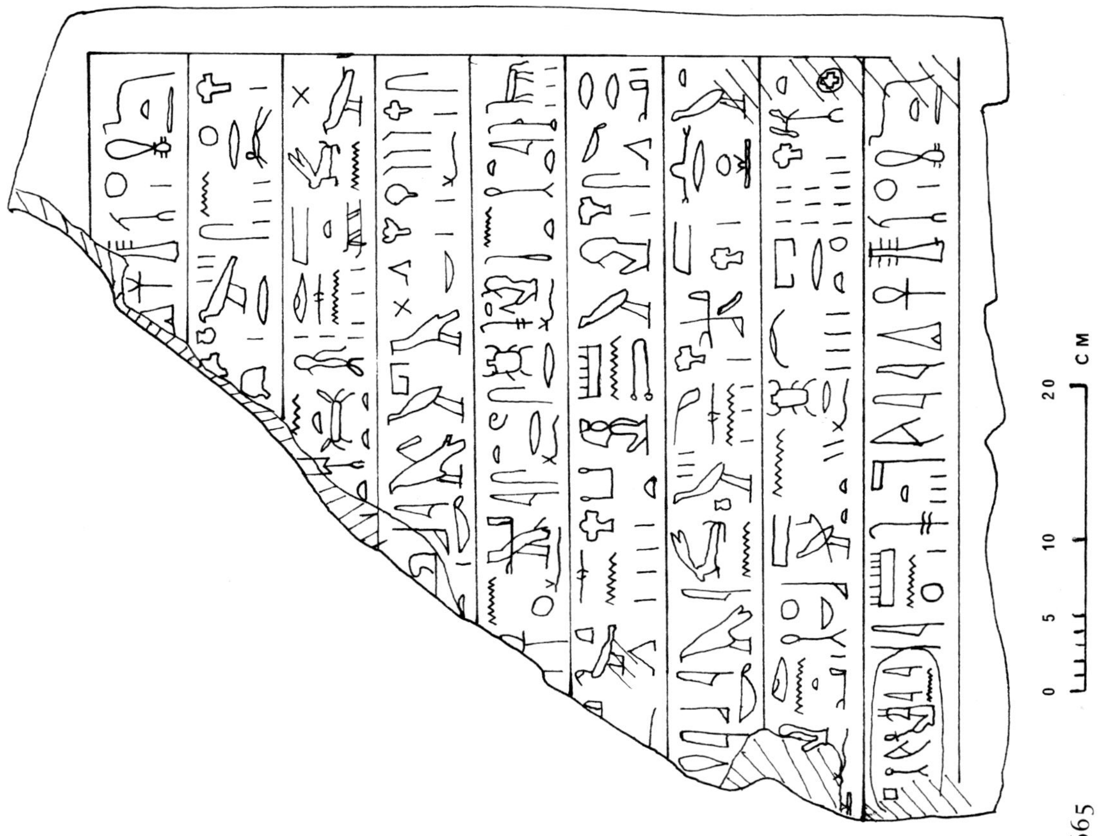

No. 1665

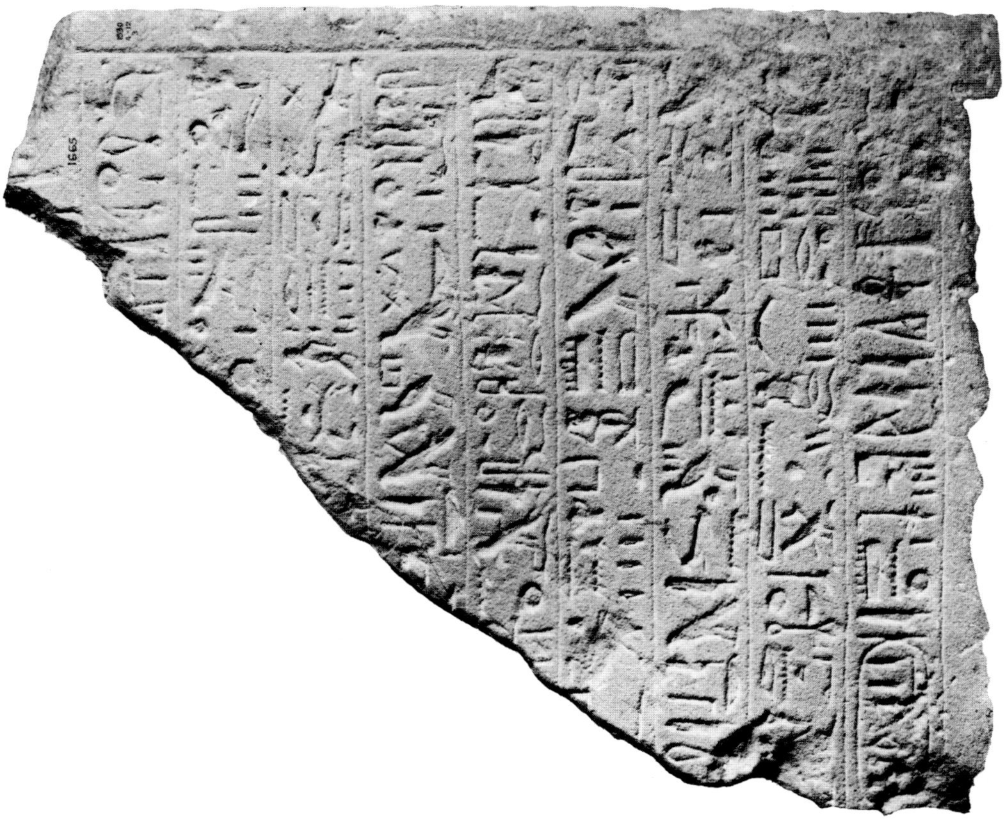

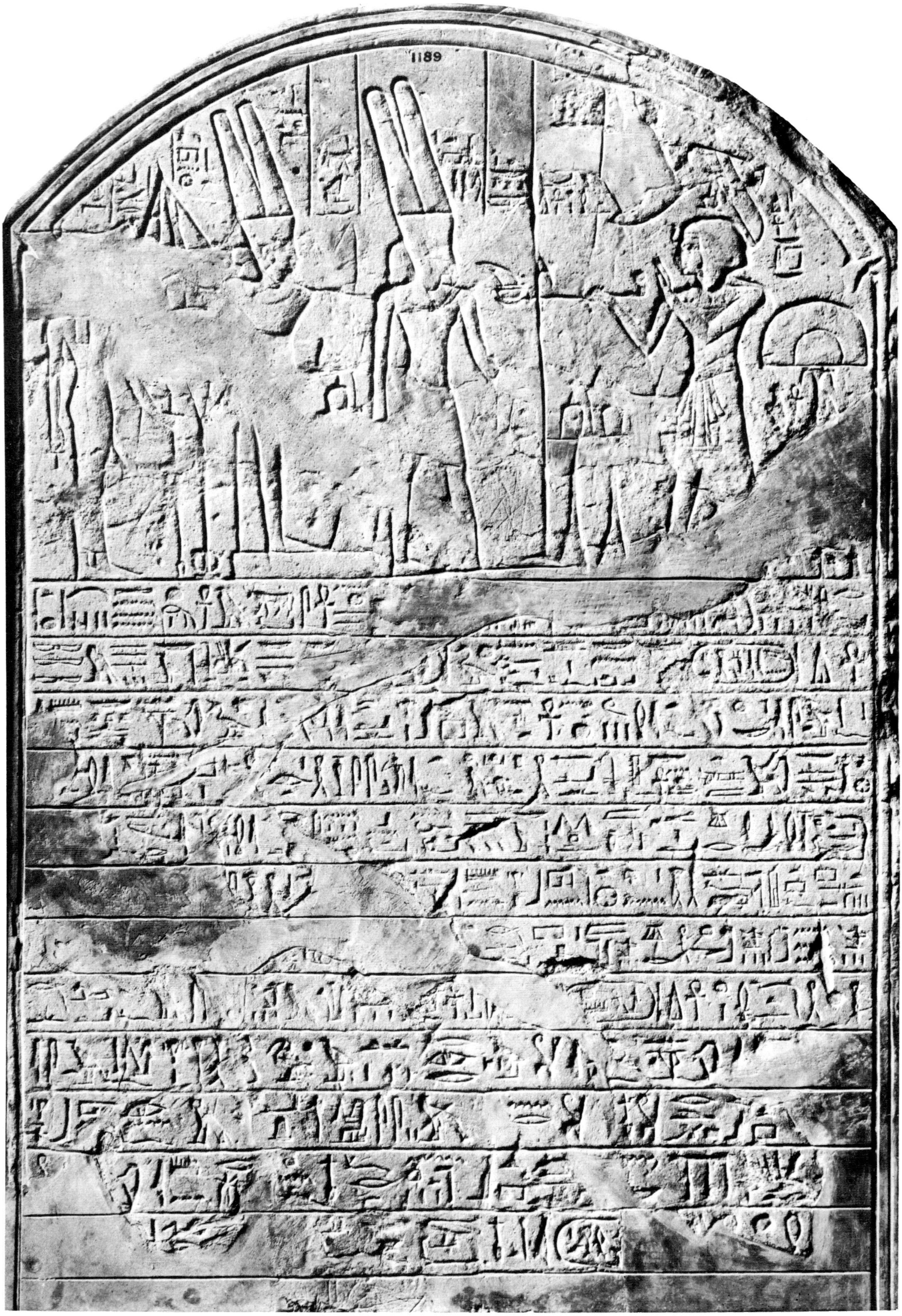

No. 1189

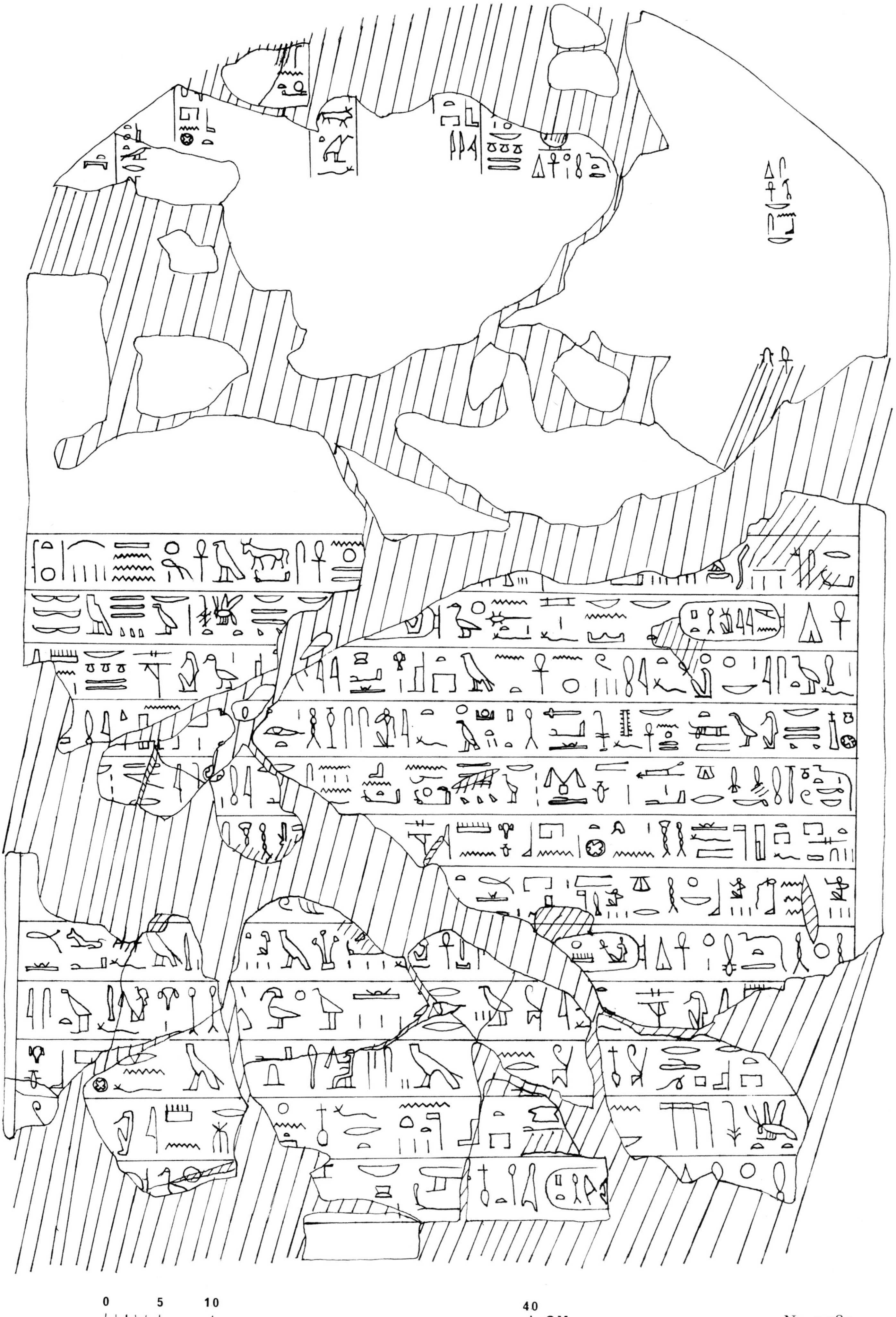

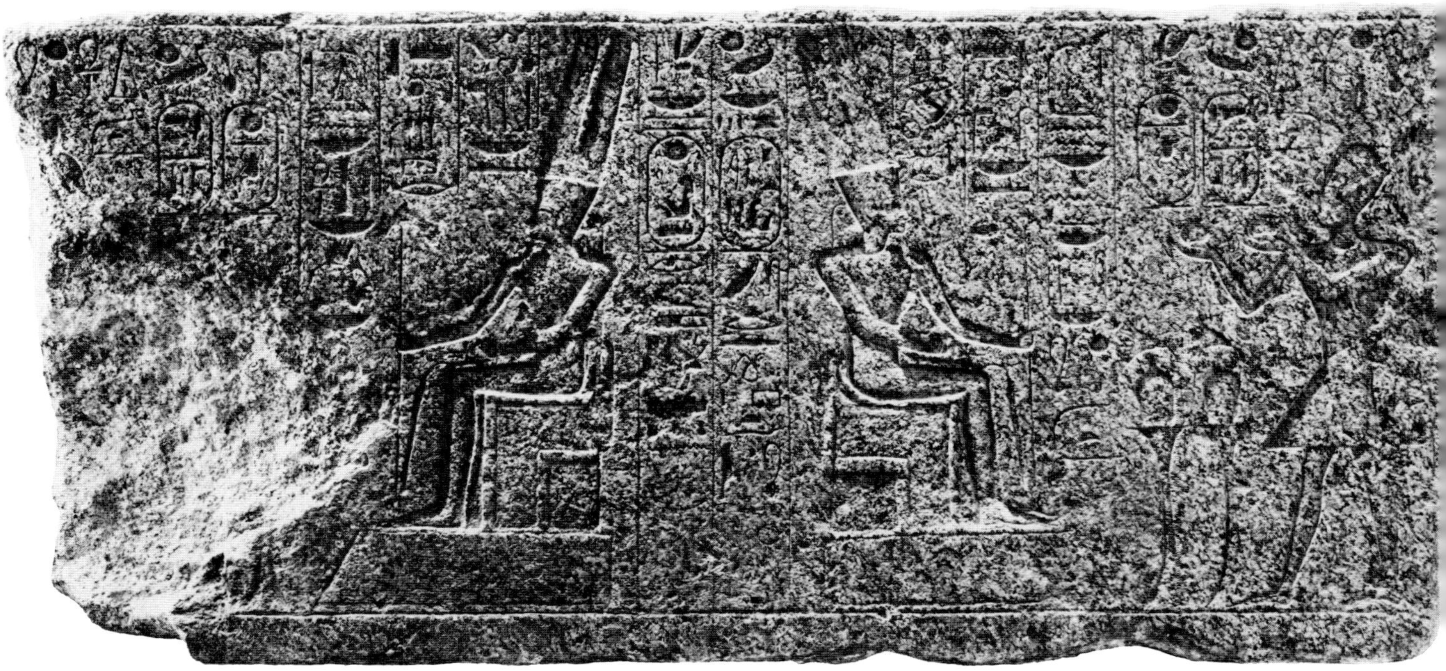

No. 1103

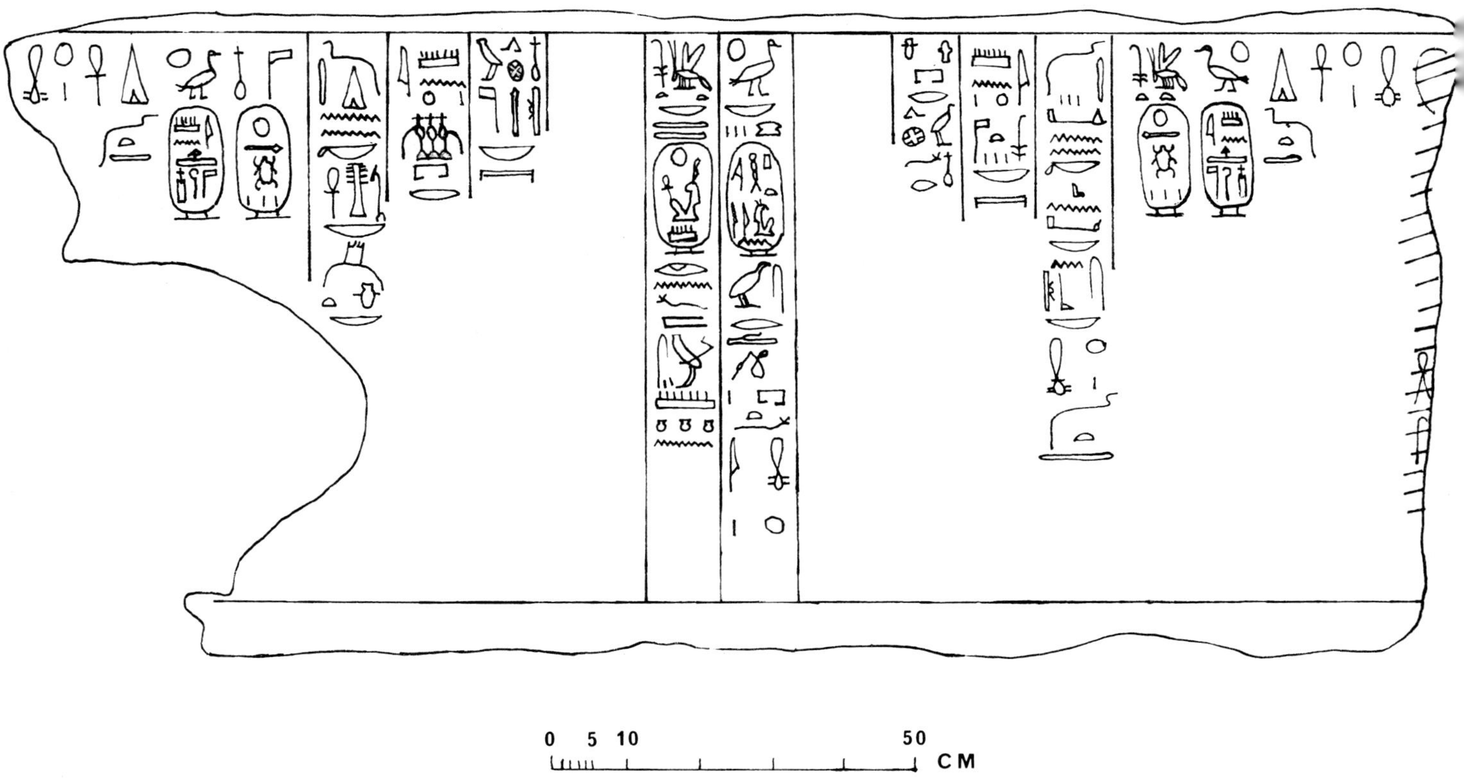

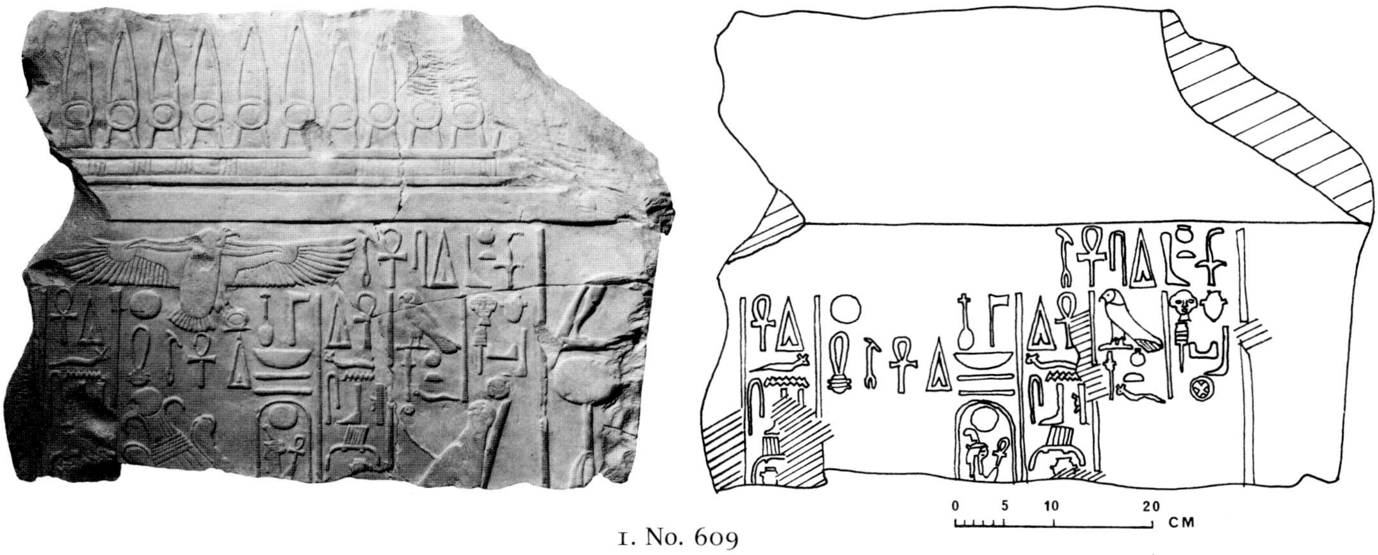

1. No. 609

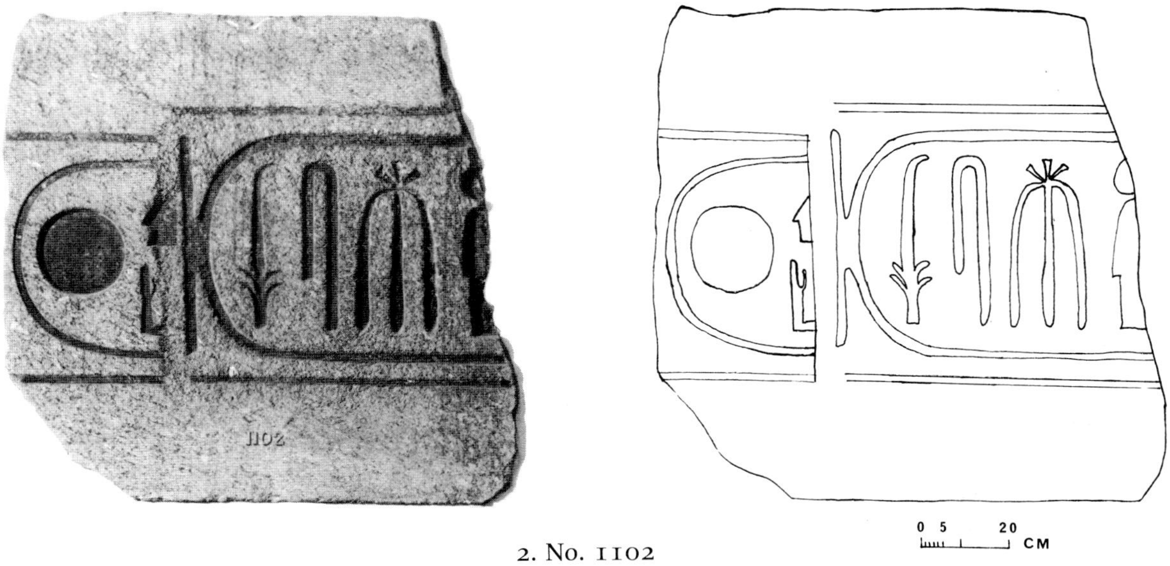

2. No. 1102

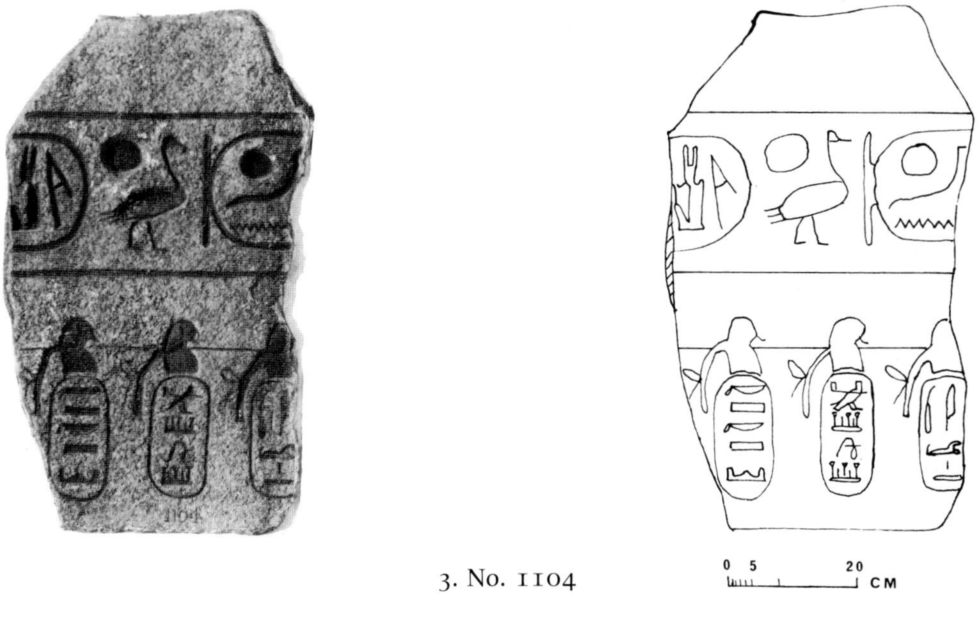

3. No. 1104

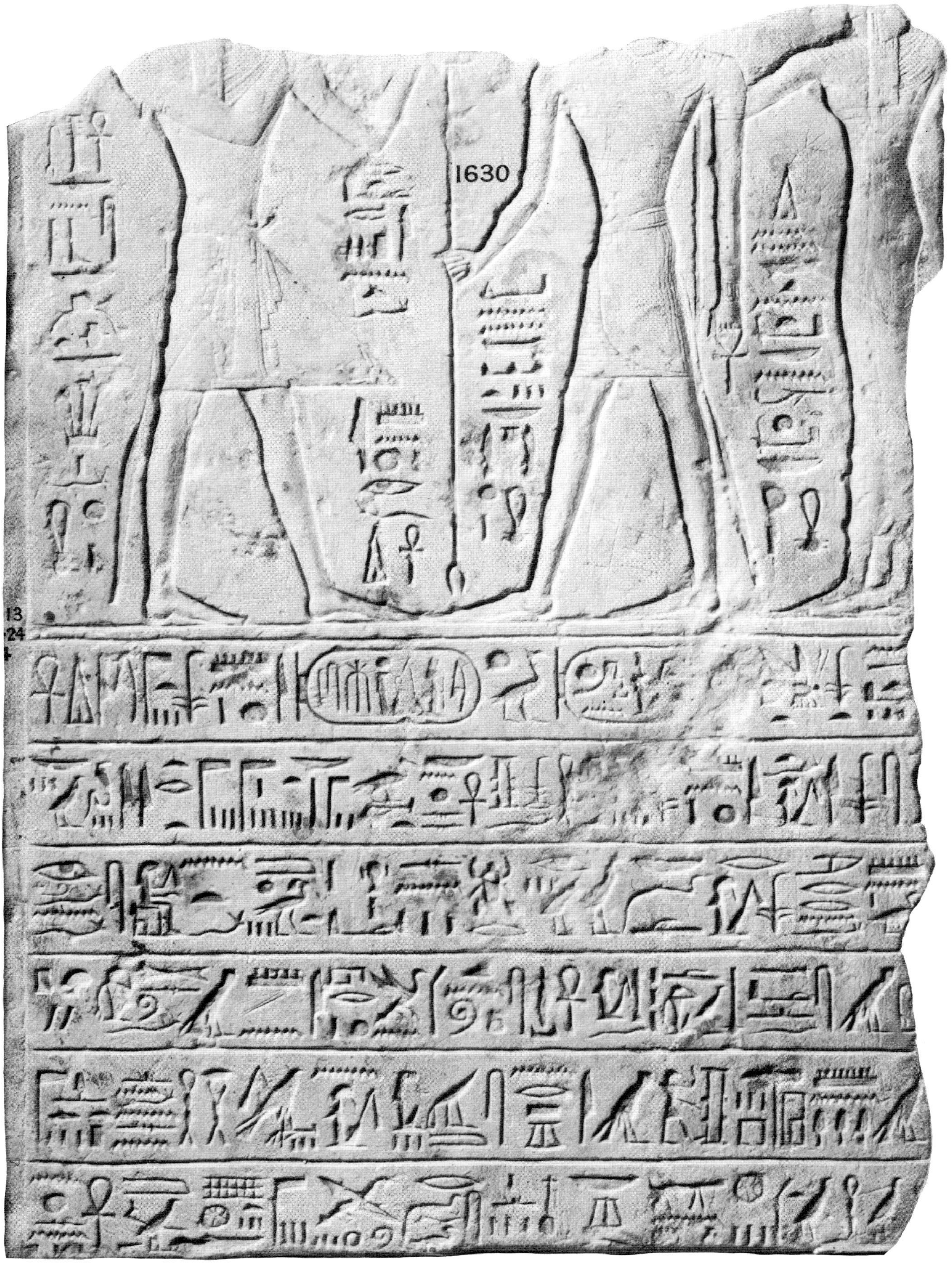

No. 1630

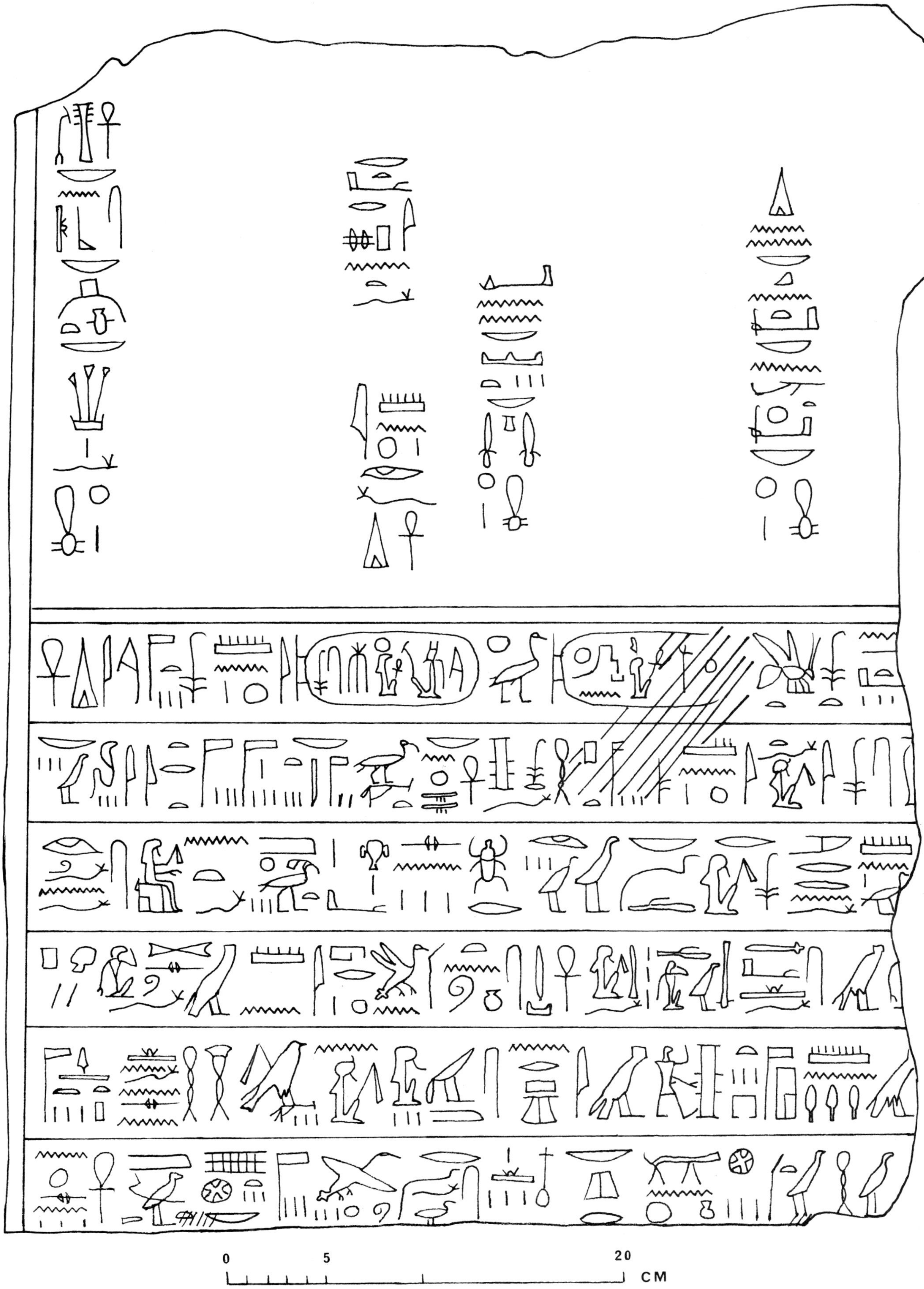

No. 1630

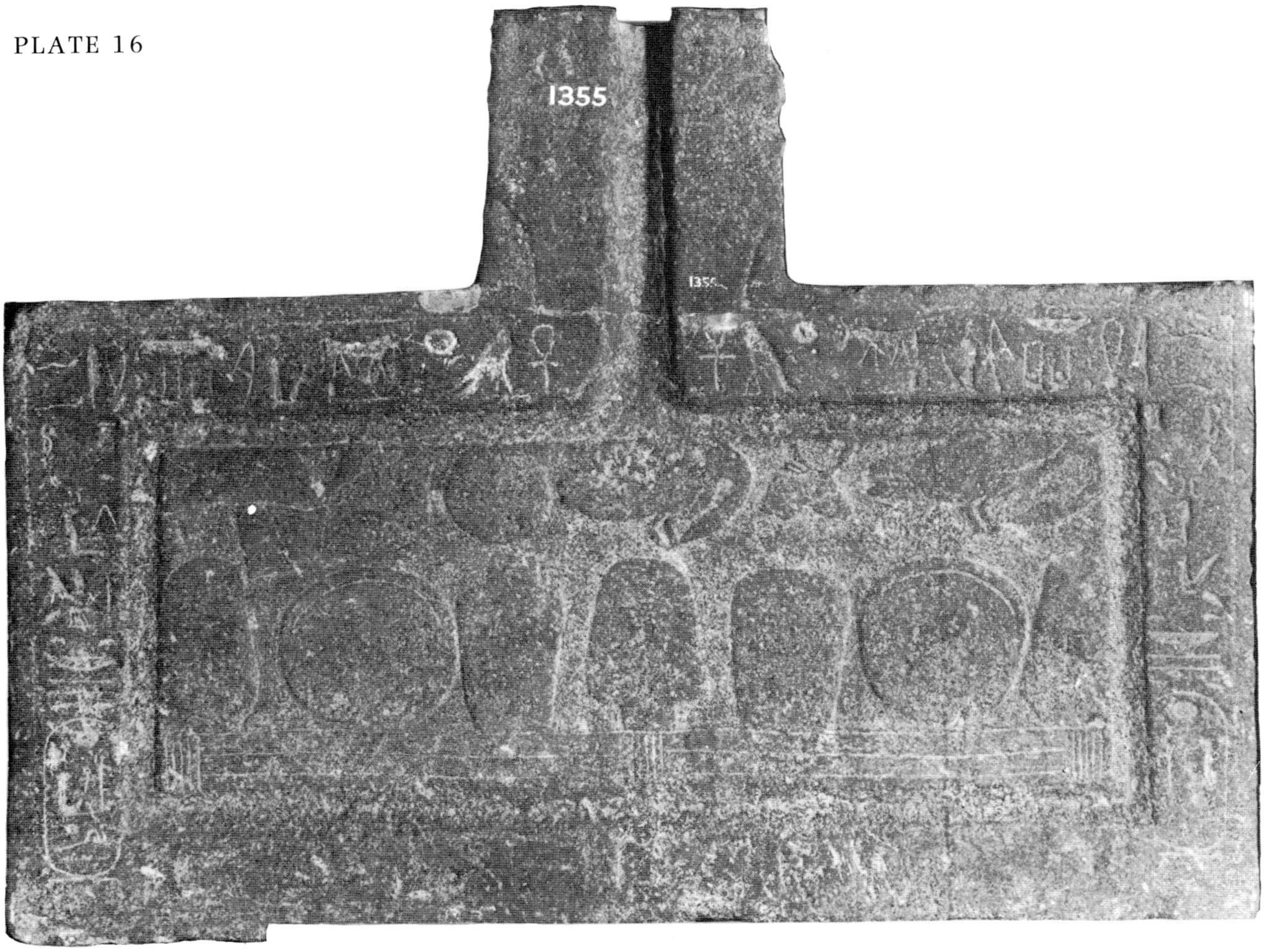

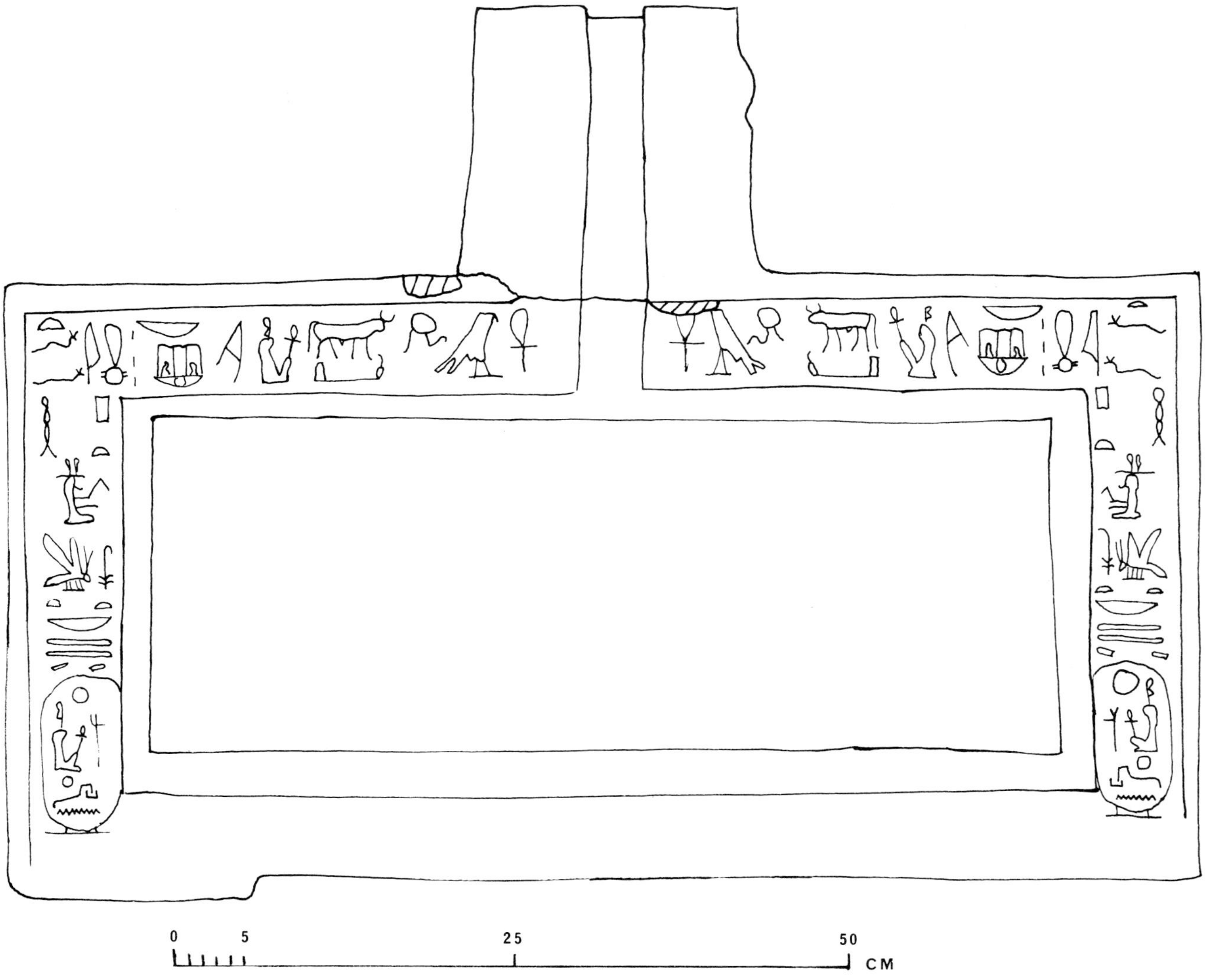

No. 1355

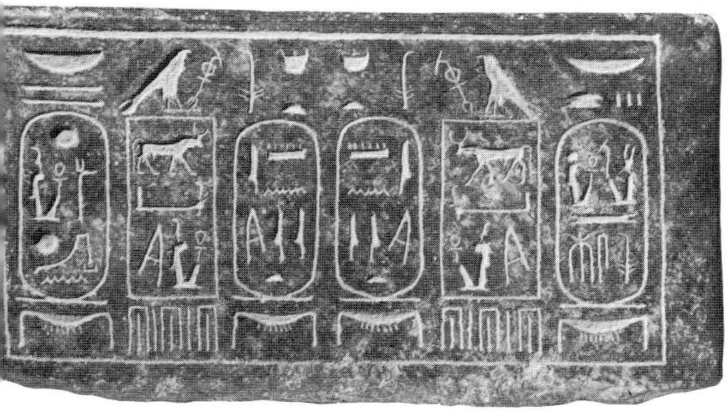

A

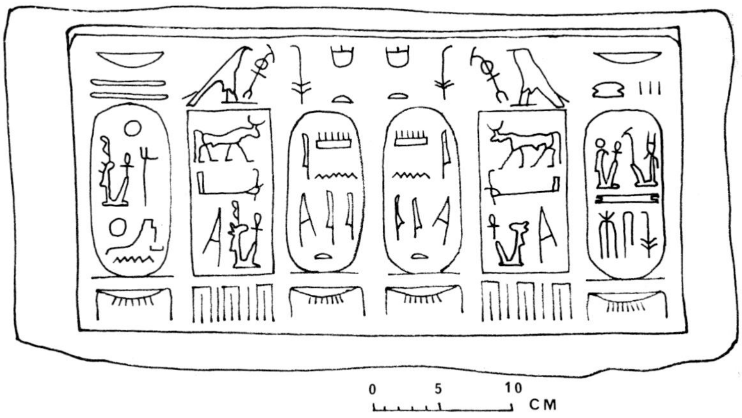

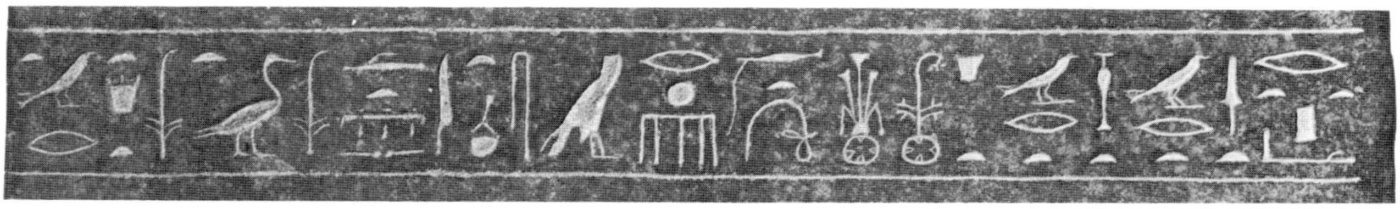

B1

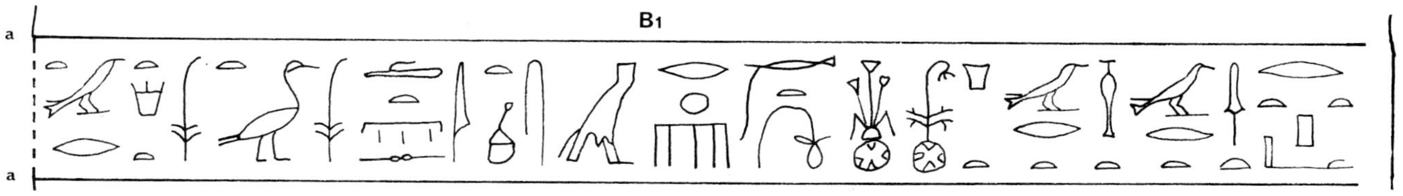

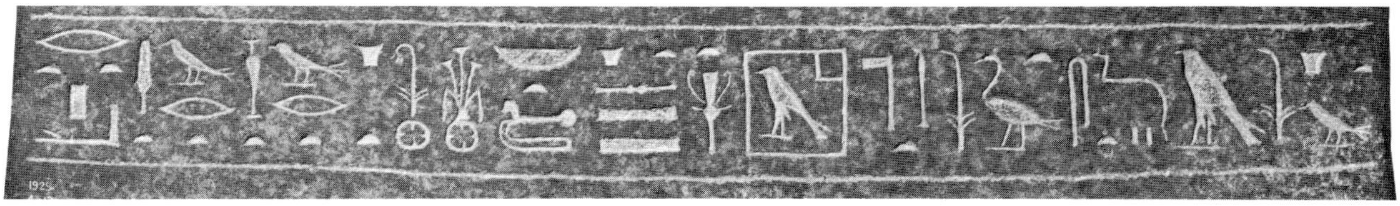

C1

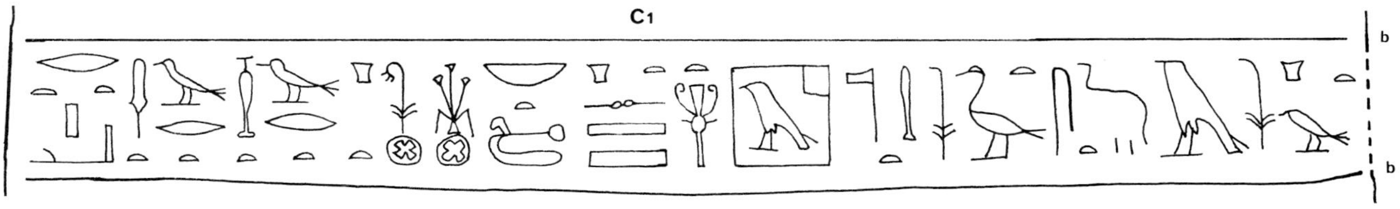

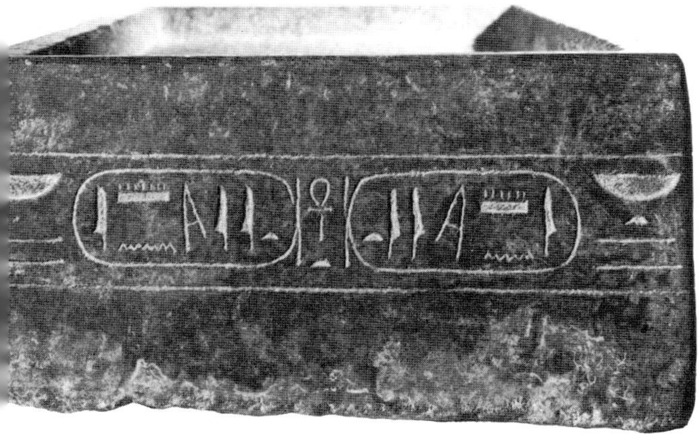

C2 B2

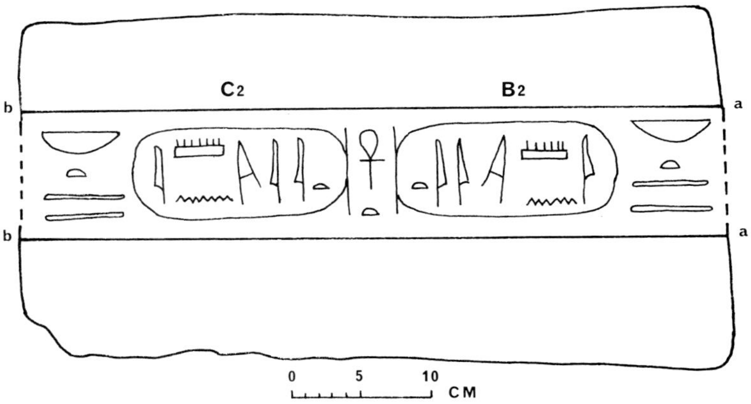

No. 1662

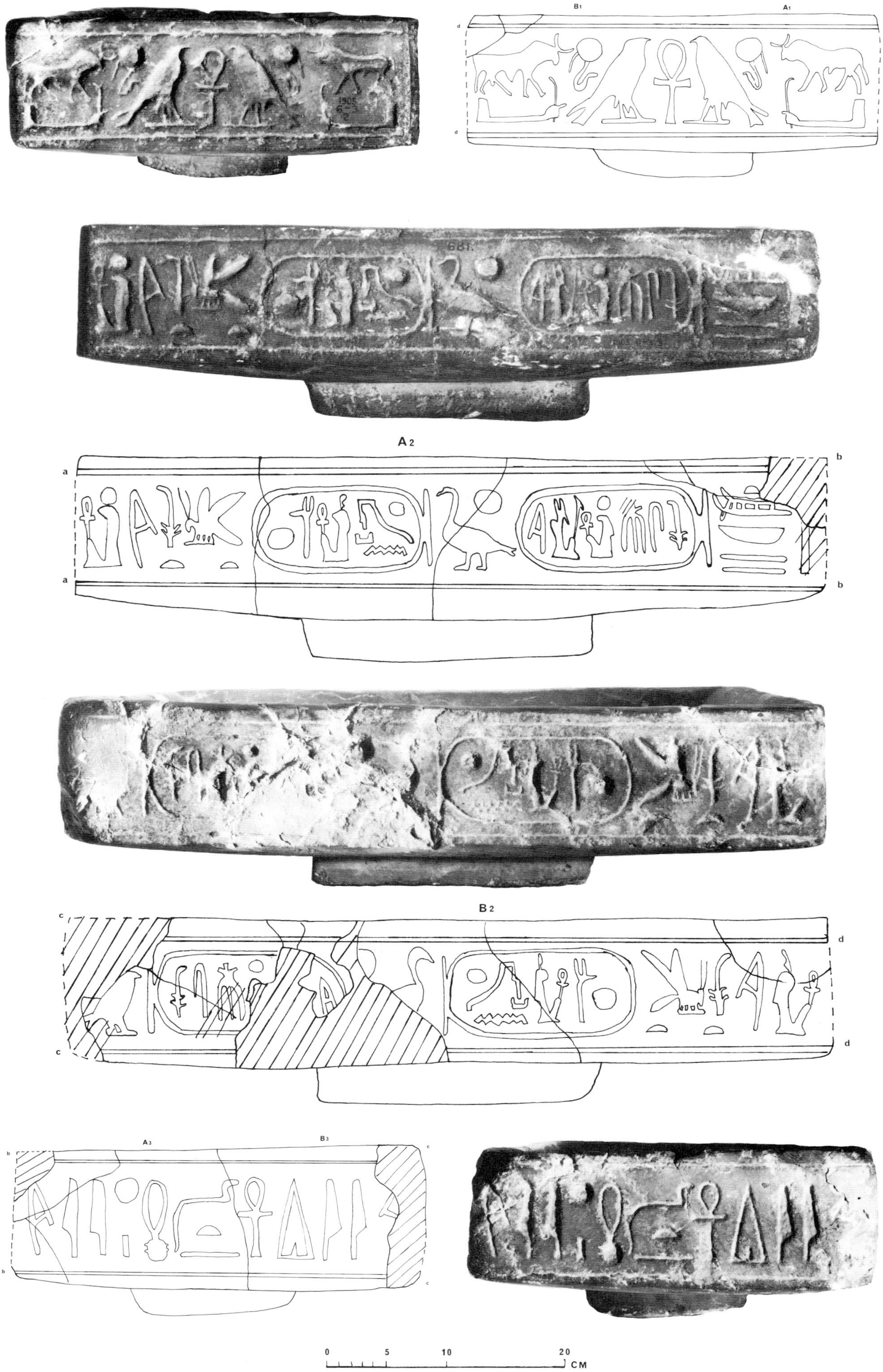

No. 681

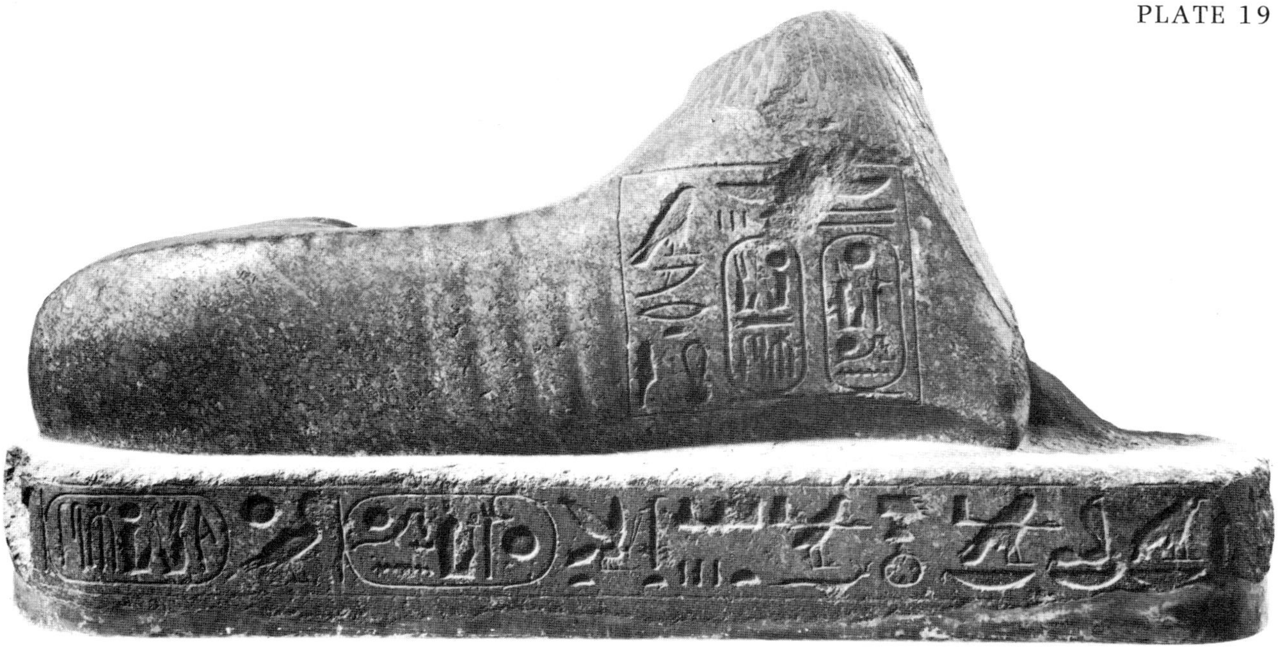

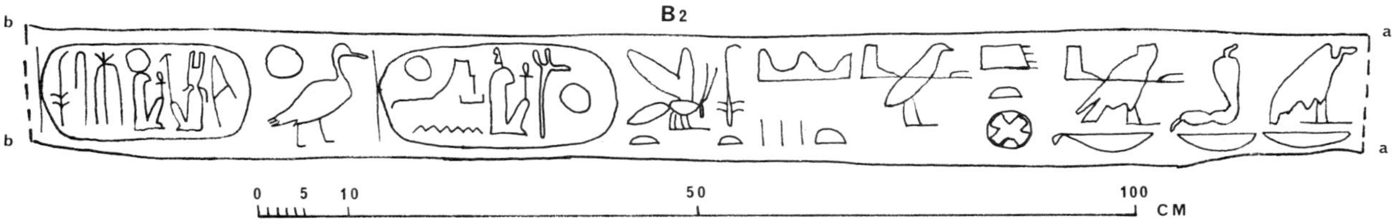

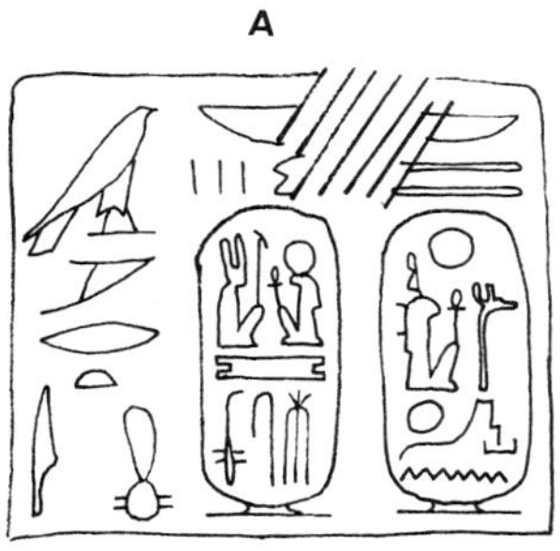

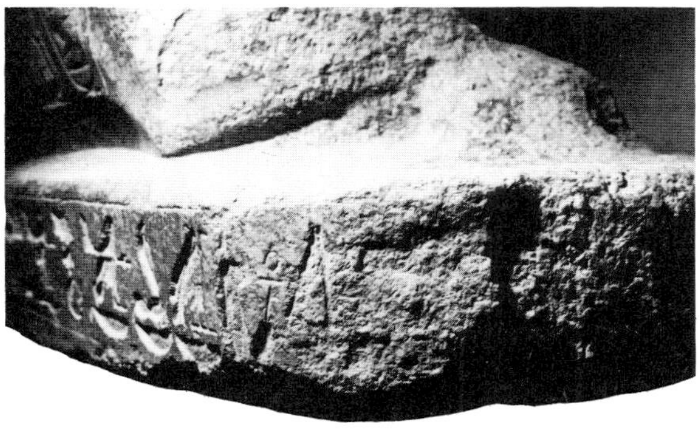

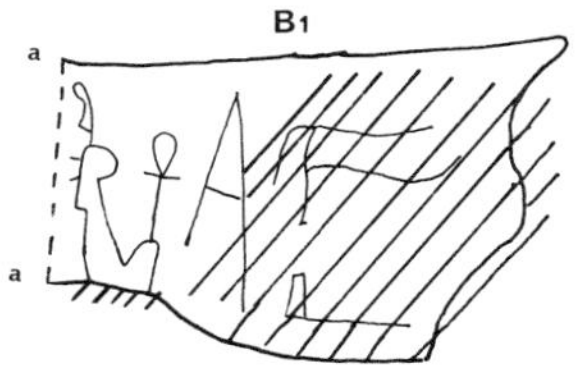

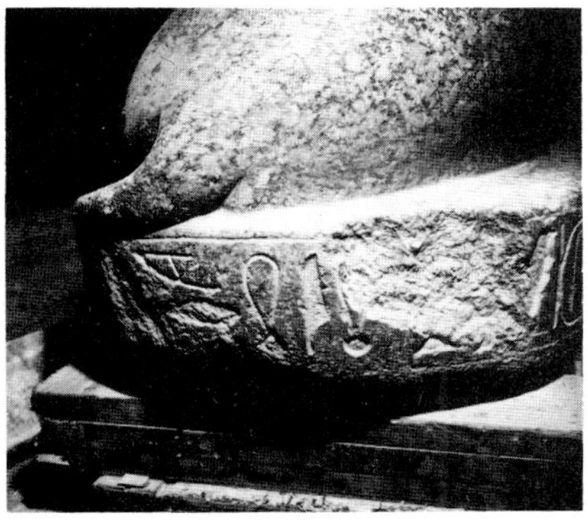

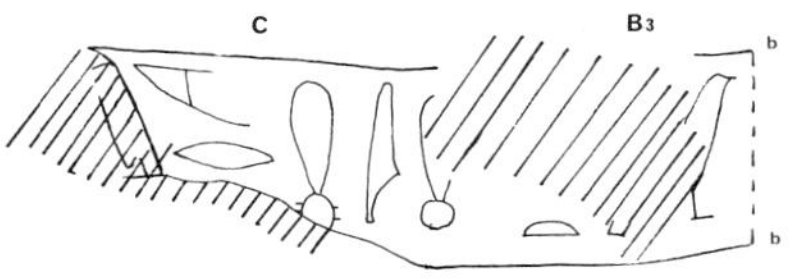

1. No. 857

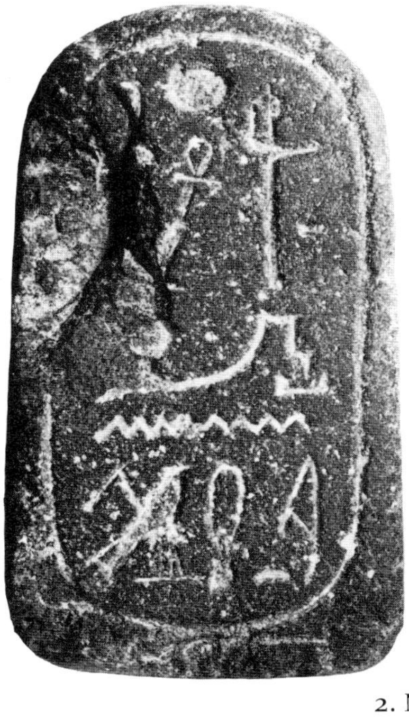

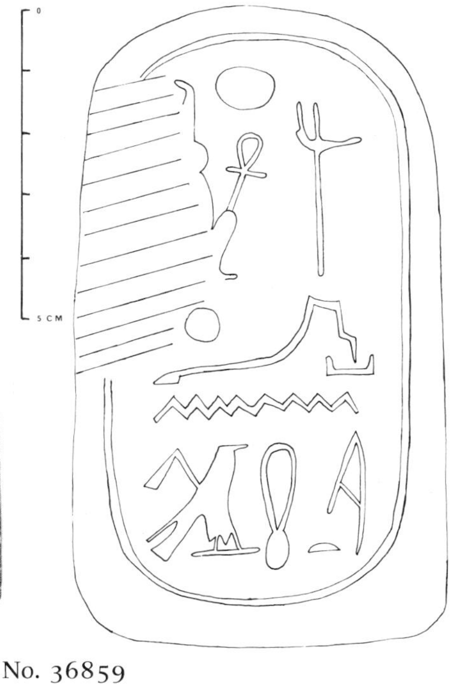

2. No. 36859

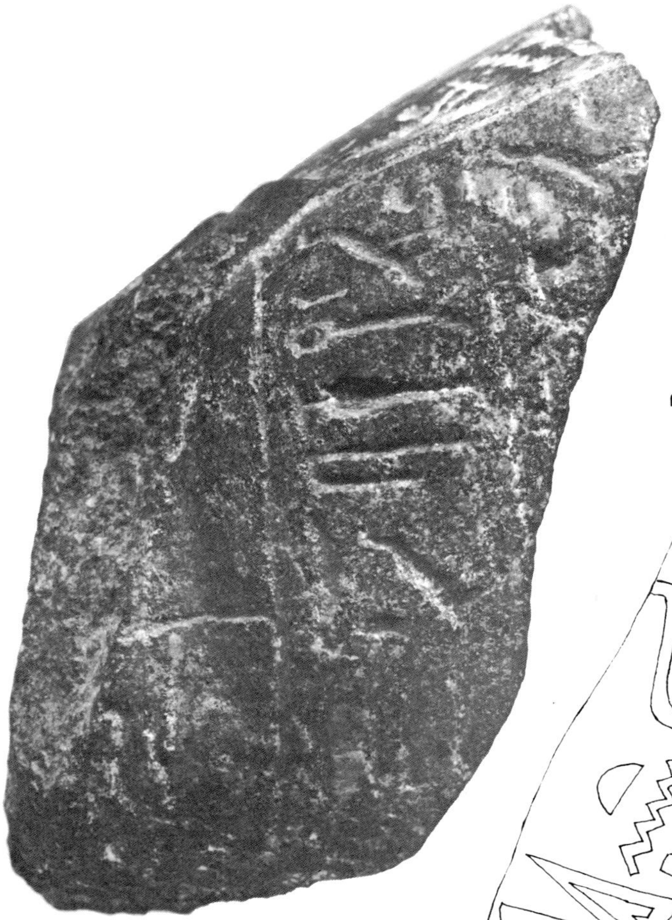

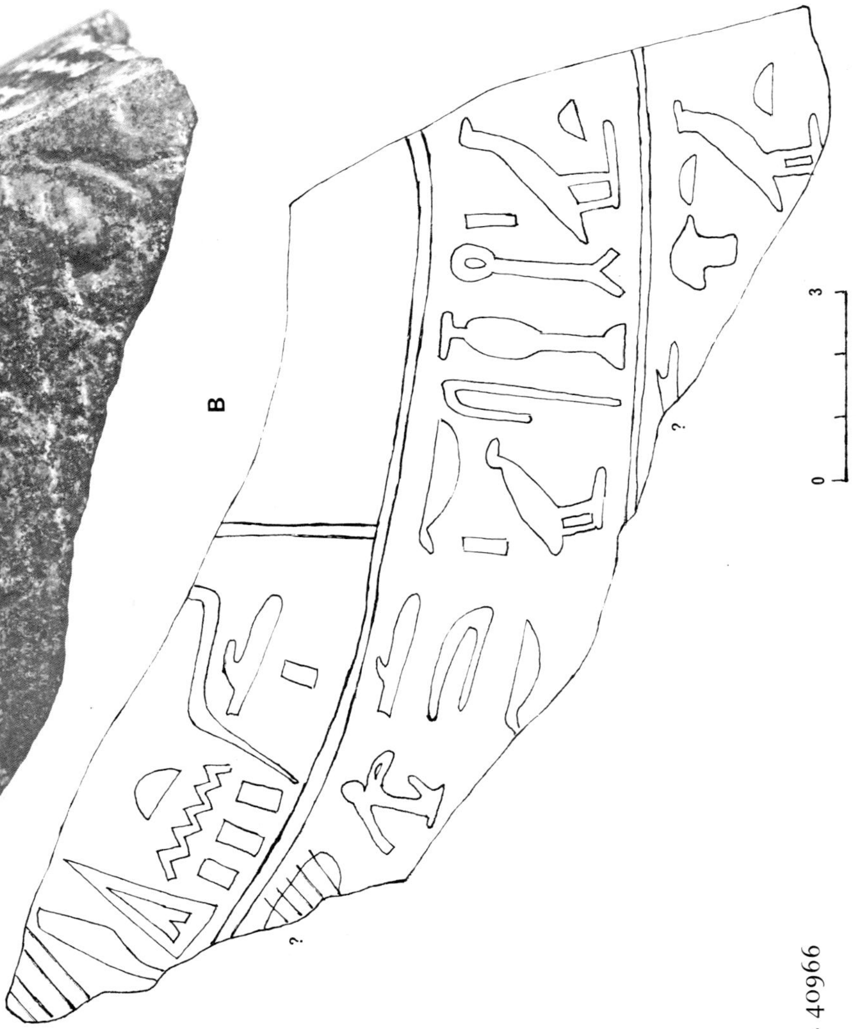

B

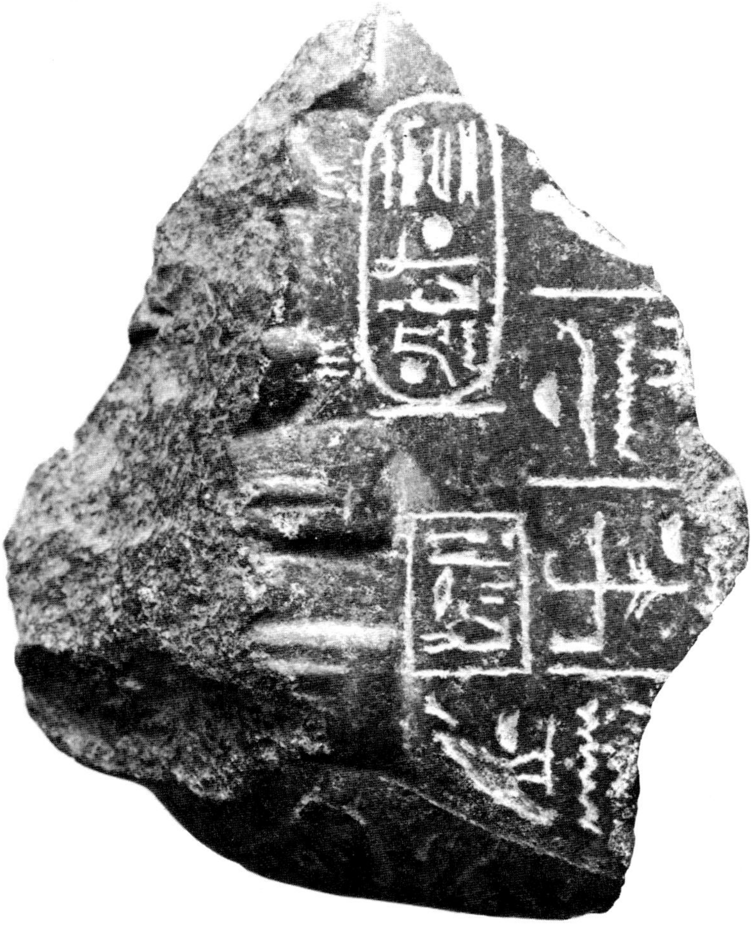

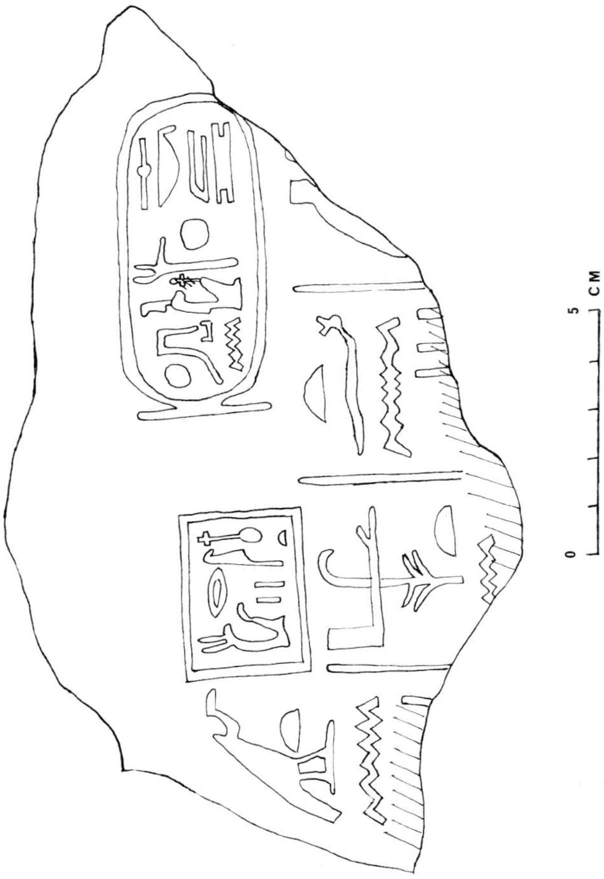

A

No. 40966

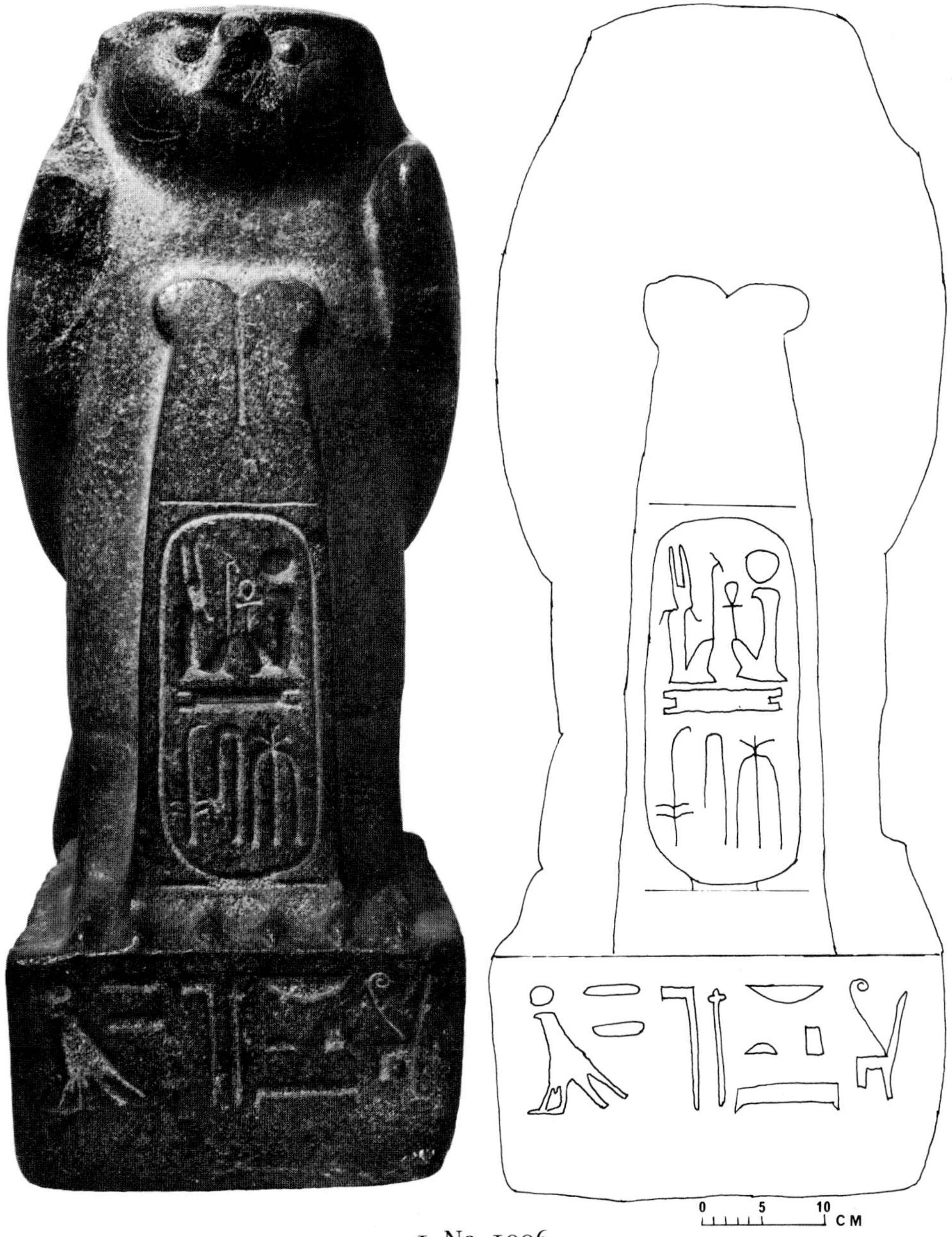

1. No. 1006

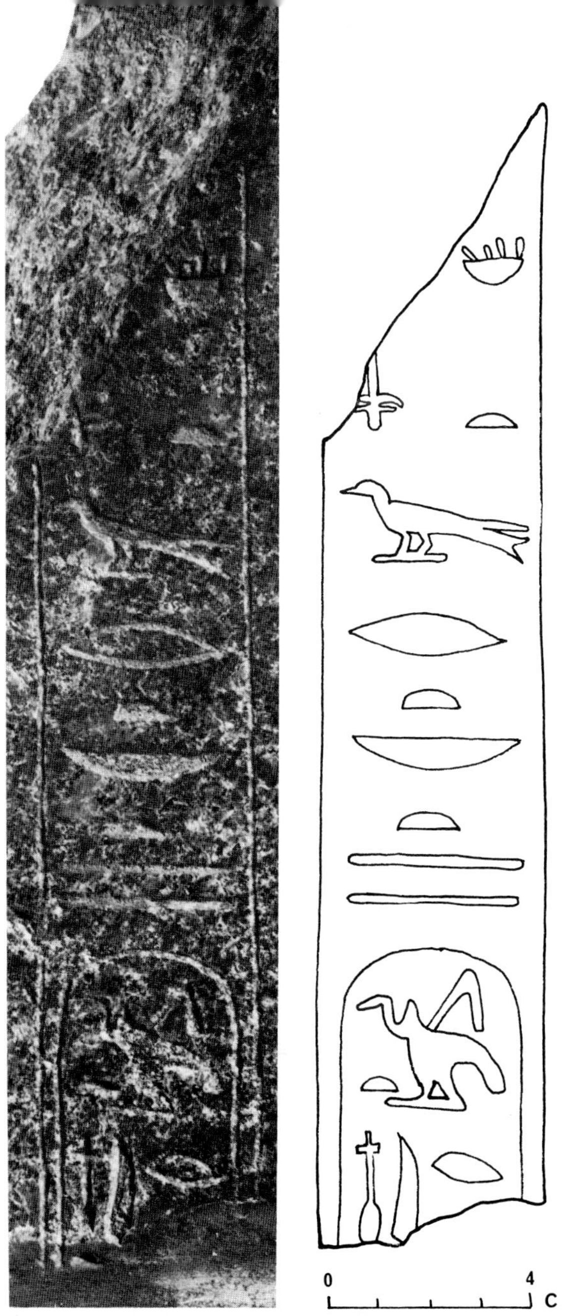

2. No. 1133

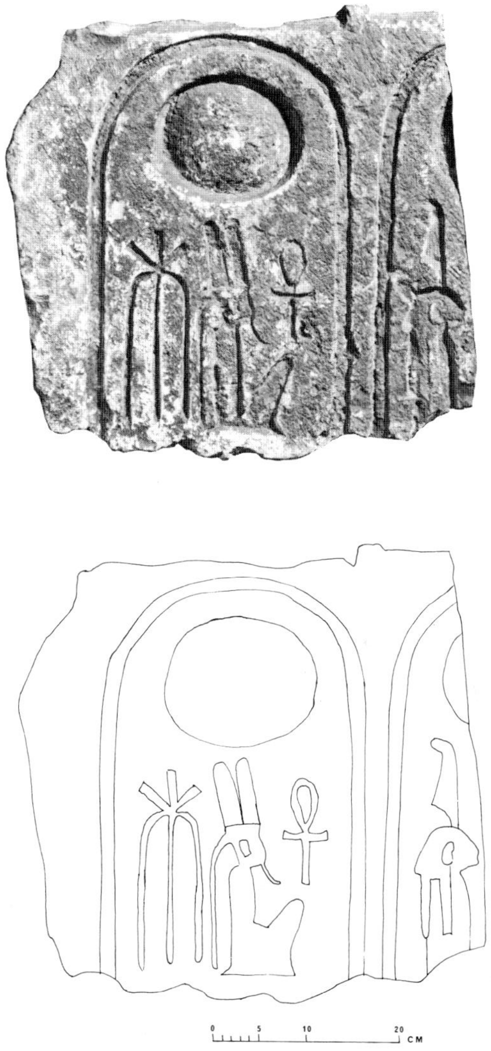

3. No. 442

B
A
0
5 CM

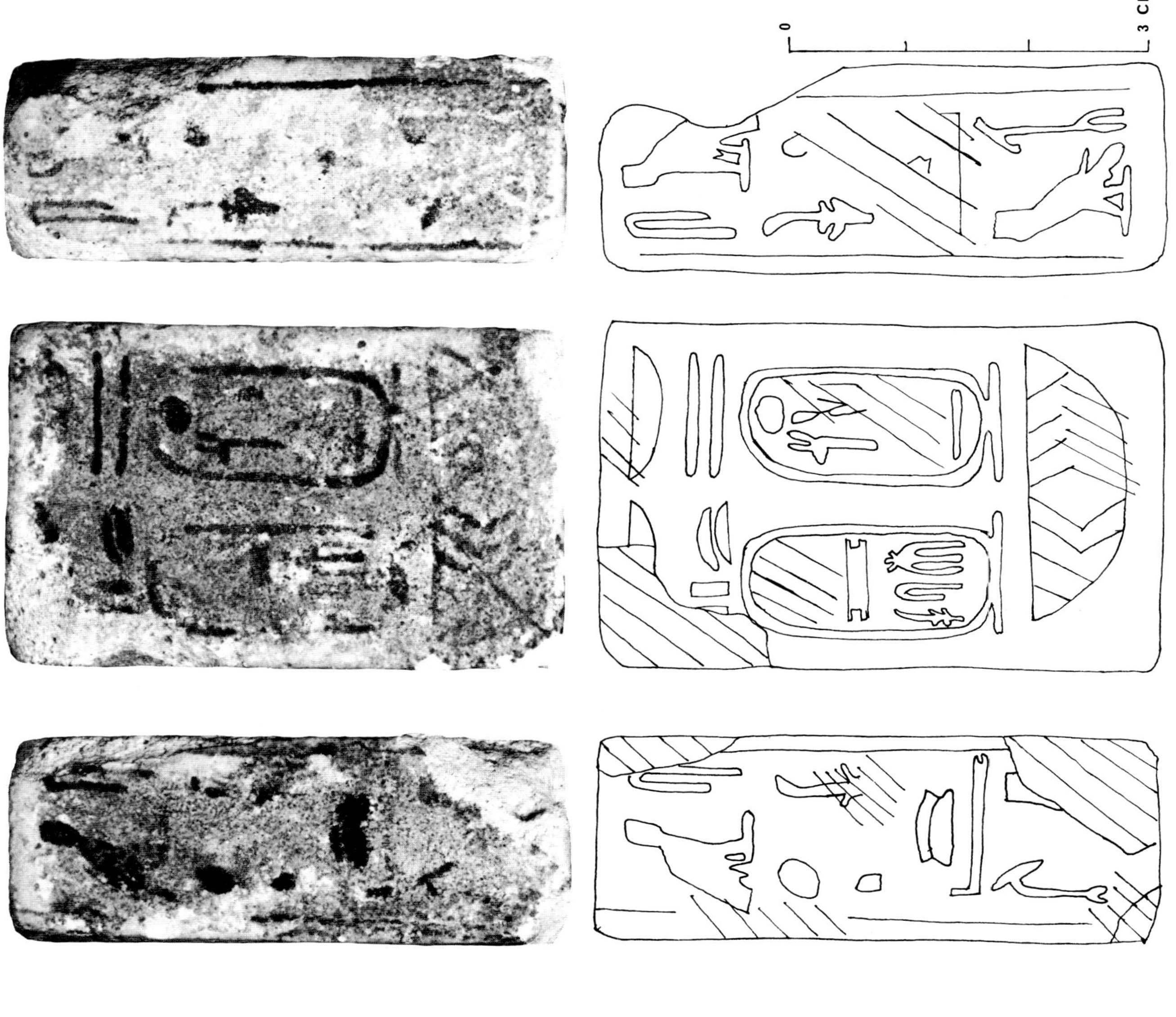
0
3 CM
C
A
B

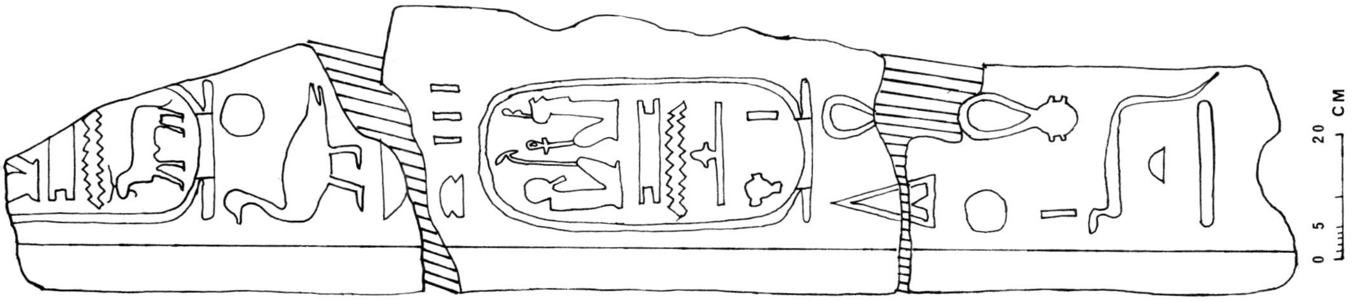

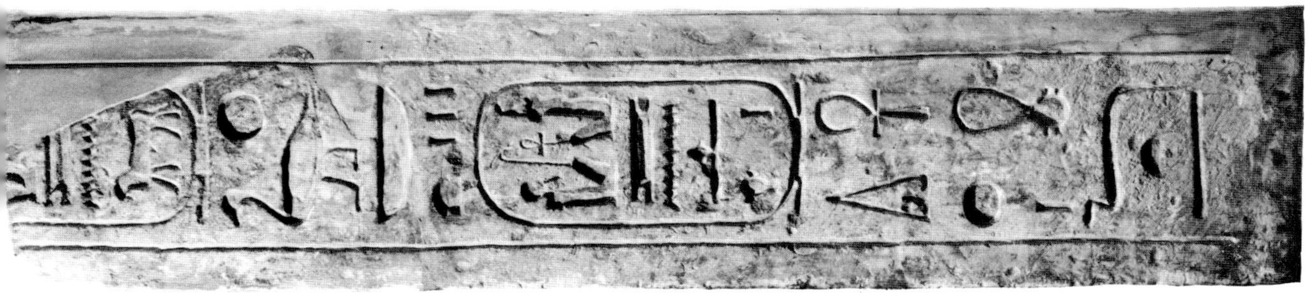

No. 1469

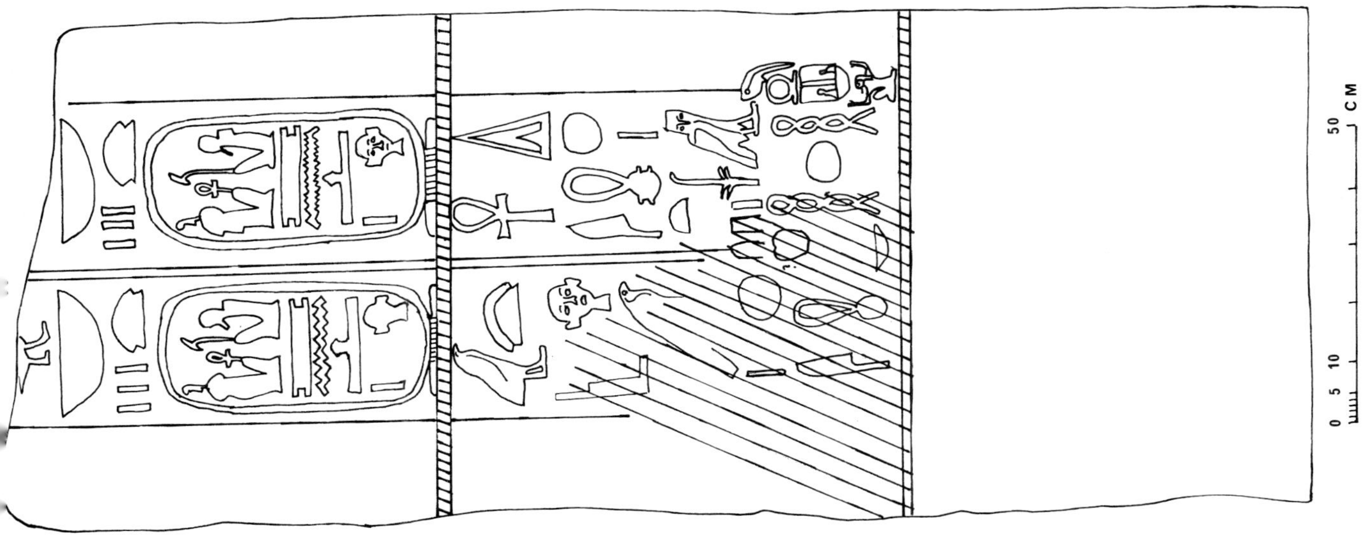

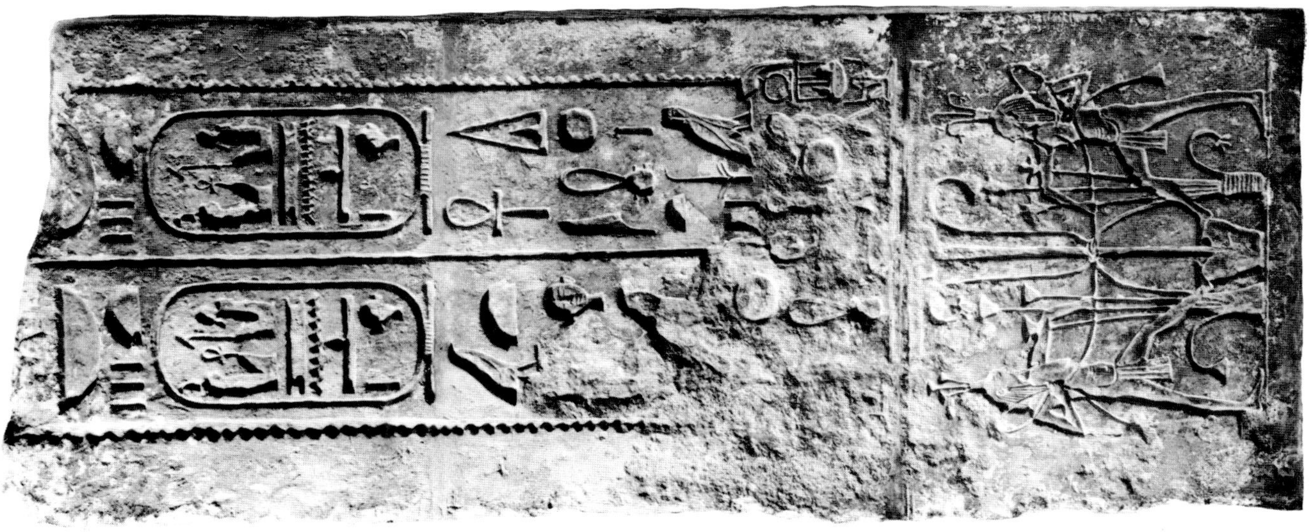

PLATE 24

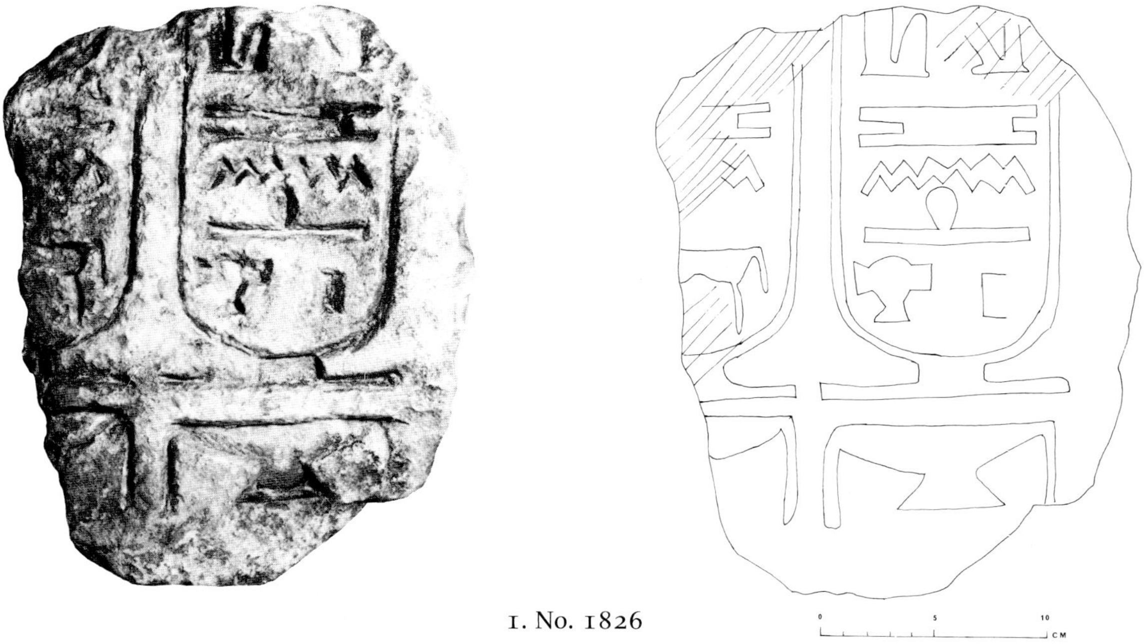

1. No. 1826

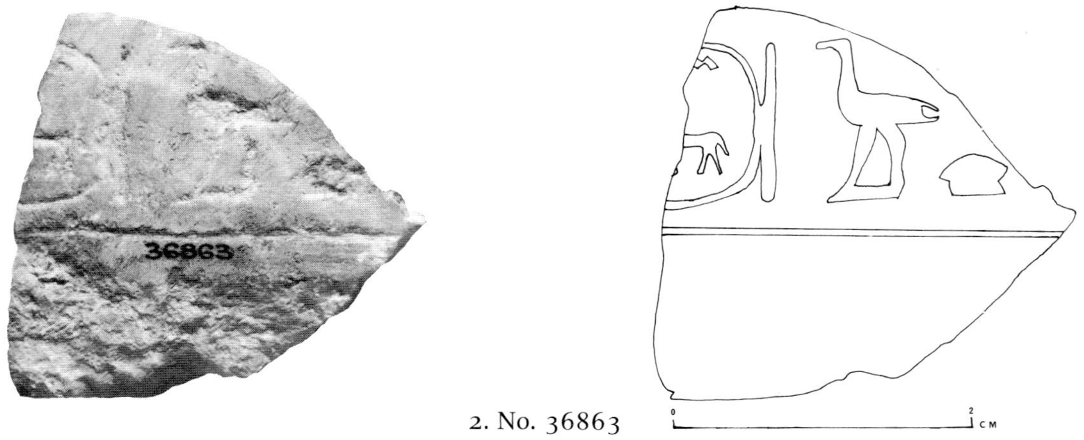

2. No. 36863

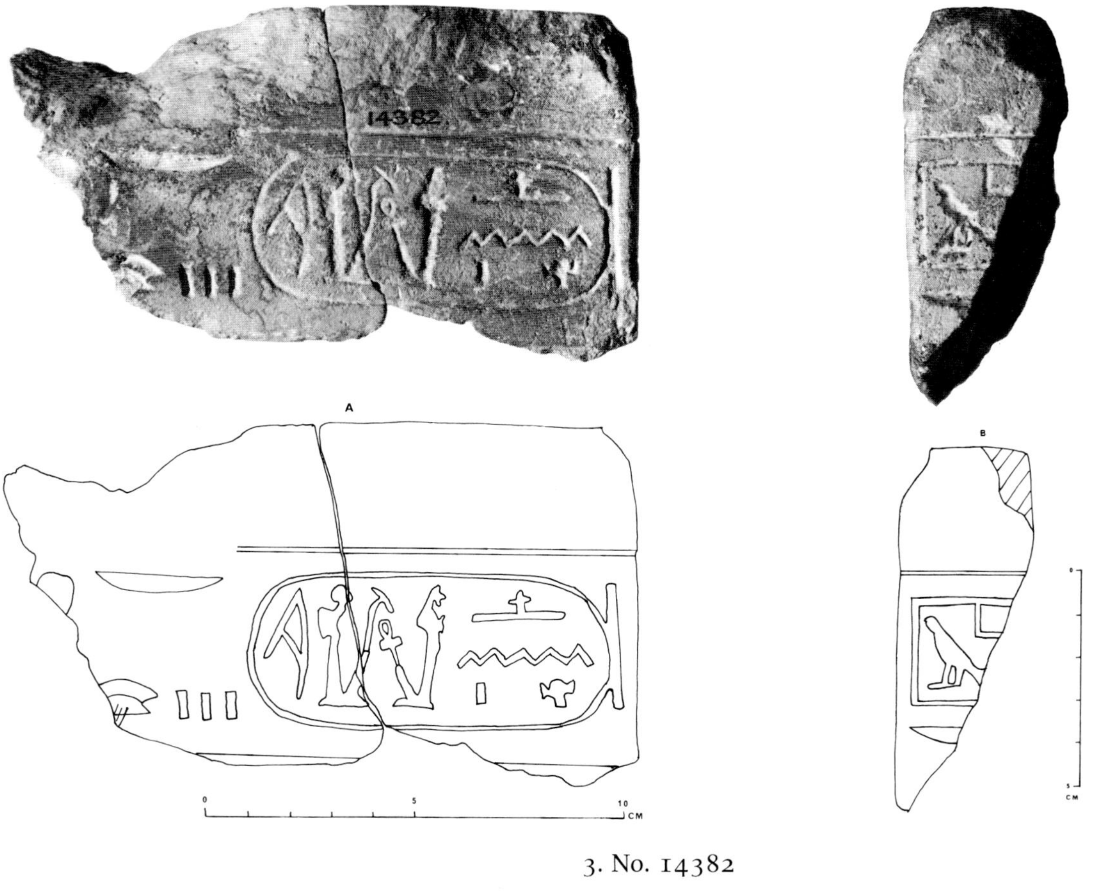

3. No. 14382

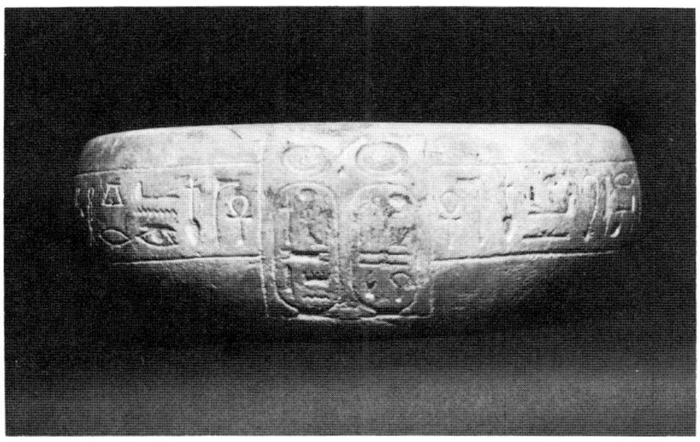

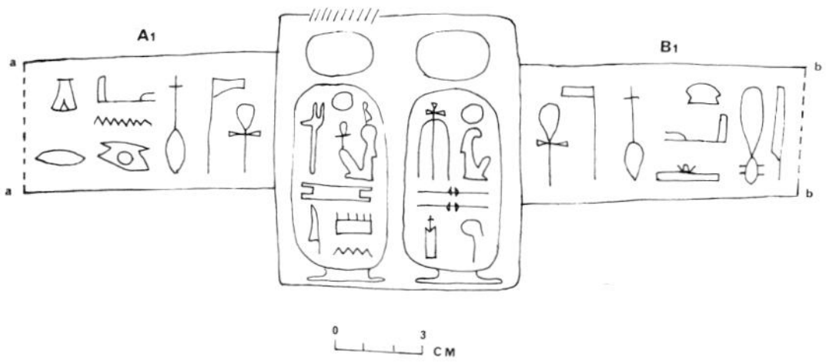

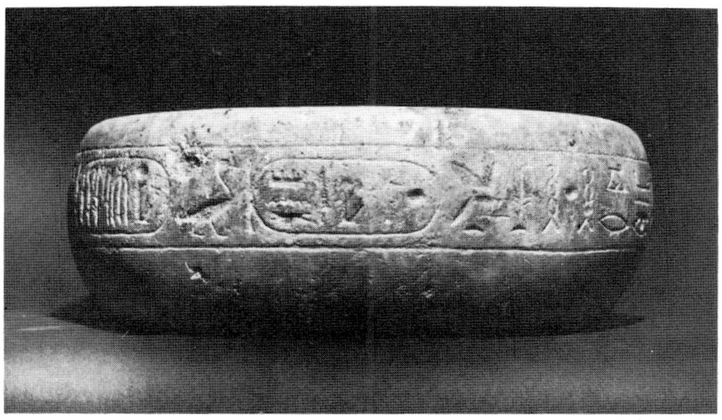

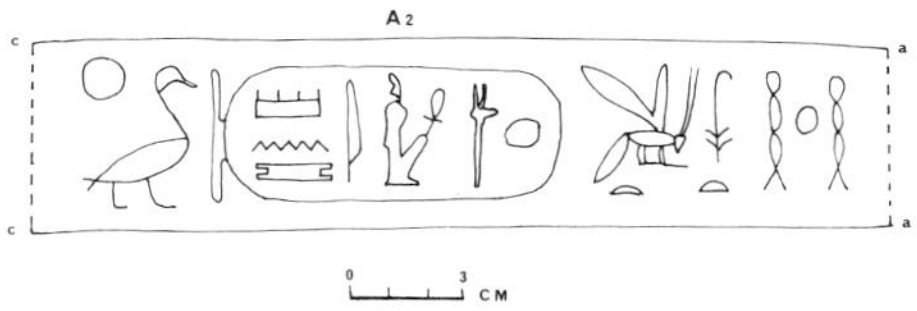

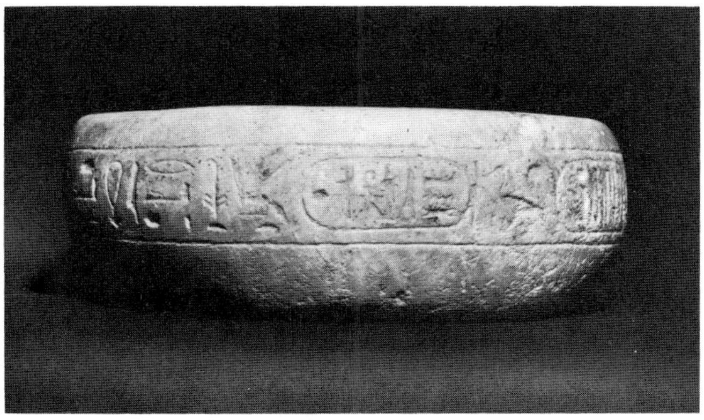

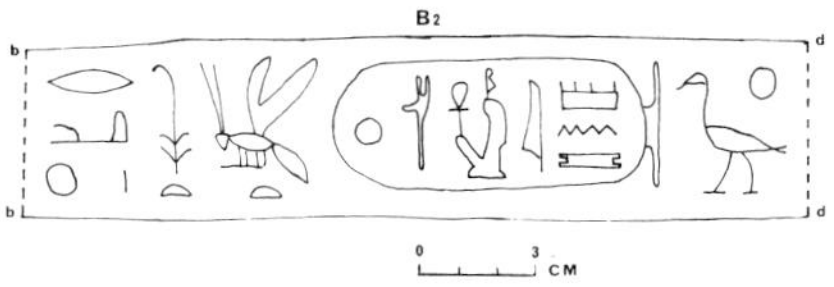

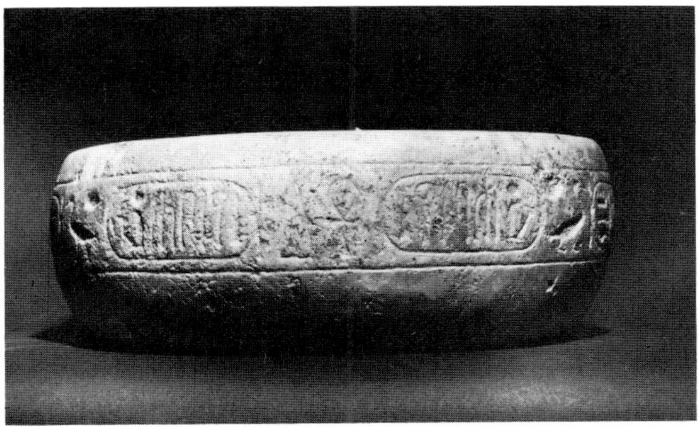

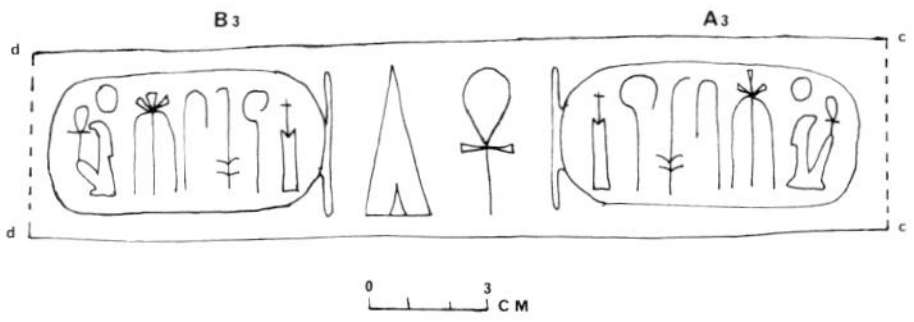

No. 634

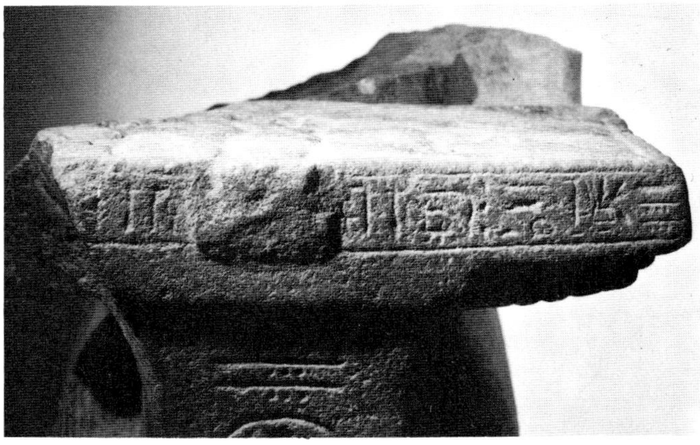

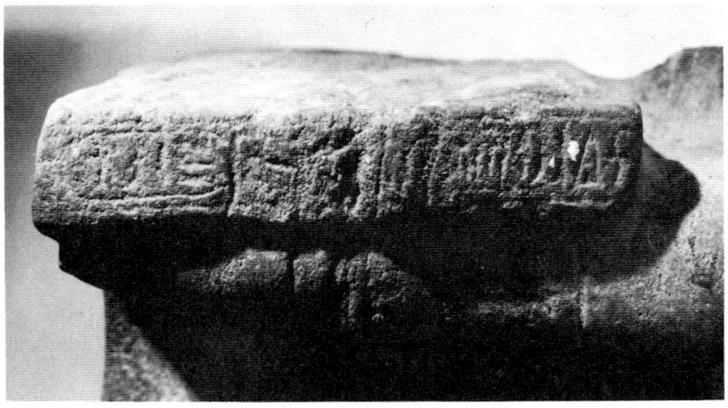

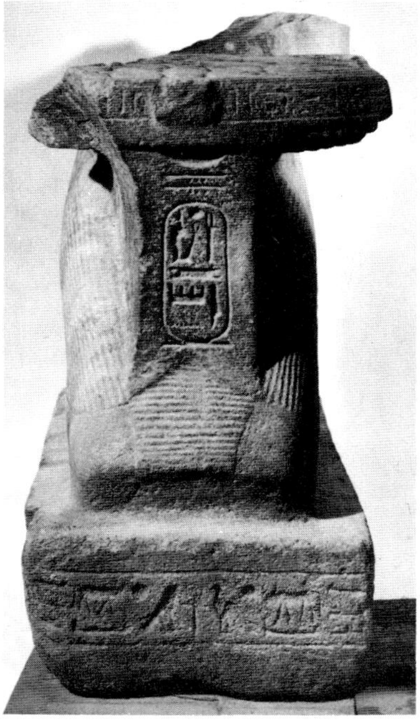

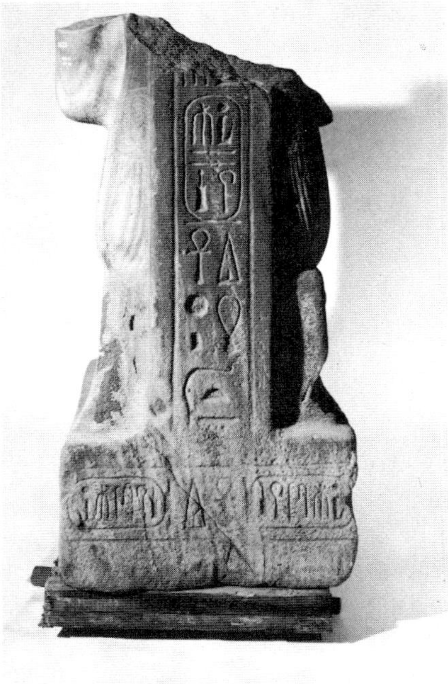

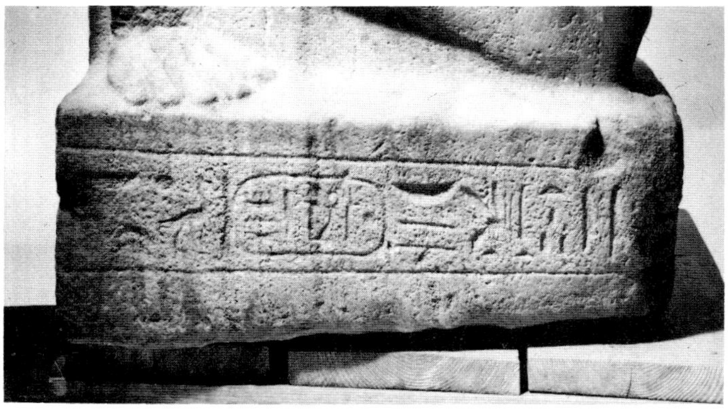

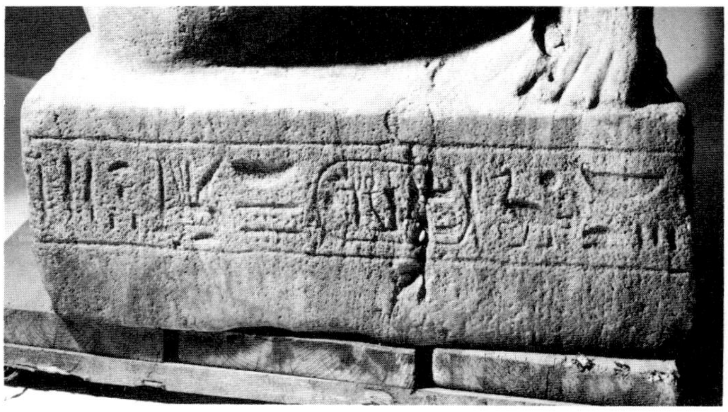

No. 1821

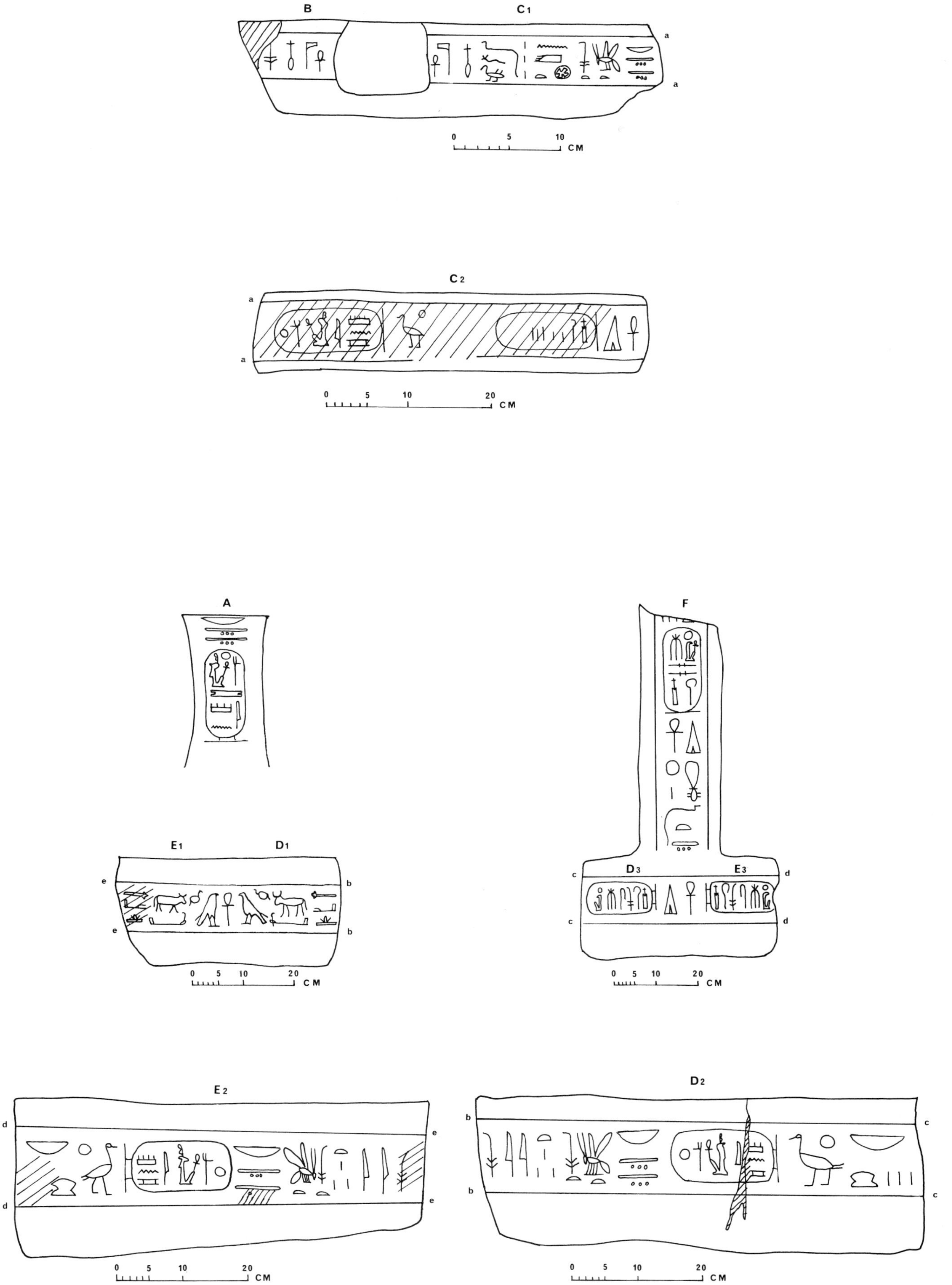
B
C1
a
a
0 5 10 CM
C2
a
a
0 5 10 20 CM
A
F
E1
D1
e
e
b
b
0 5 10 20 CM
c
c
D3
E3
d
d
0 5 10 20 CM
E2
d
d
e
e
0 5 10 20 CM
D2
b
b
c
c
0 5 10 20 CM

No. 1821

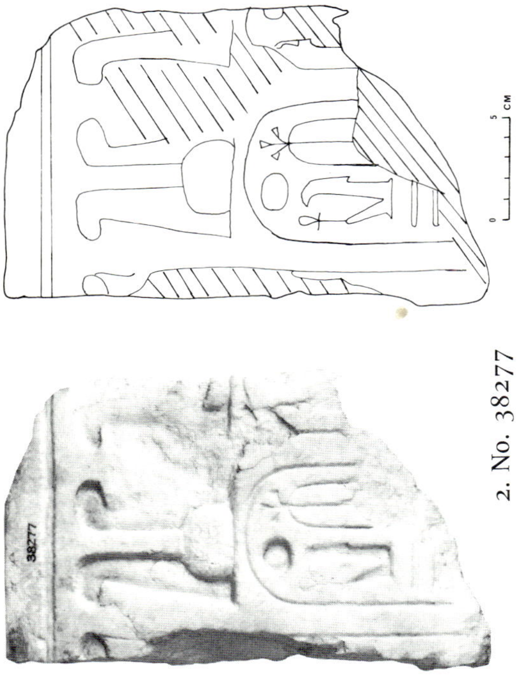

2. No. 38277

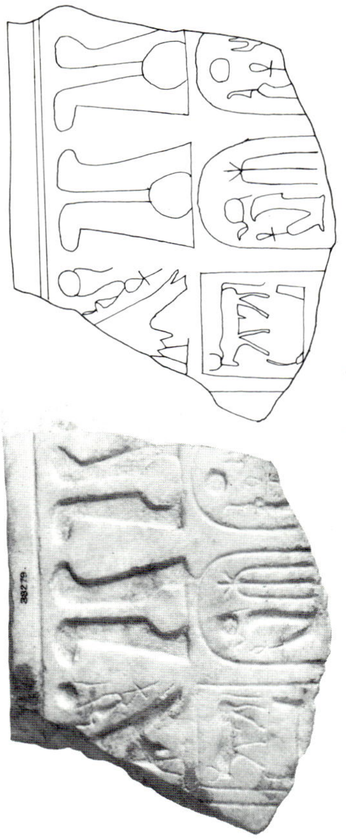

3. No. 38279

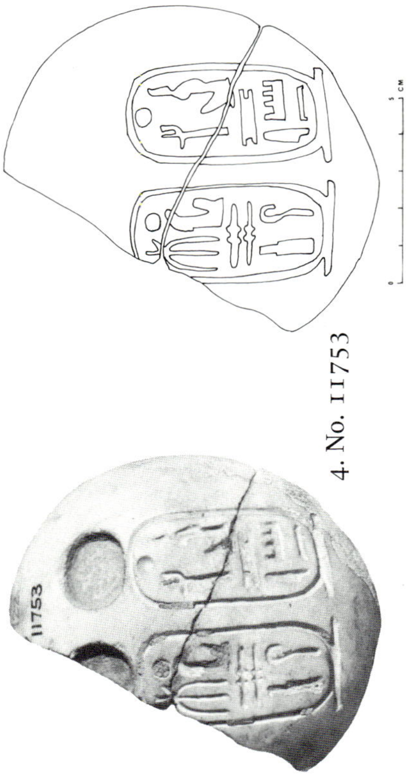

4. No. 11753

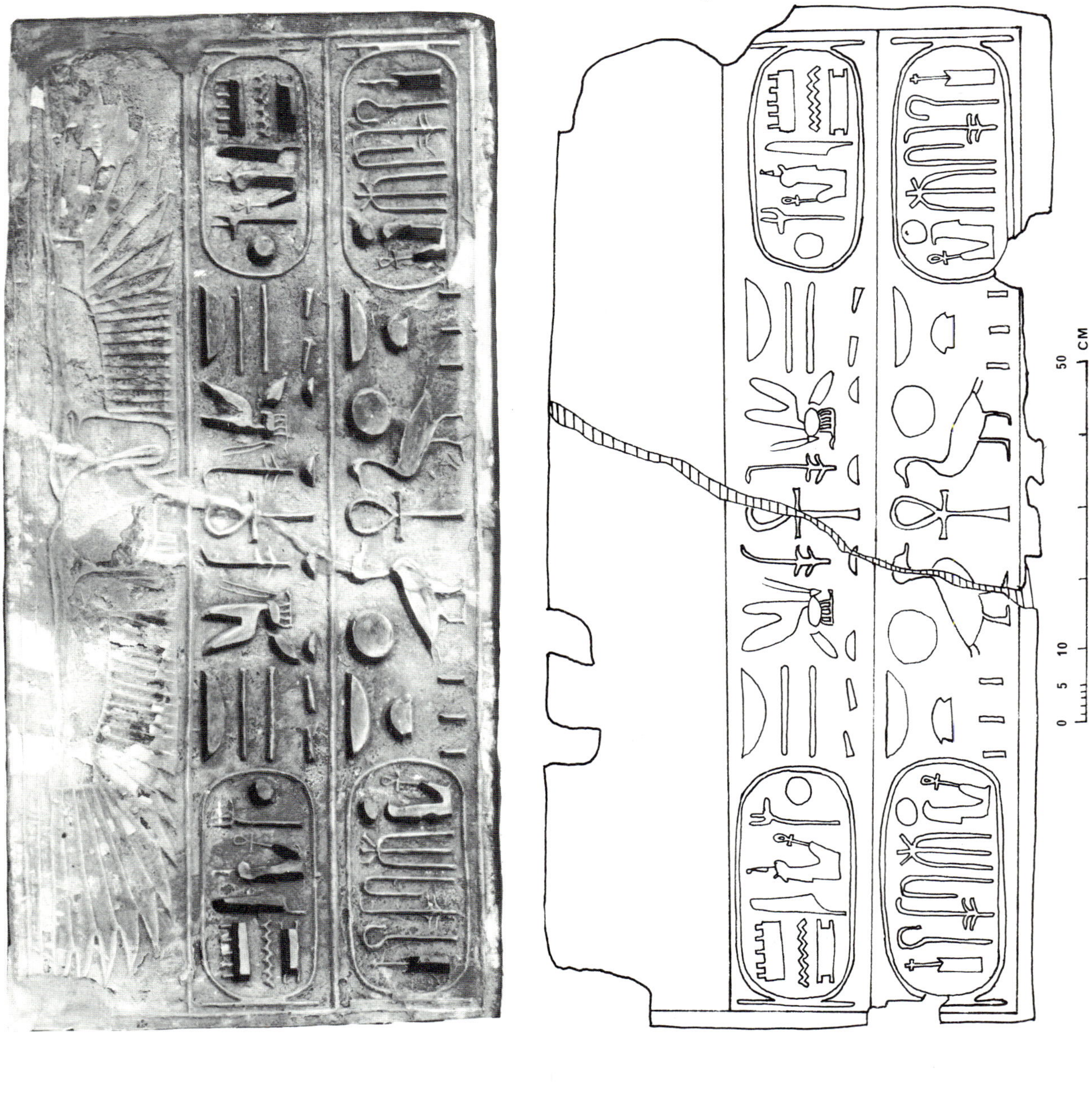

1. No. 1344

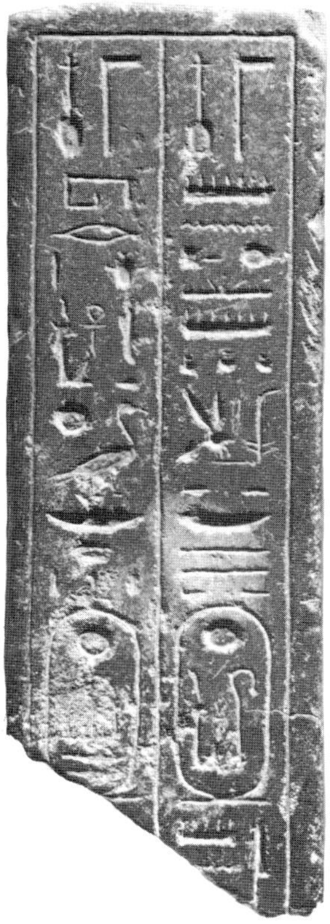

A1

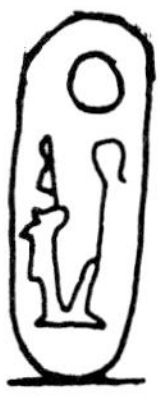

A2

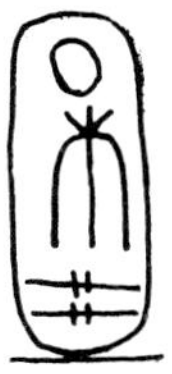

A3

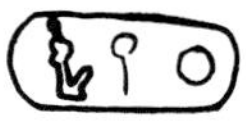

B

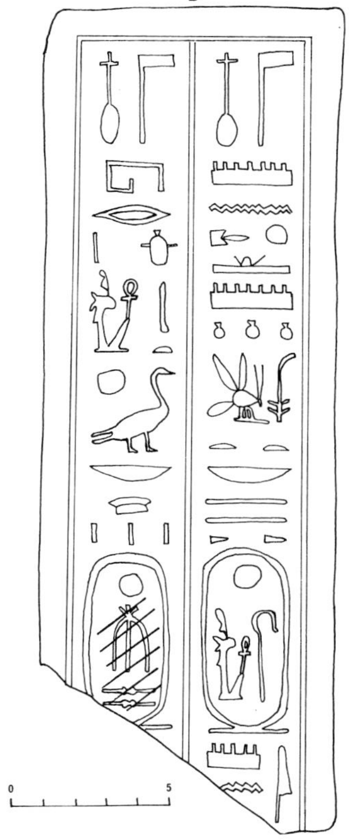

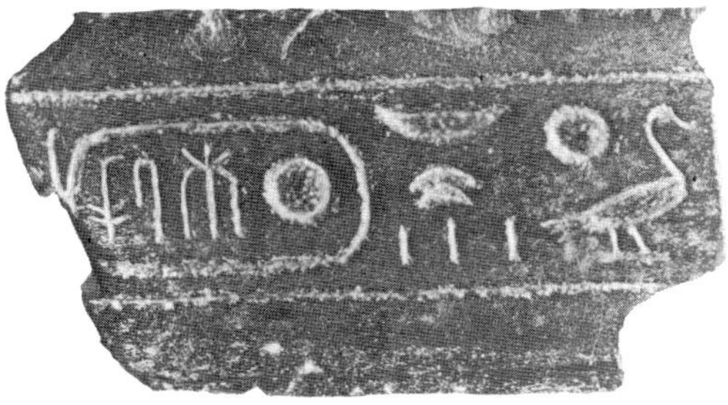

C

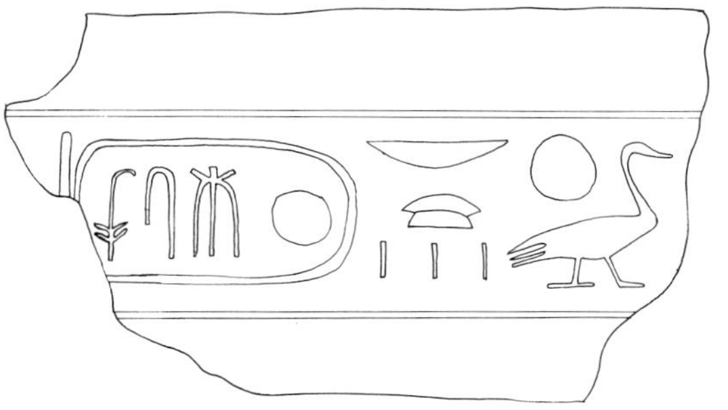

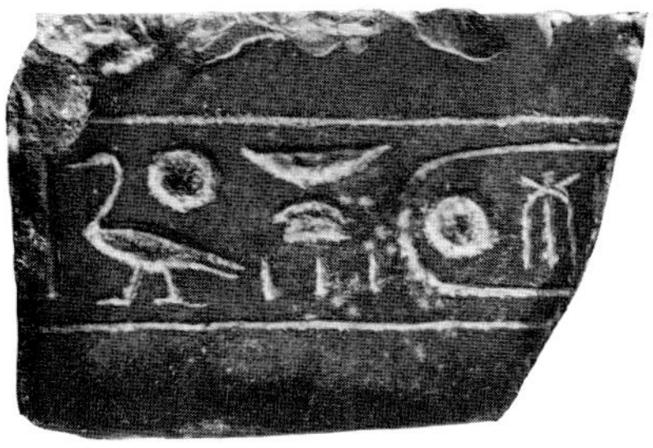

D

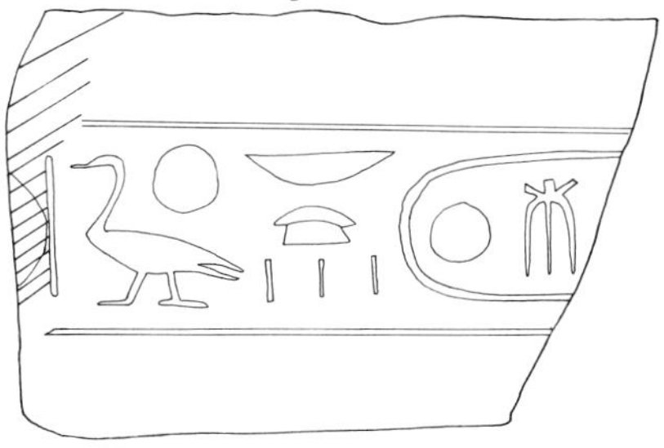

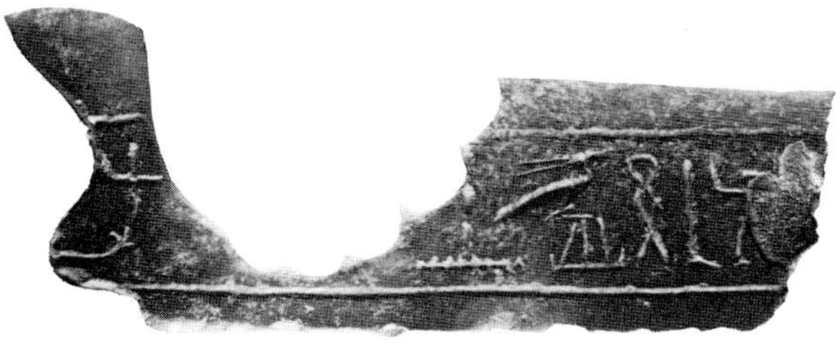

E

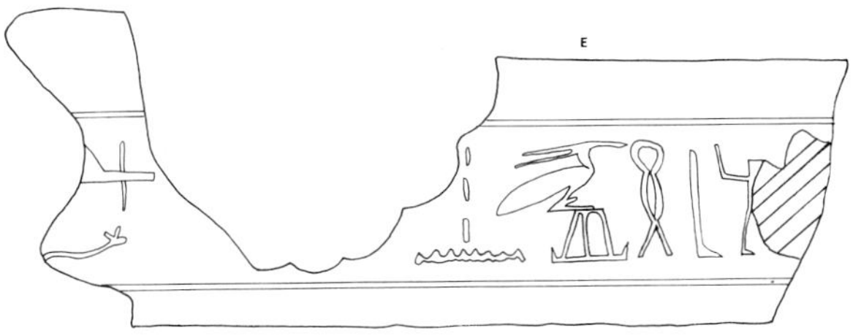

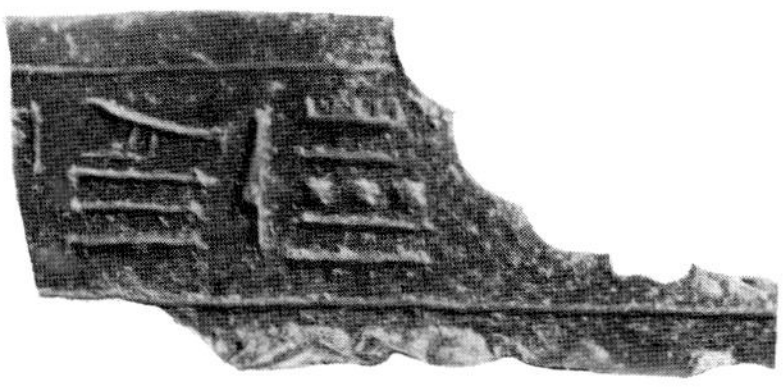

F

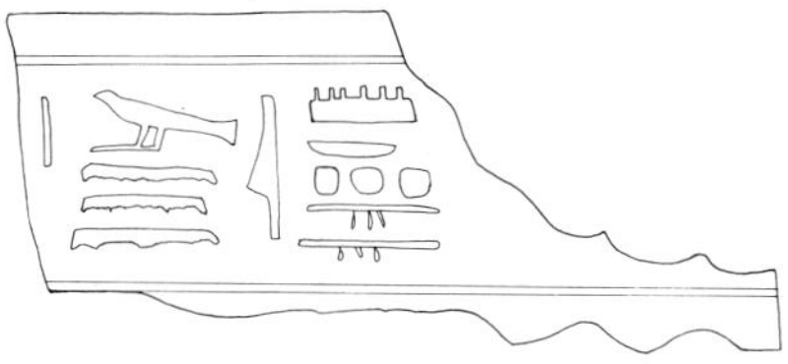

No. 1816

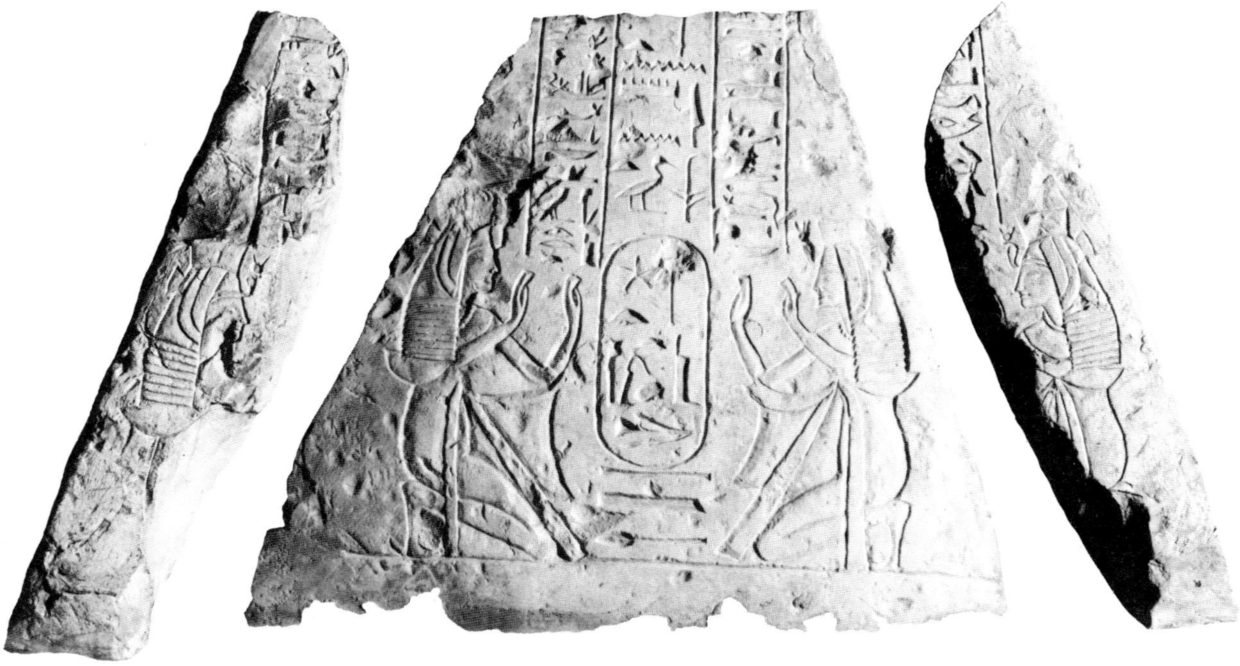

1. No. 1742

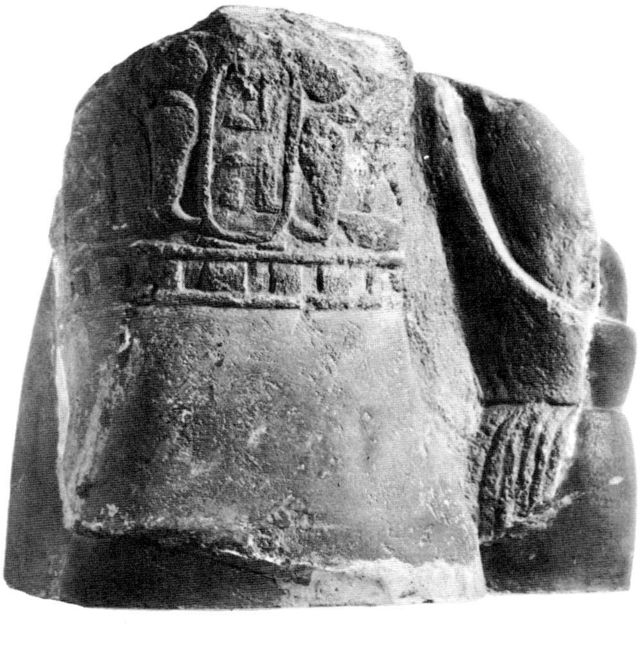

2. No. 481

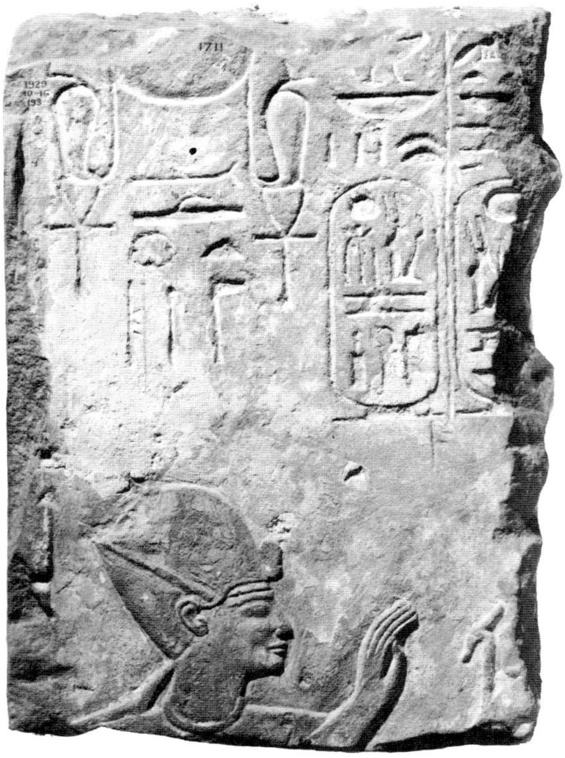

3. No. 1711

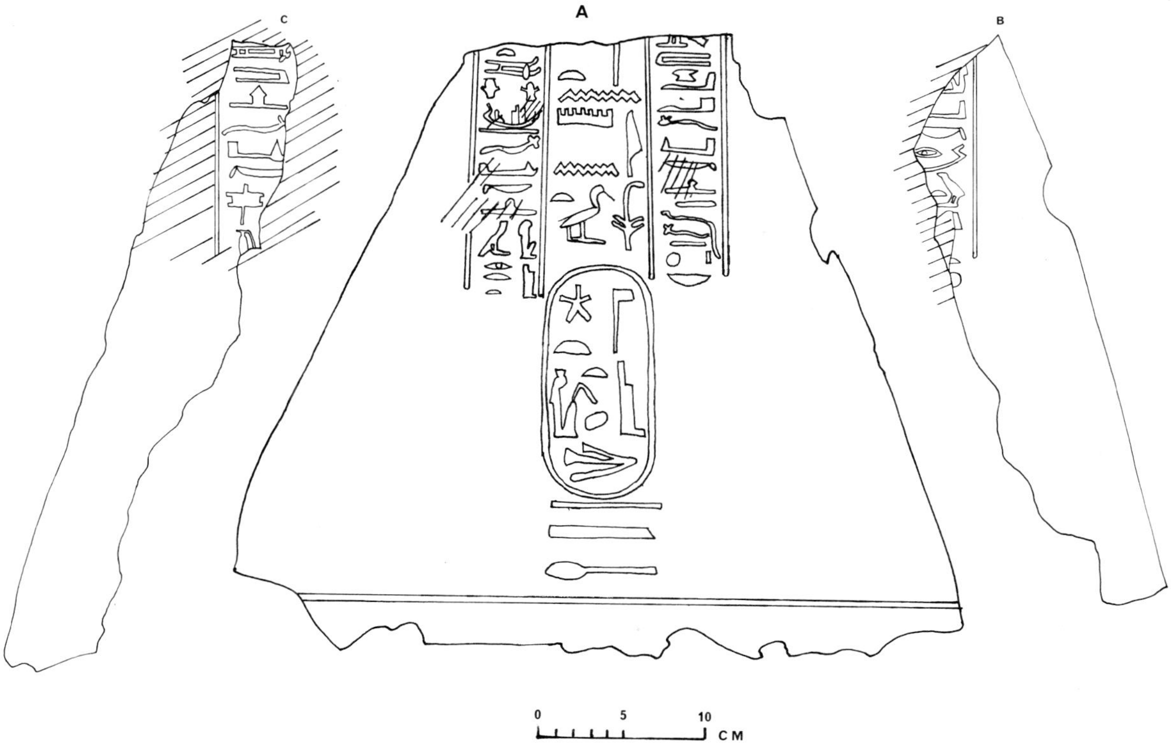

1. No. 1742

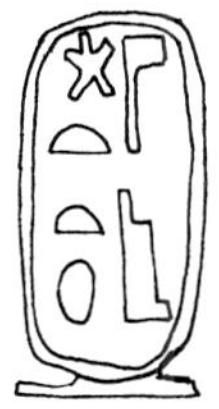

2. No. 481

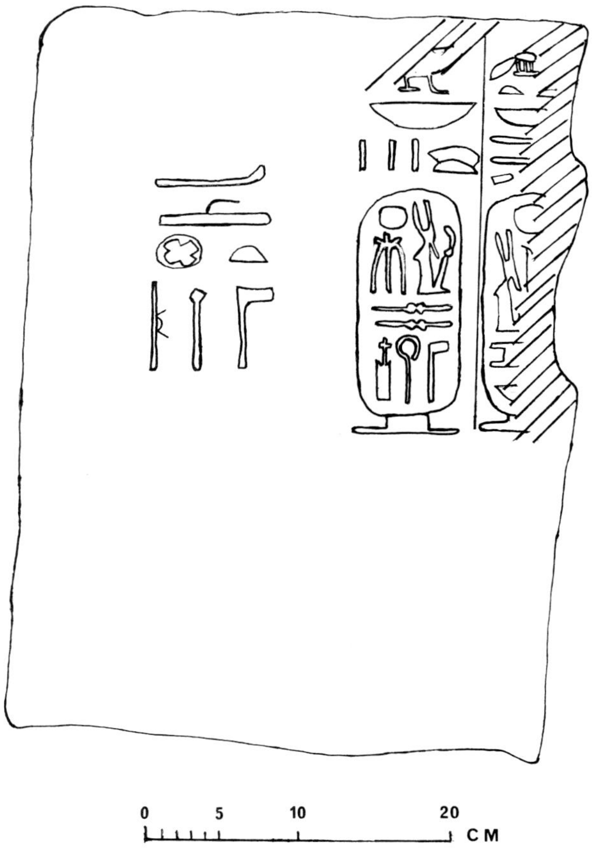

3. No. 1711

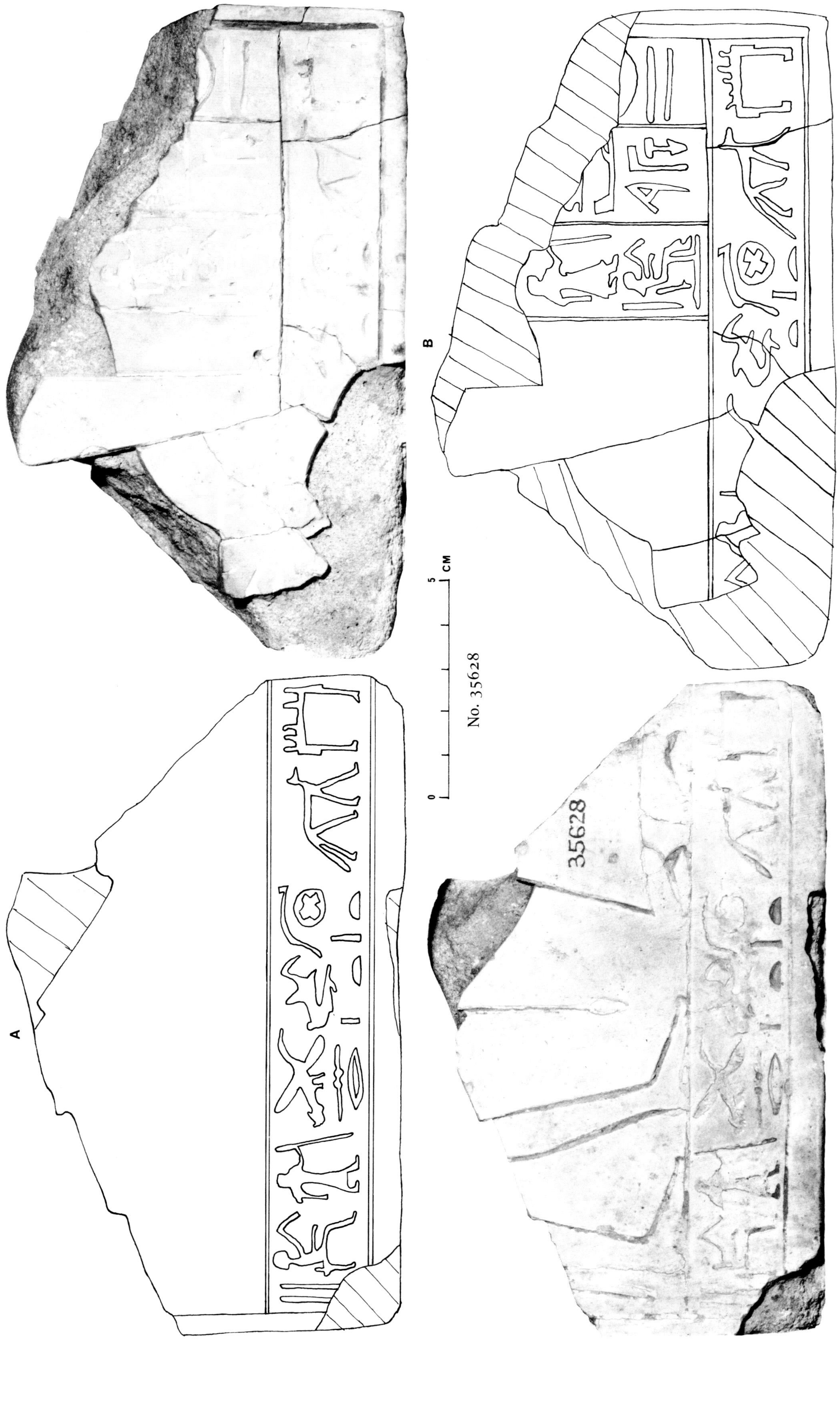

No. 35628

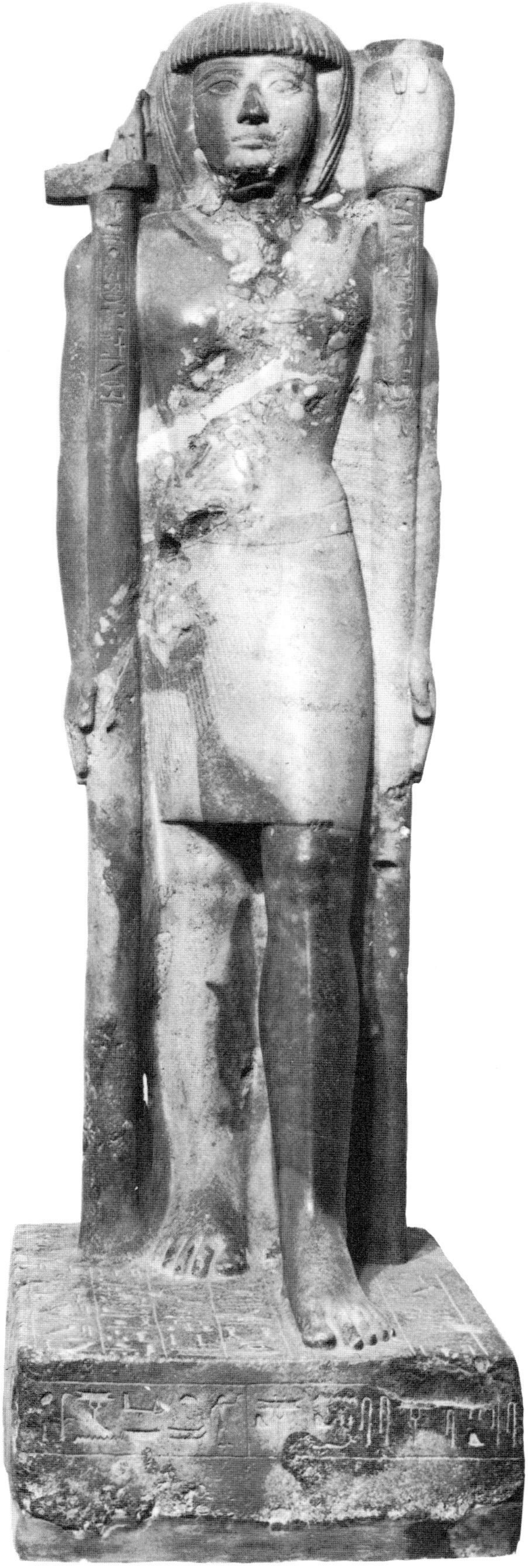

No. 947

A1

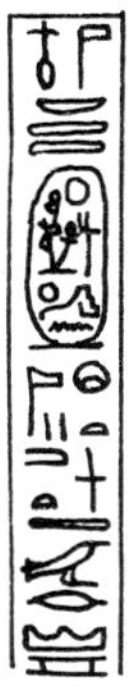

A2

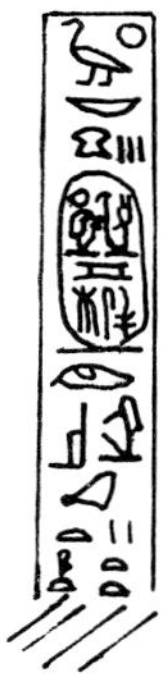

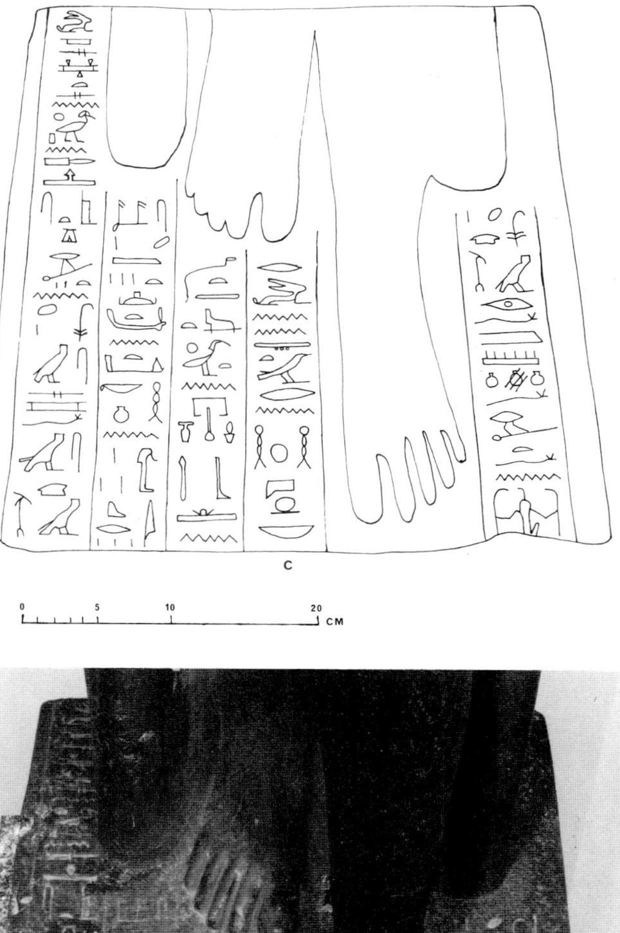

B1 B5

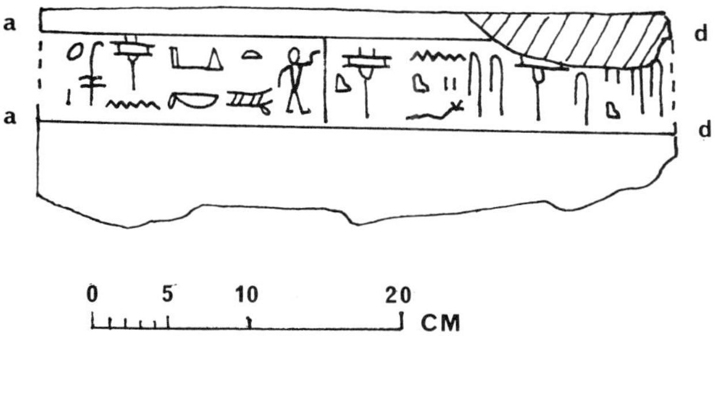

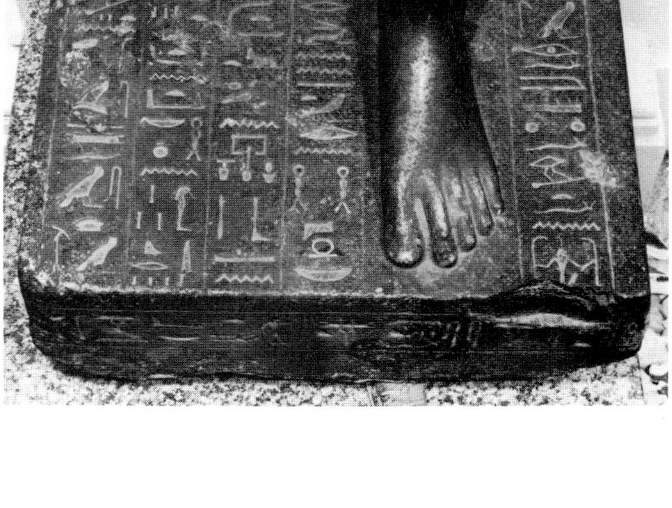

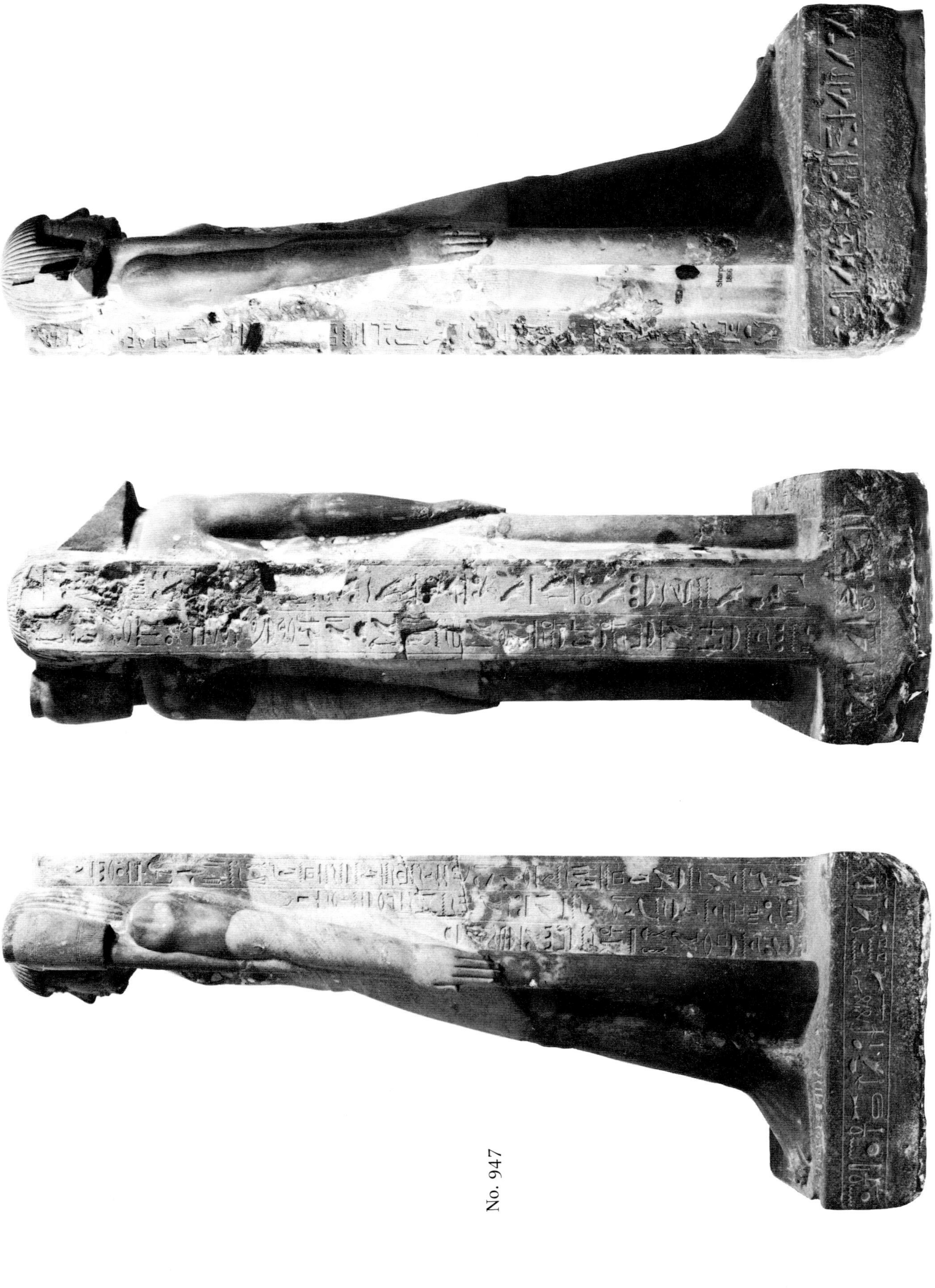

No. 947

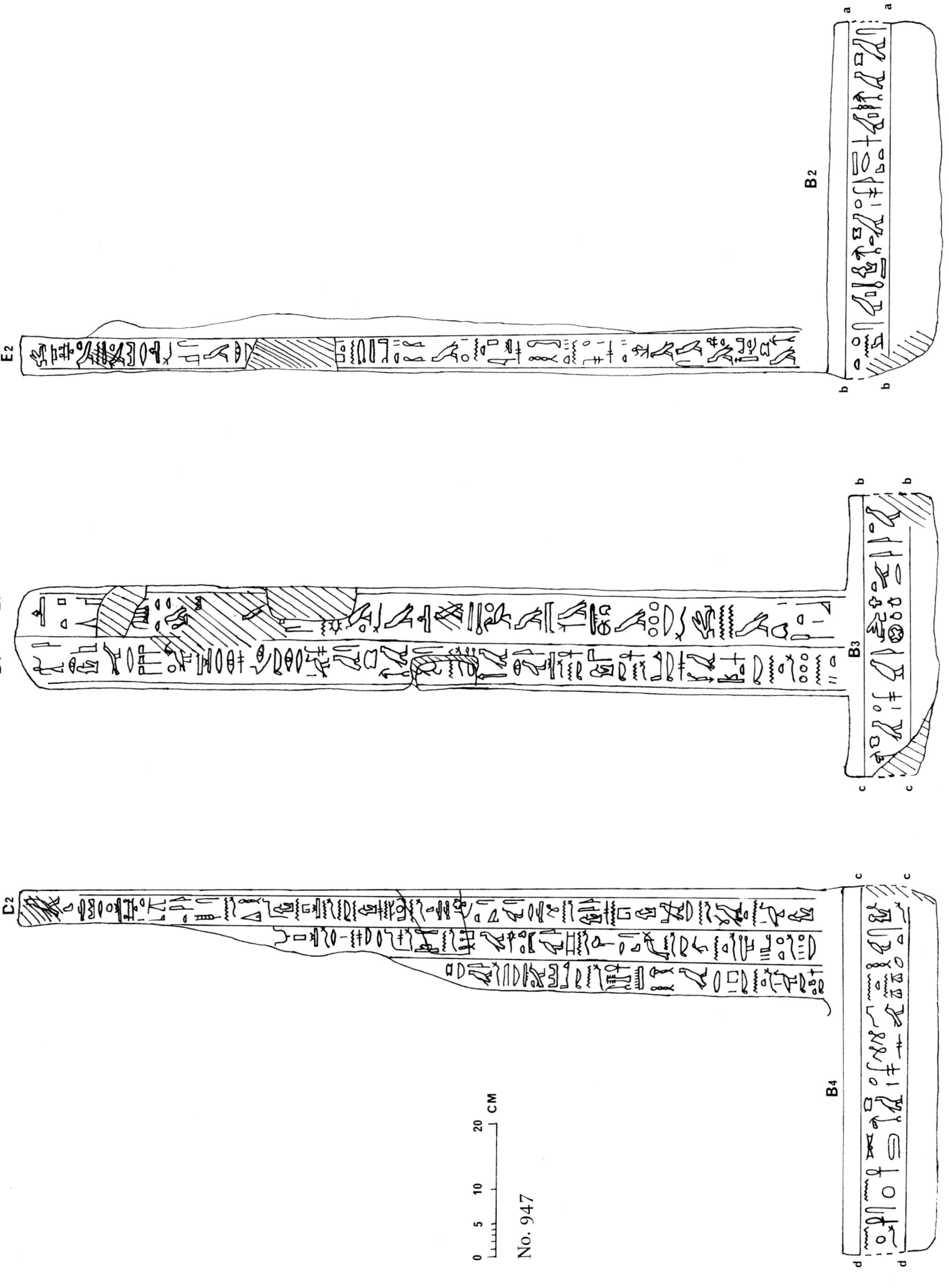
B2
E2
a
b
E1
D1
B3
C2
B4
c
d
0 5 10 20 CM
No. 947

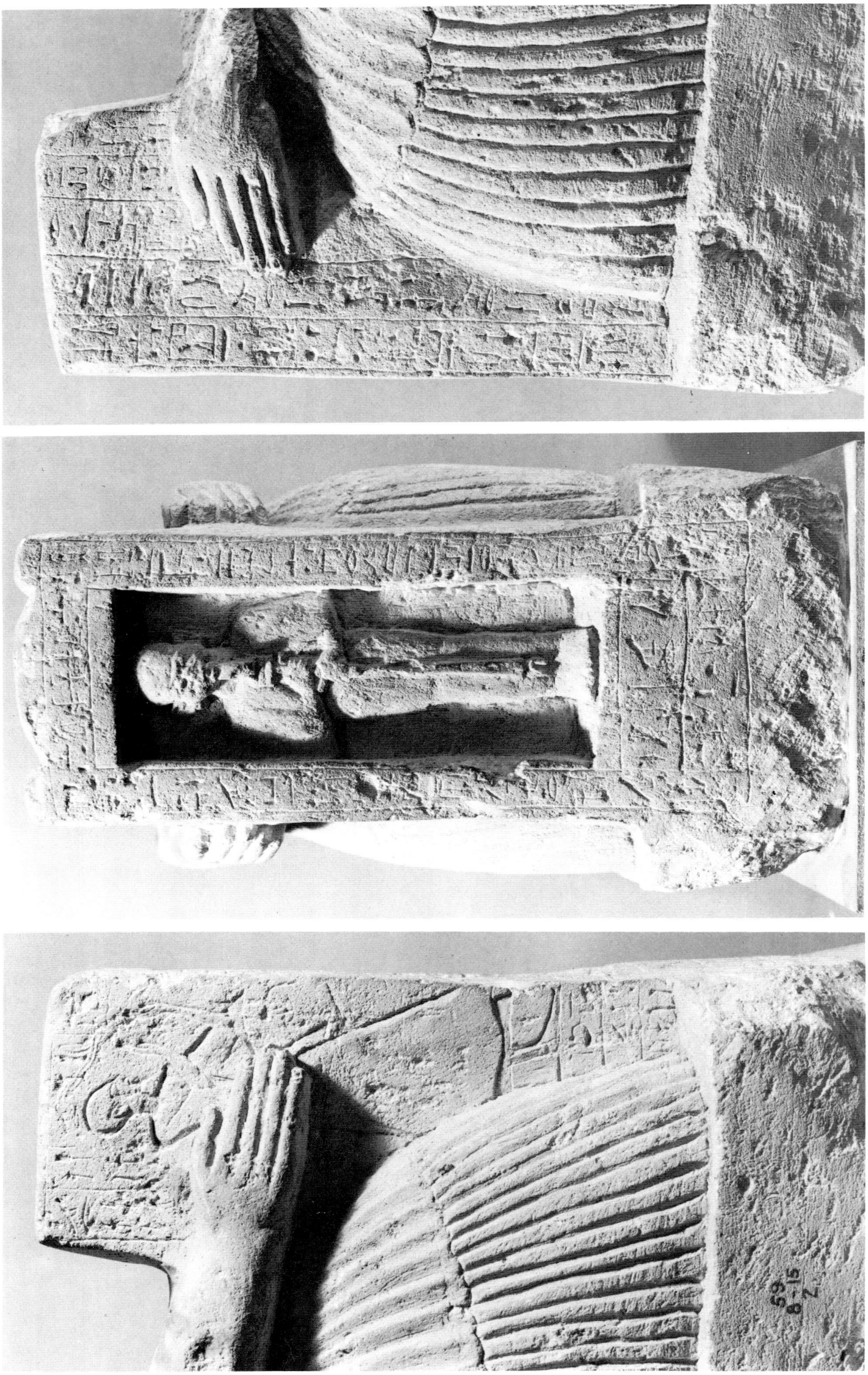

No. 845

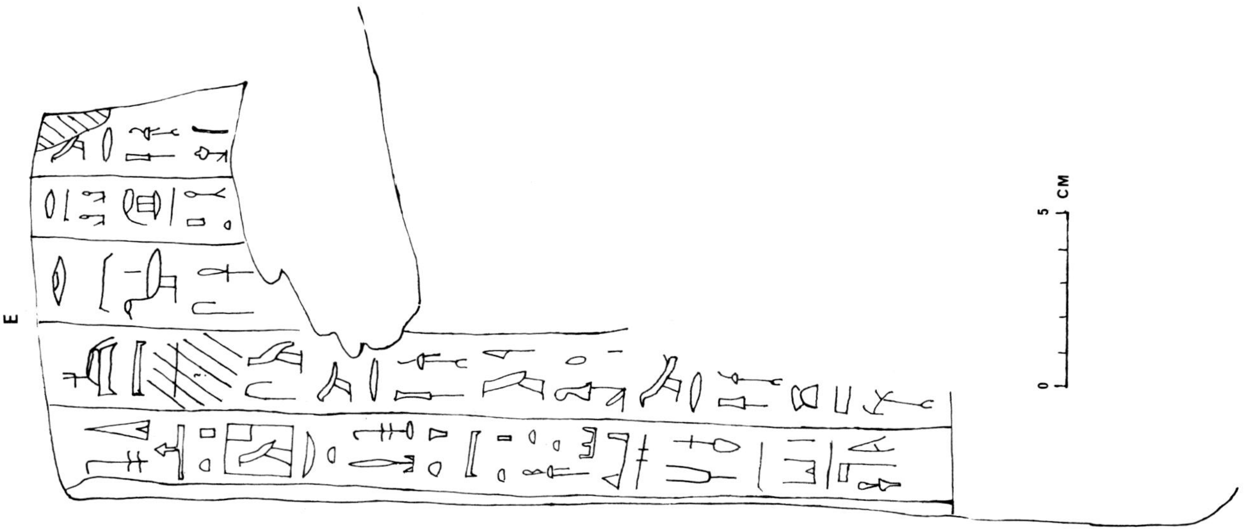

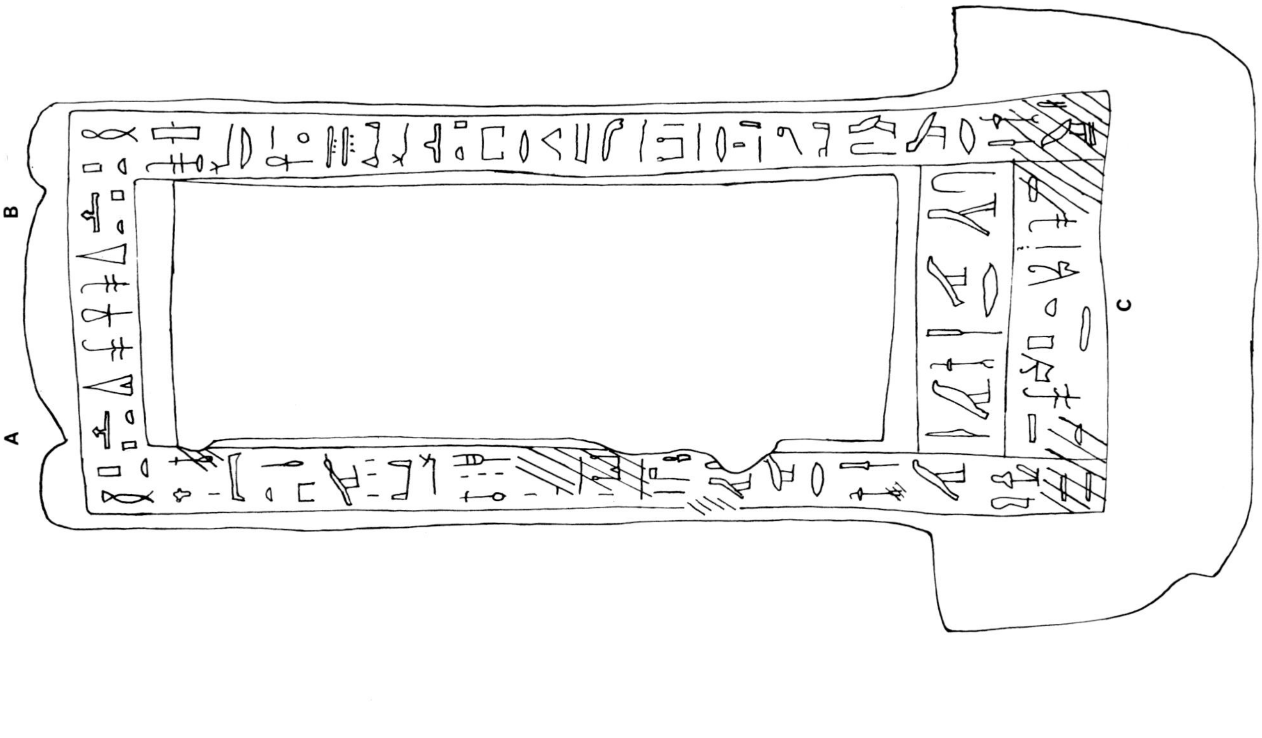

No. 845

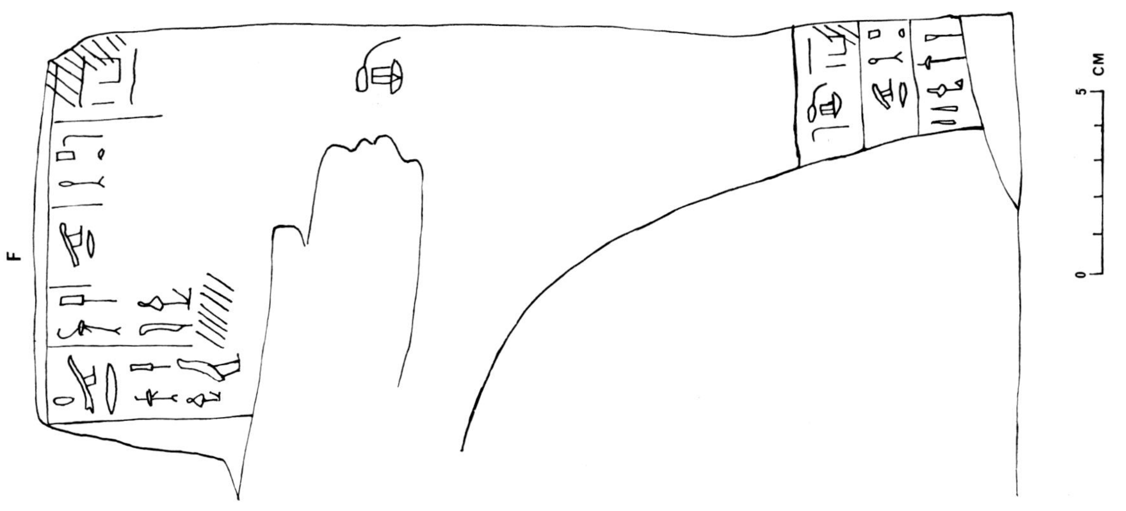

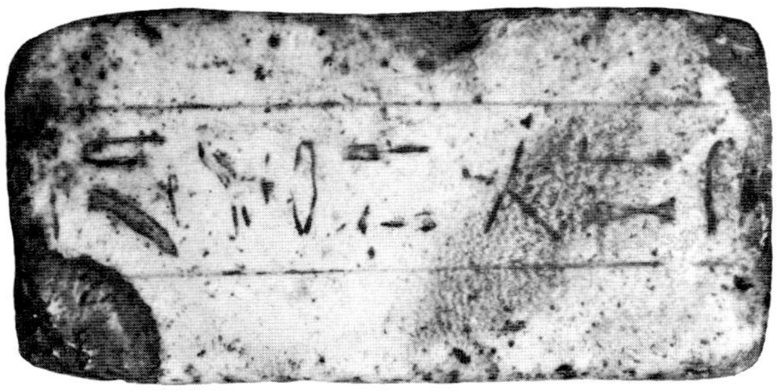
4. No. 59259

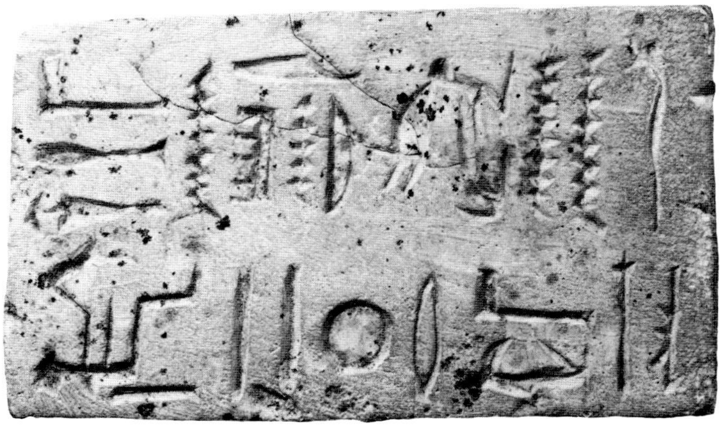
3. No. 57690

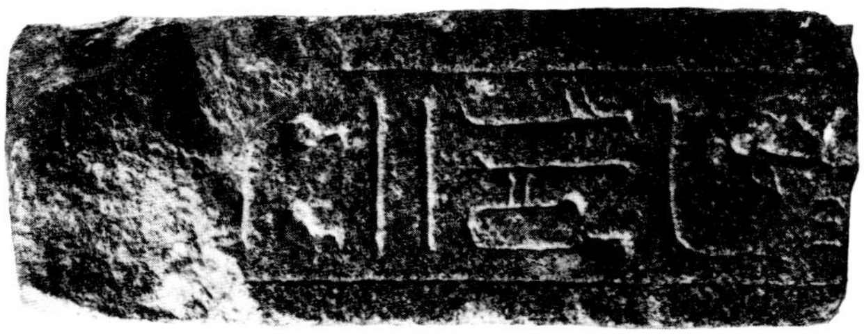
2. No. 68682

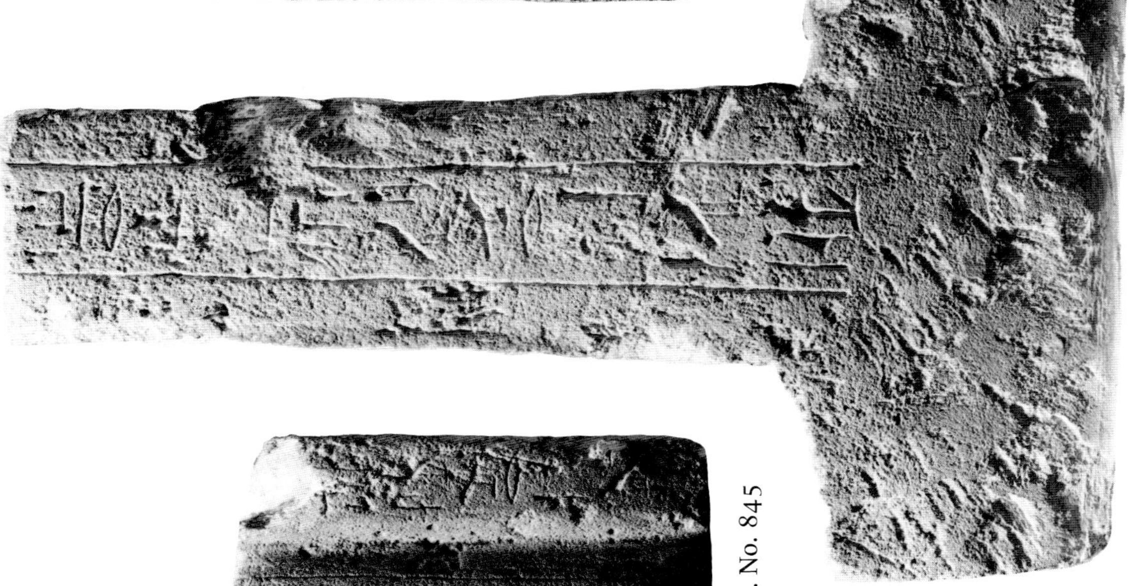

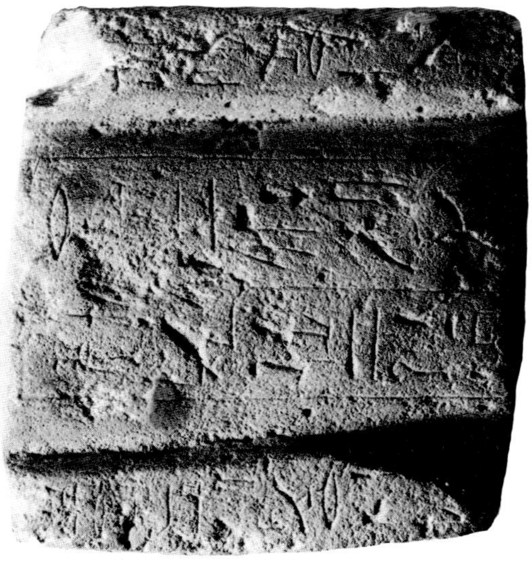
1. No. 845

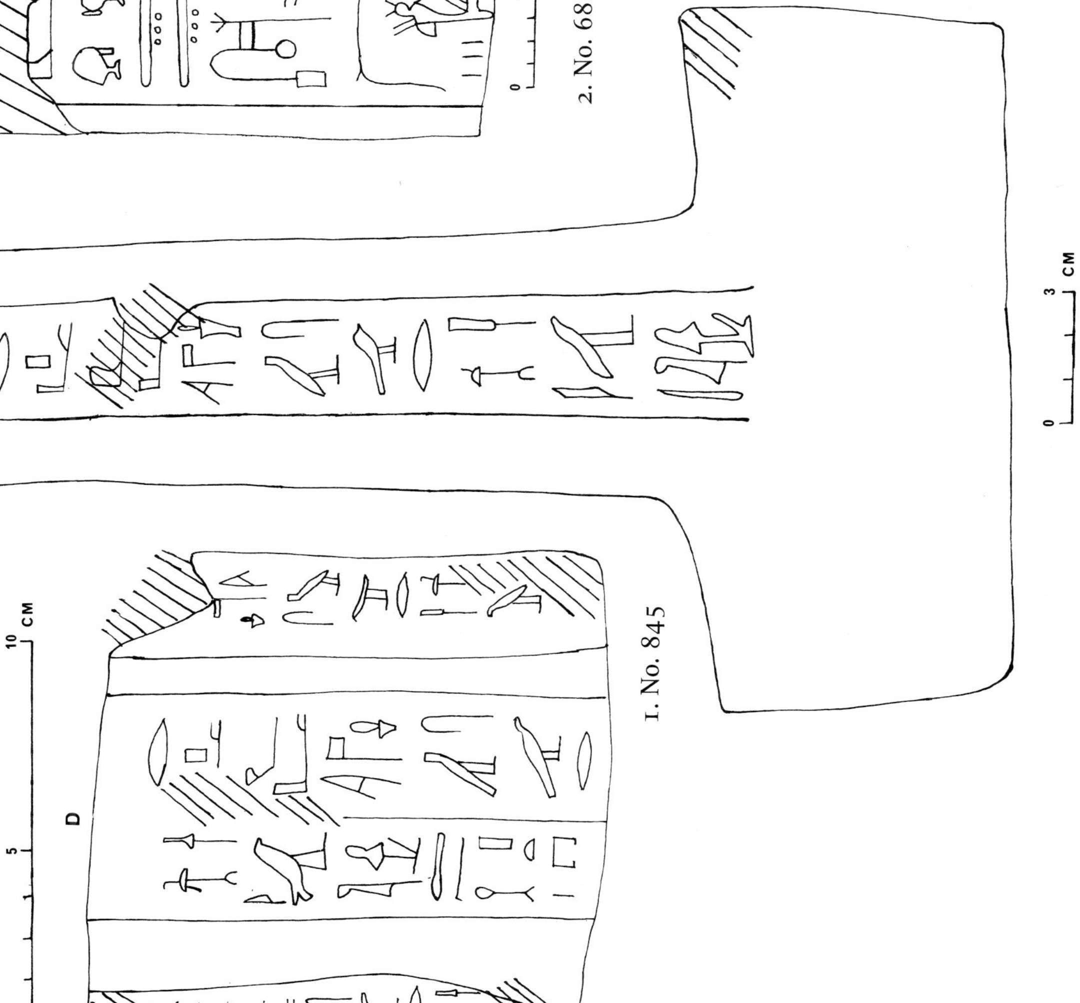

1. No. 845

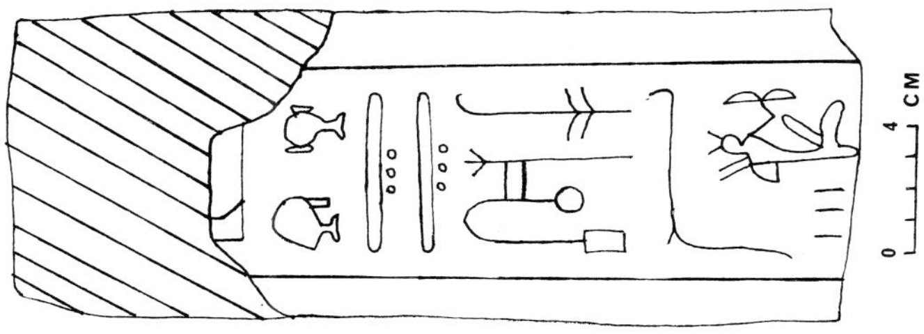

2. No. 68682

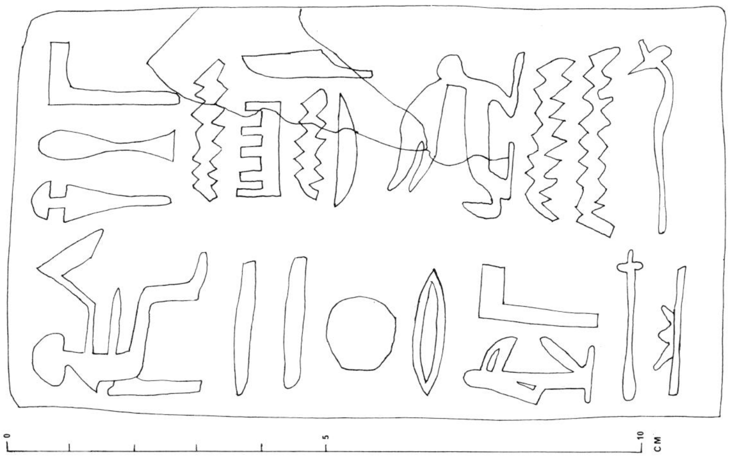

3. No. 57690

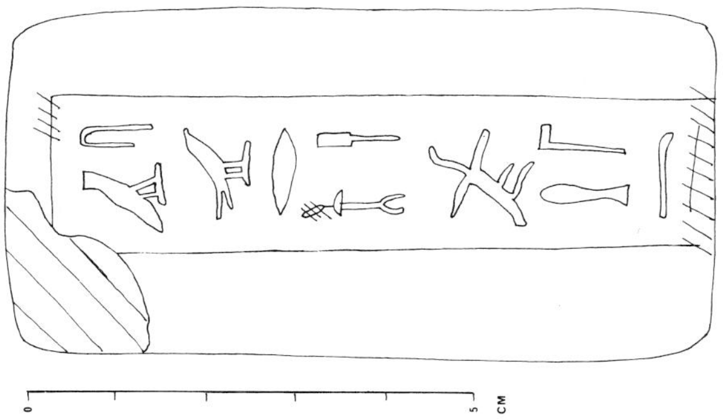

4. No. 59259

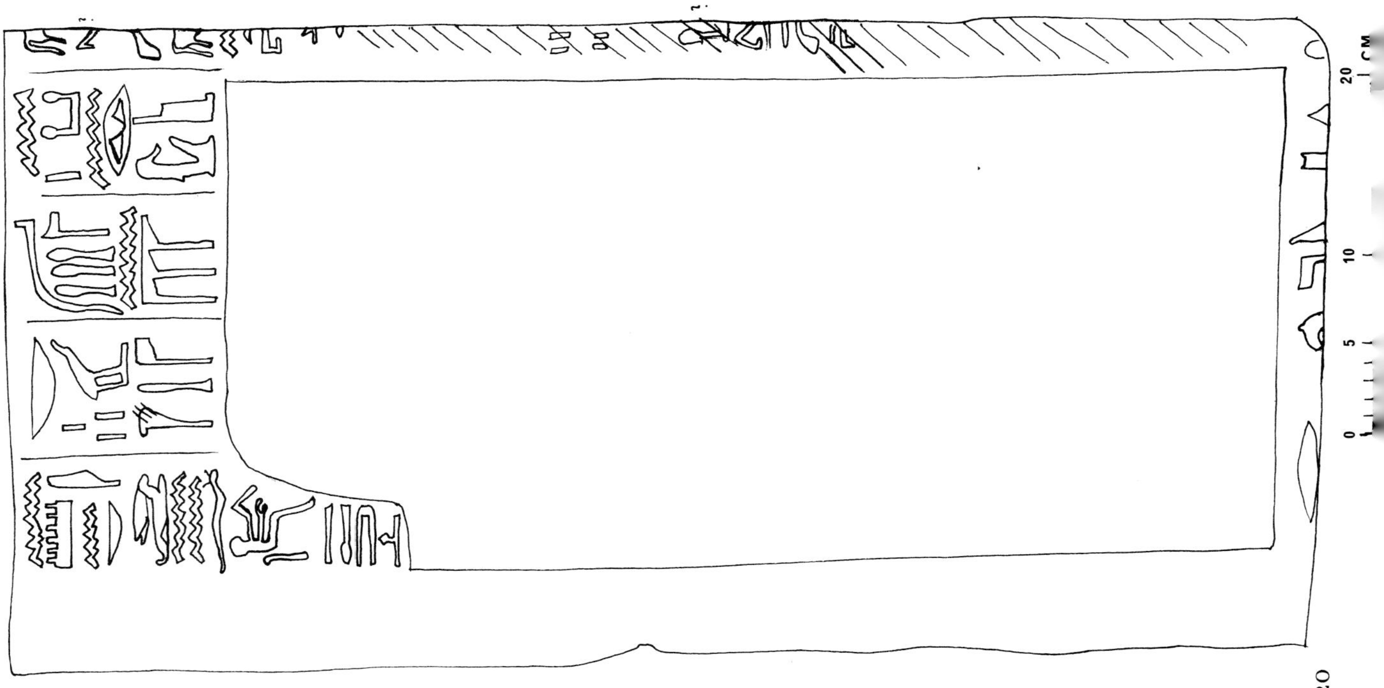

No. 1820

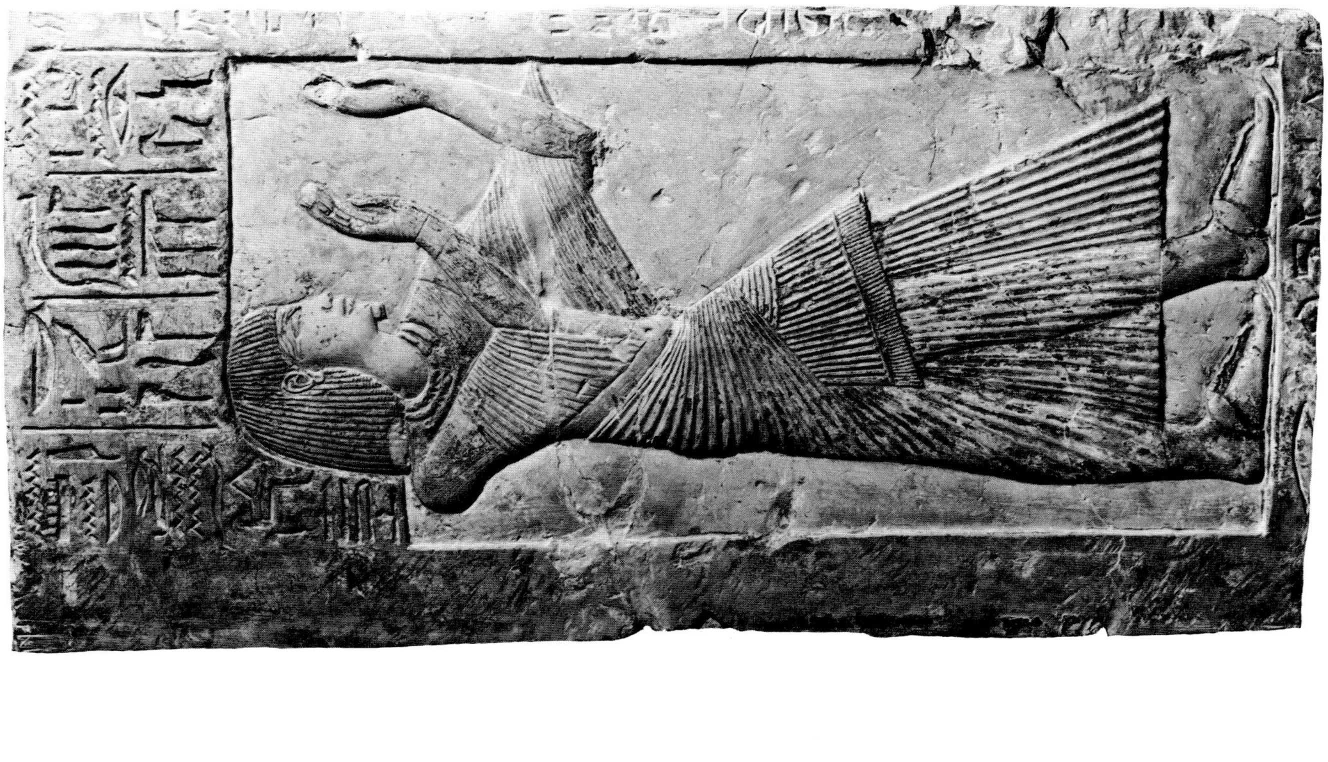

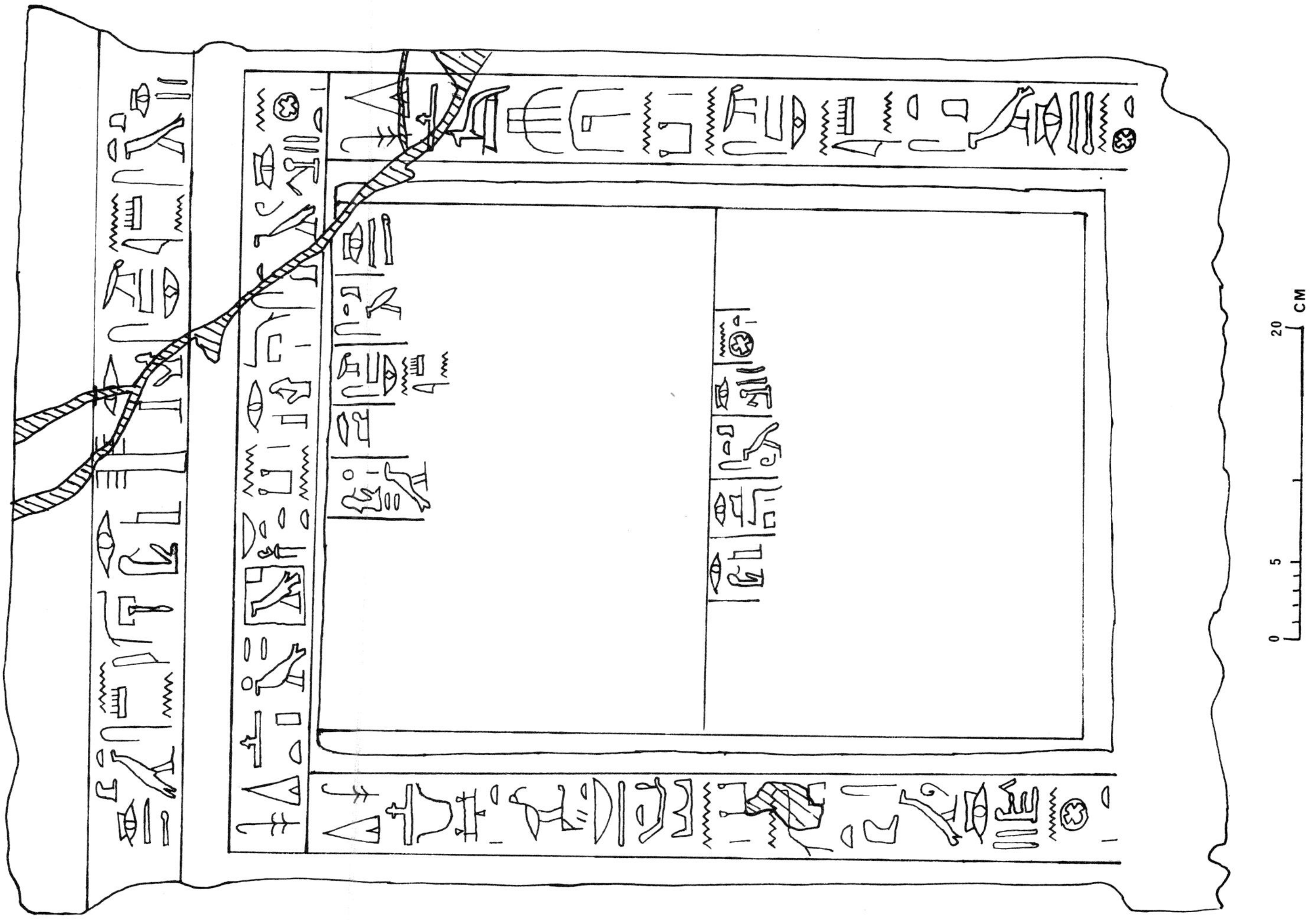

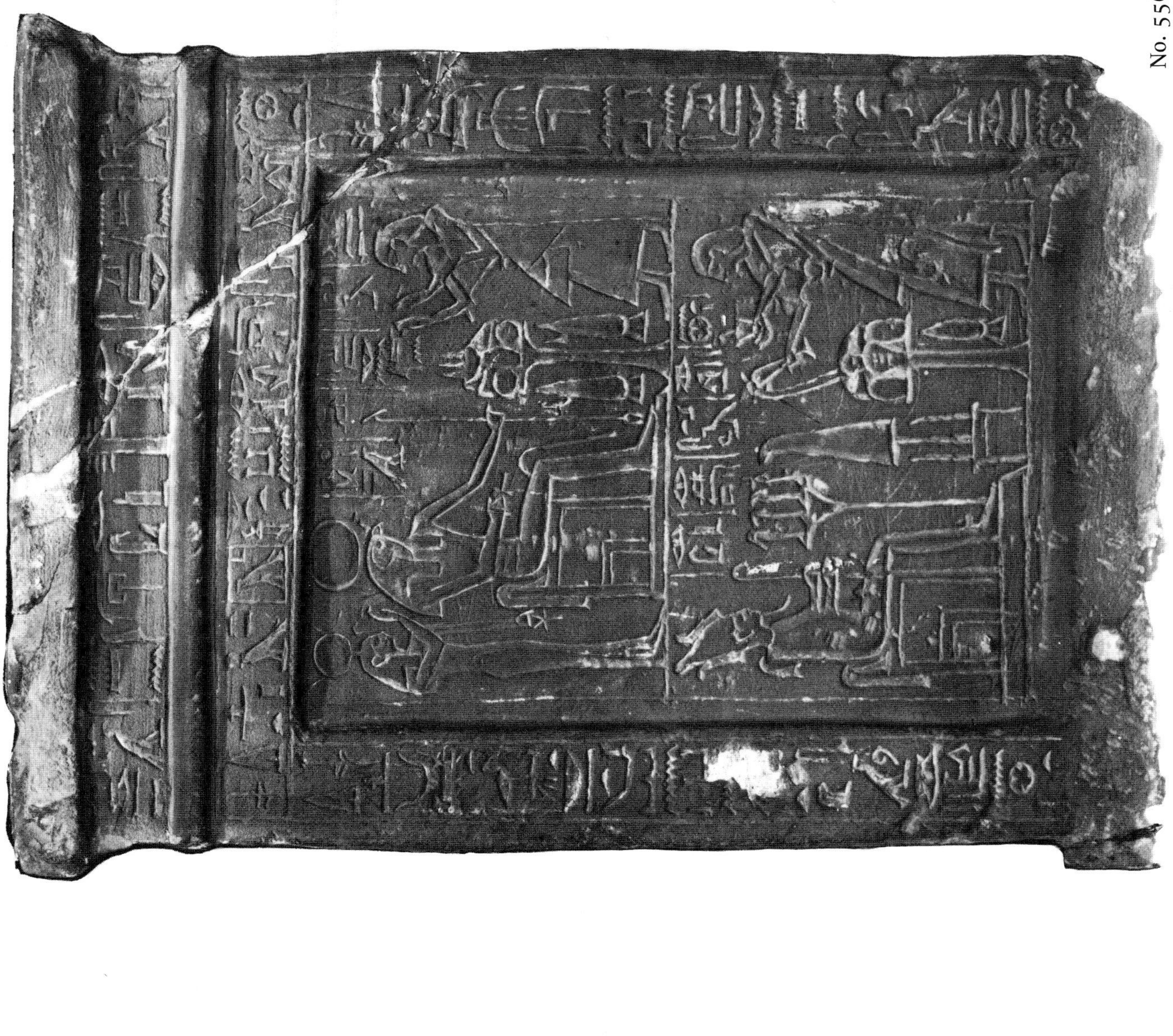

No. 556

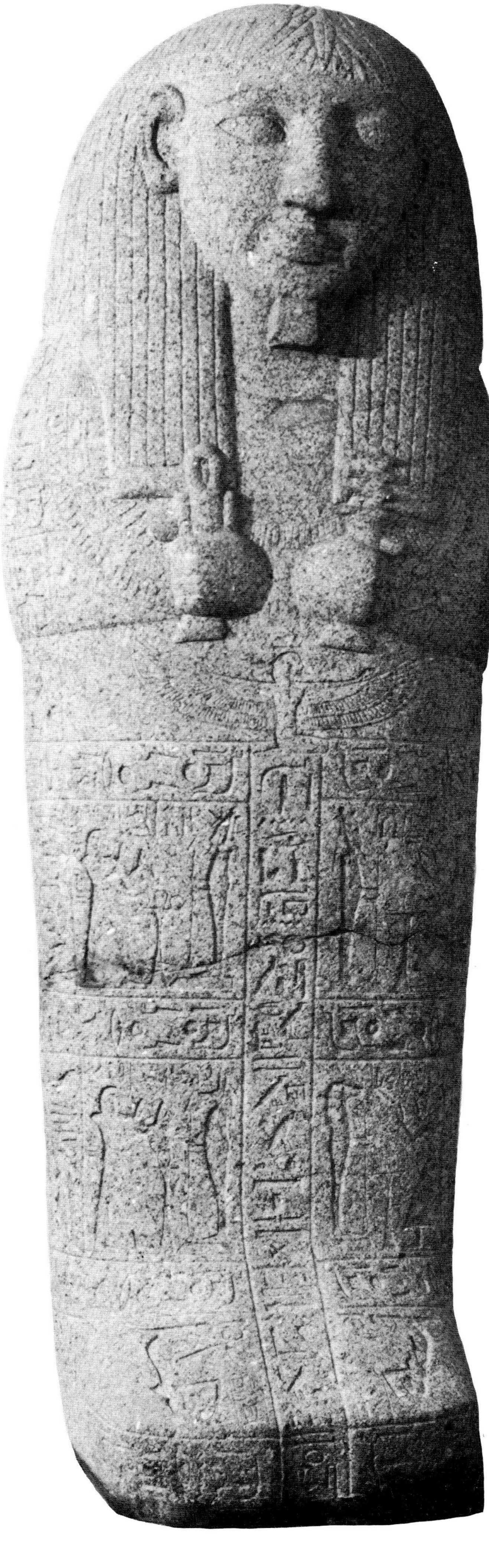

No. 78

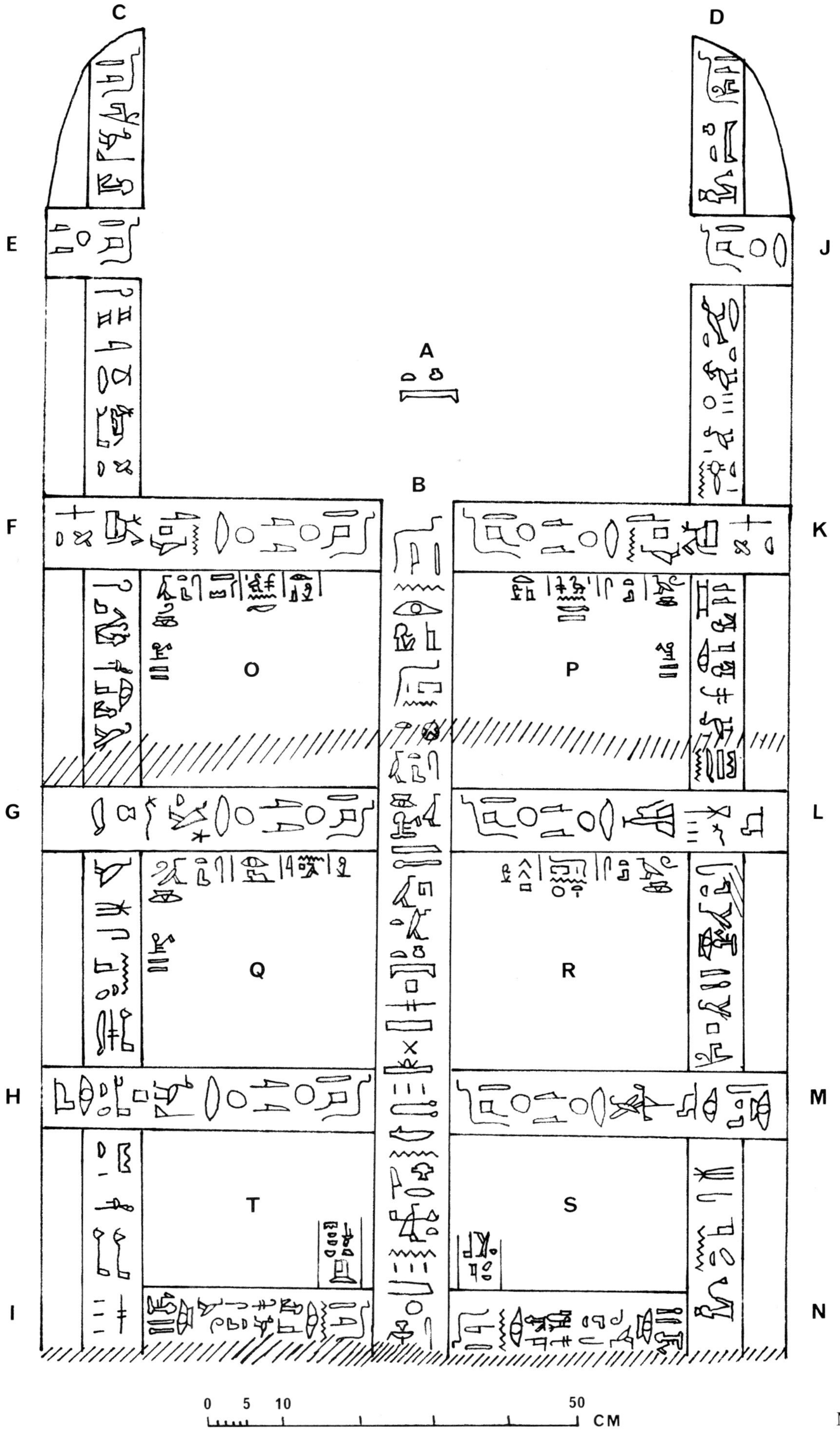
C
D
E
J
A
B
F
K
O
P
G
L
Q
R
H
M
T
S
I
N
0 5 10 50 CM

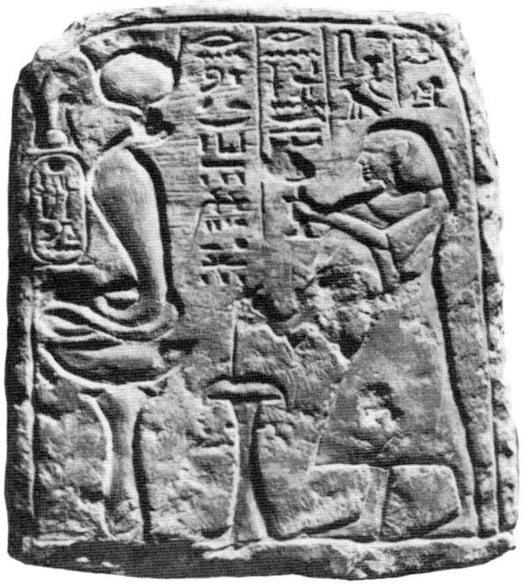

1. No. 1055

2. No. 792

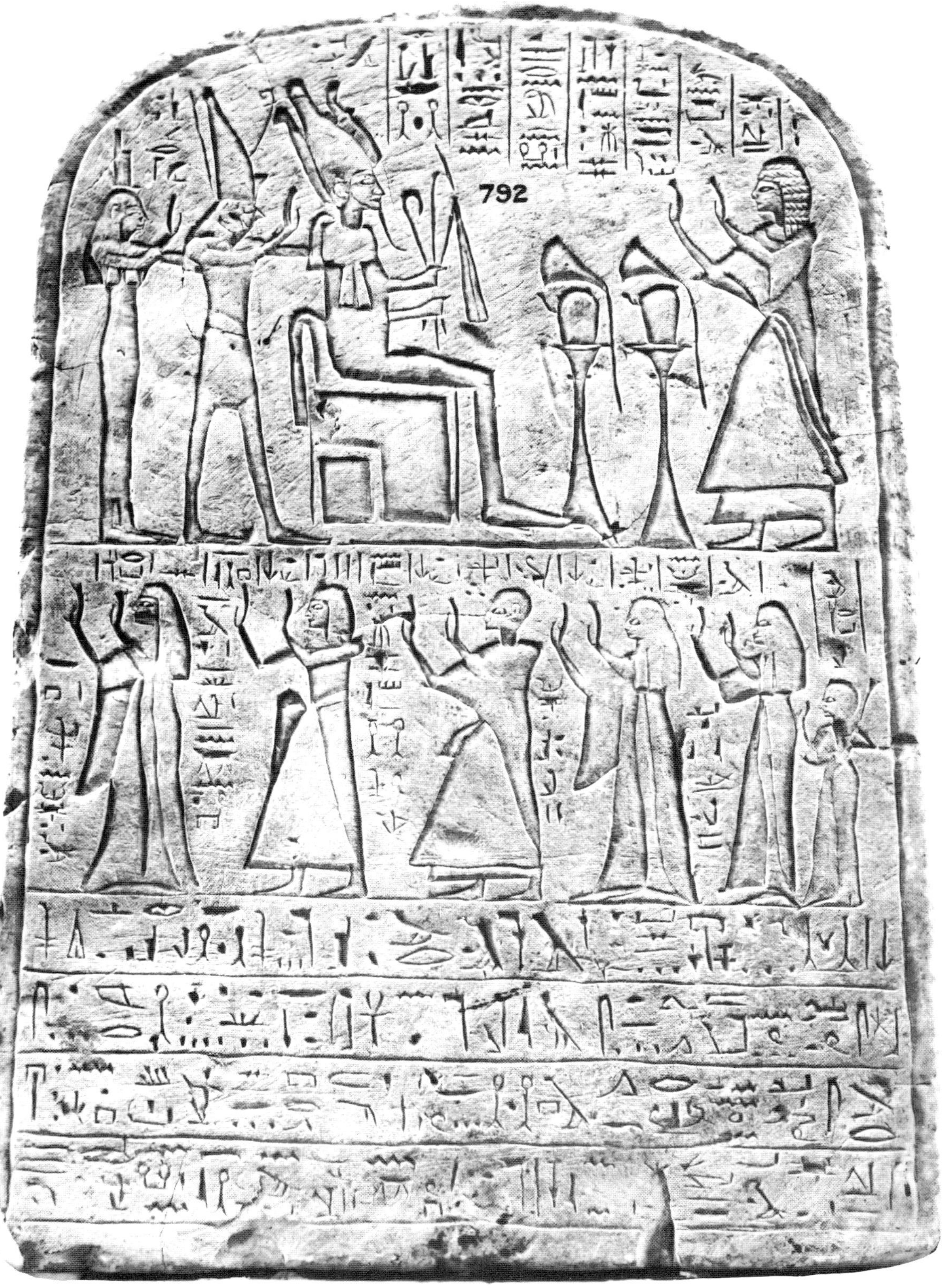

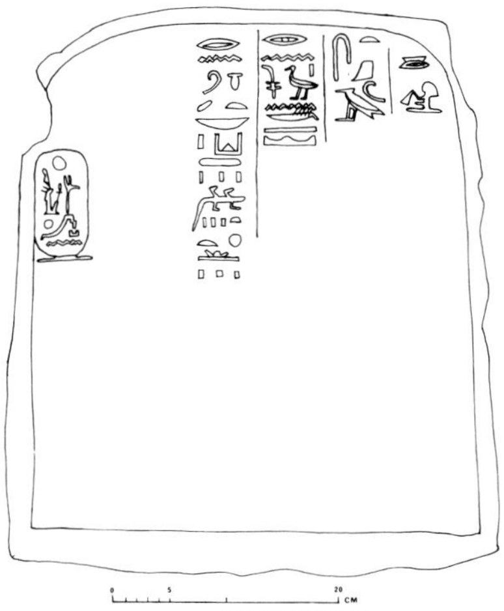

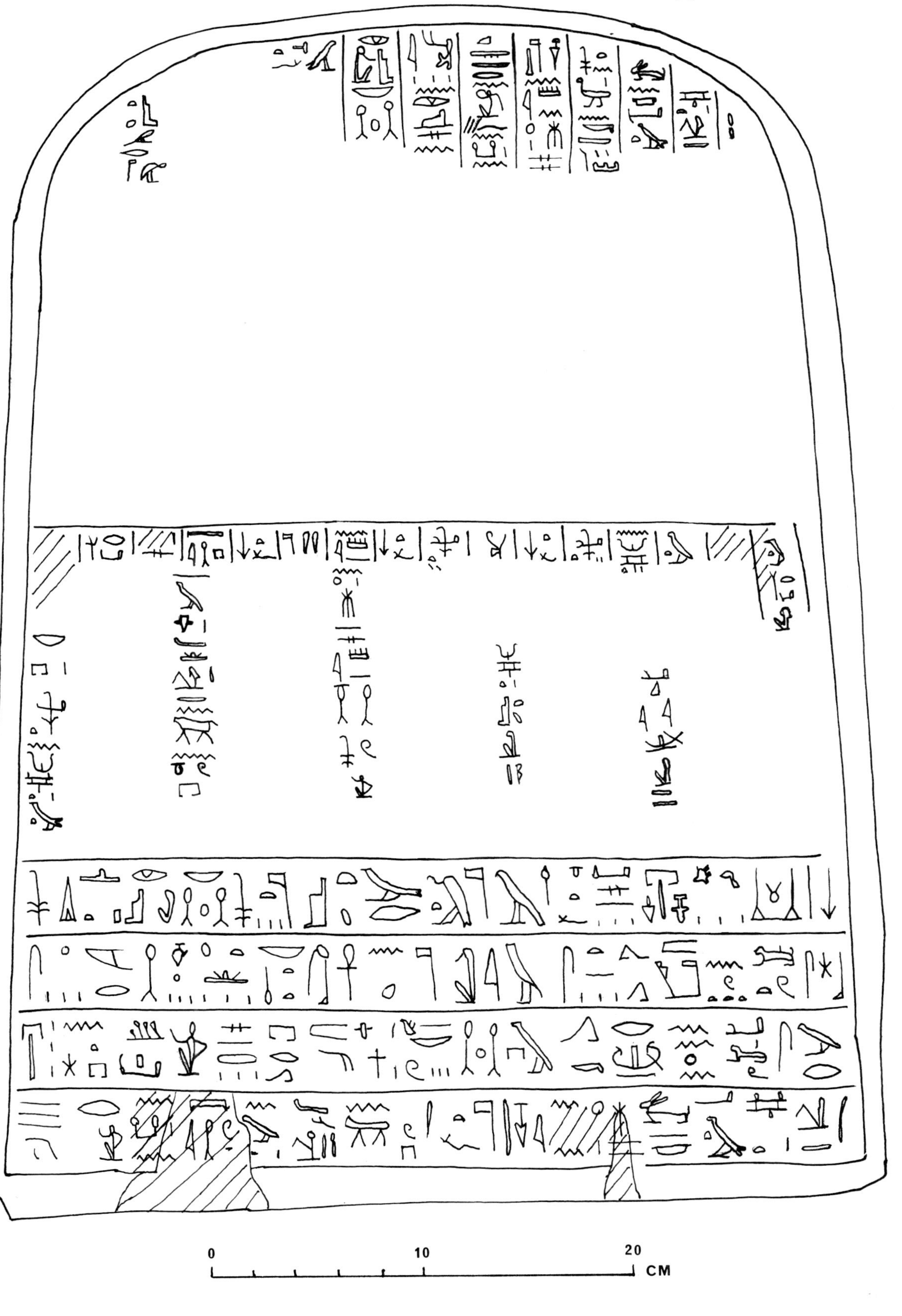

1. No. 1055

2. No. 792

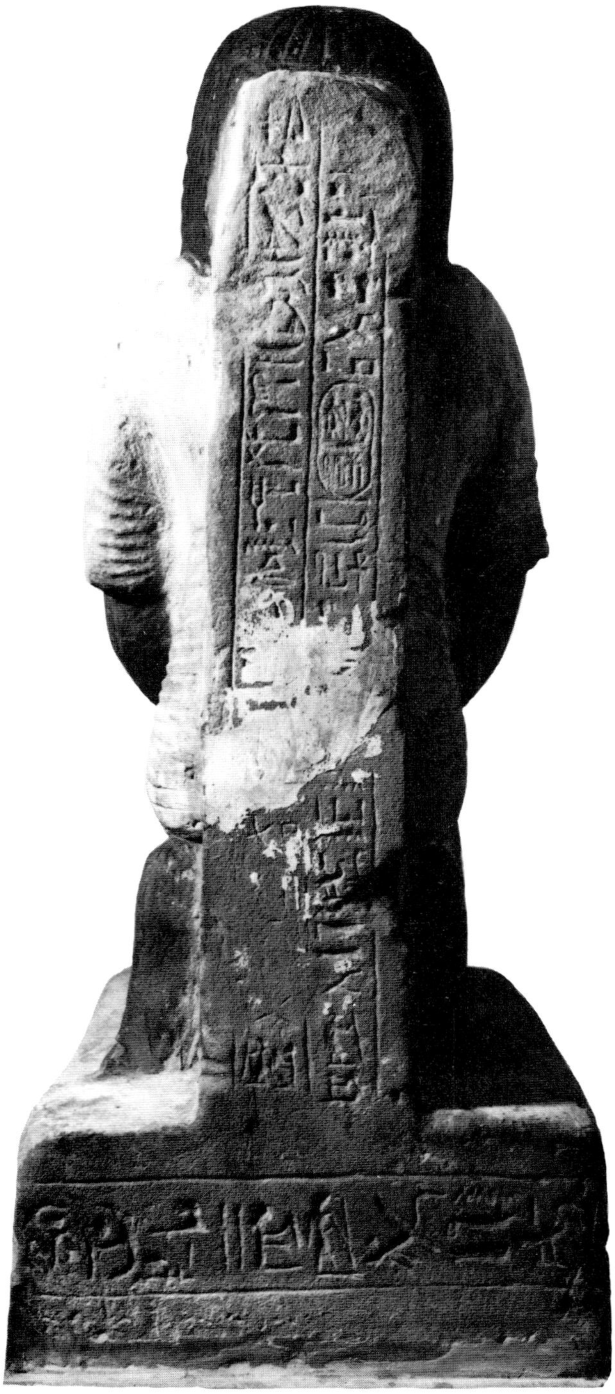

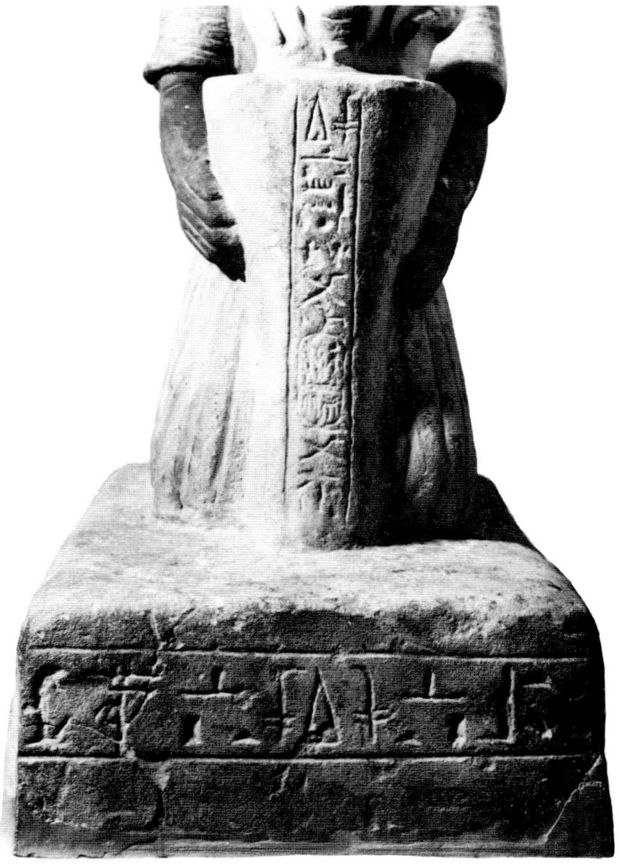

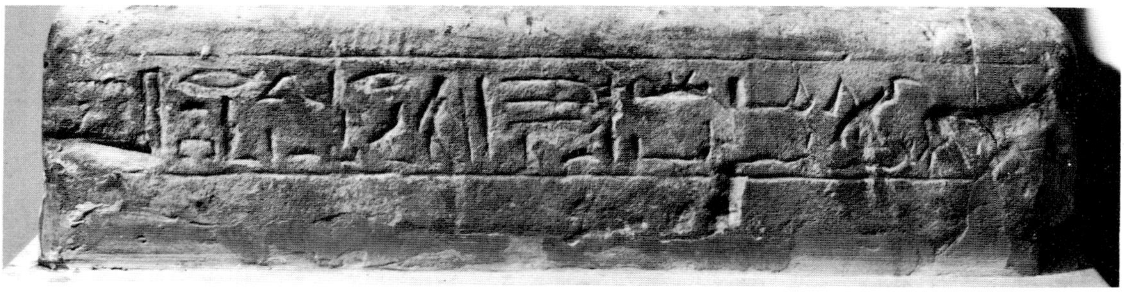

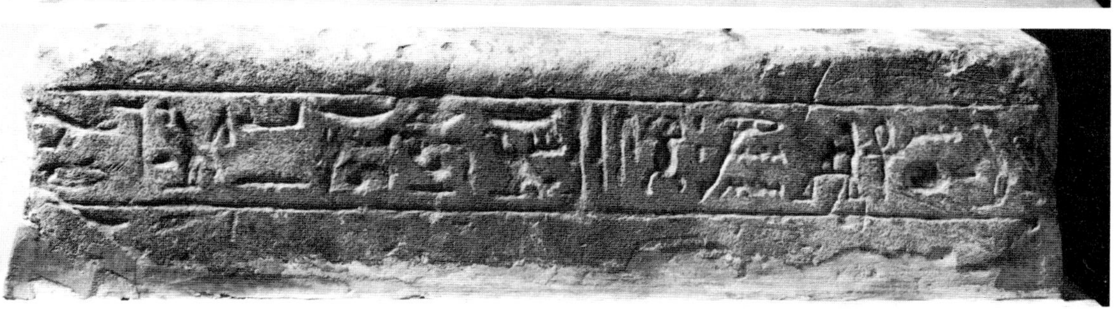

No. 1376

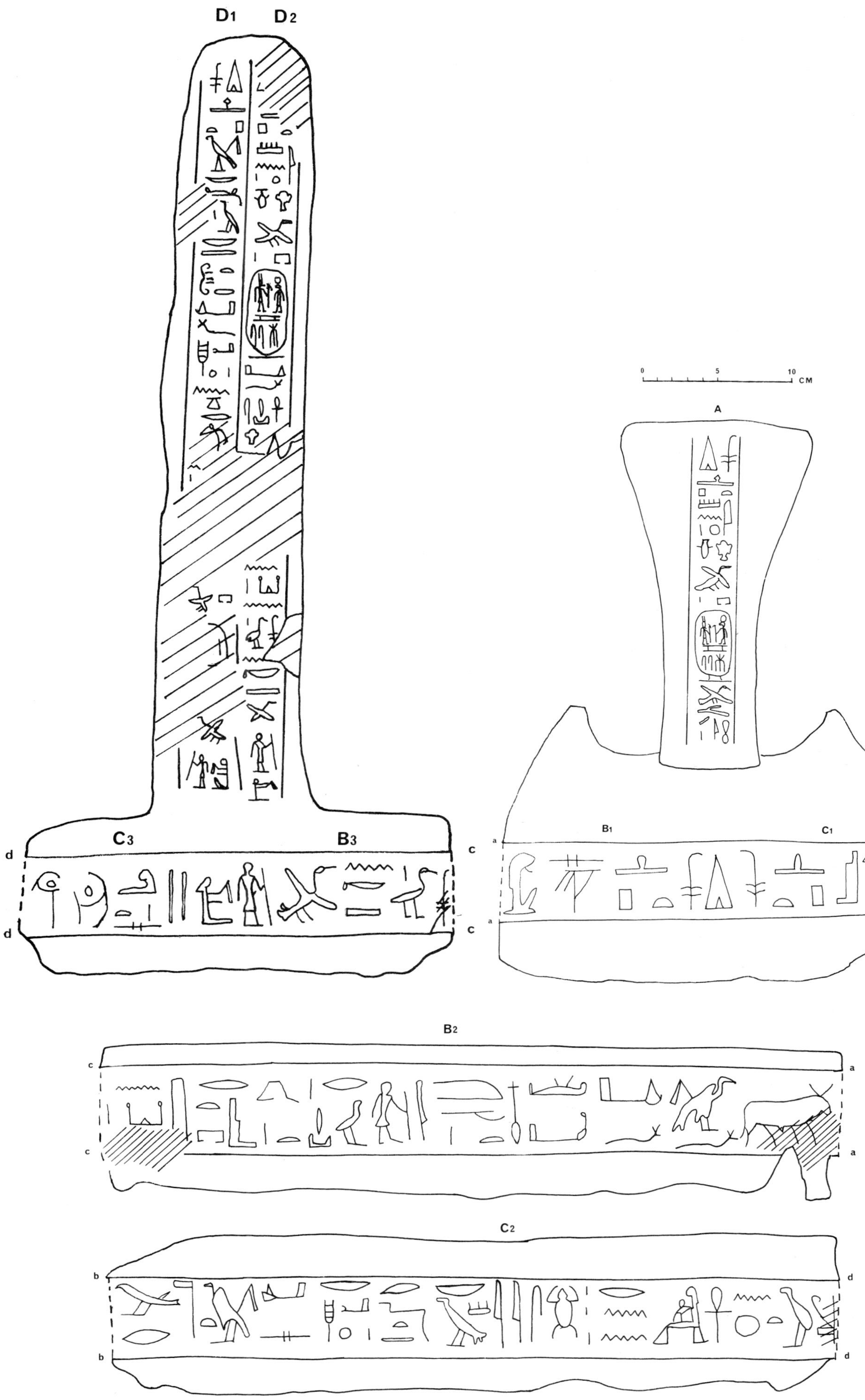

No. 1376

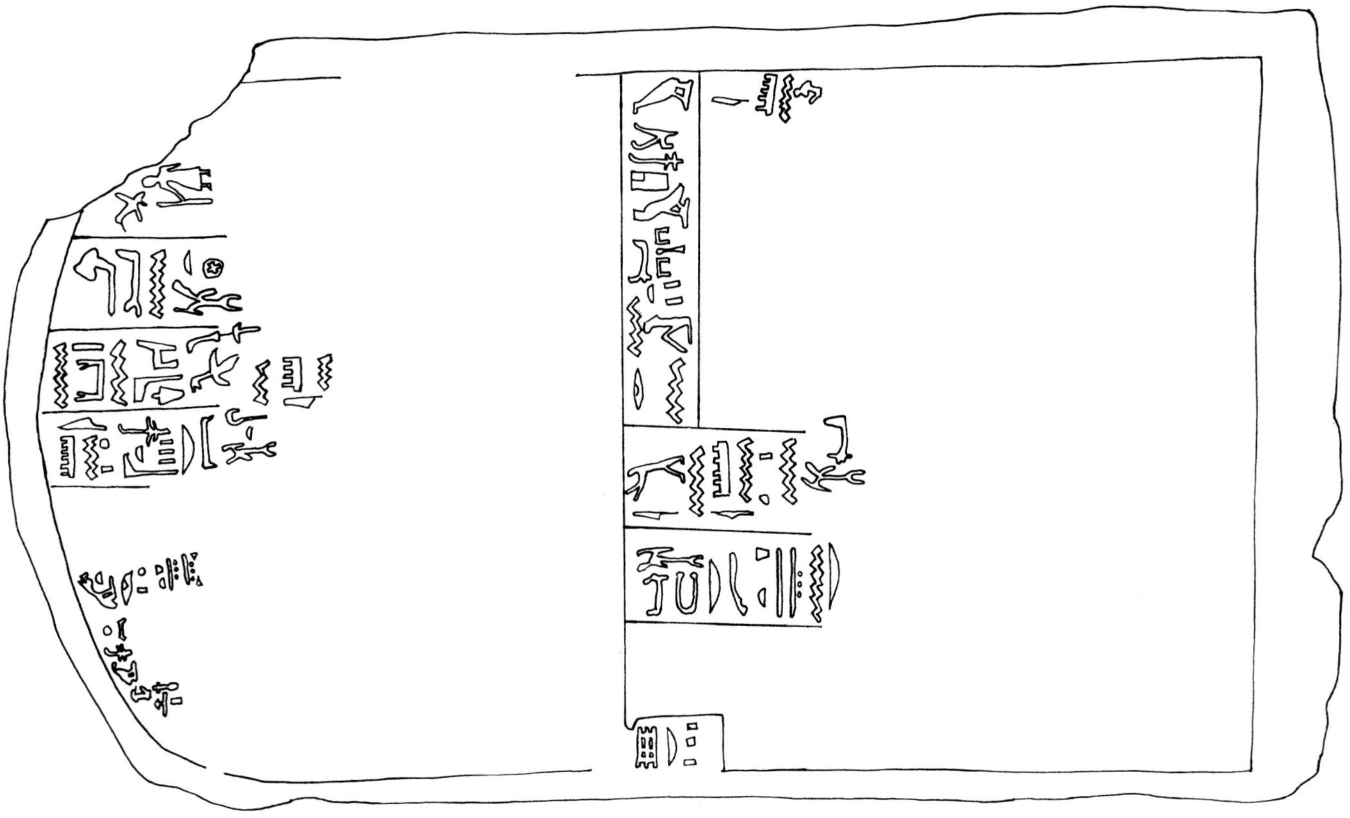

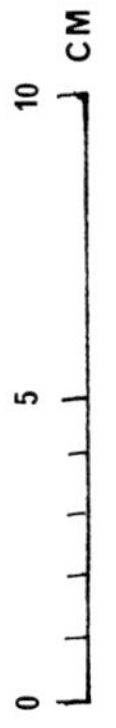

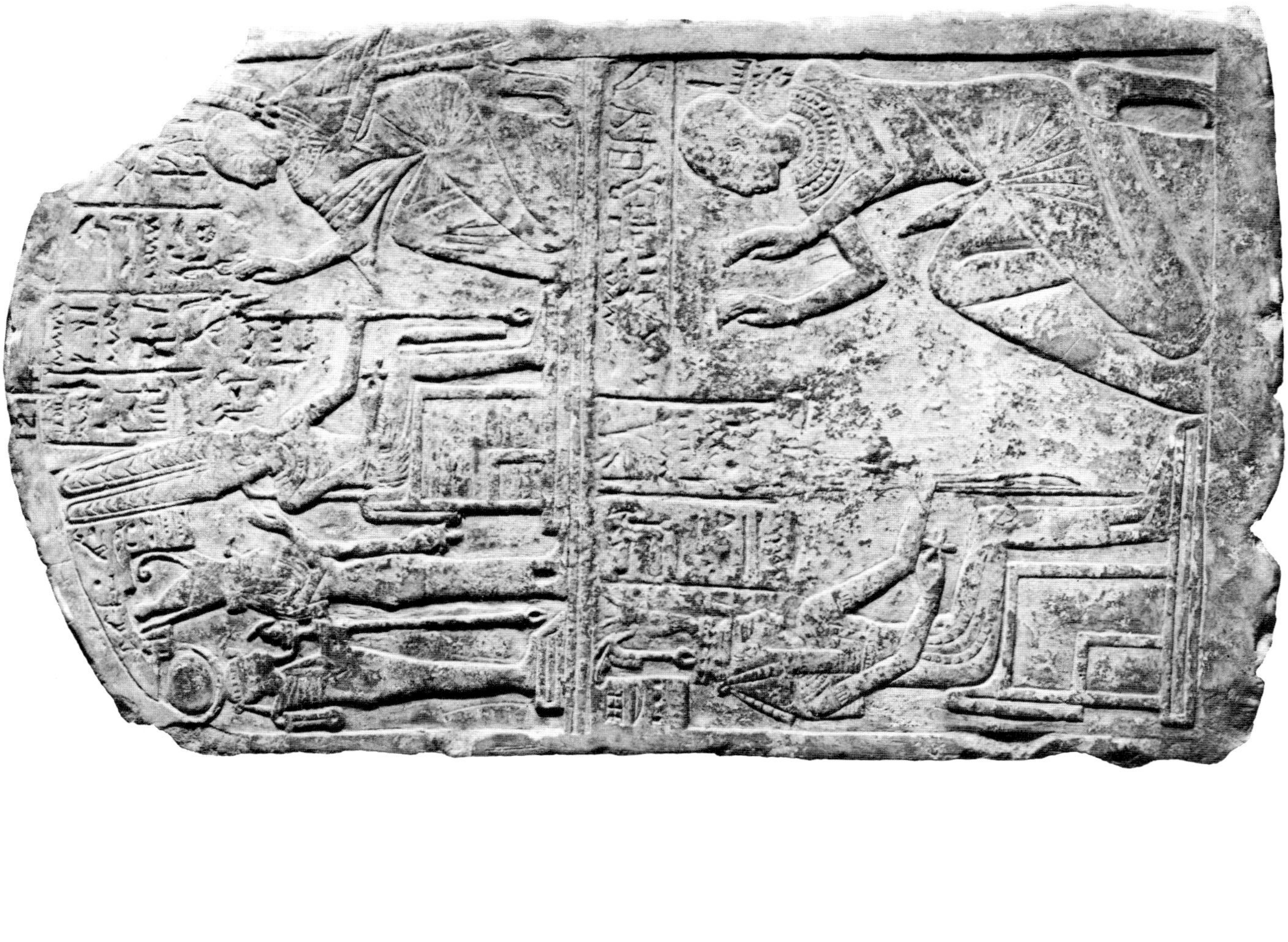

No. 1214

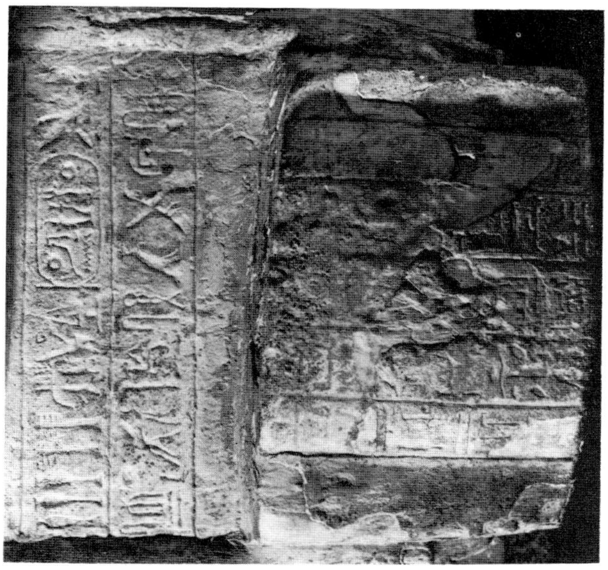

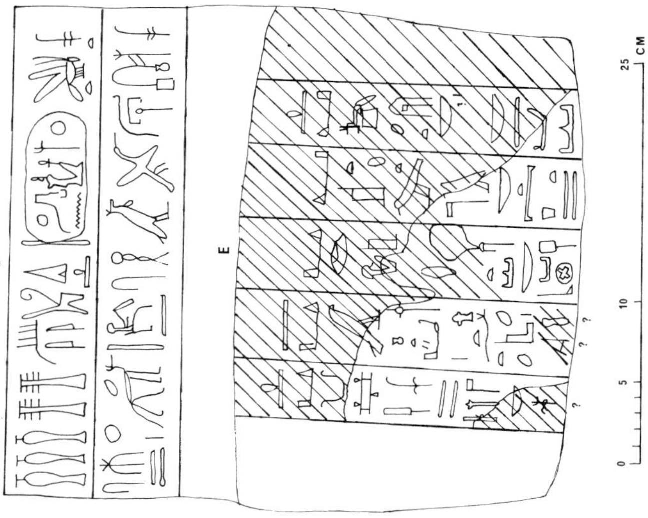

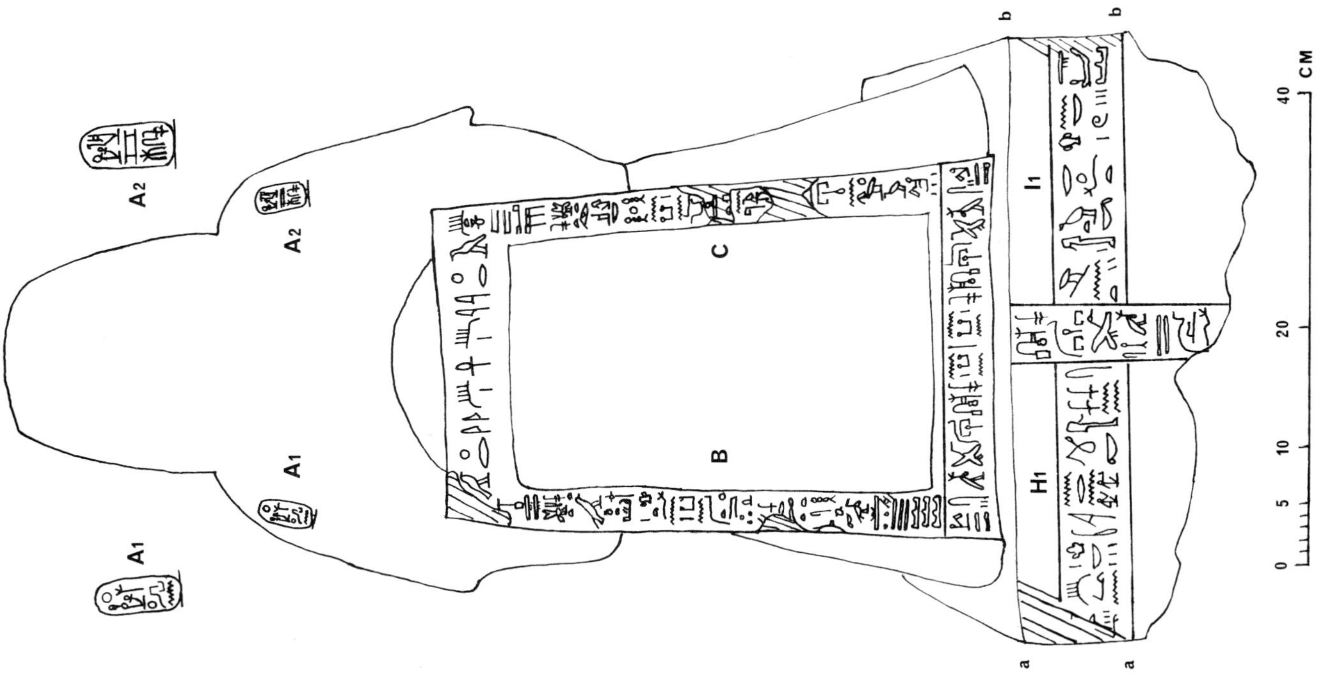

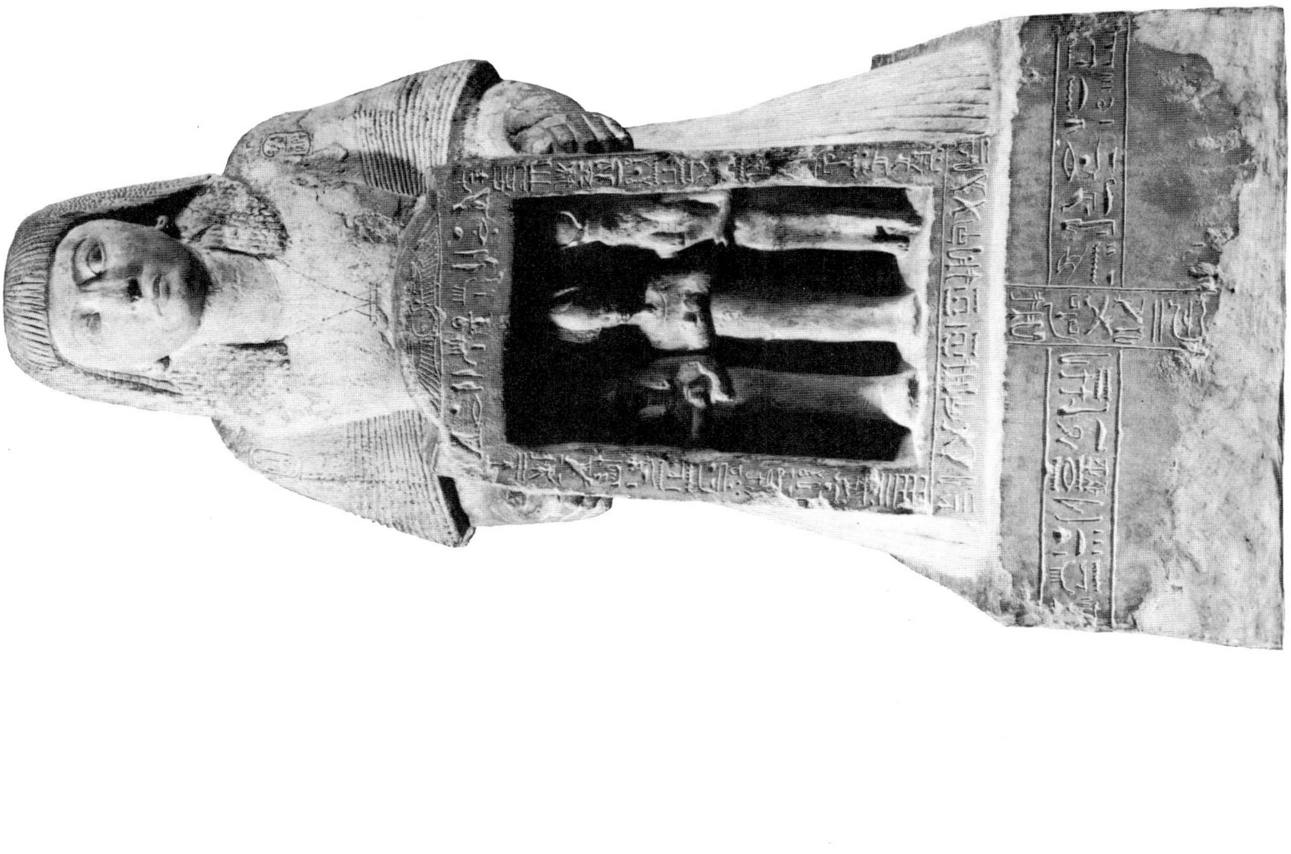

No. 1377

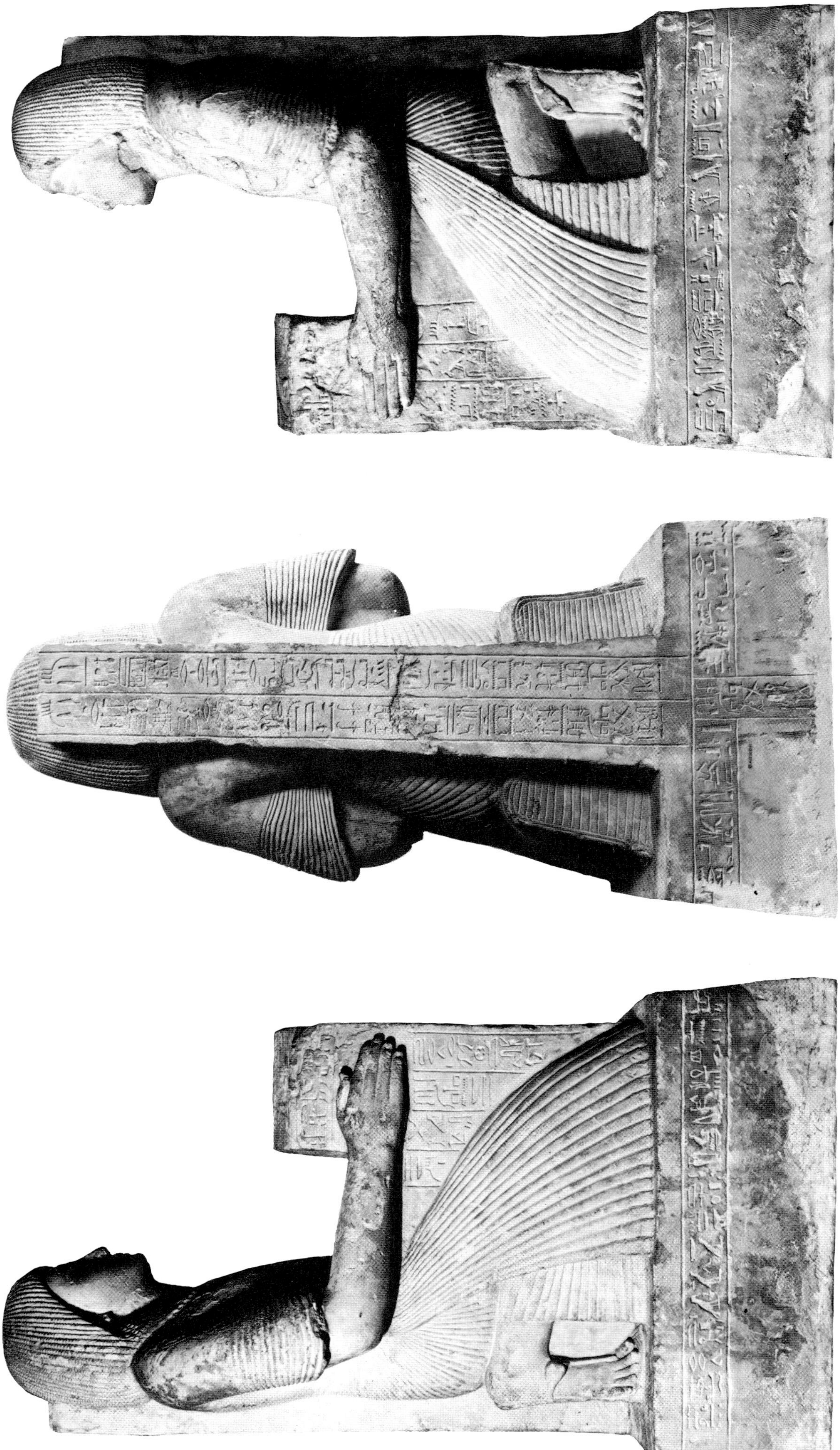

No. 1377

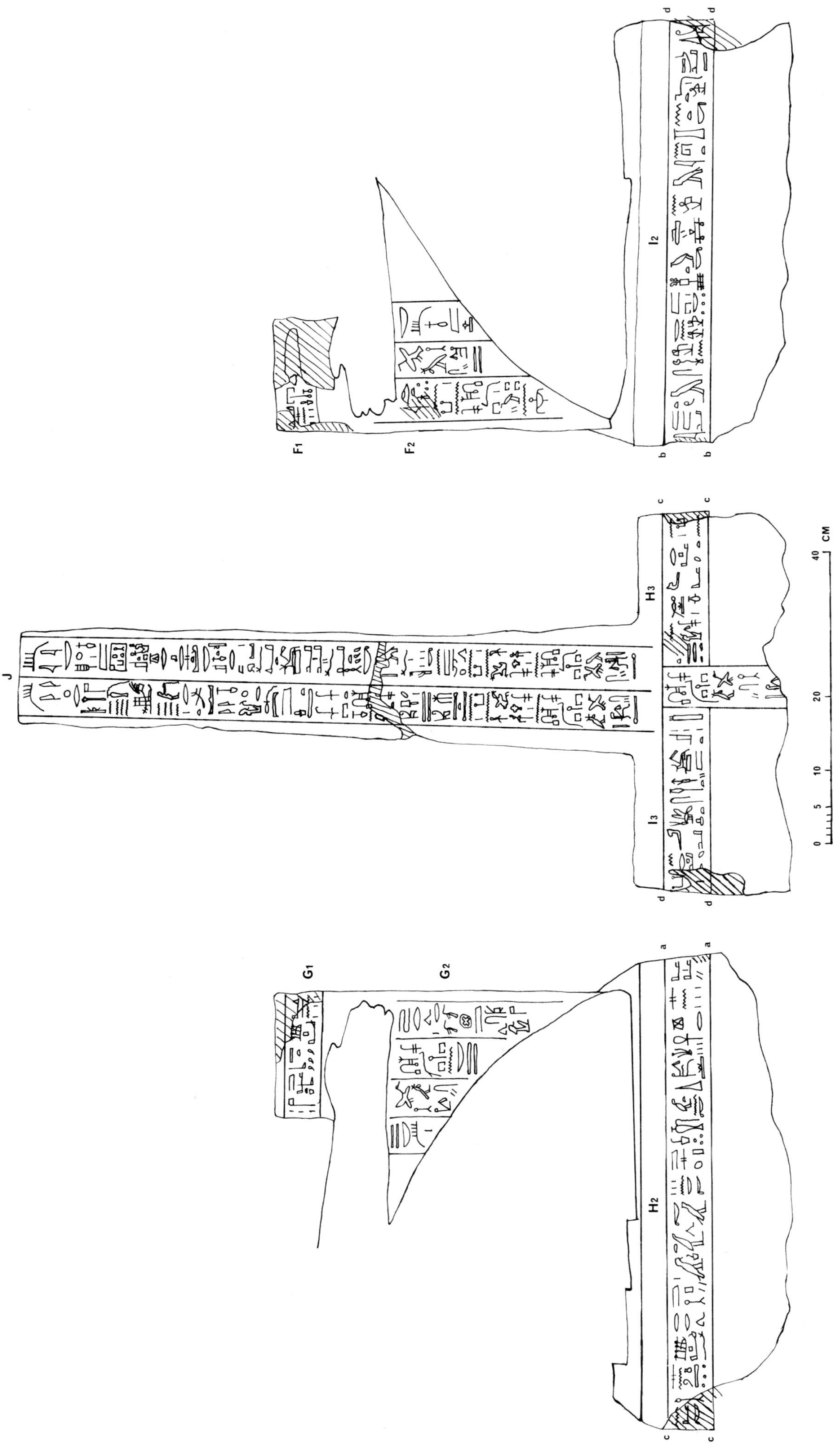

No. 1377

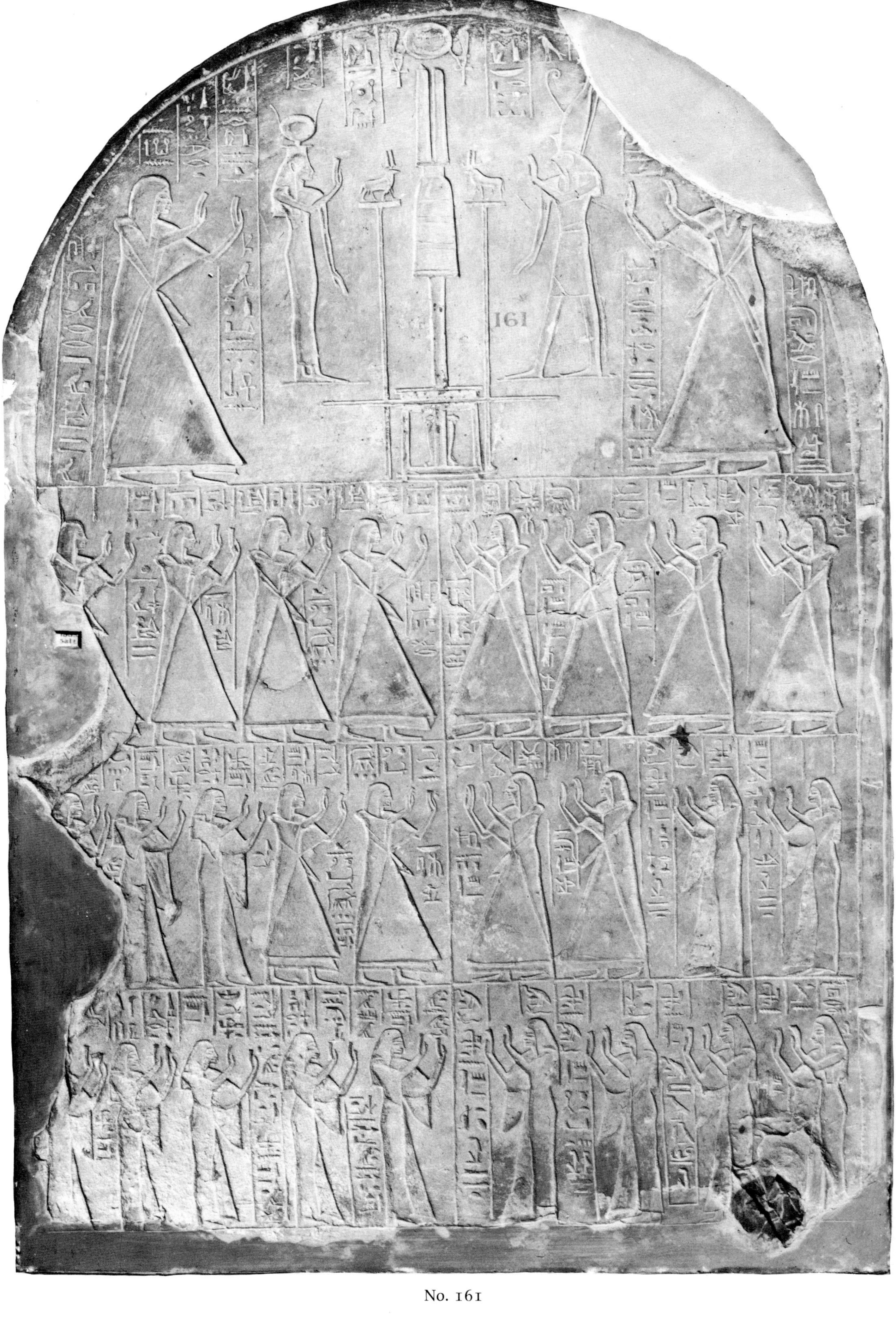

No. 161

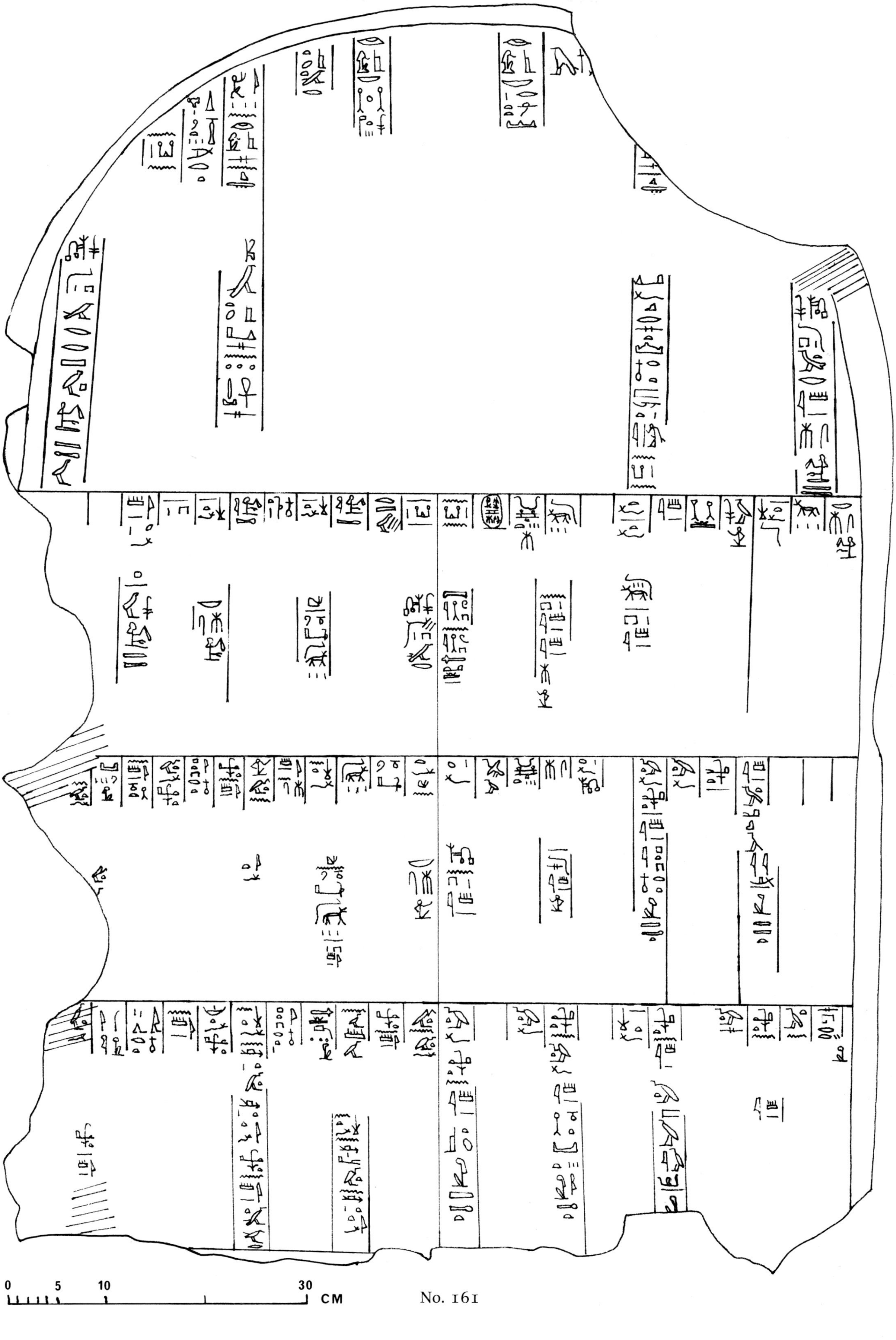

0 5 10 30 CM

No. 161

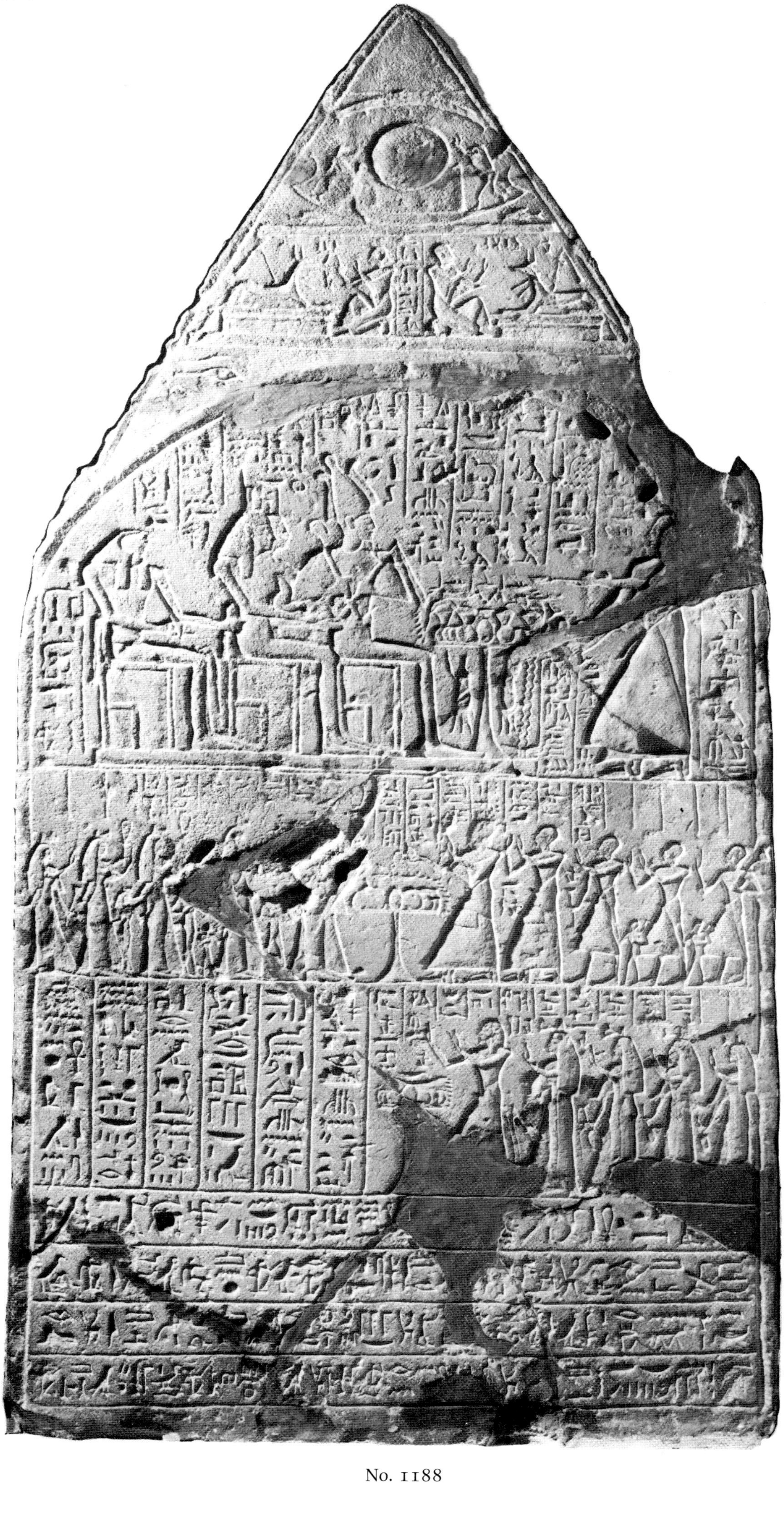

No. 1188

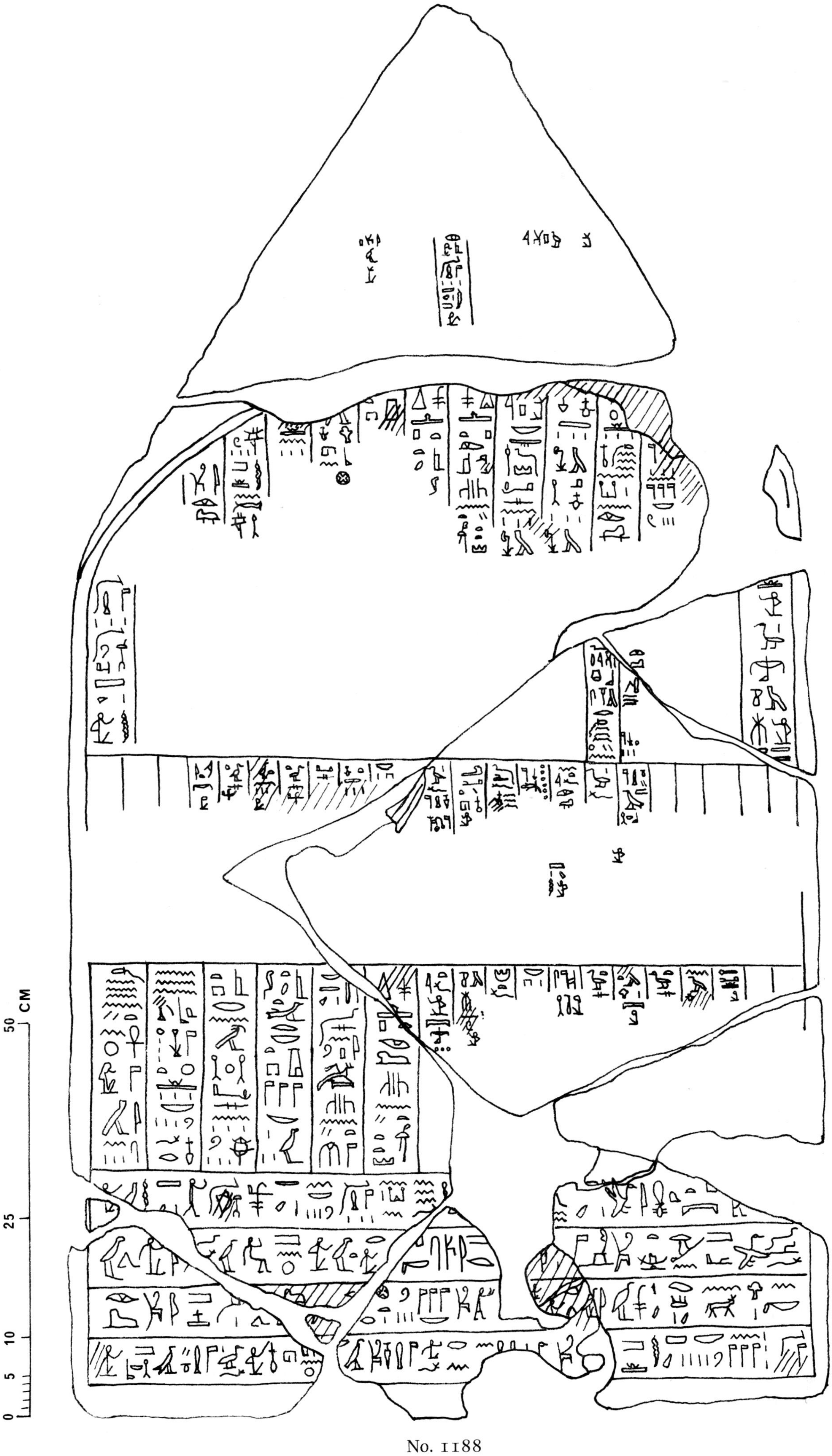

No. 1188

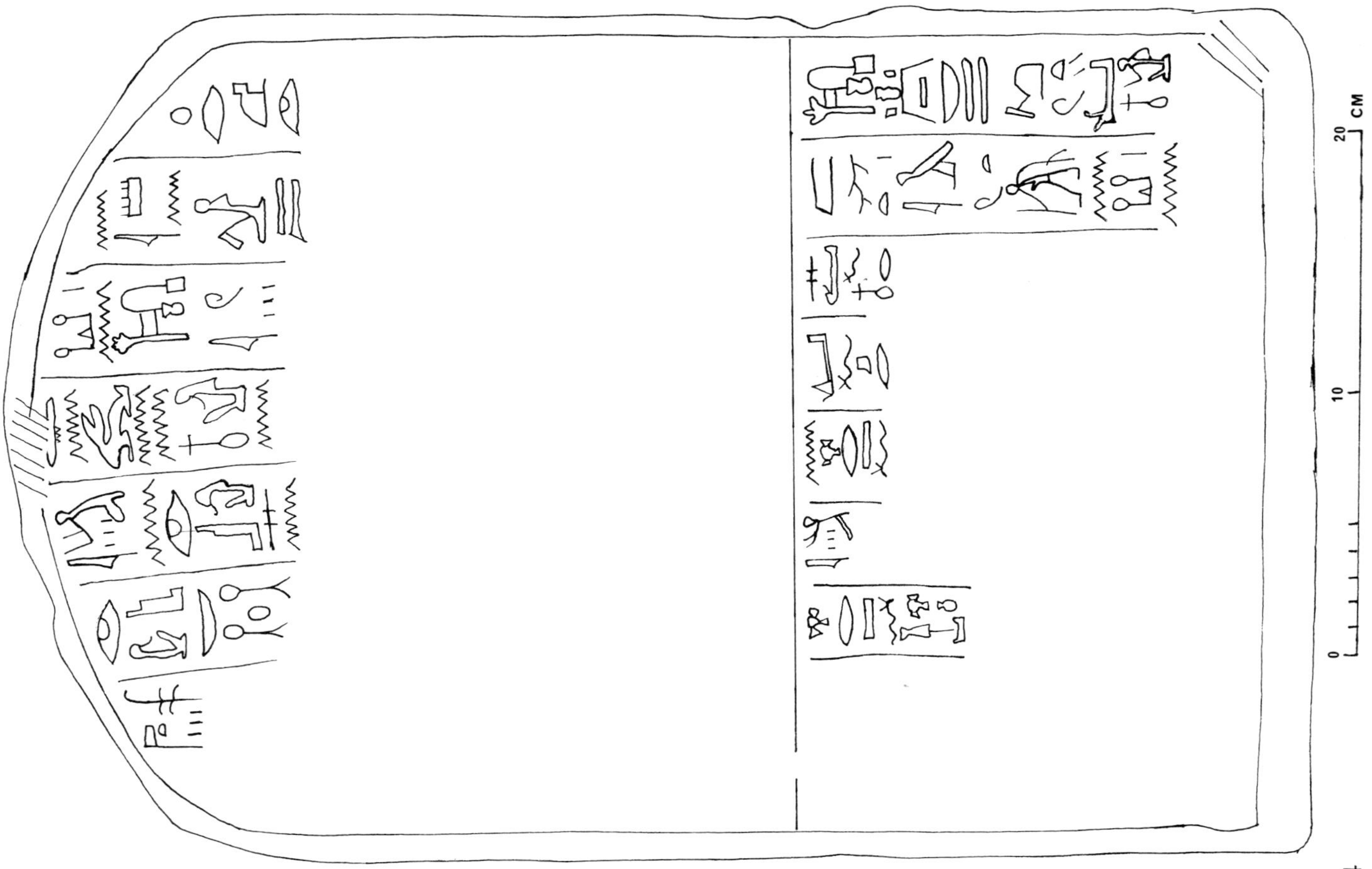

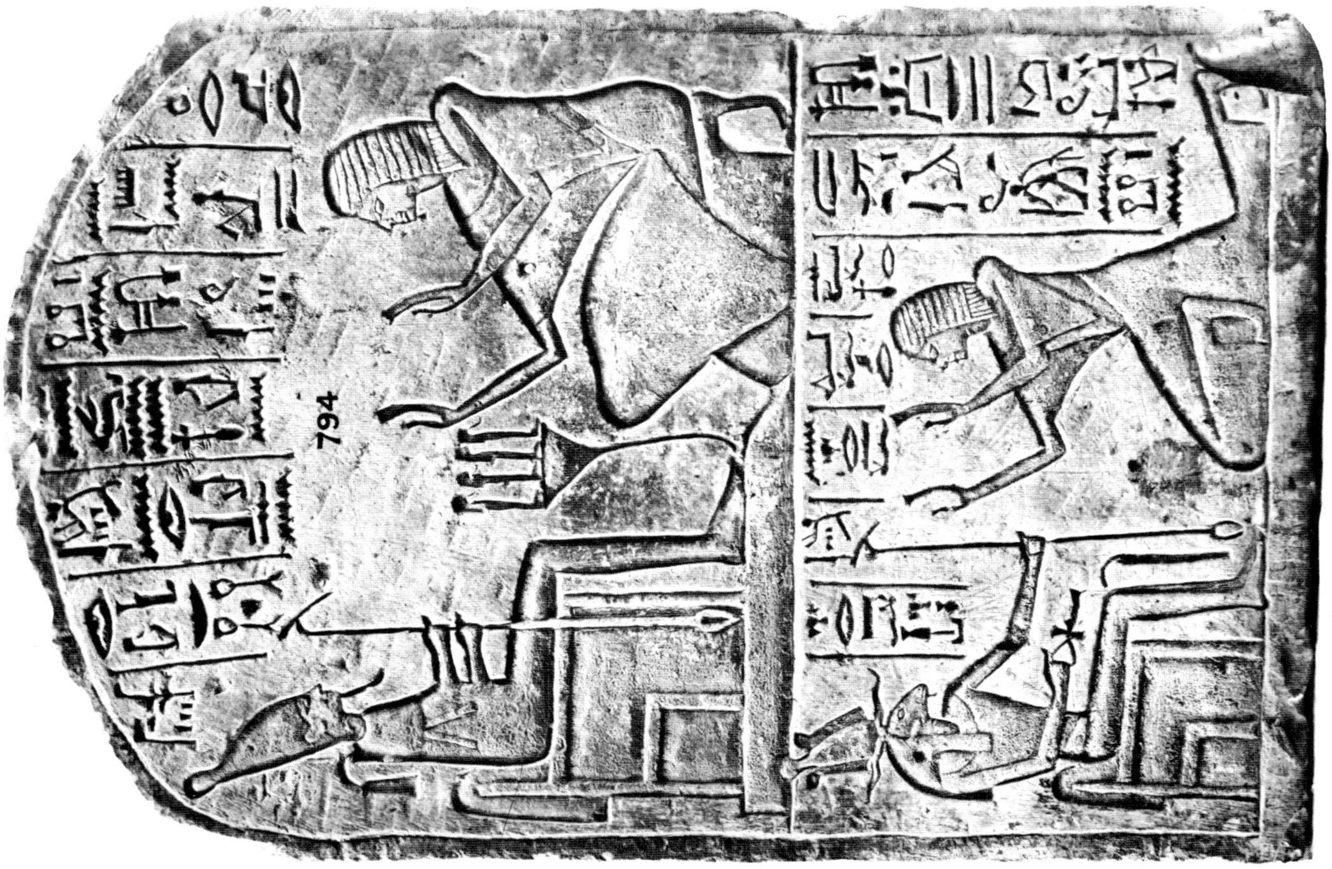

No. 794

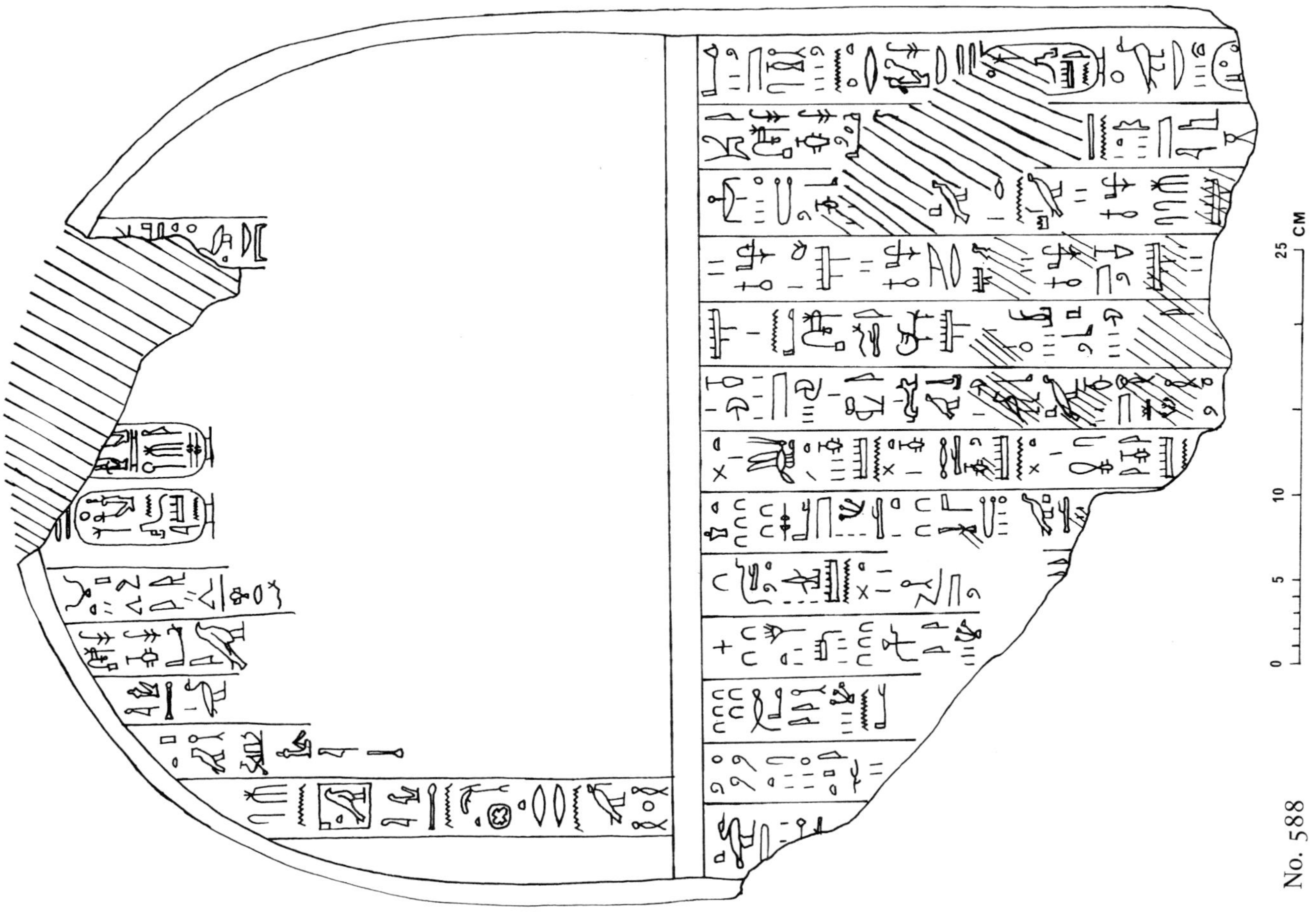

No. 588

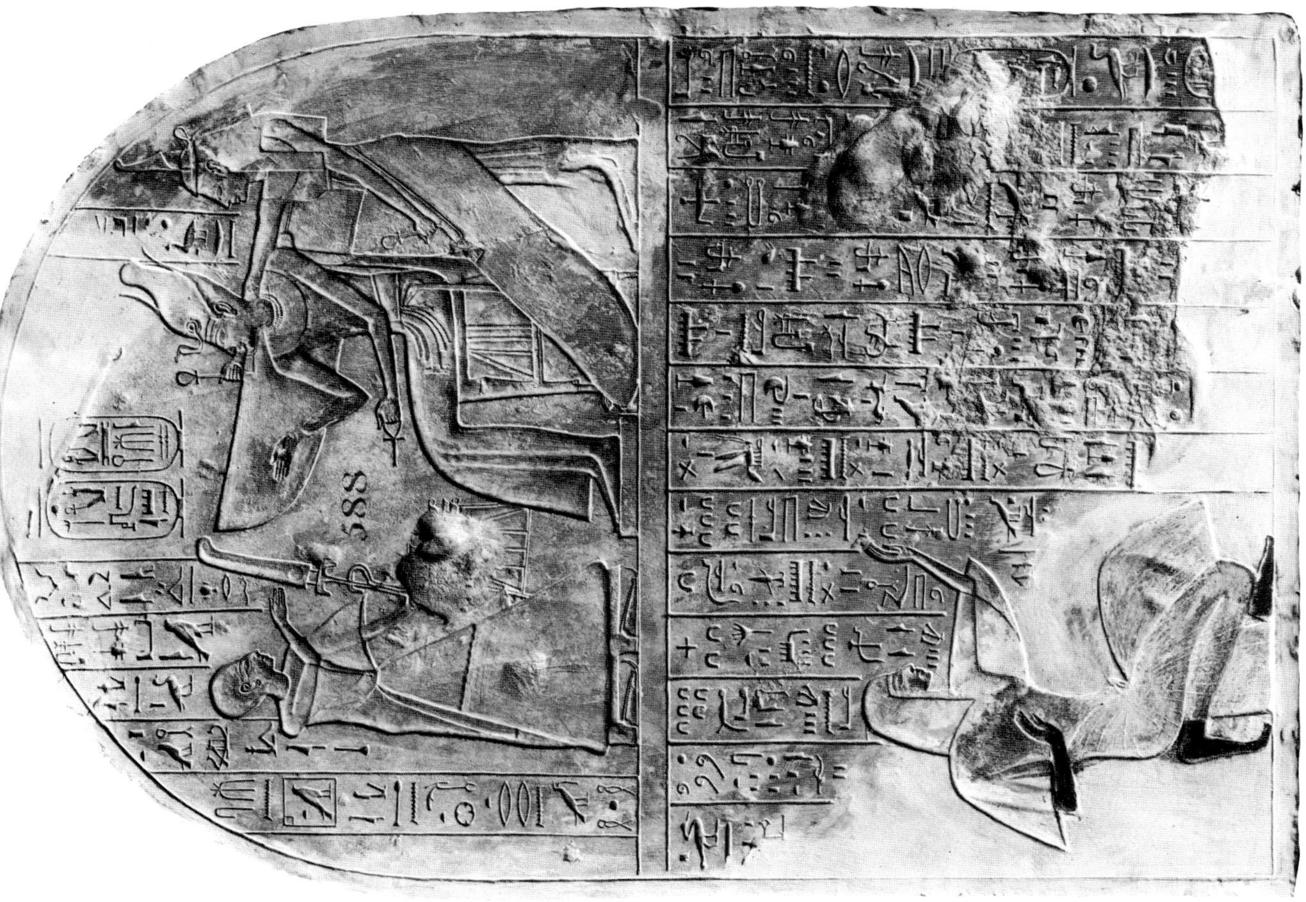

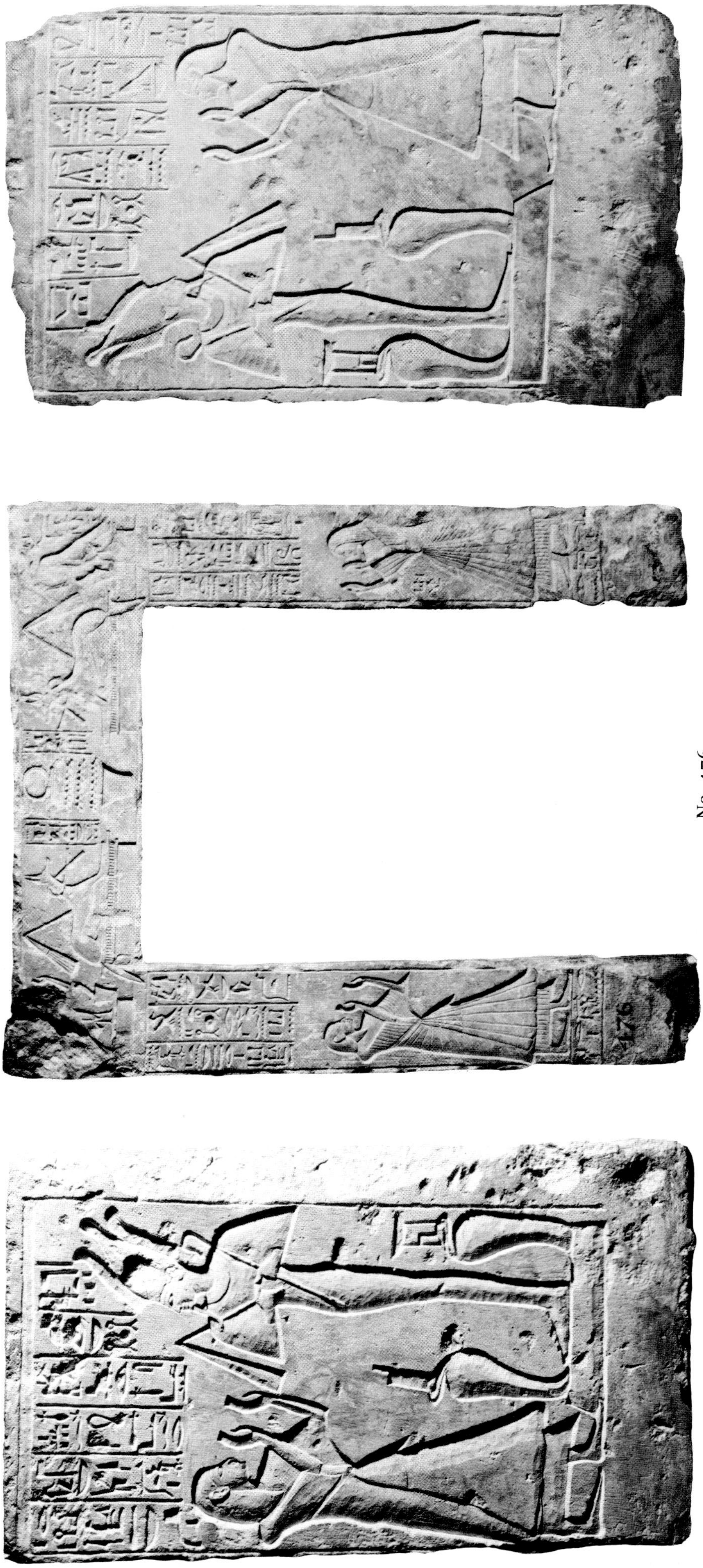

No. 476

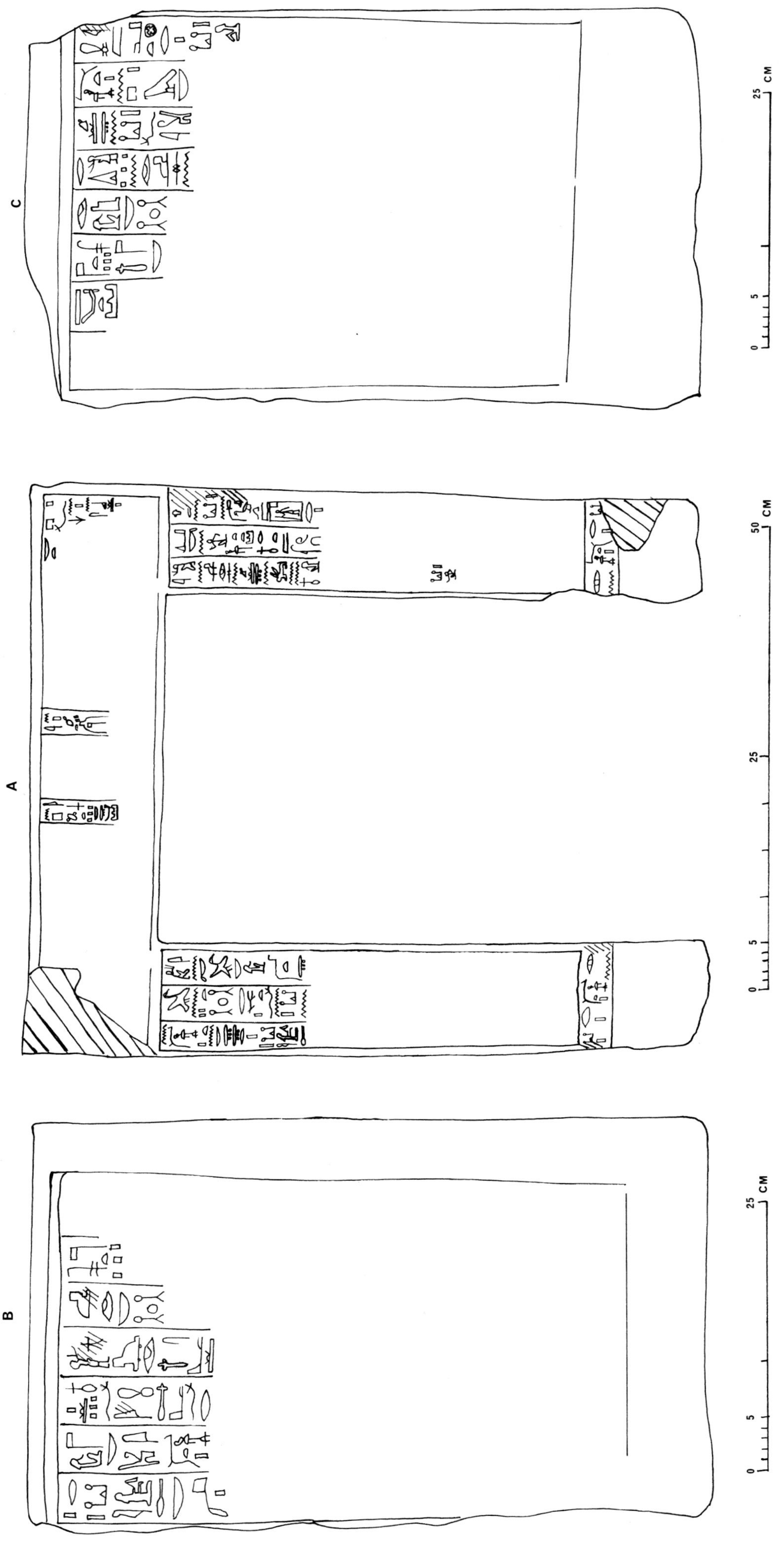

No. 476

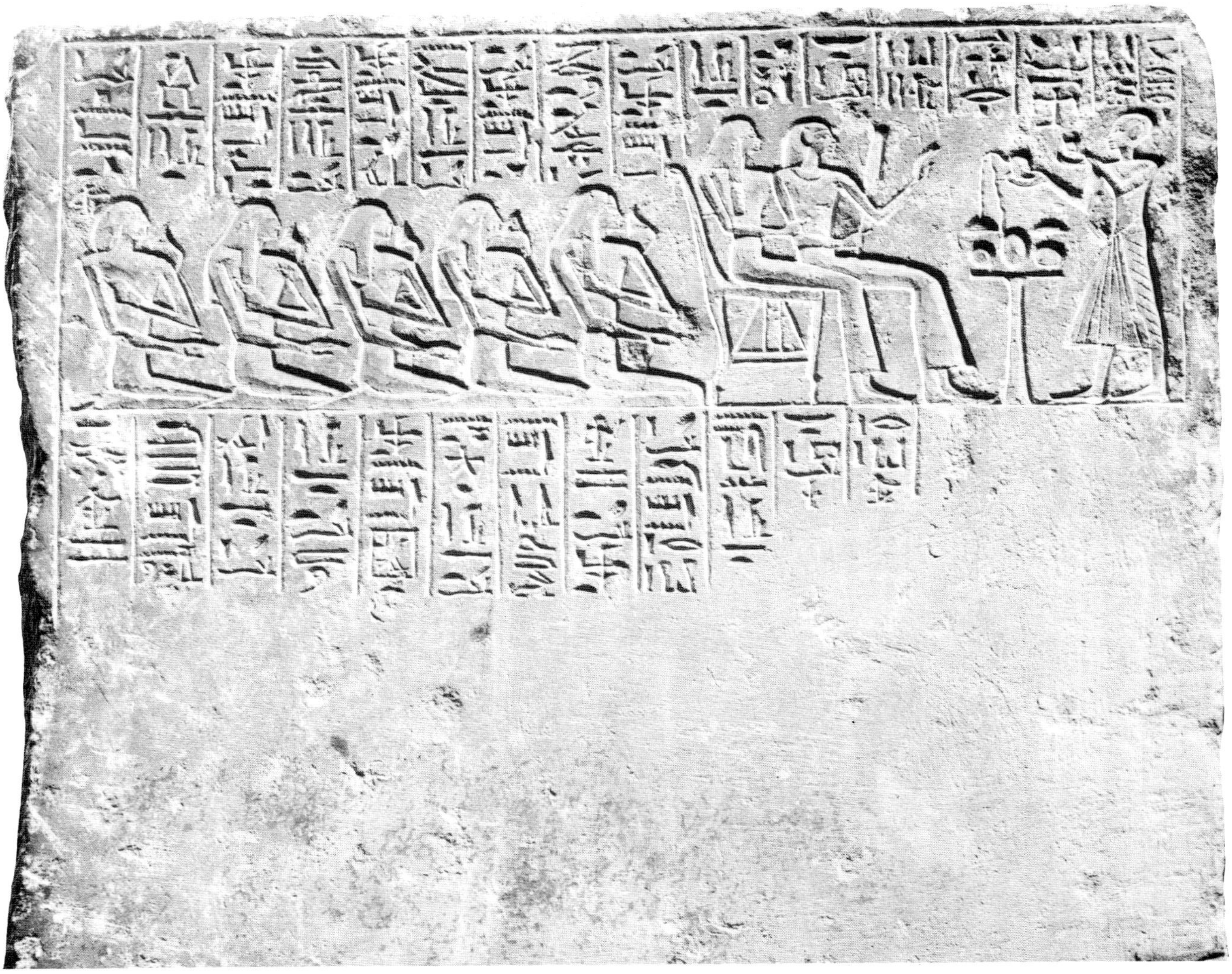

D

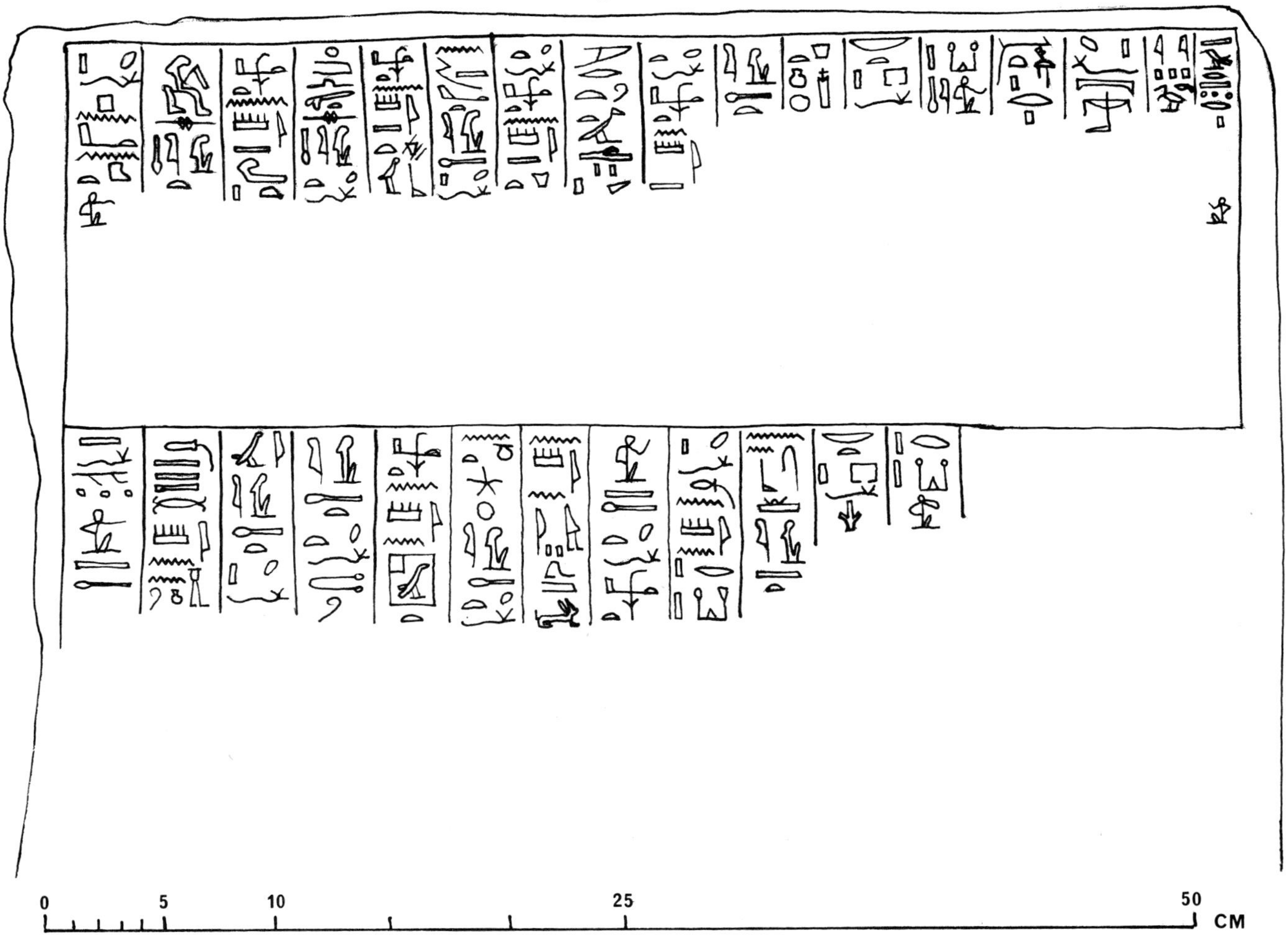

No. 476

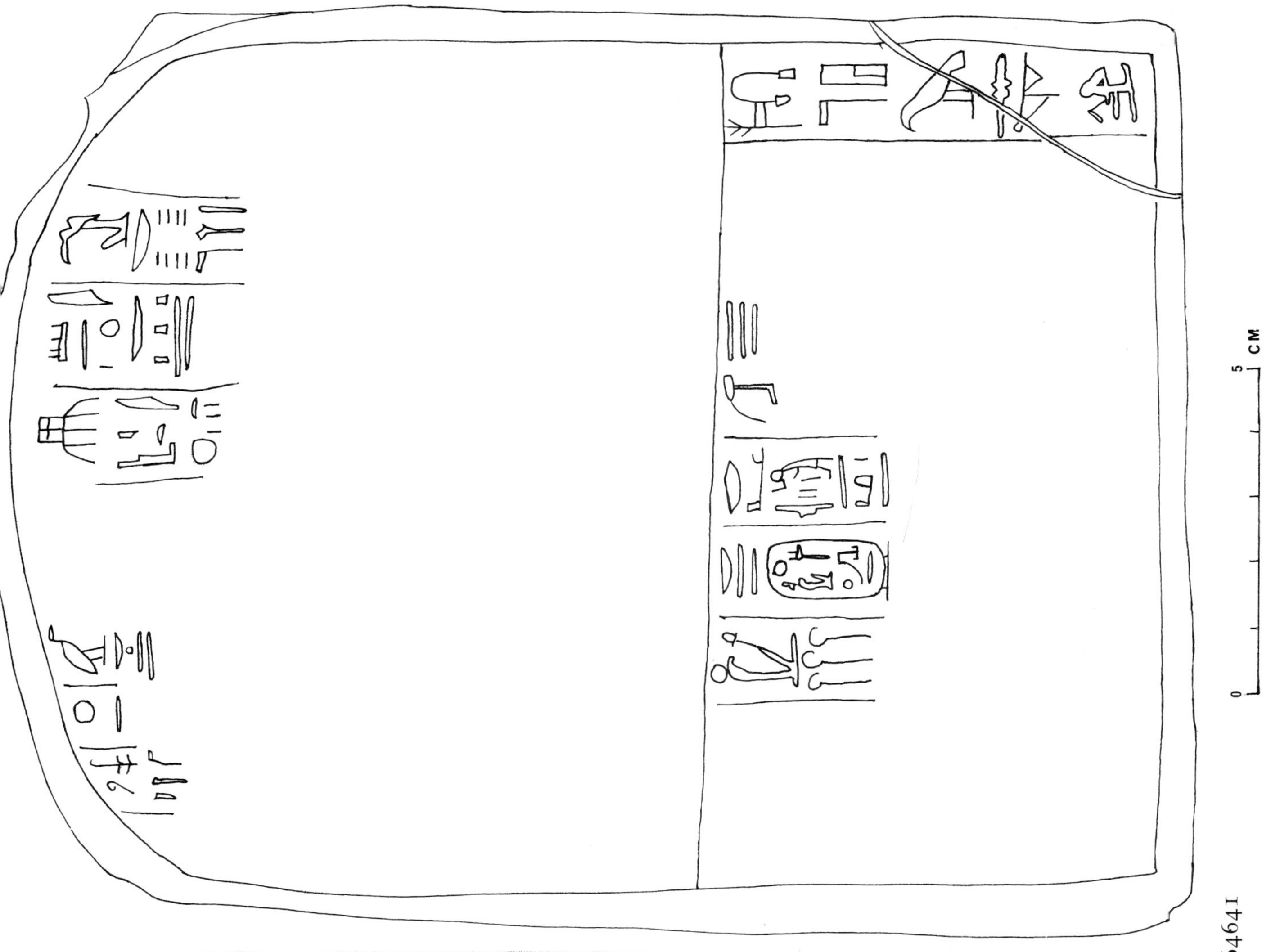

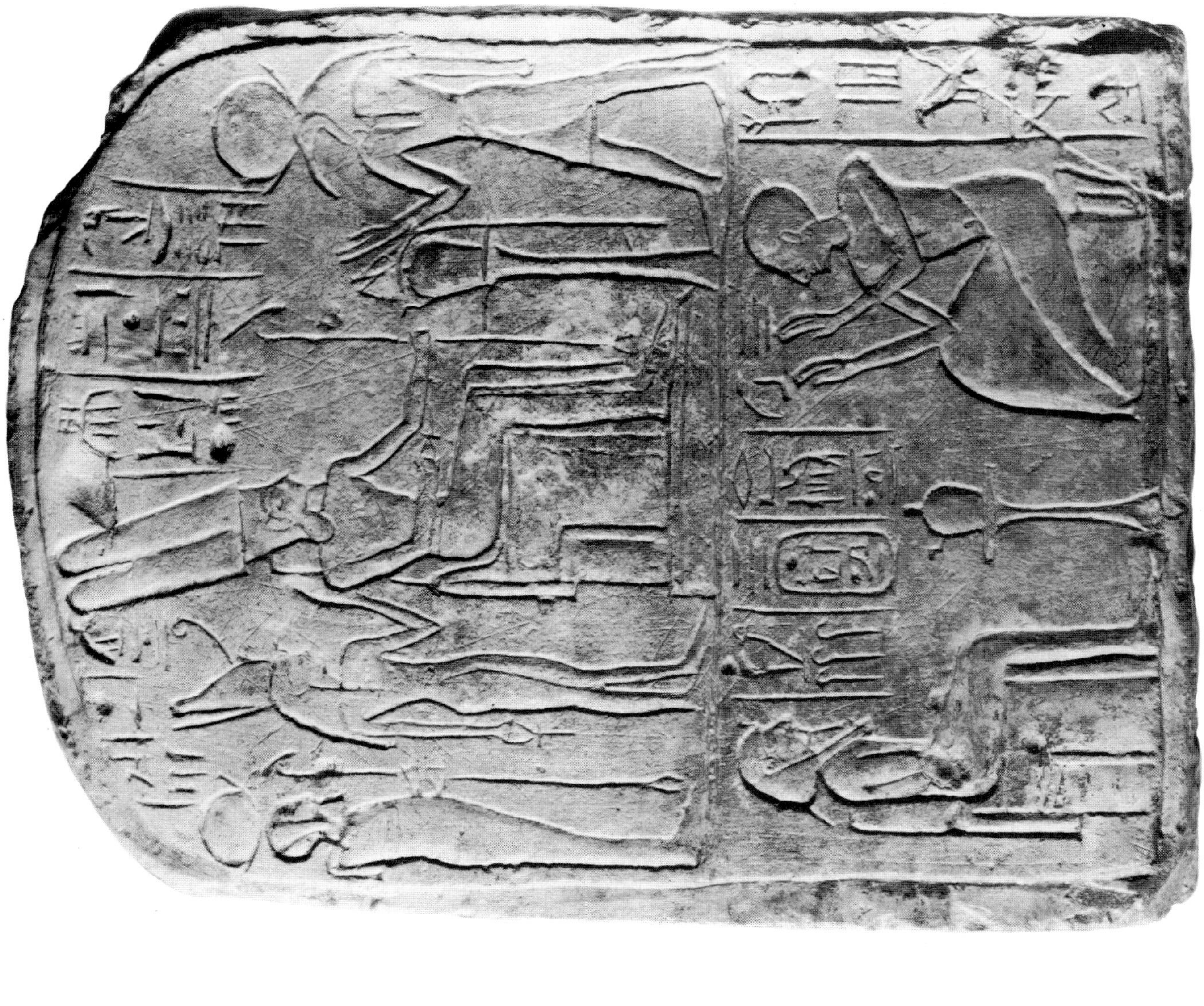

No. 64641

B

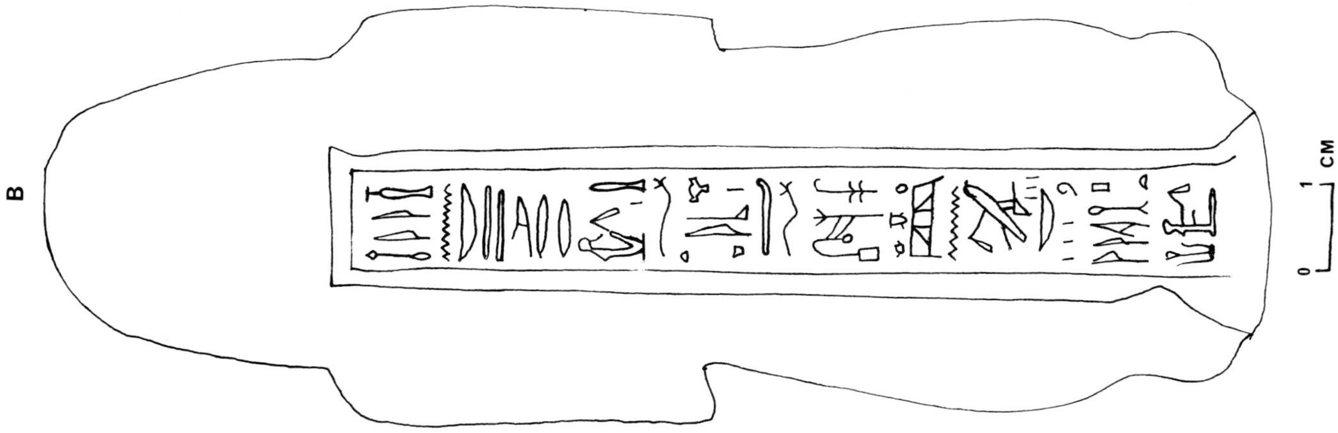

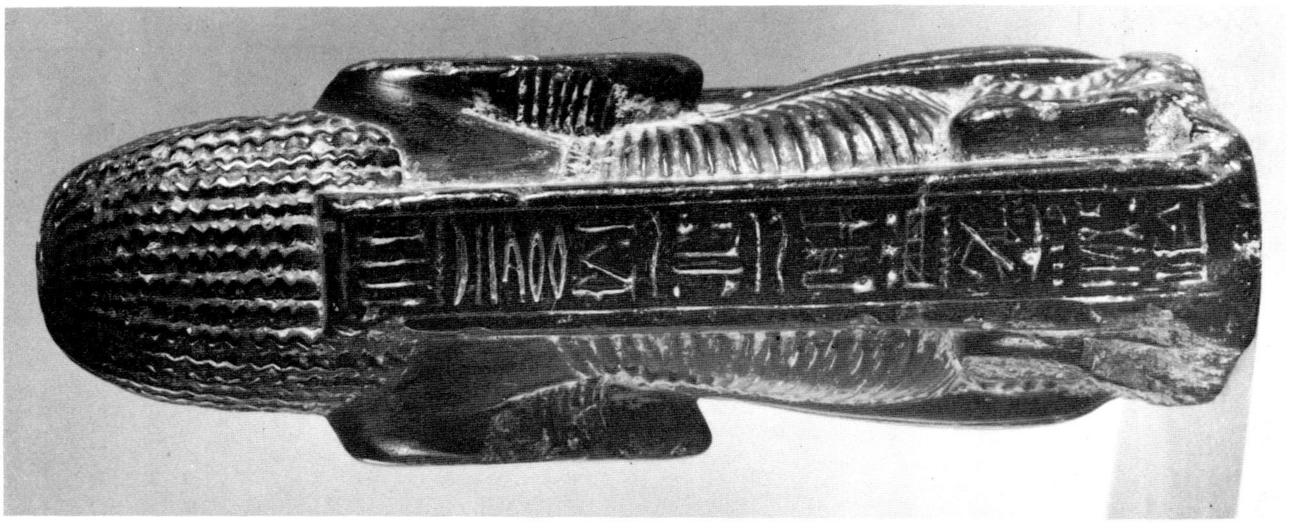

No. 2291

A

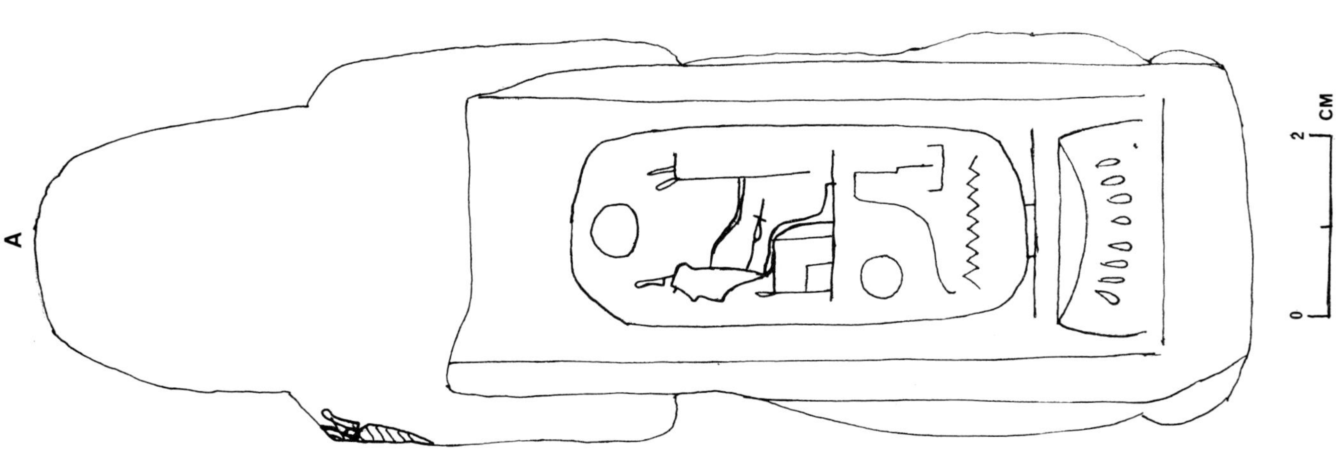

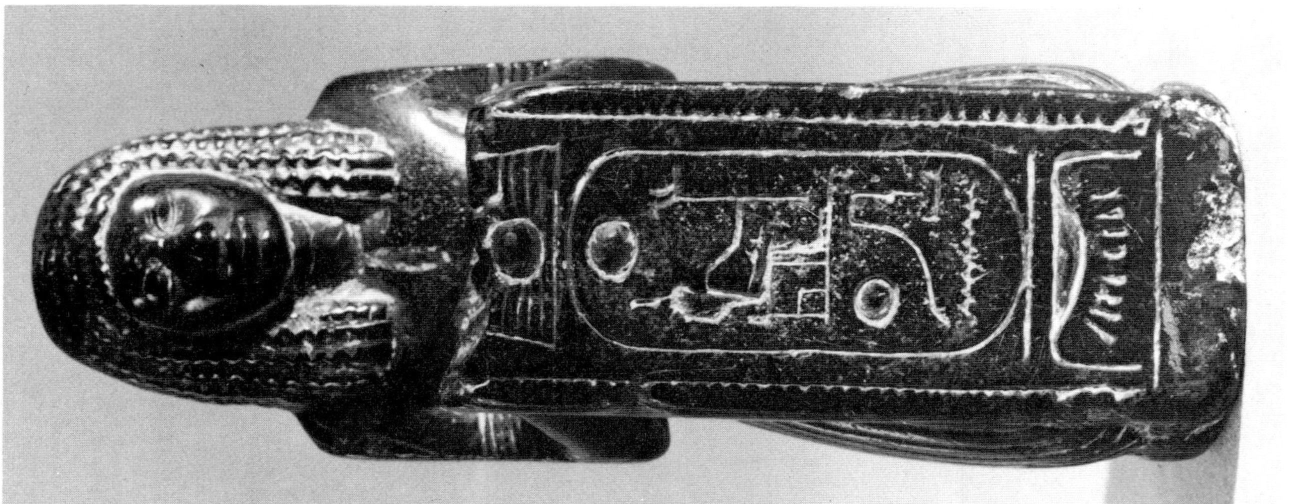

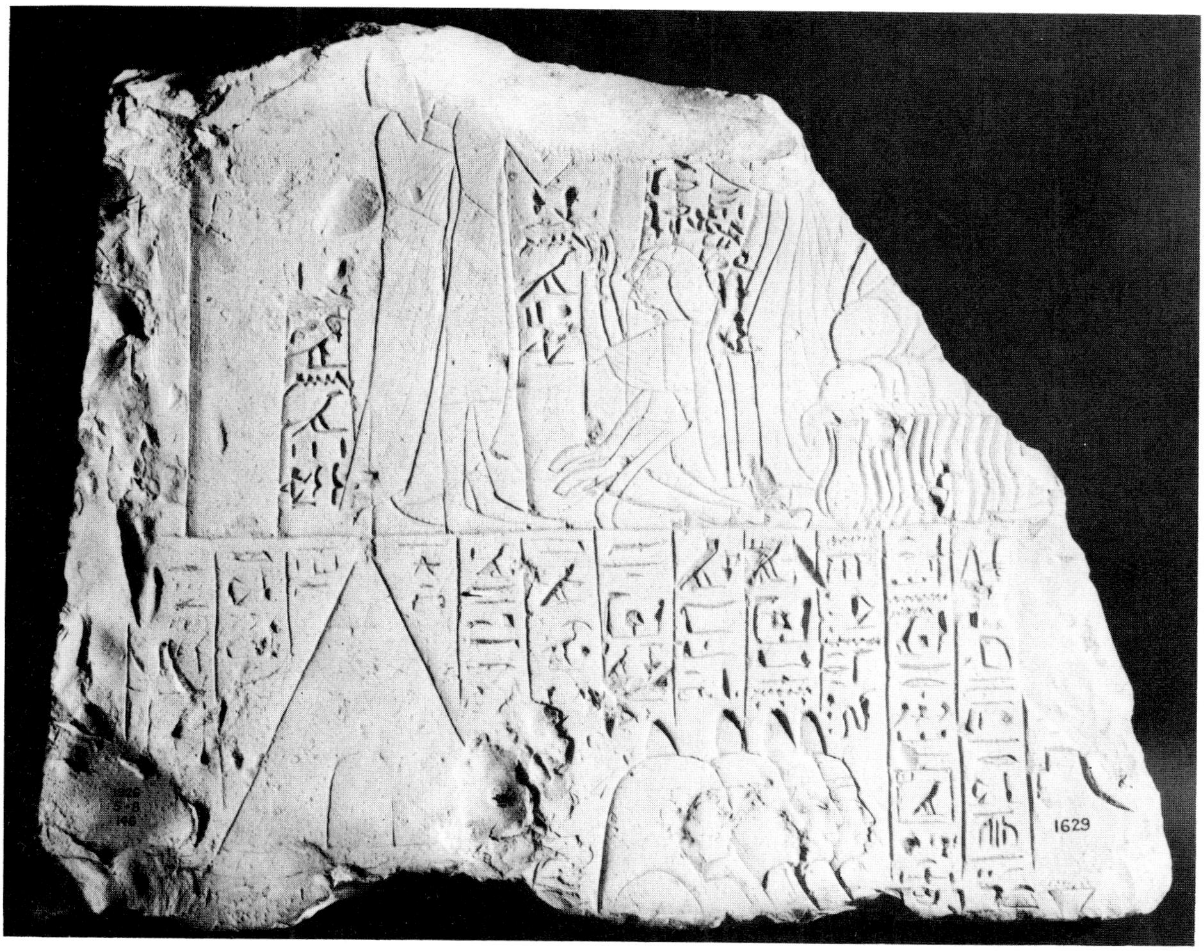

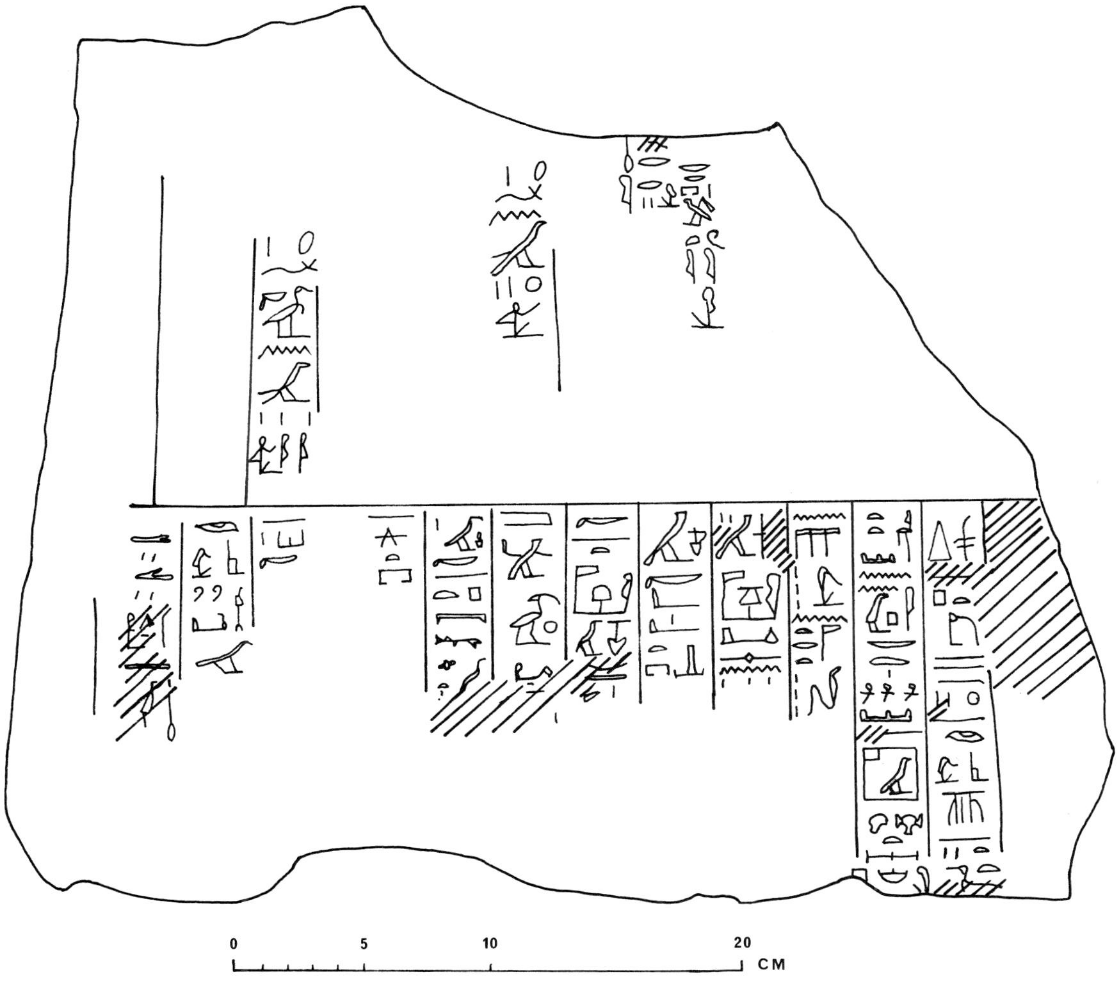

No. 1629

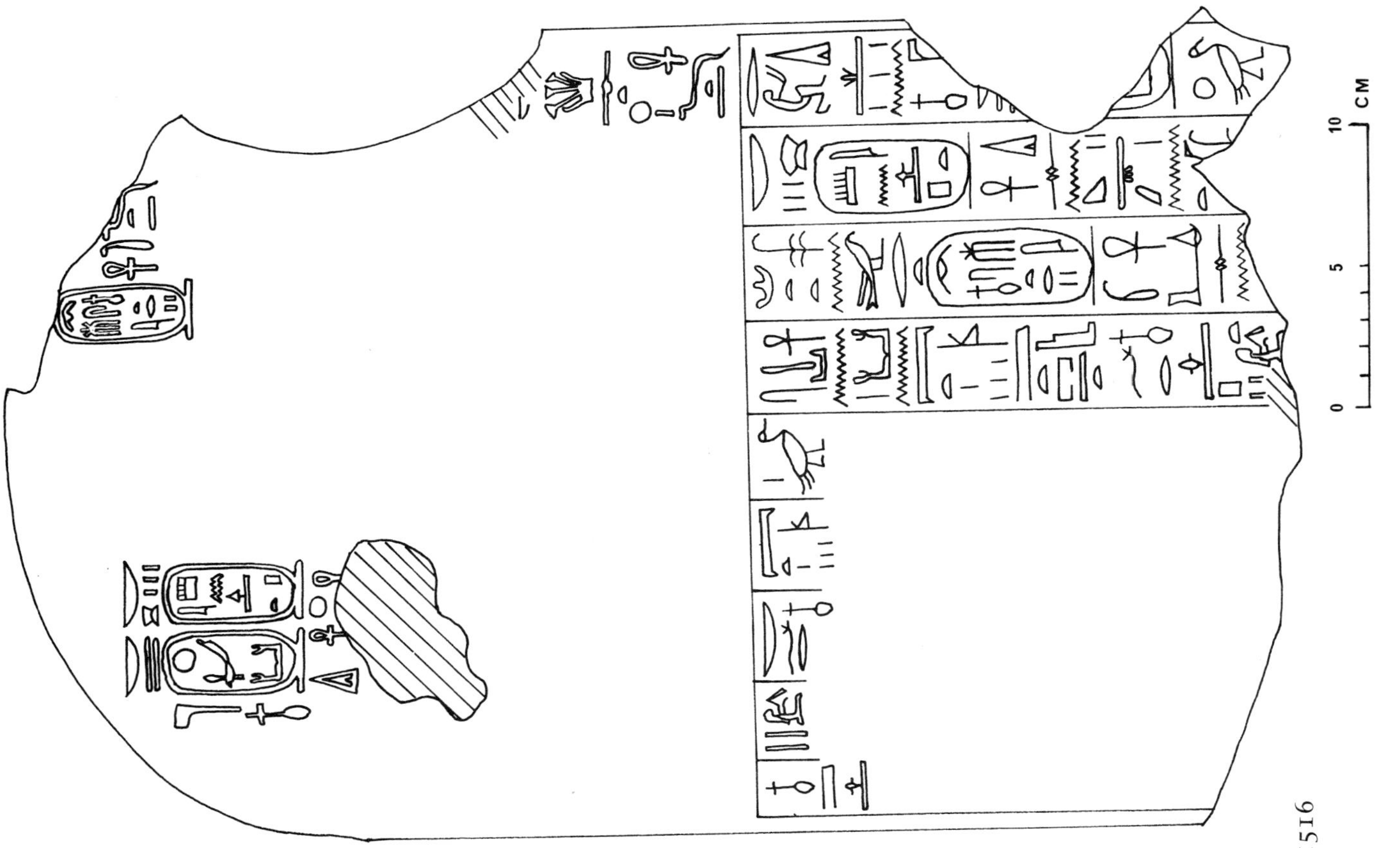

No. 1516

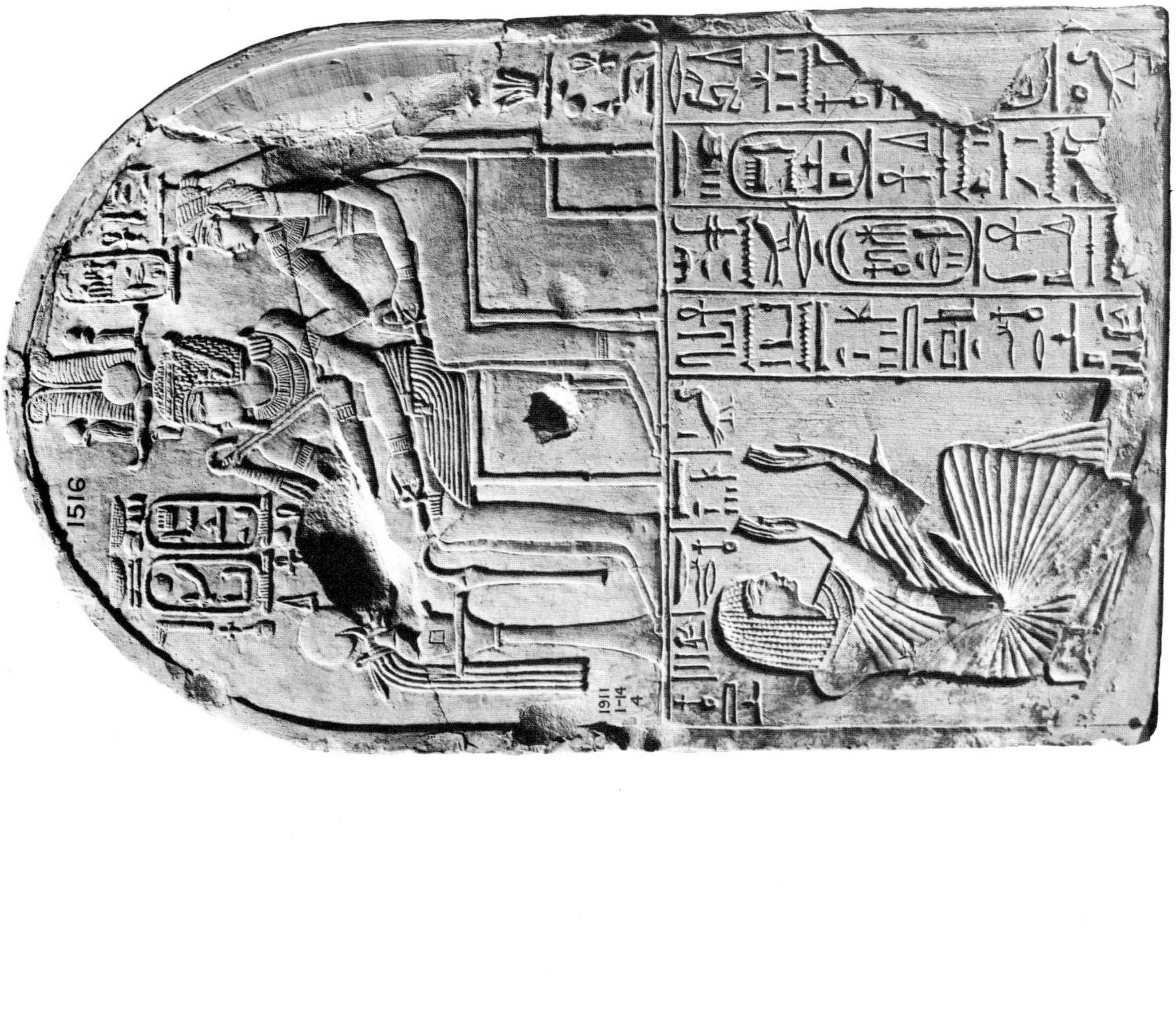

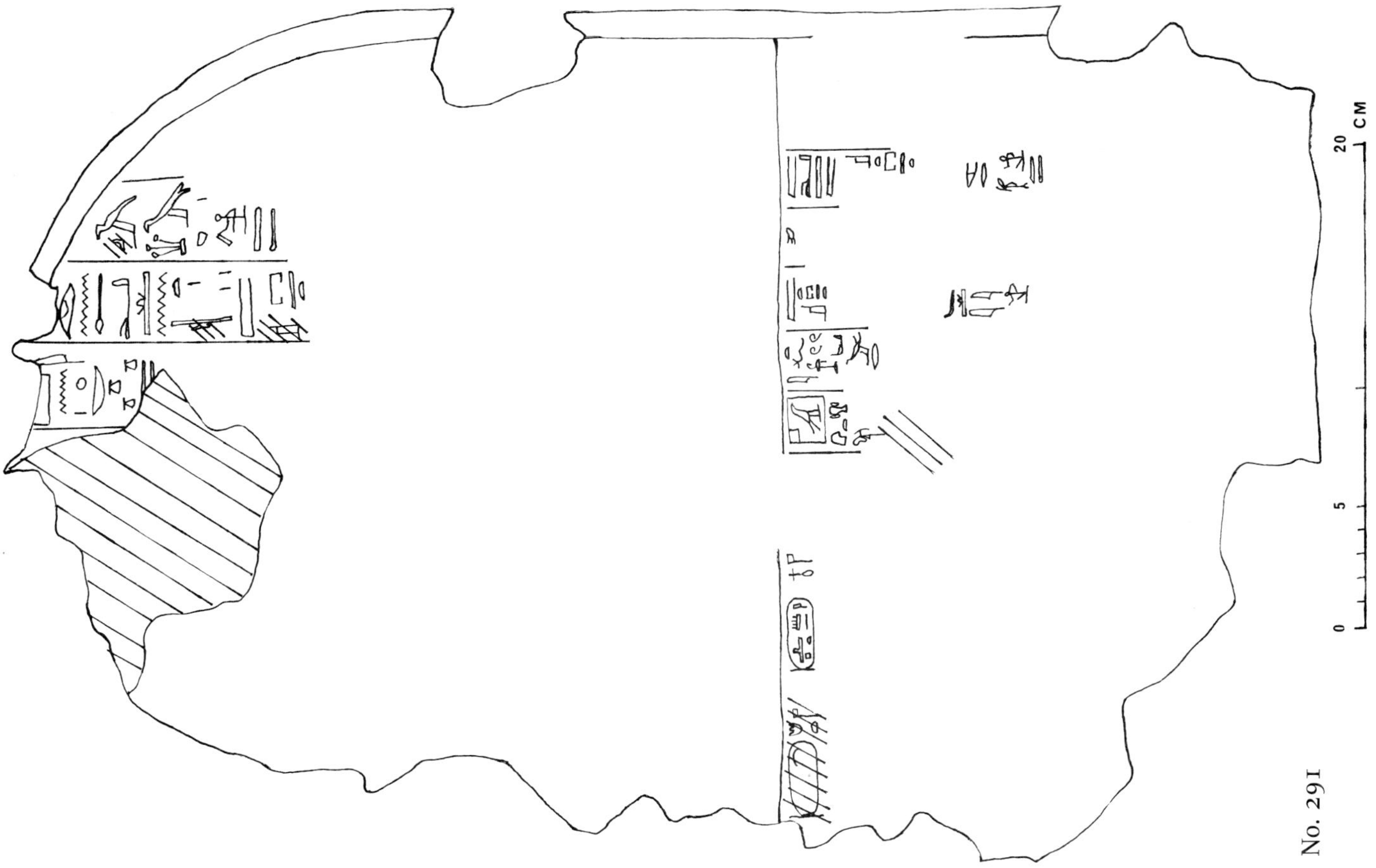

No. 291

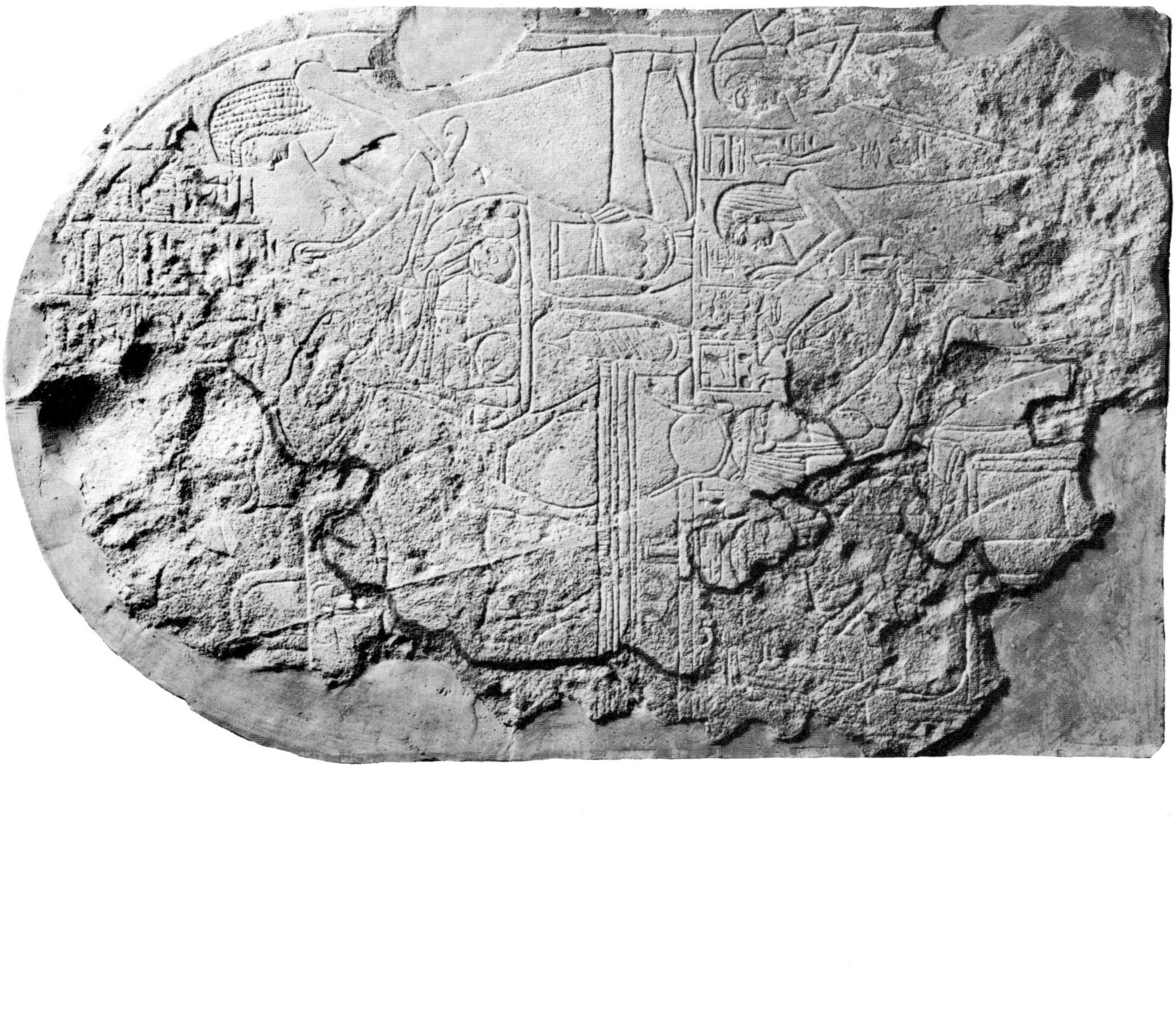

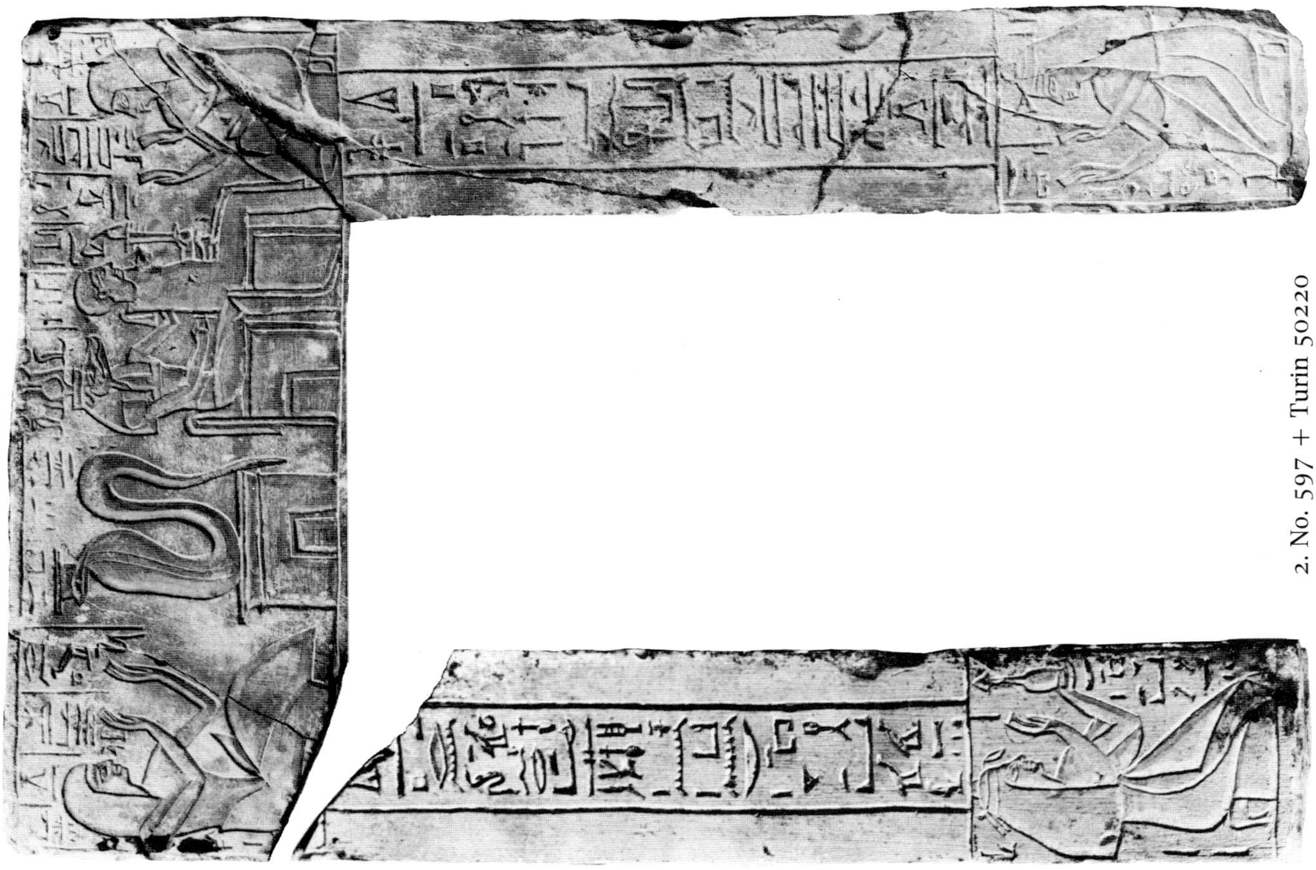

2. No. 597 + Turin 50220

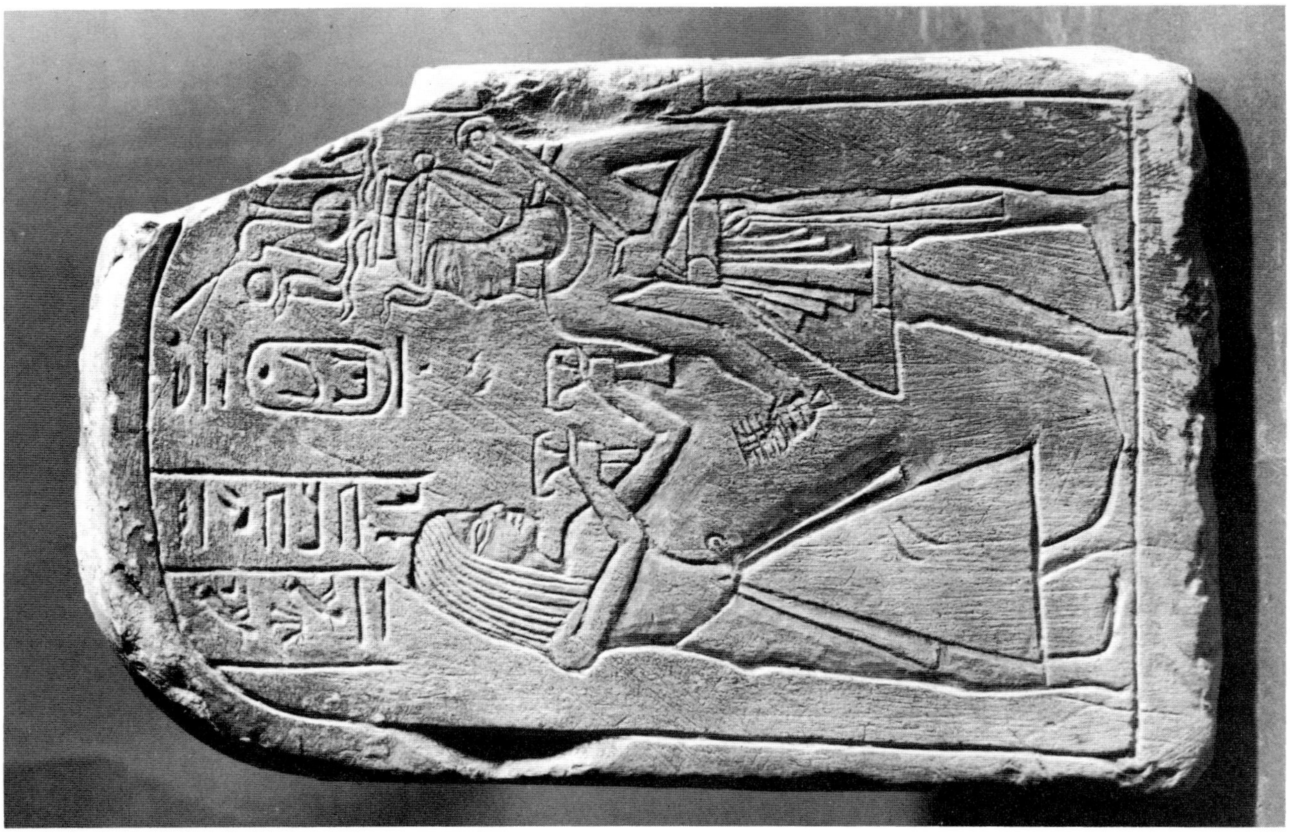

1. No. 274

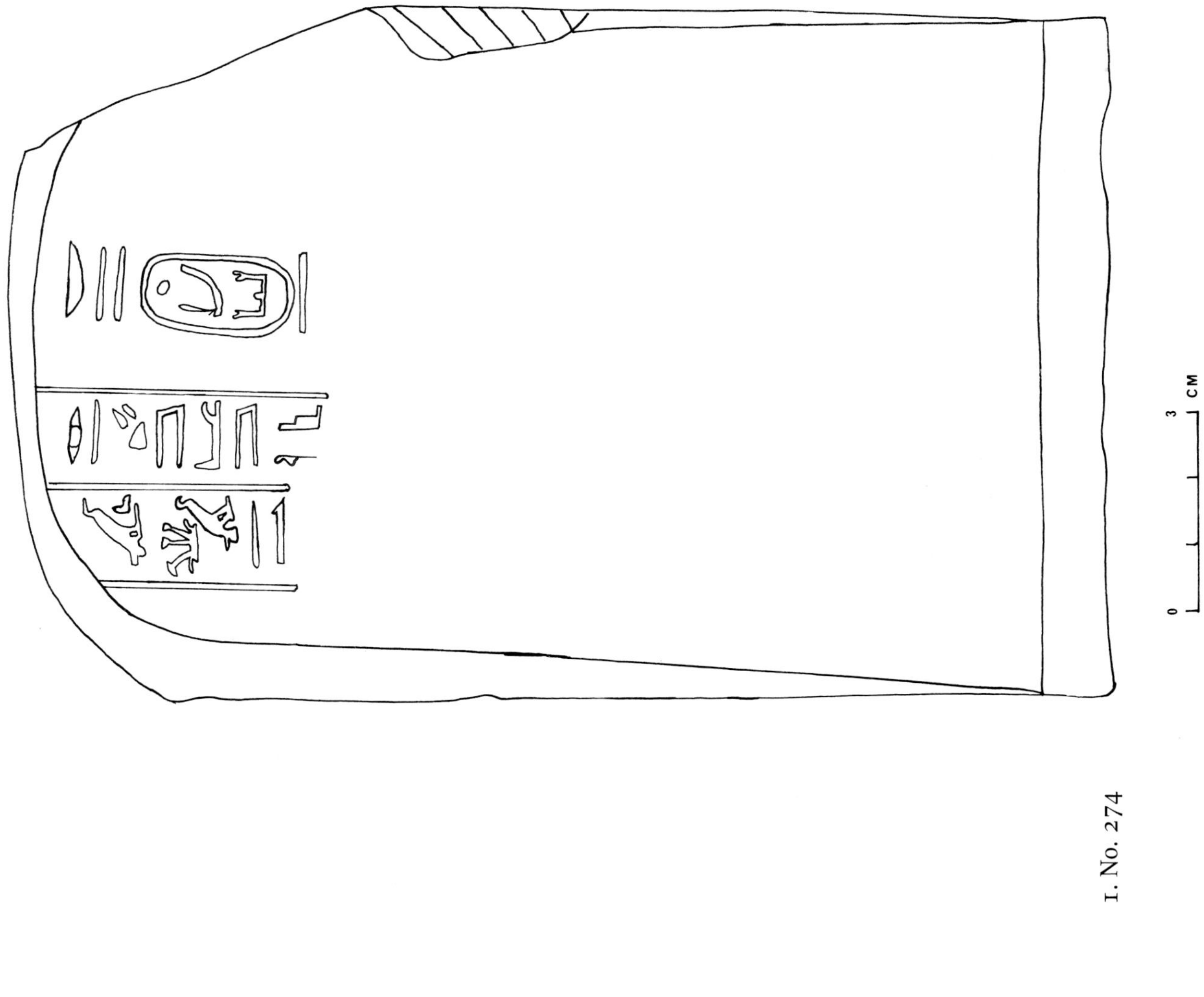

1. No. 274

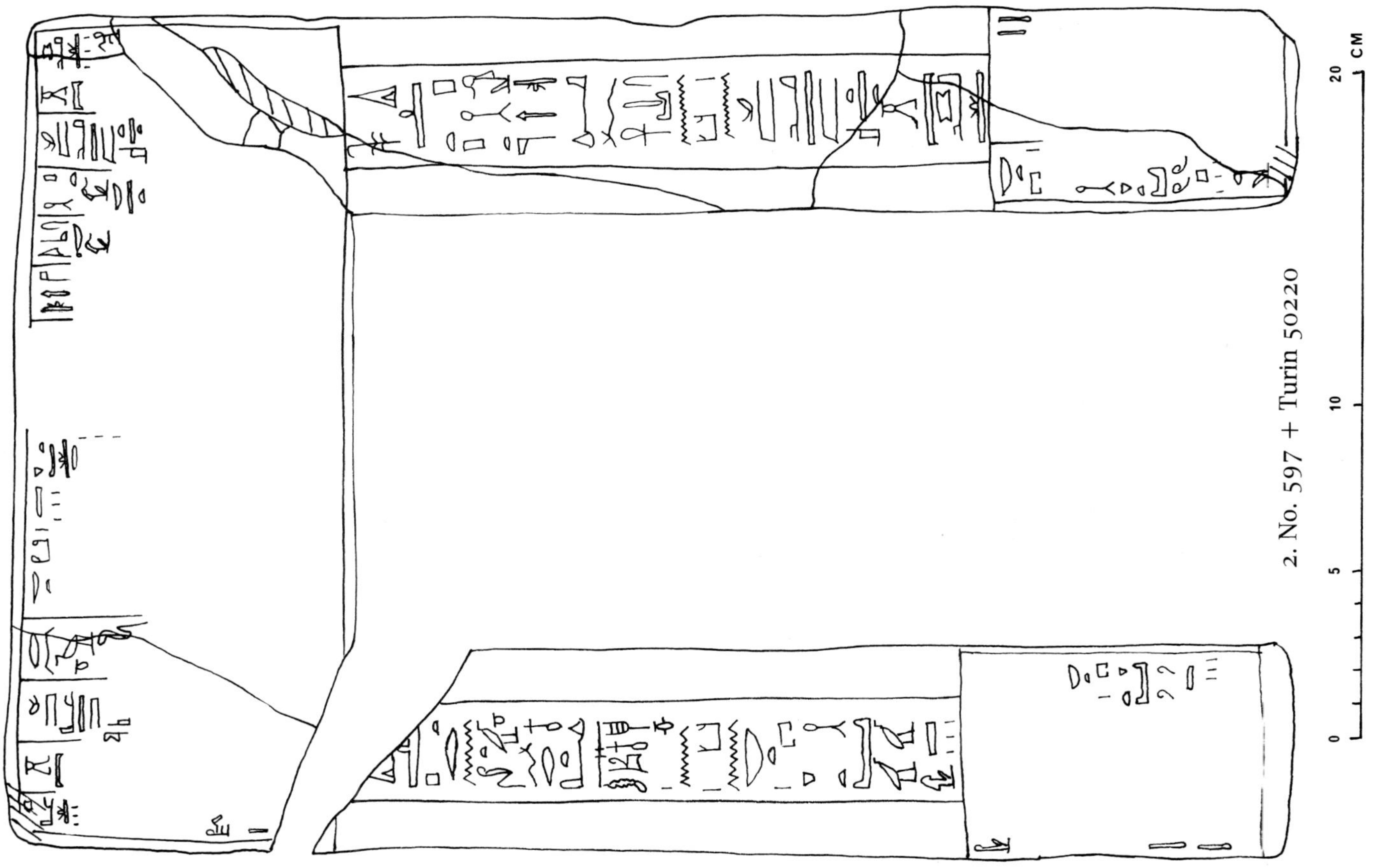

2. No. 597 + Turin 50220

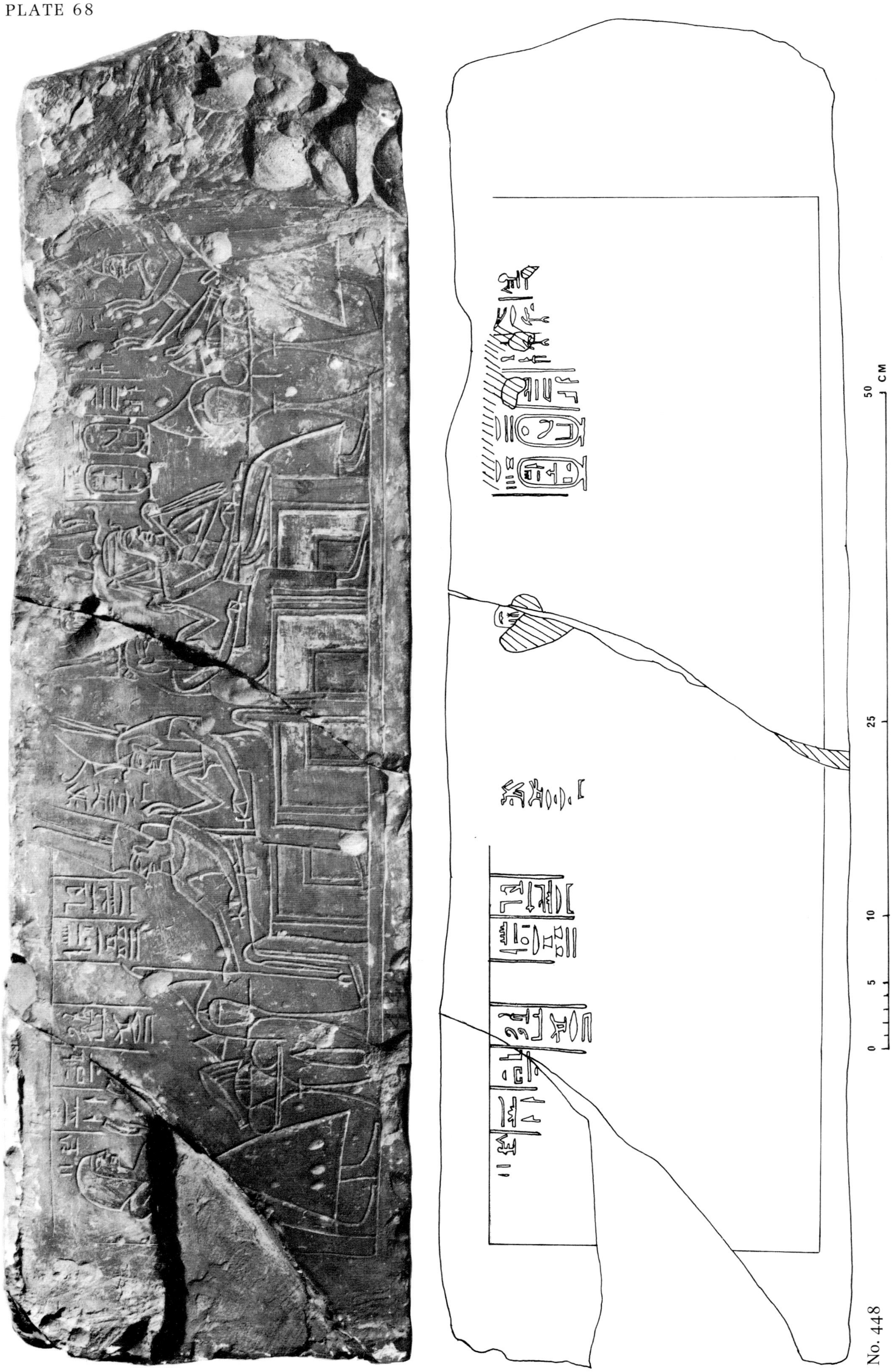

No. 448

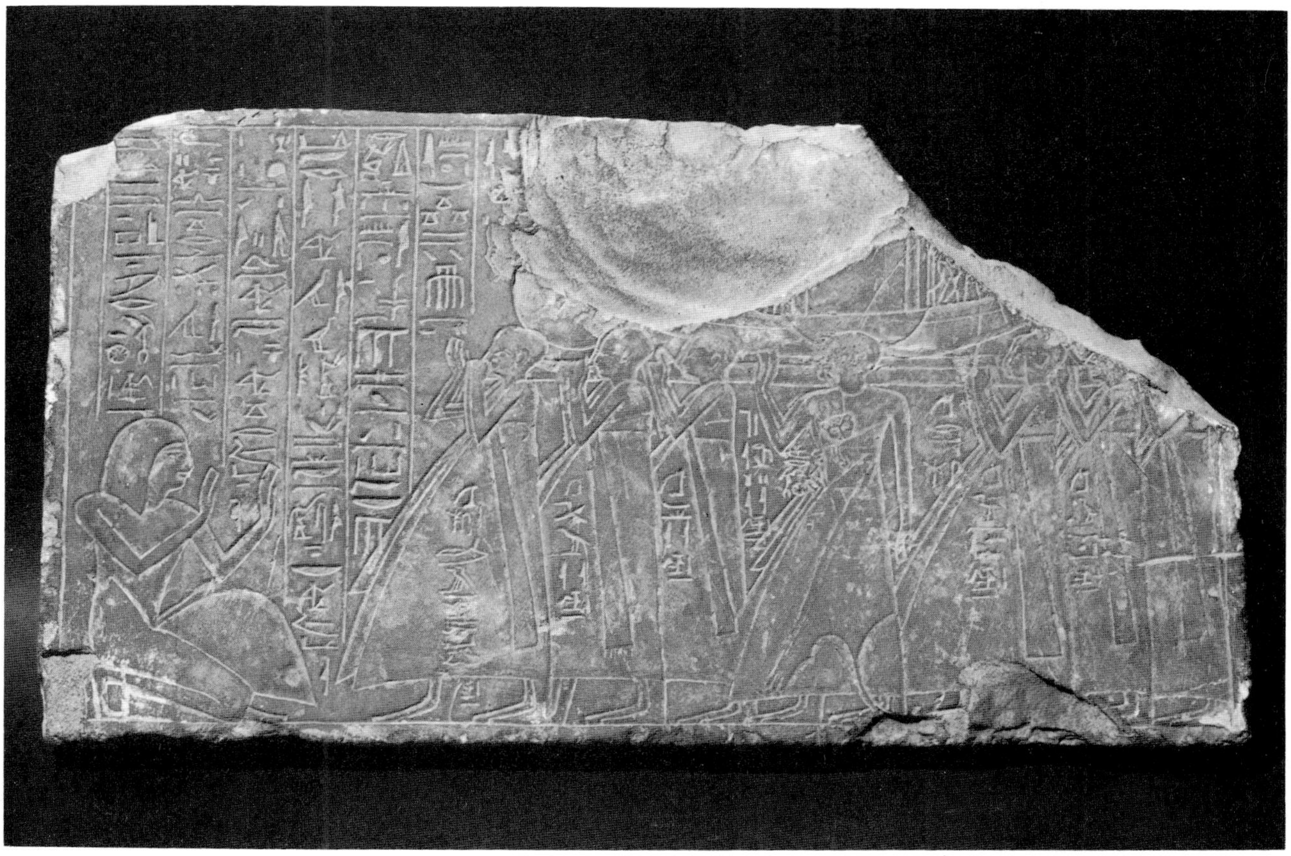

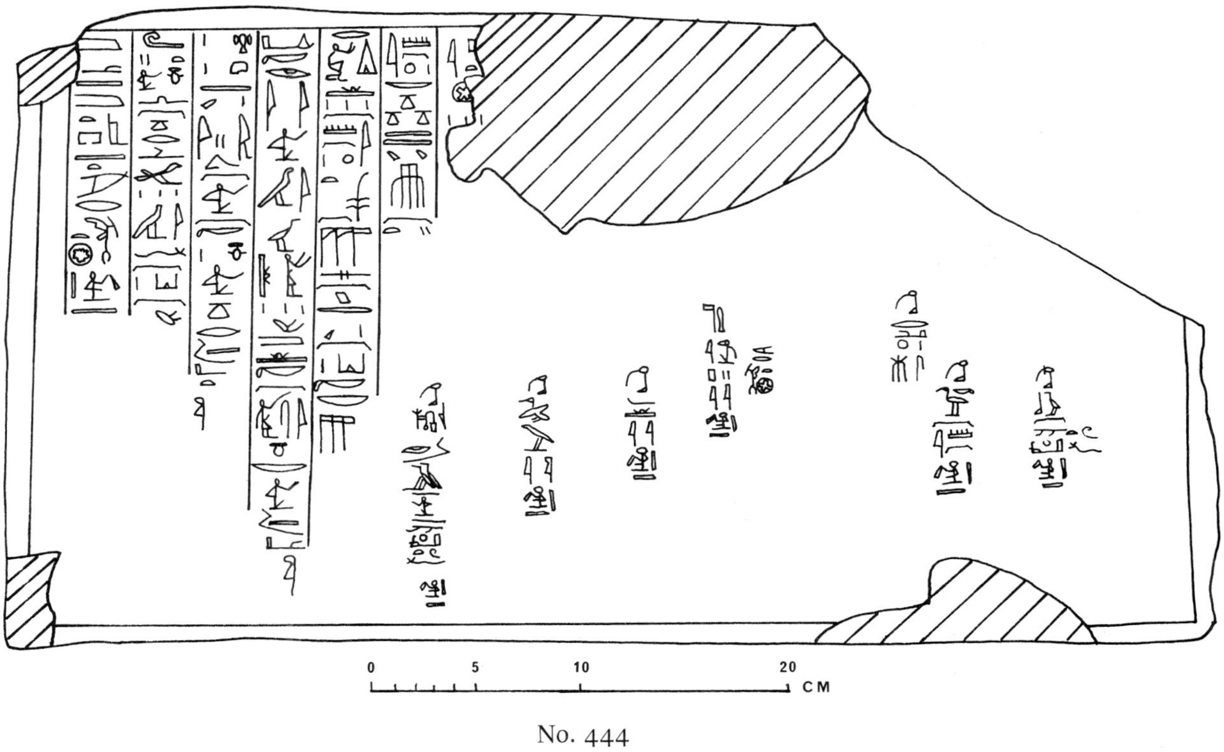

No. 444

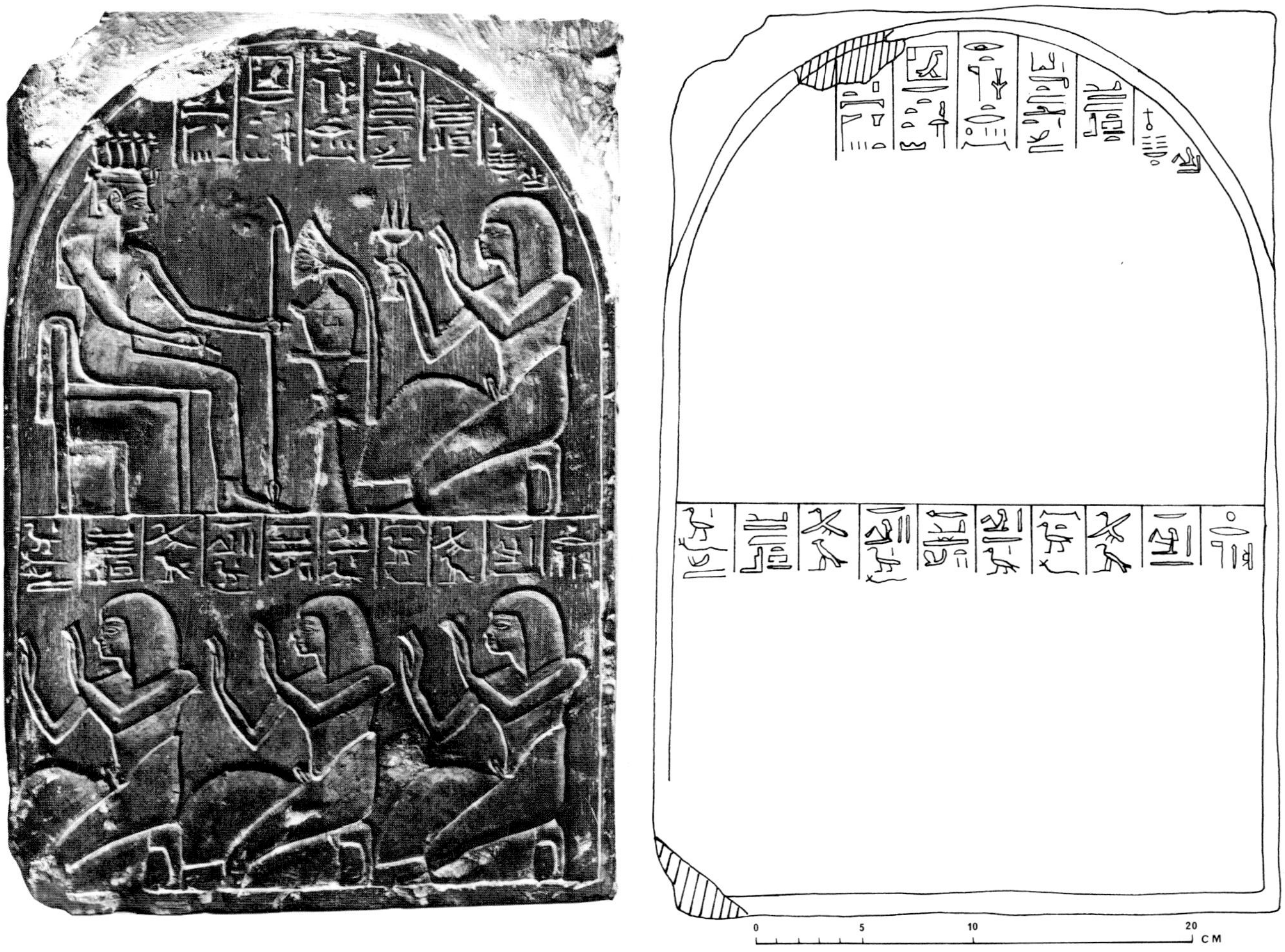

1. No. 316

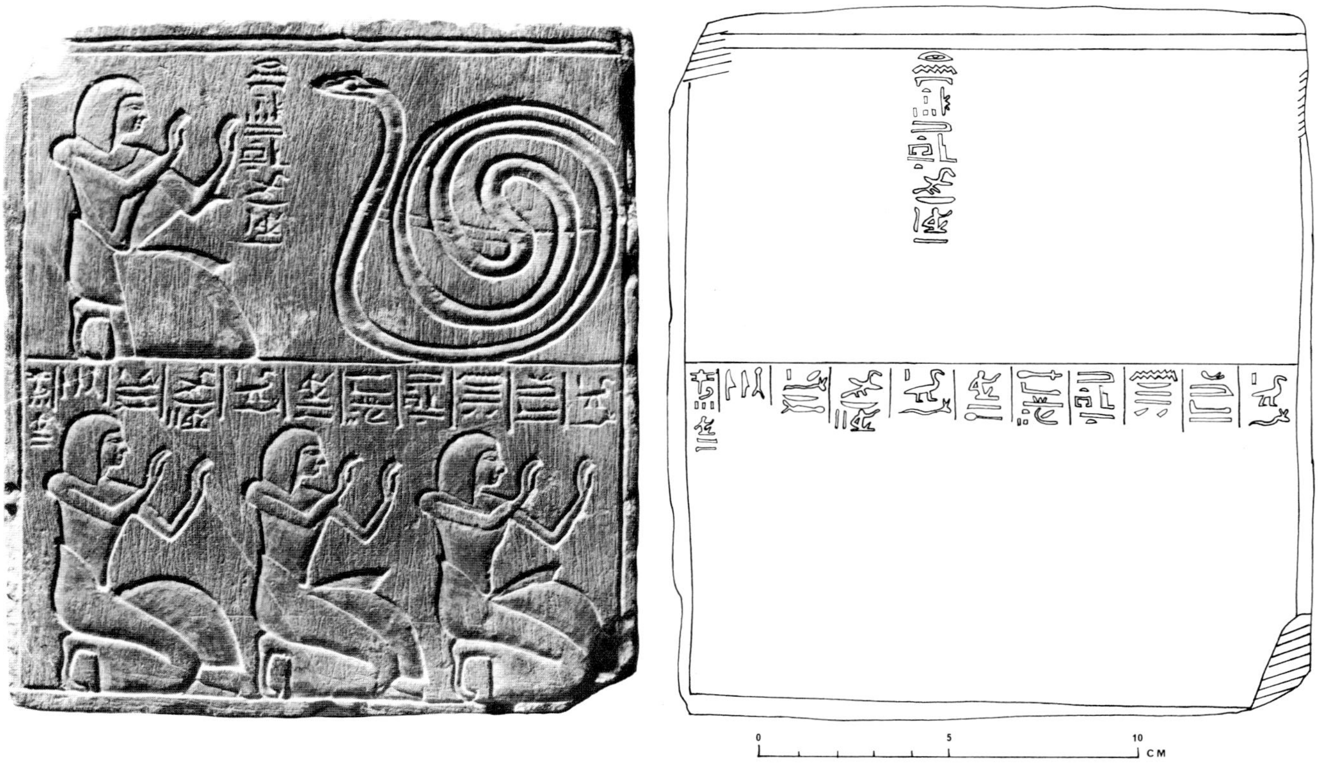

2. No. 272

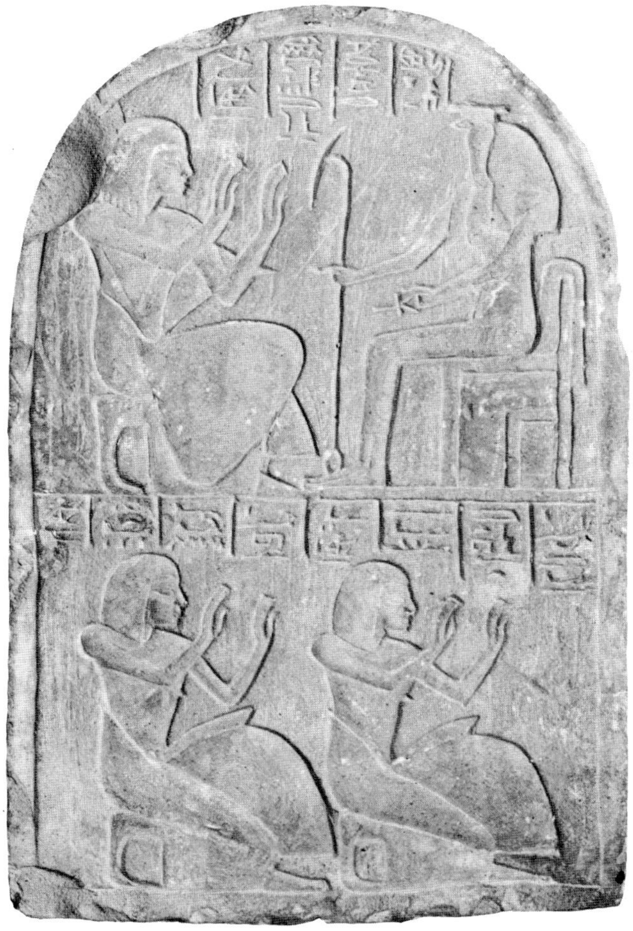

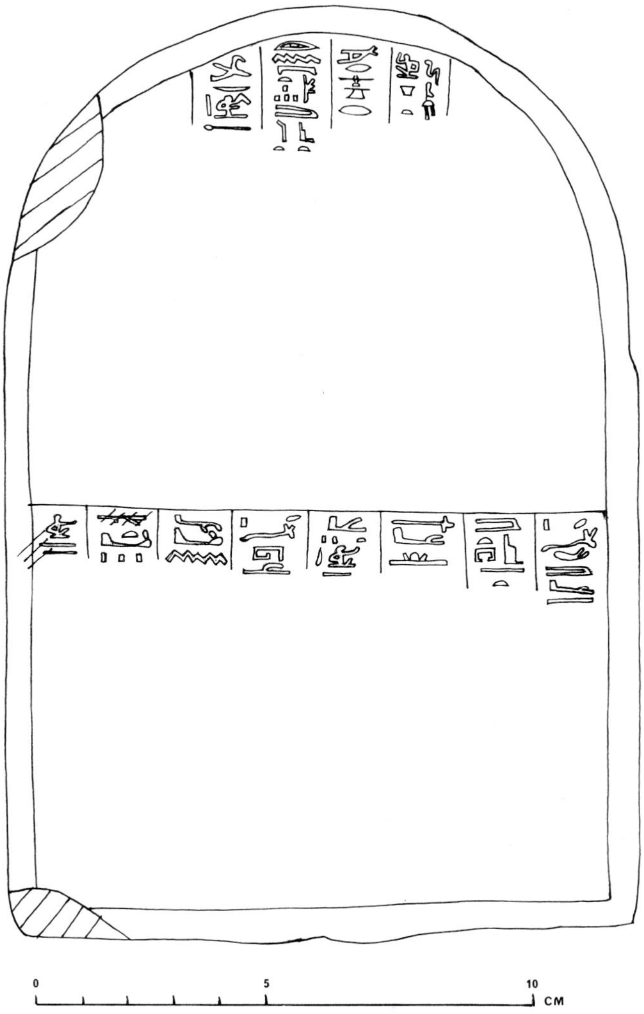

1. No. 273

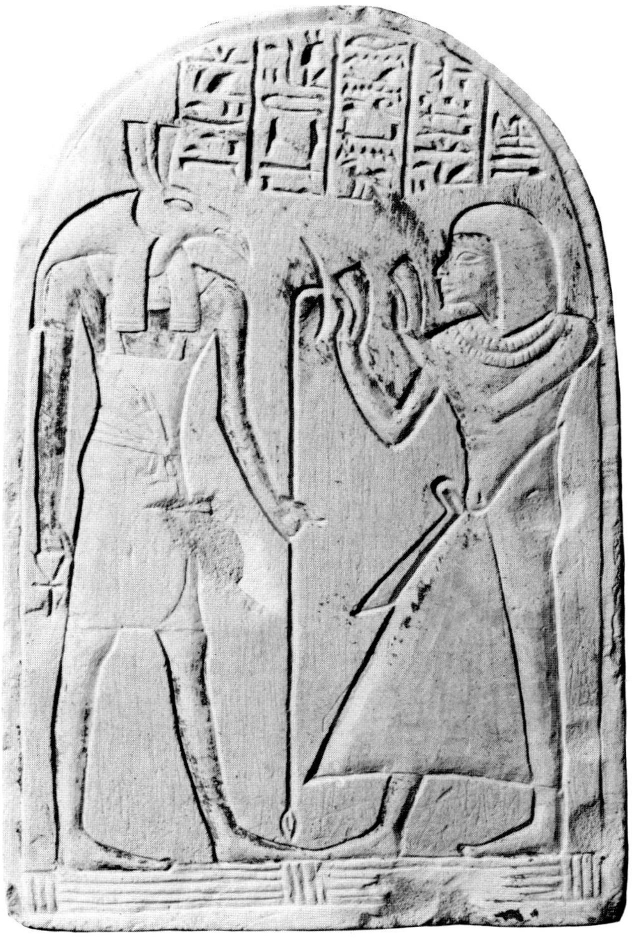

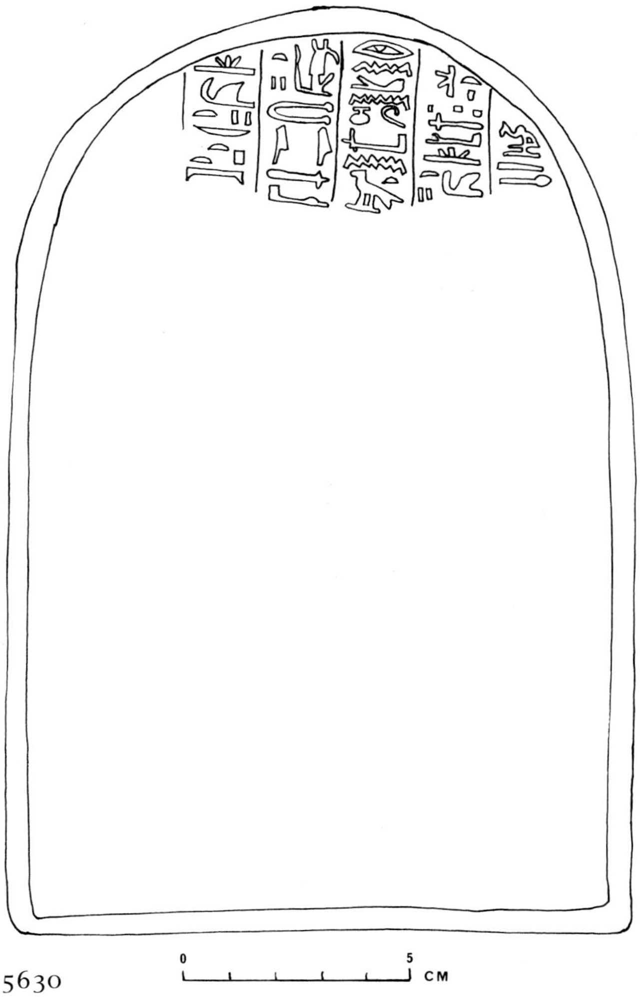

2. No. 35630

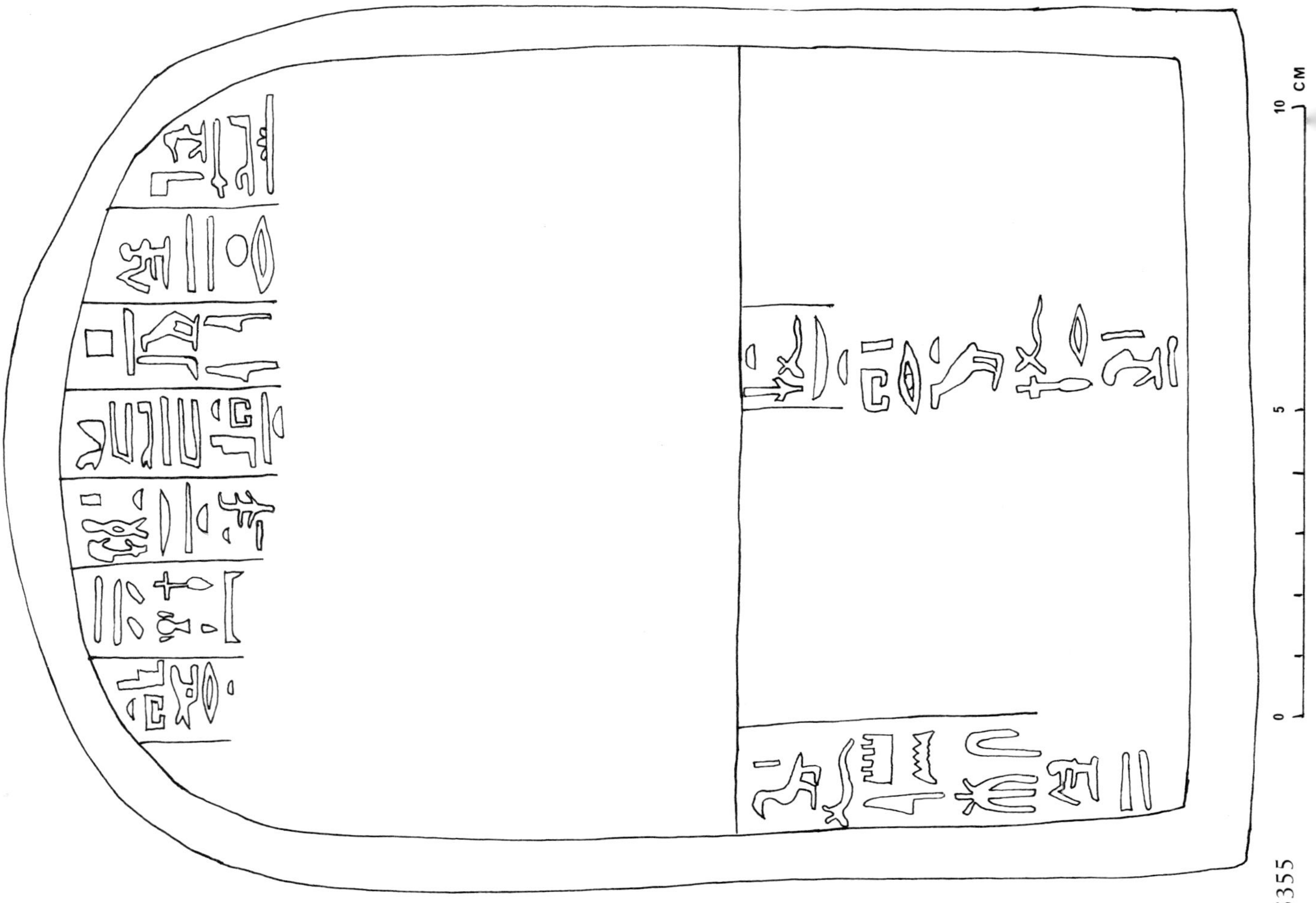

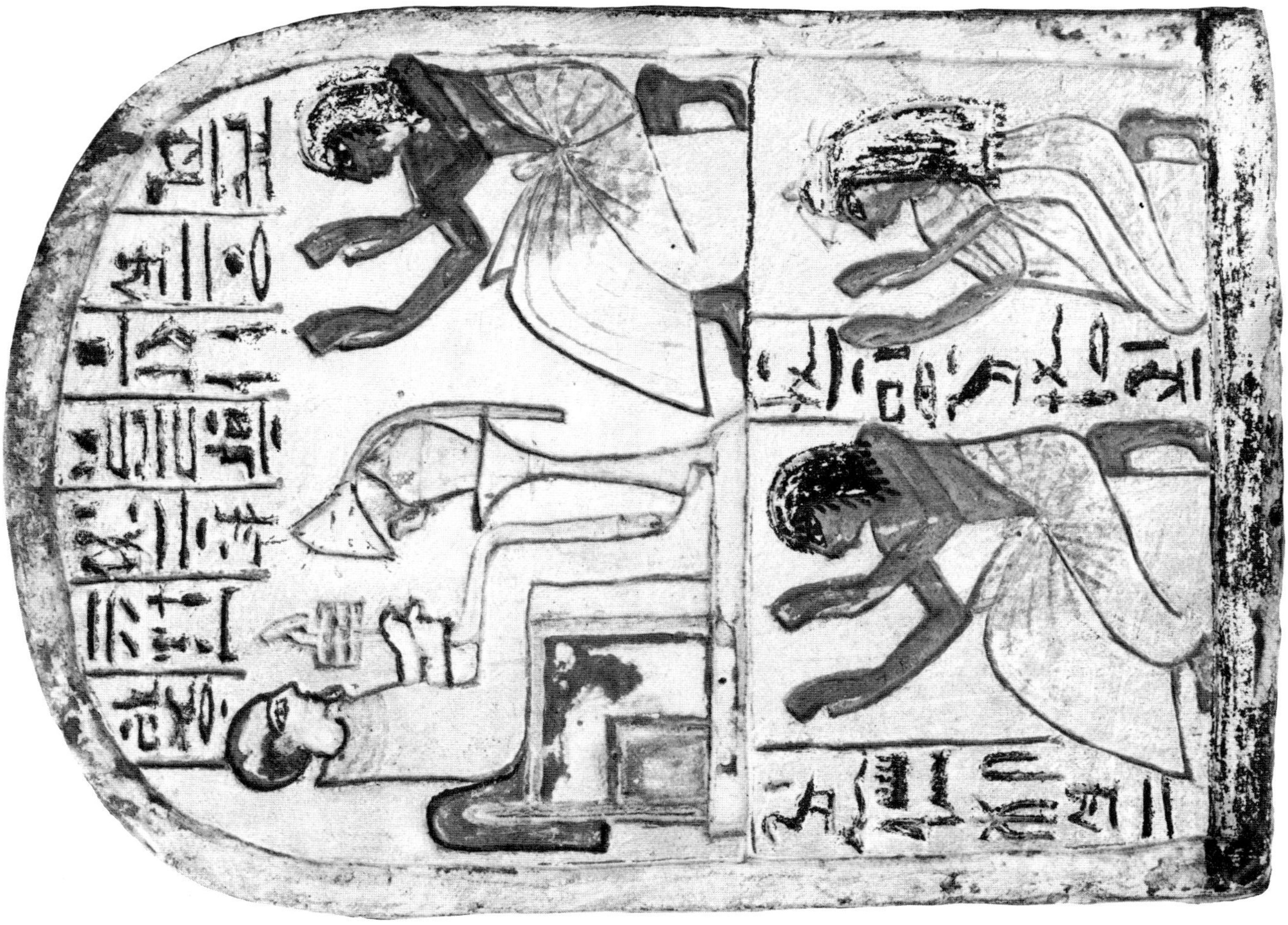

No. 65355

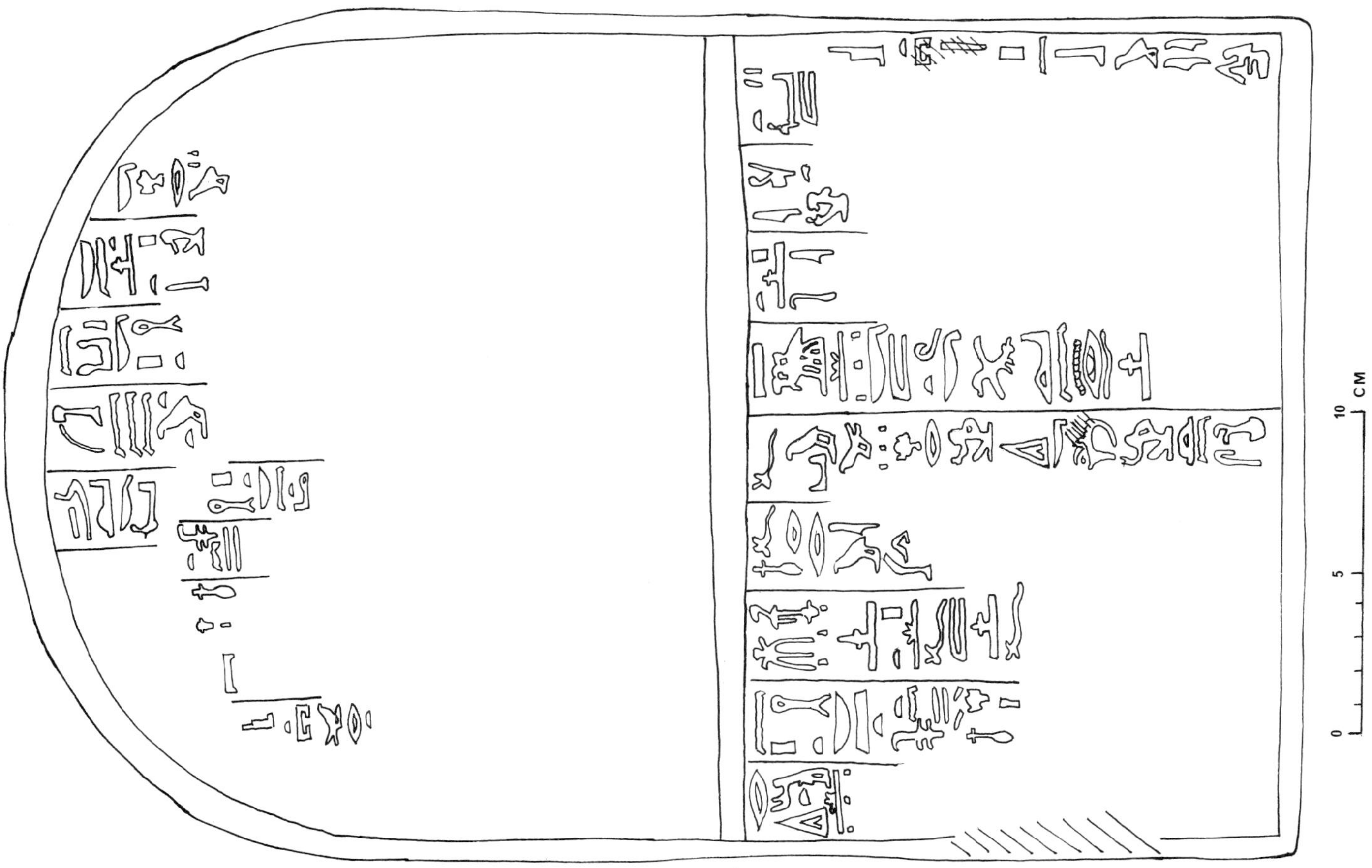

No. 1466

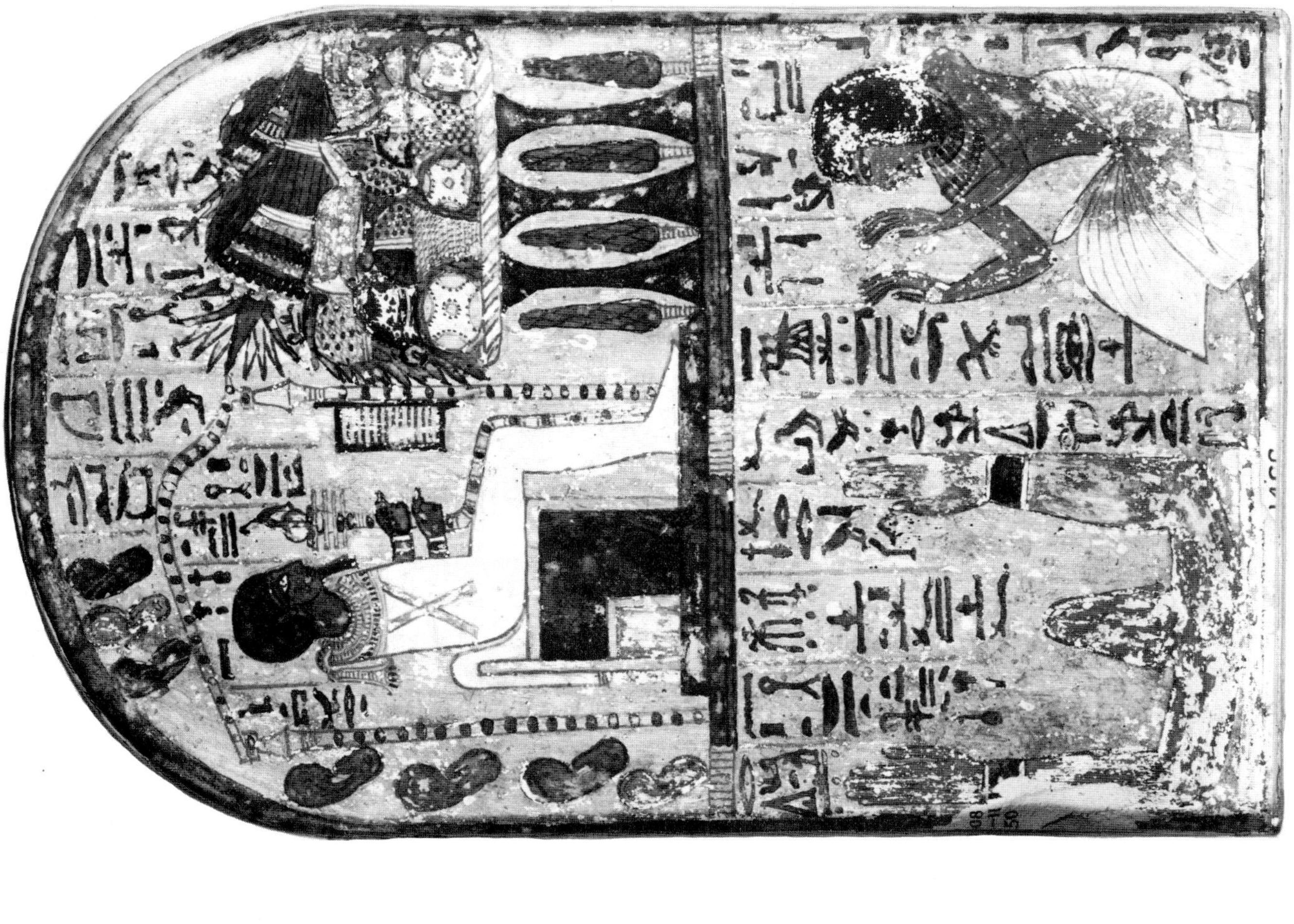

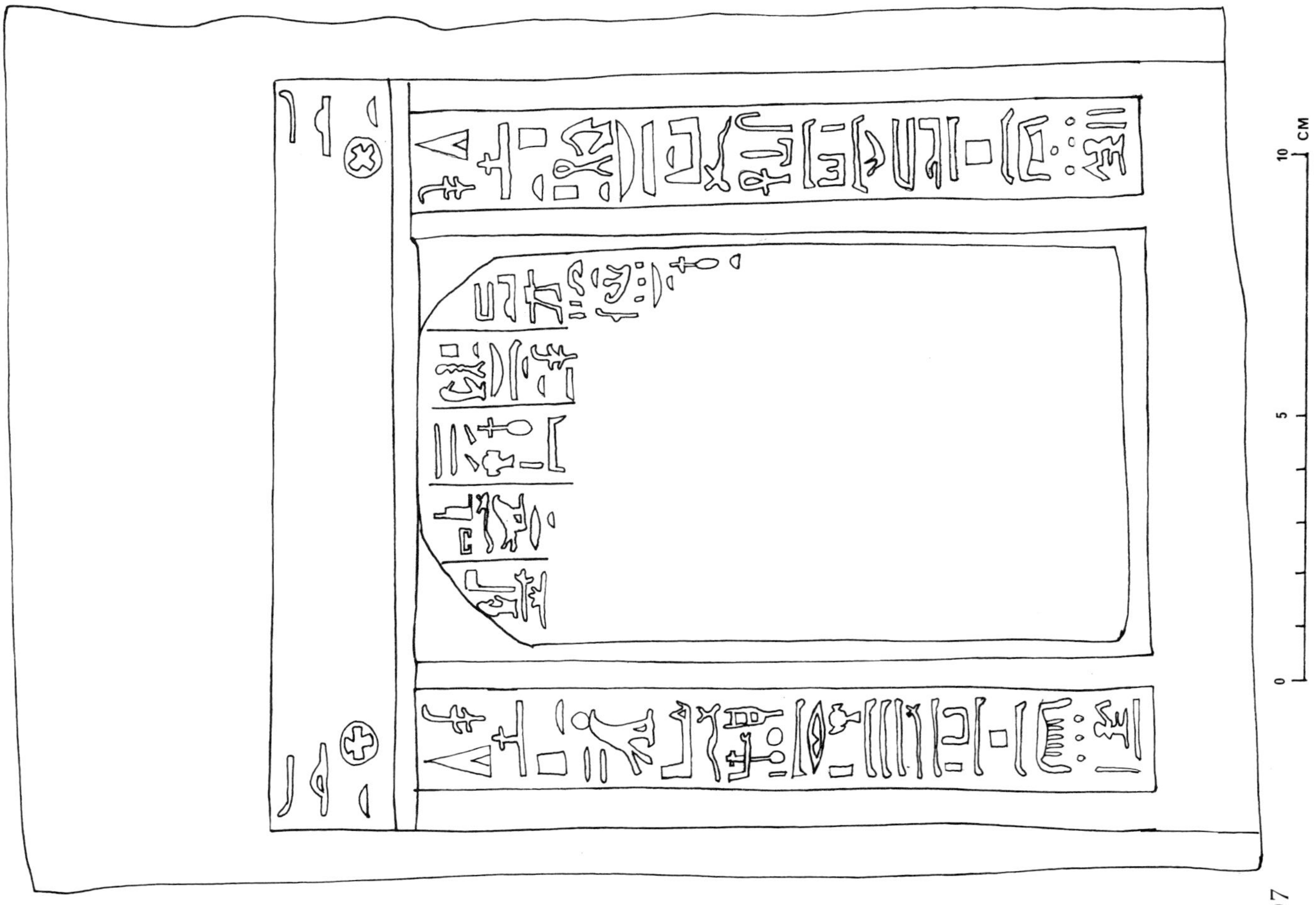

No. 8497

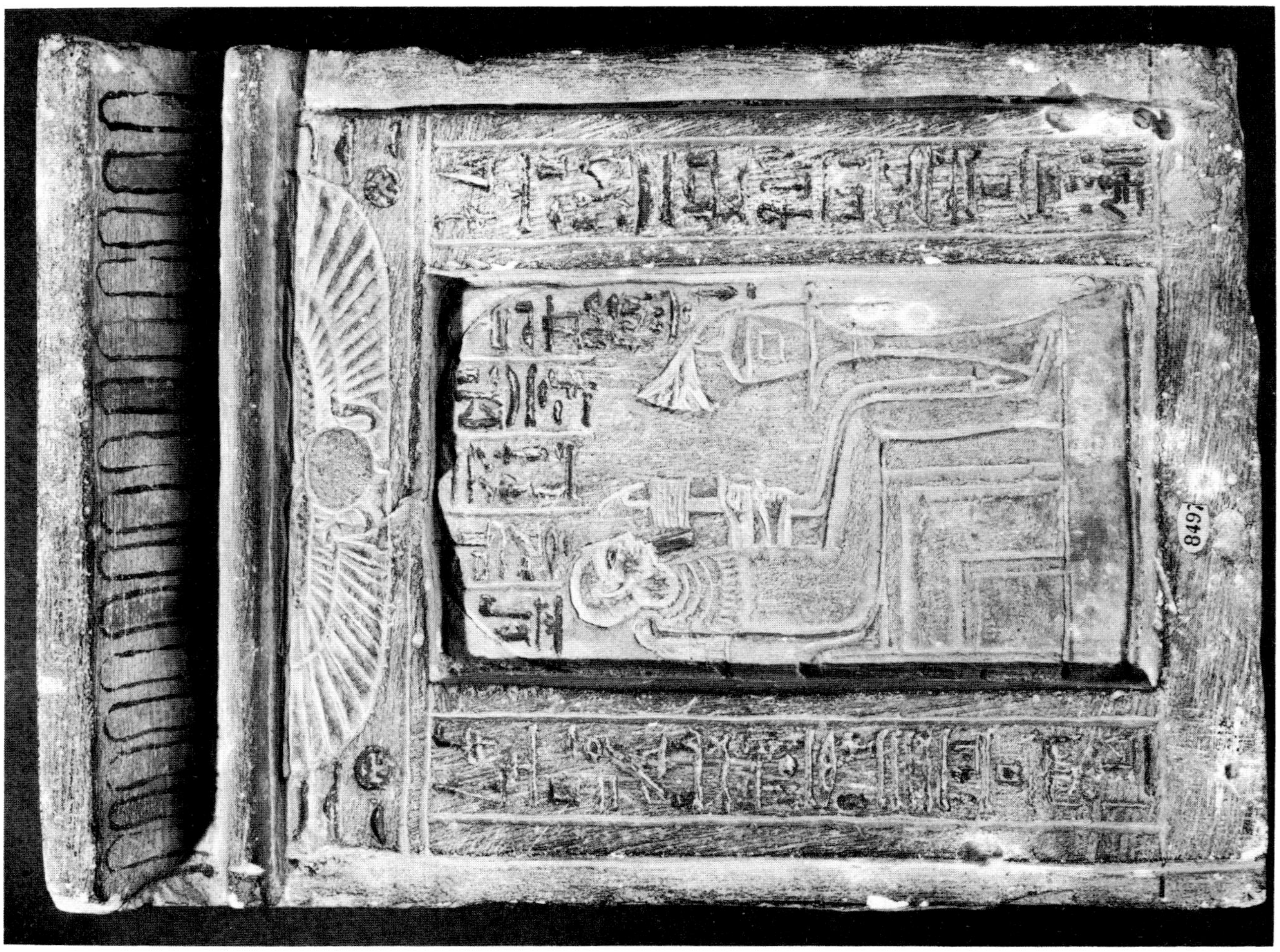

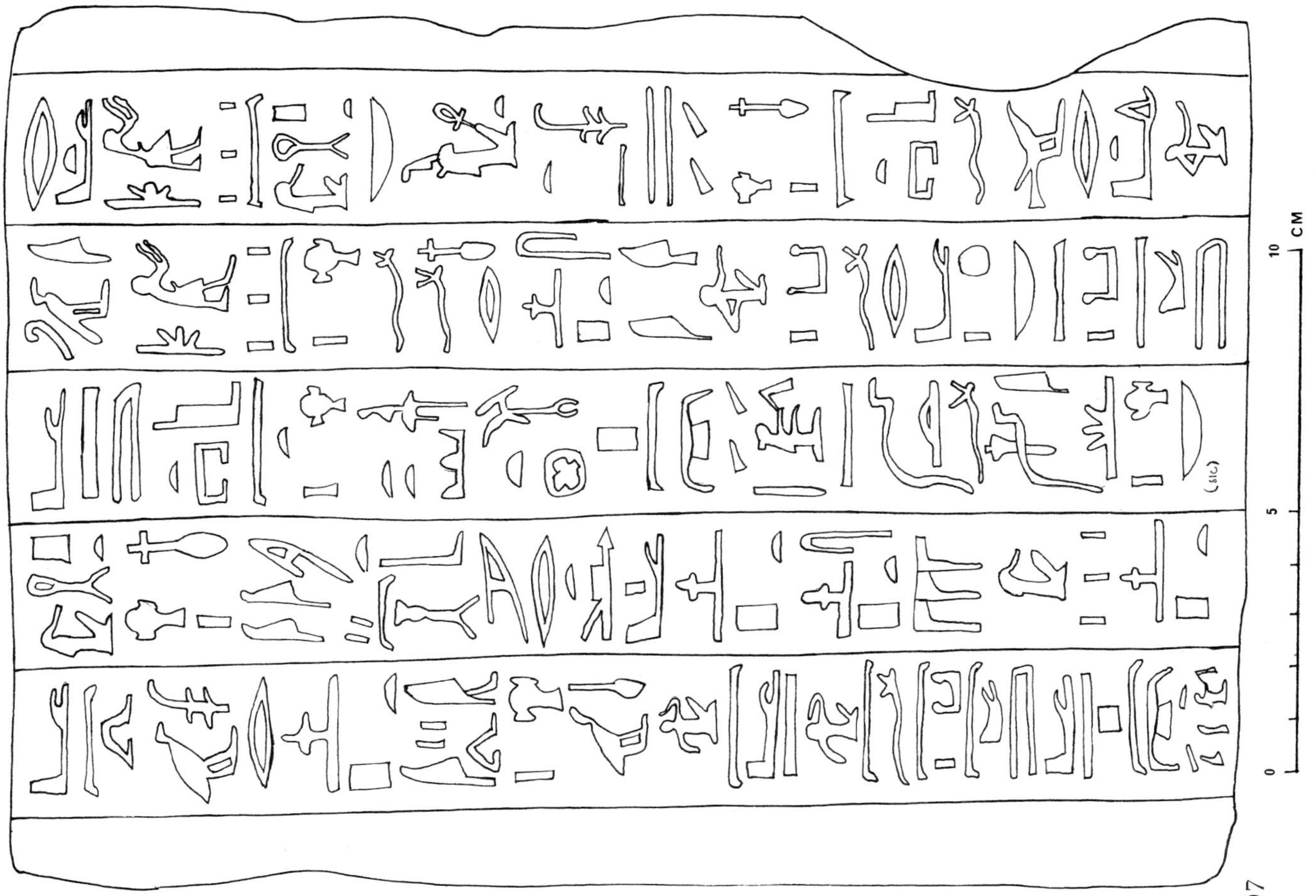

No. 8497

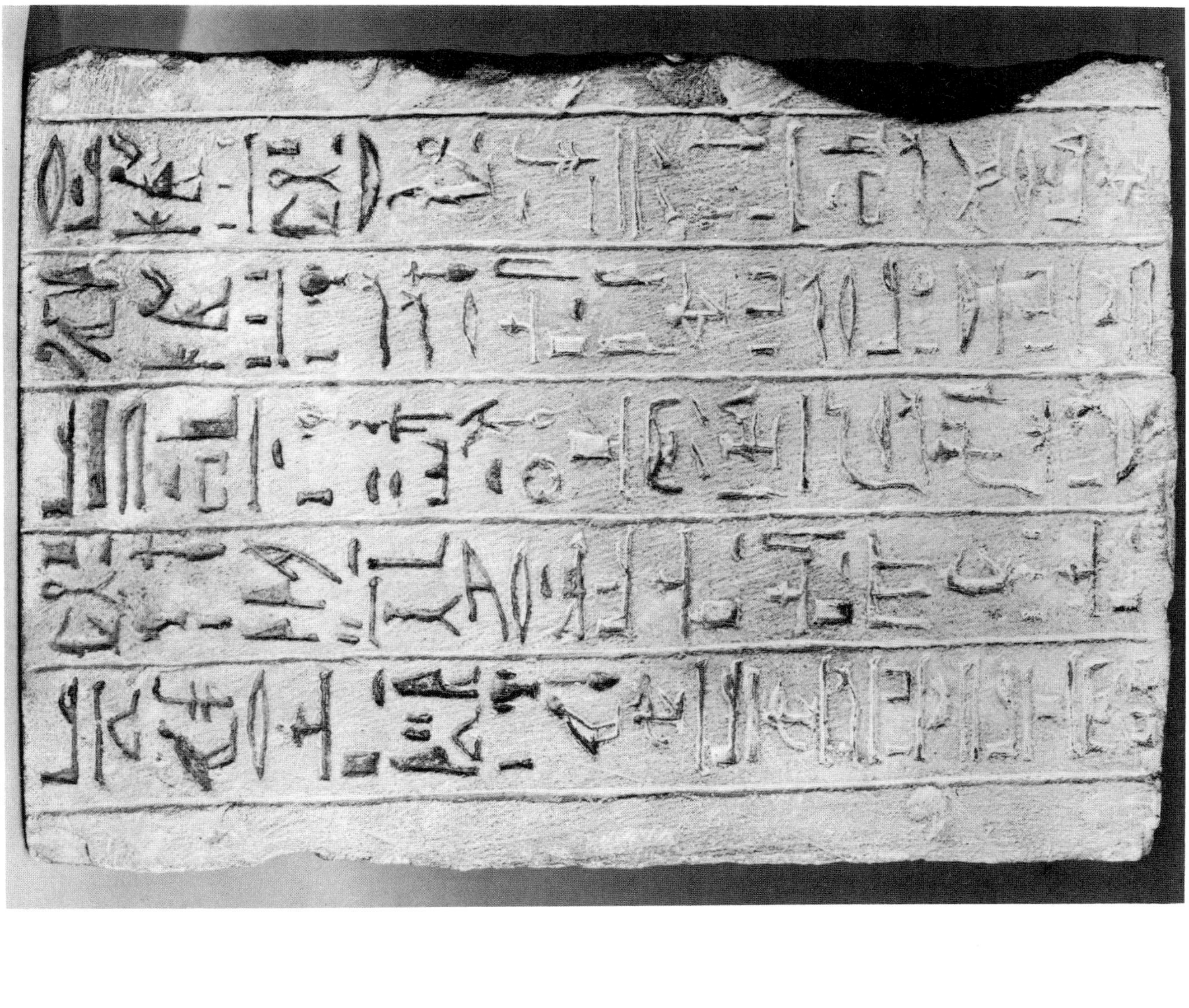

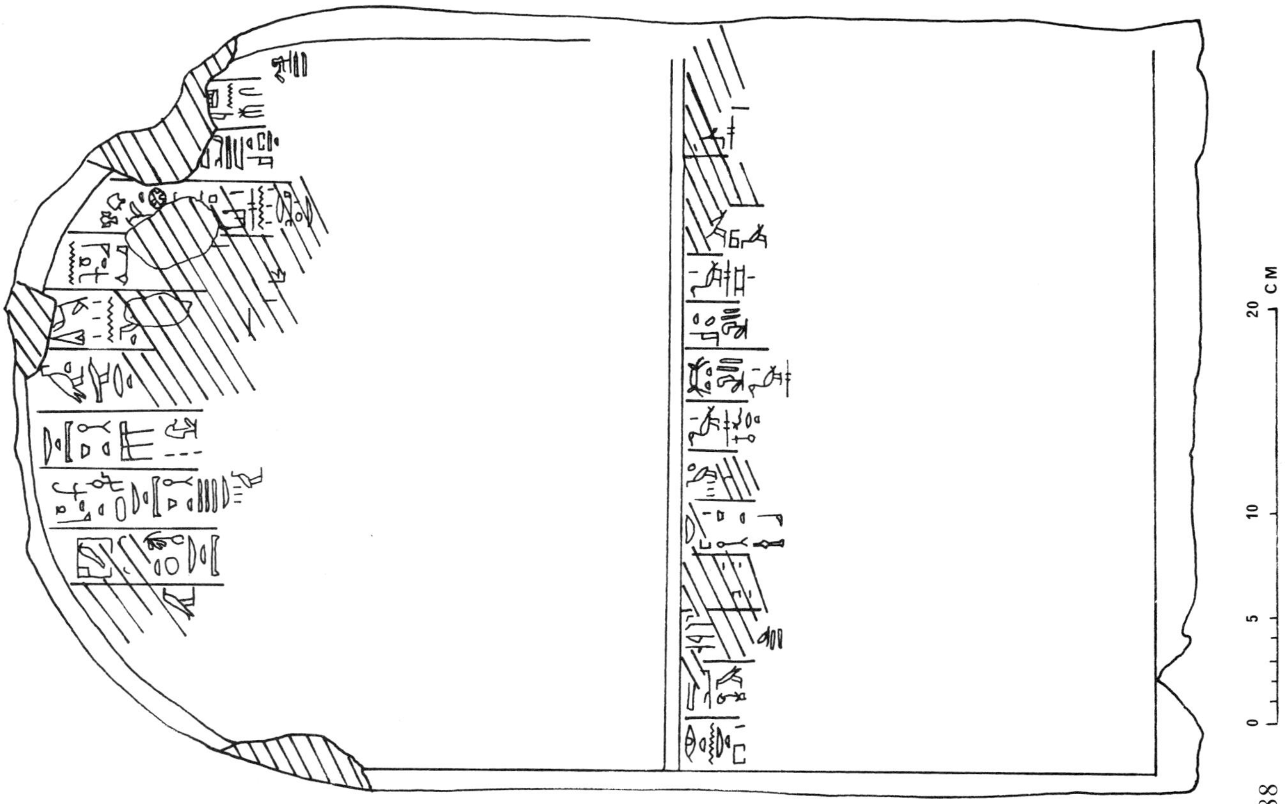

No. 1388

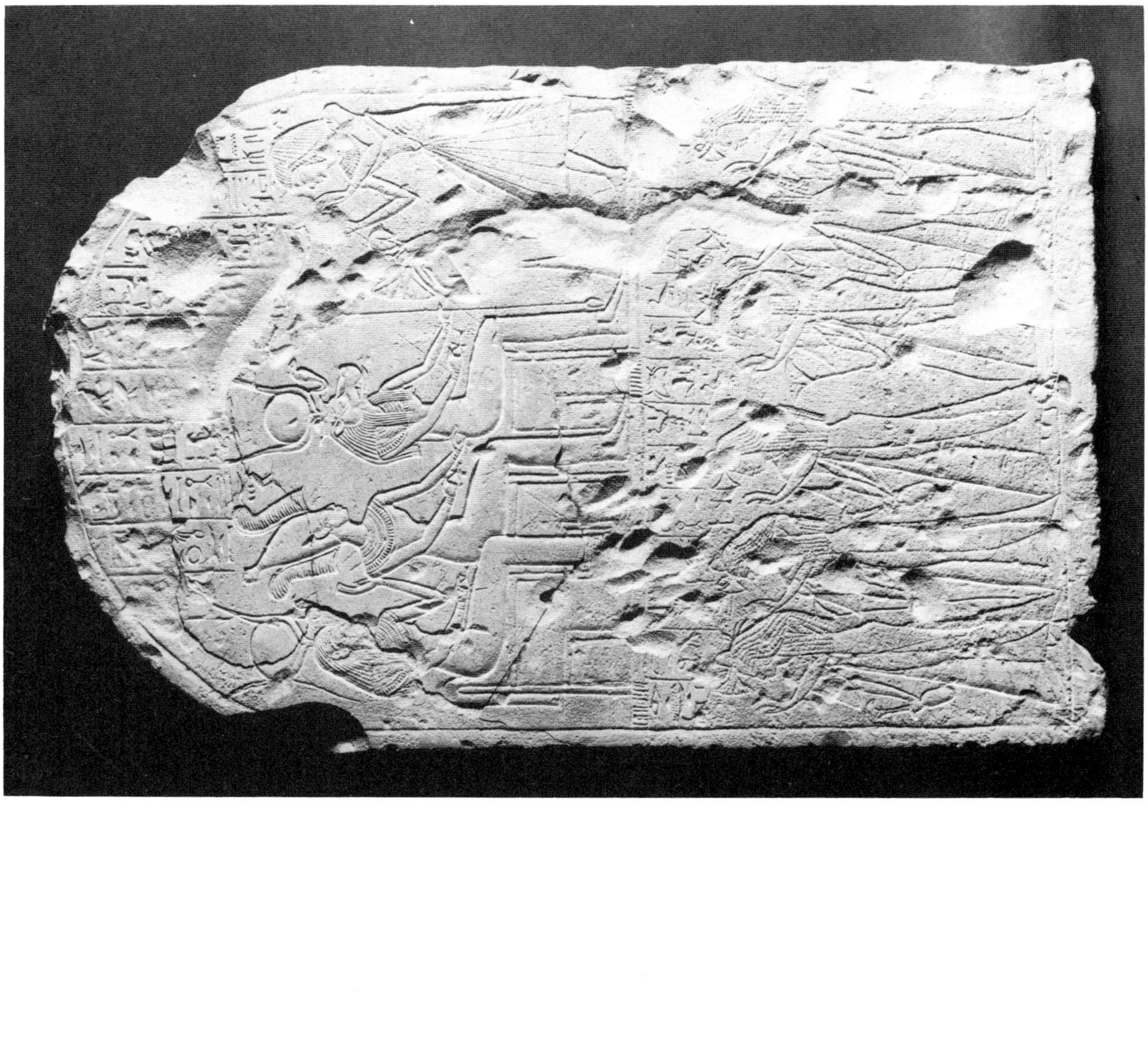

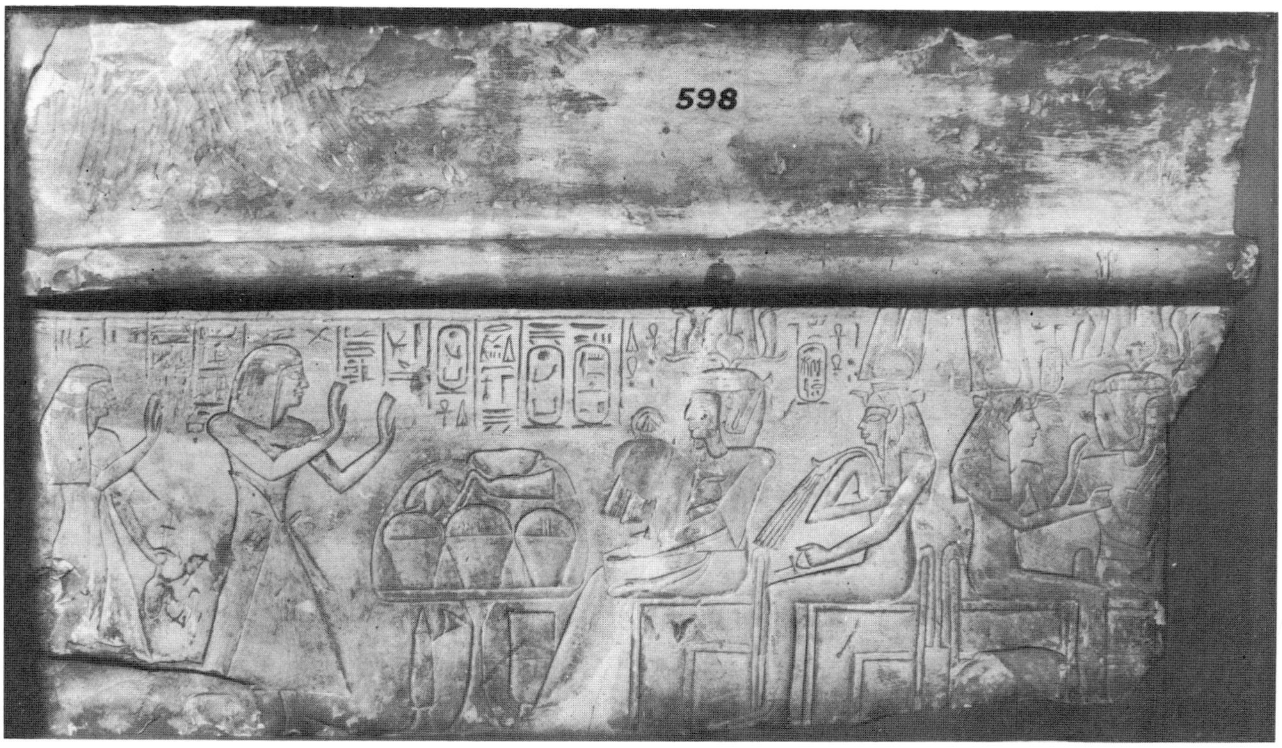

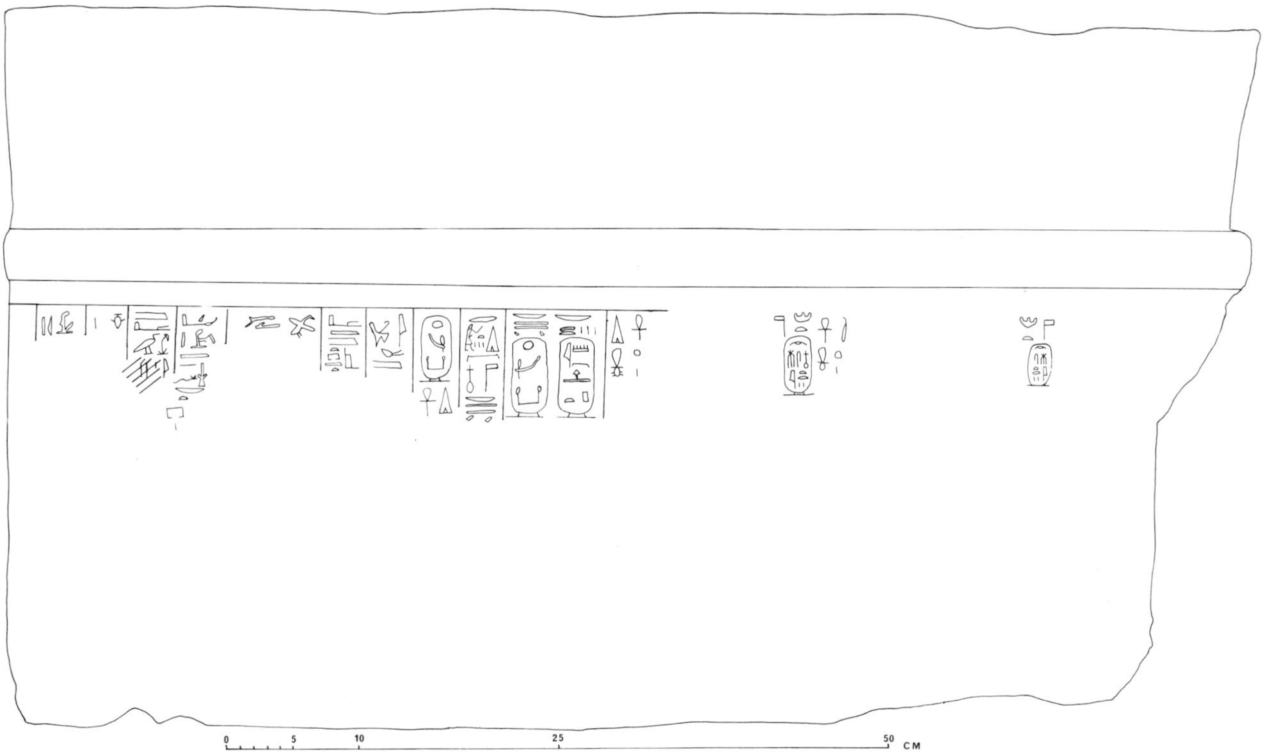

No. 598

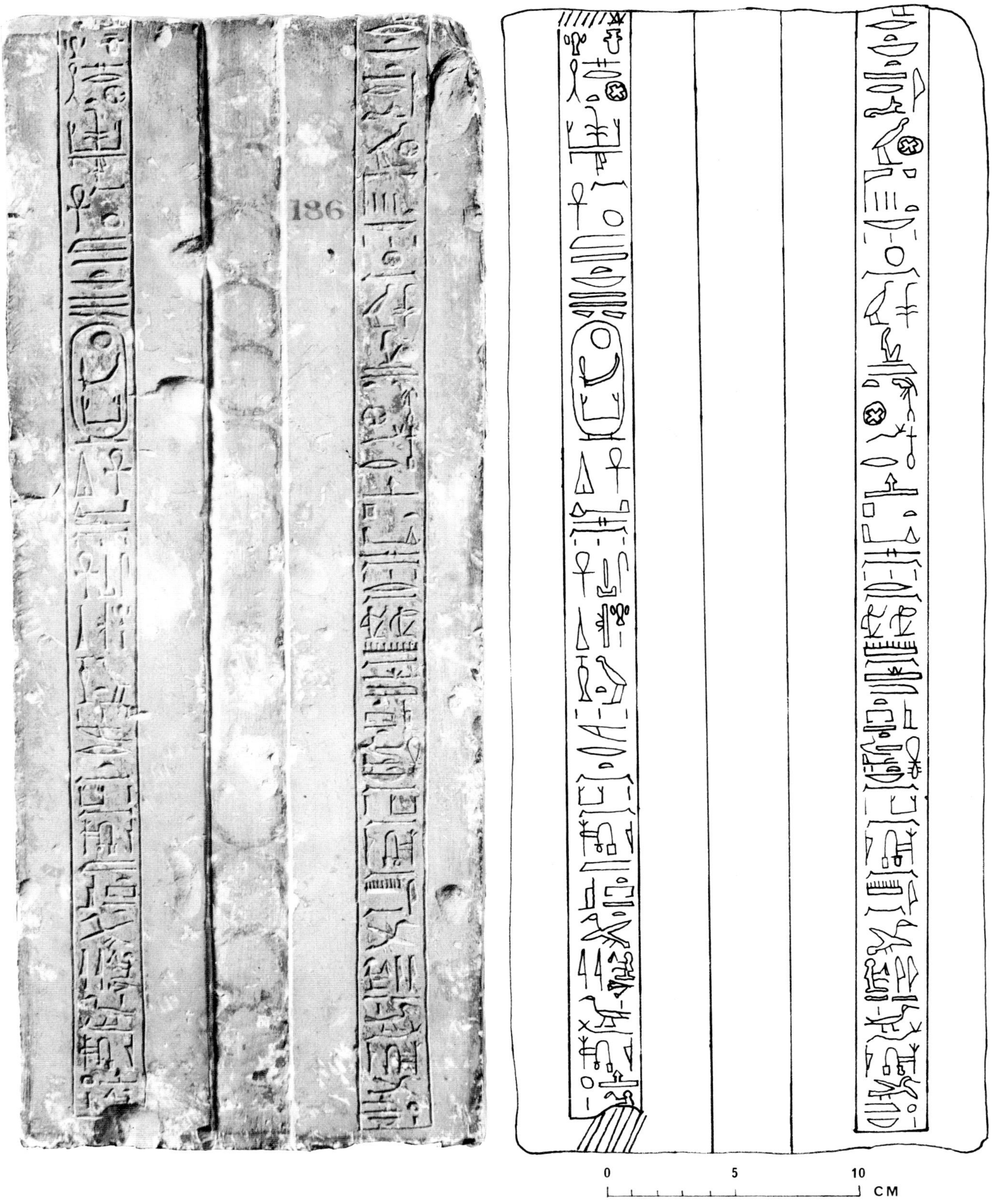

No. 186

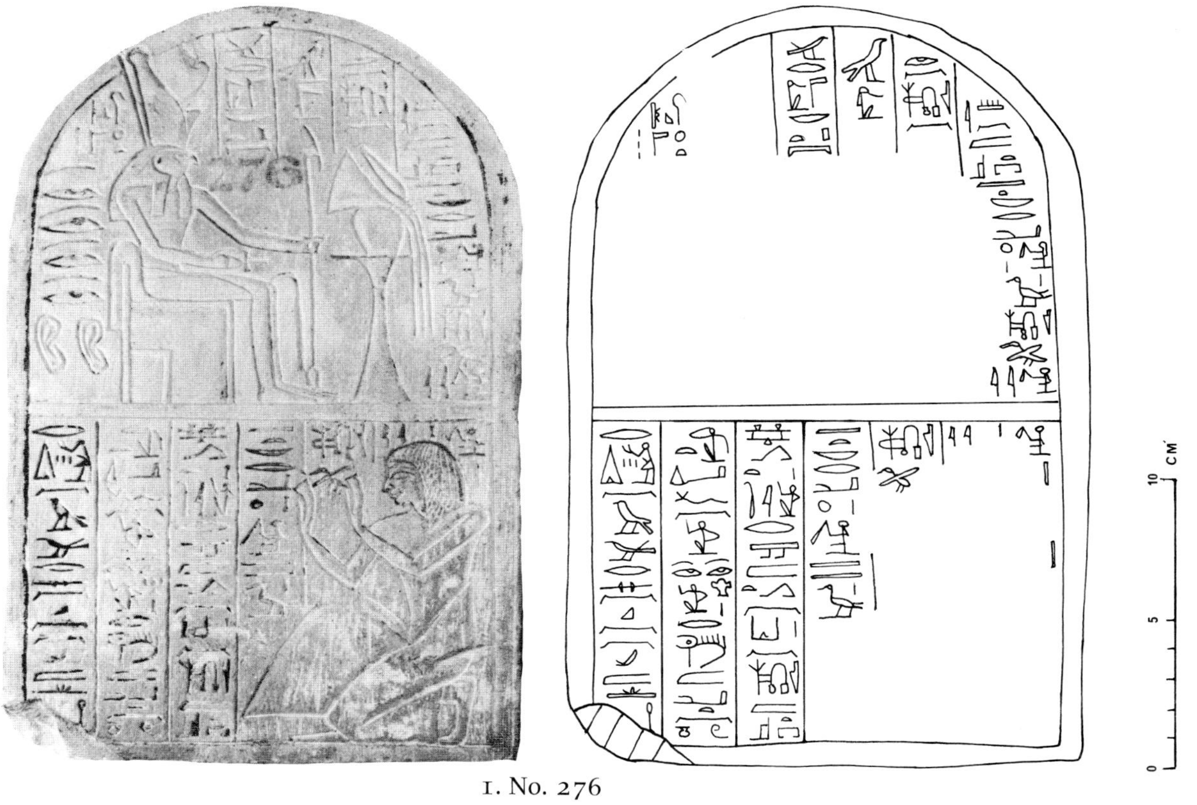

1. No. 276

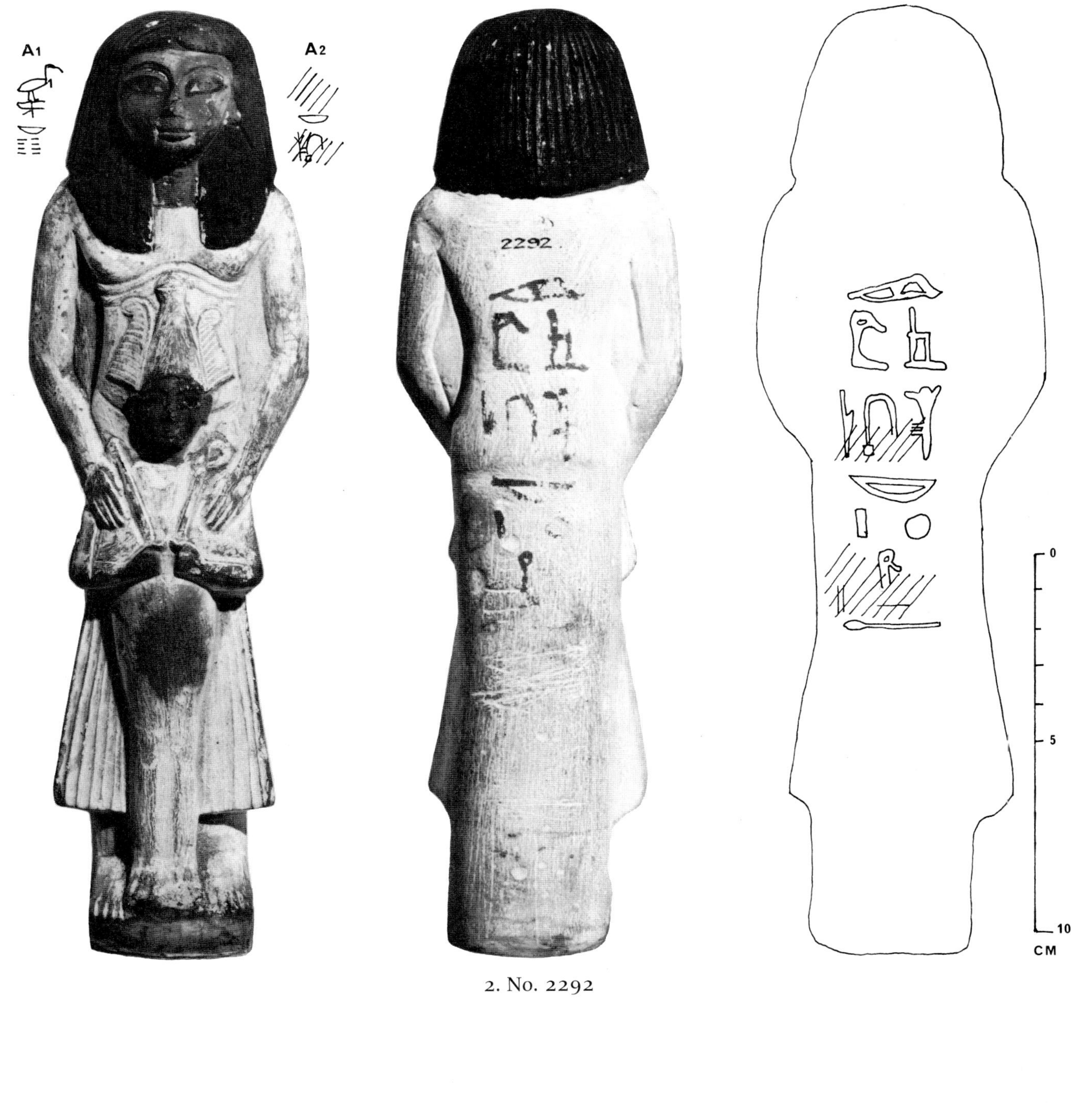

2. No. 2292

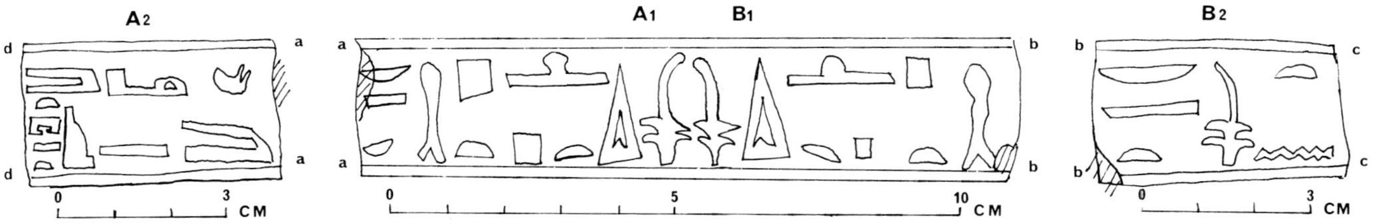

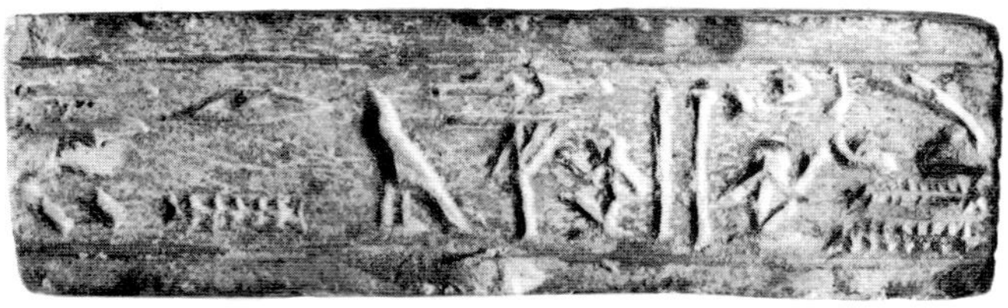

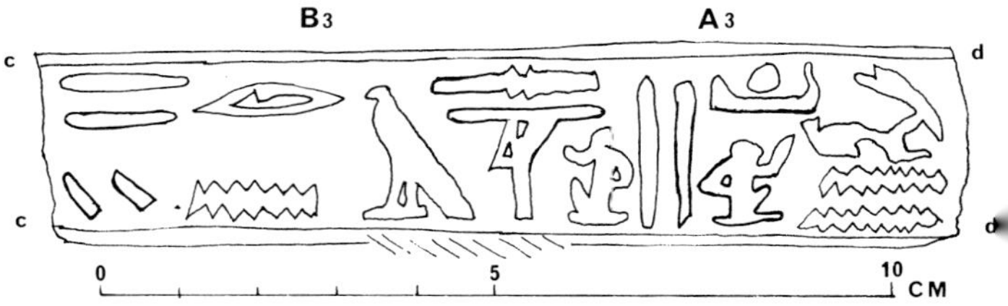

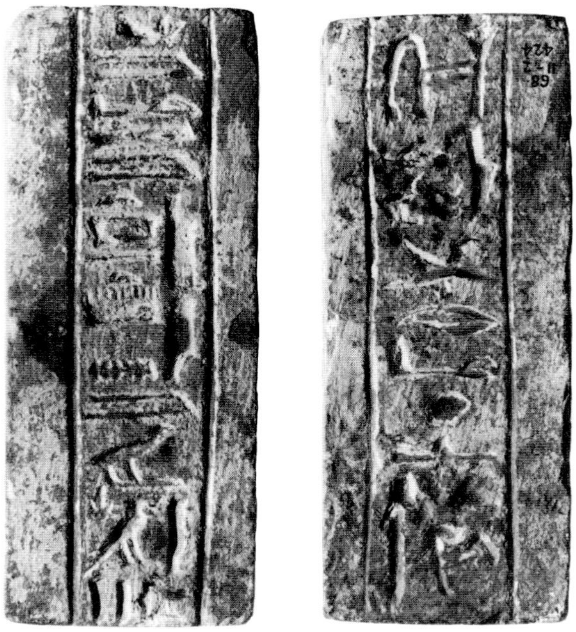

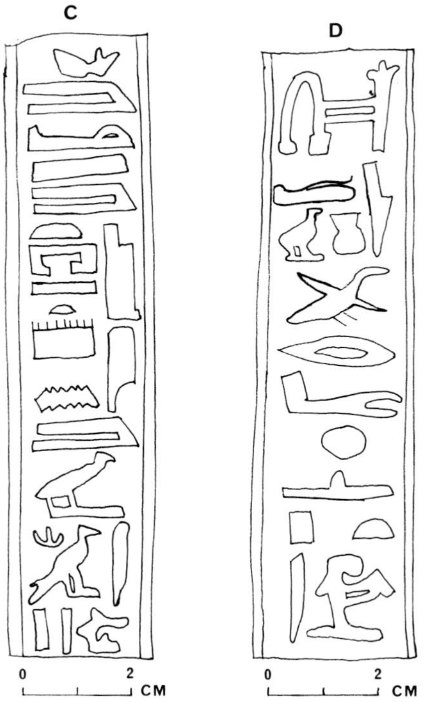

No. 36861

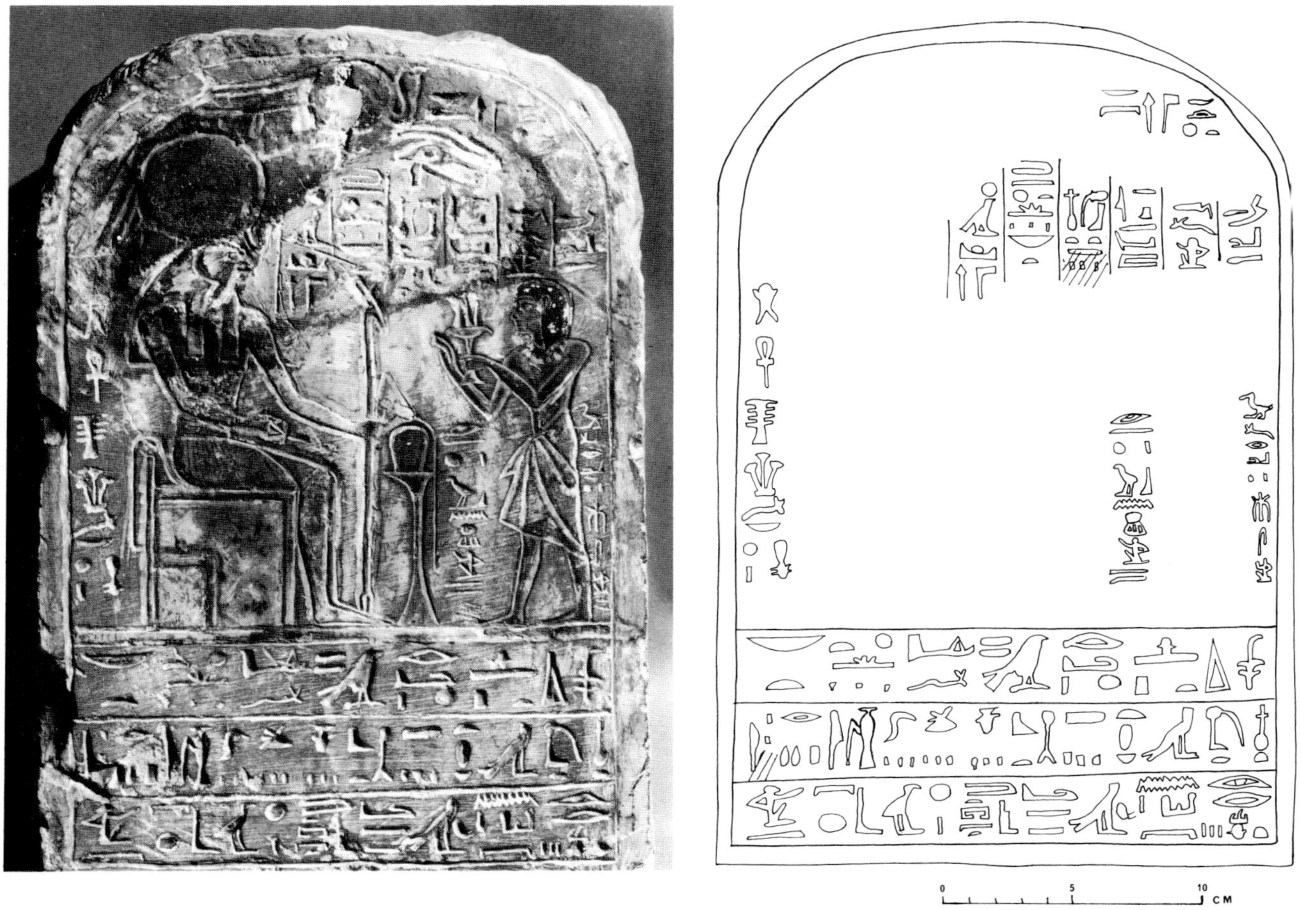

1. No. 1248

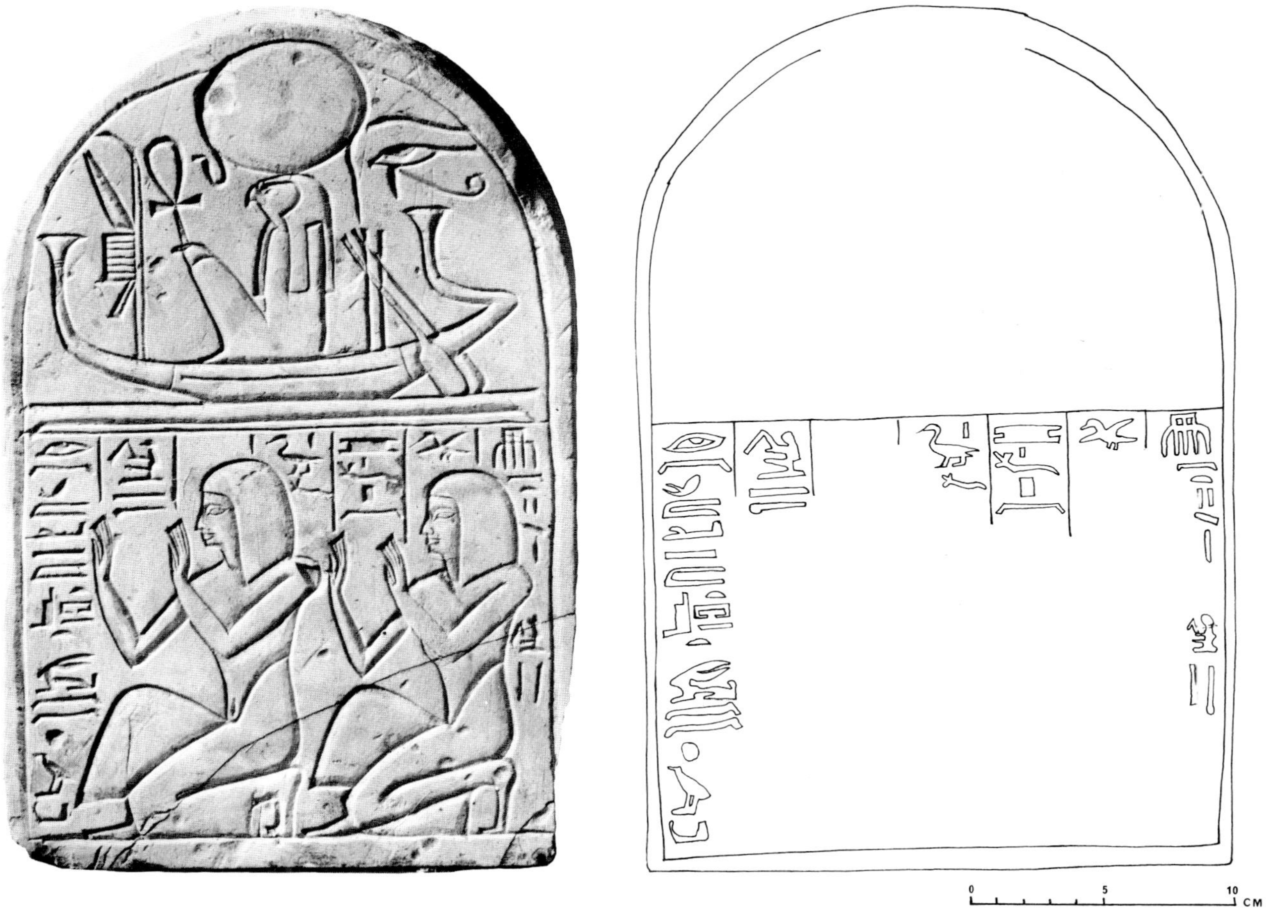

2. No. 320

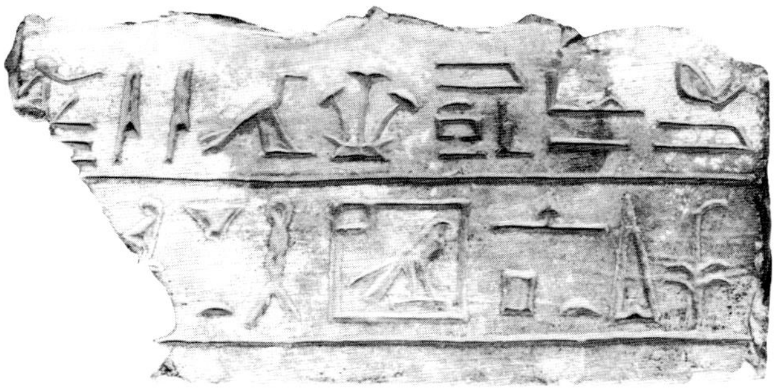

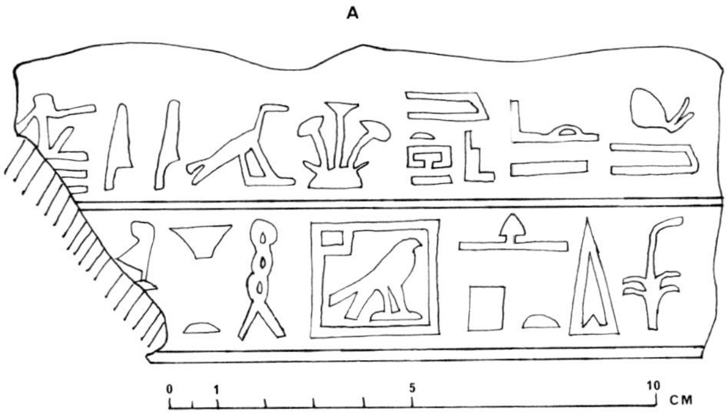
A
0 1 5 10 CM

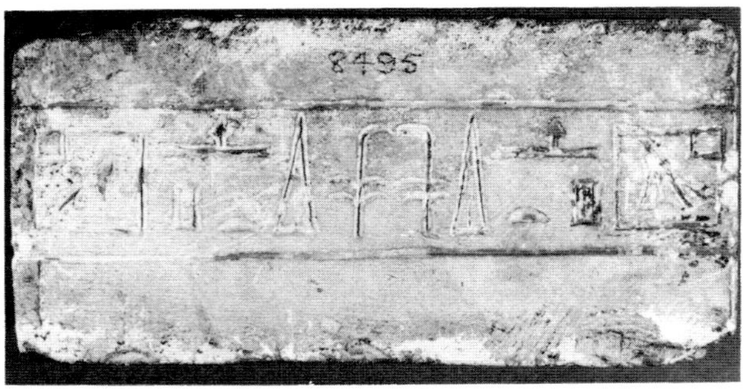
8495

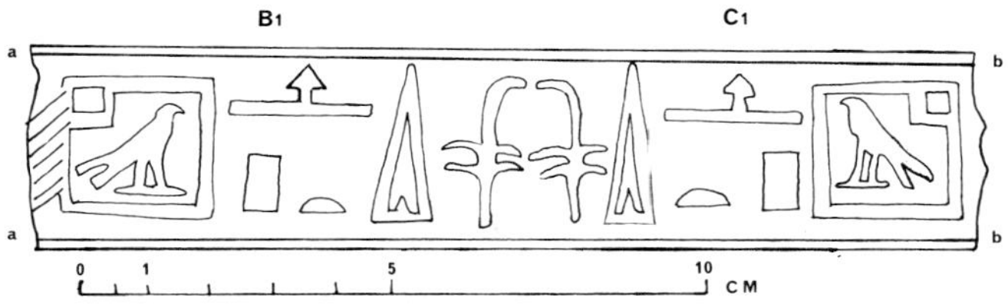
B1
C1
a
b
0 1 5 10 CM

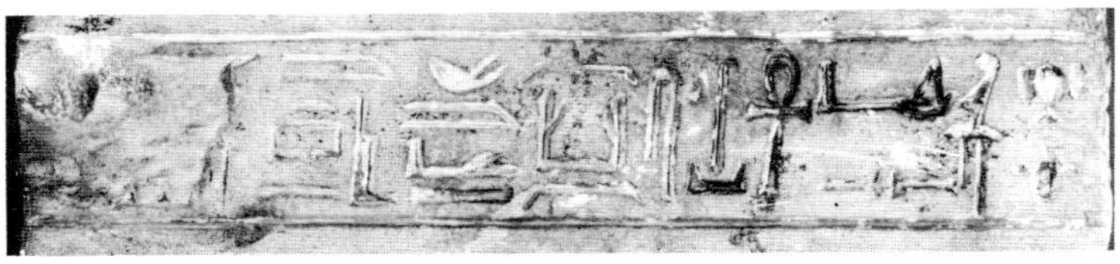

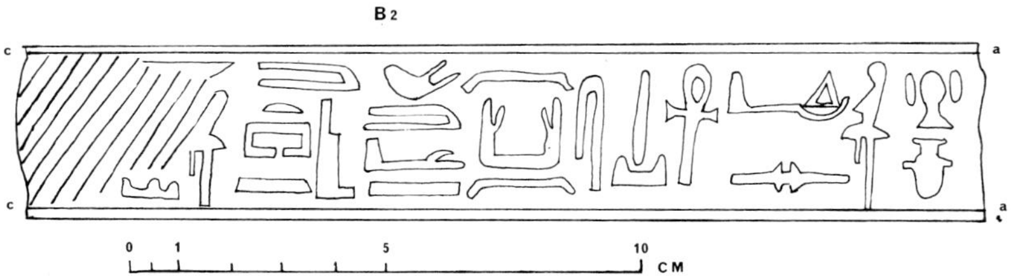
B2
c
a
0 1 5 10 CM

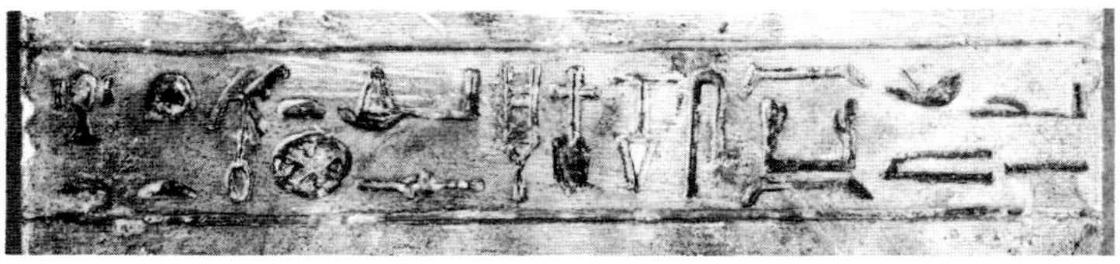

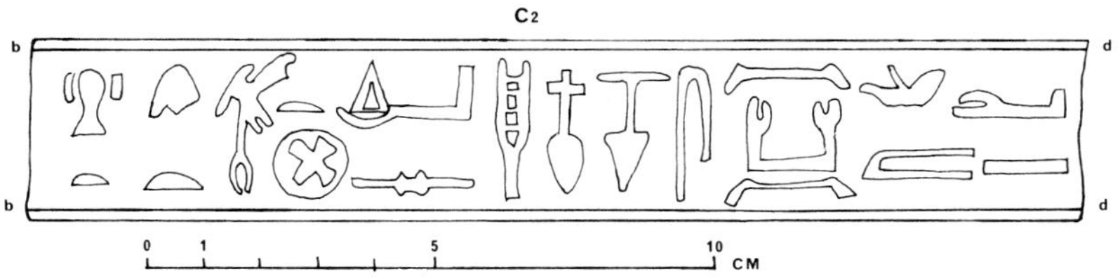
C2
b
d
0 1 5 10 CM

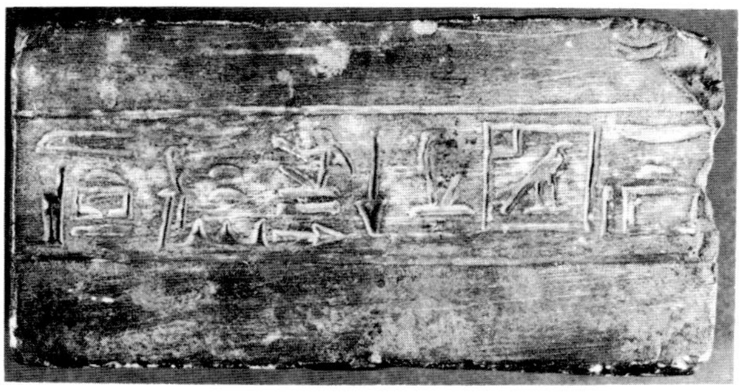

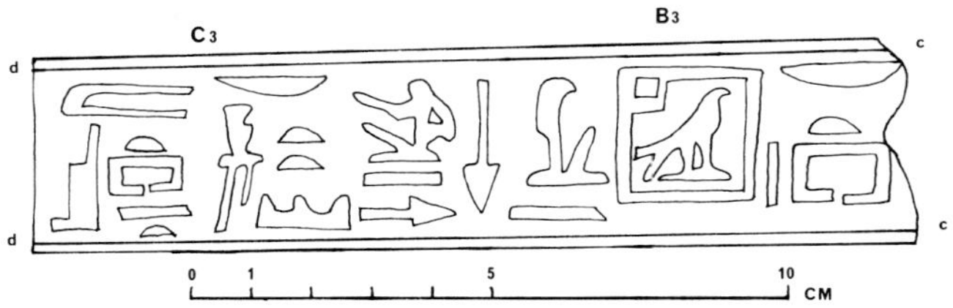
C3
B3
d
c
0 1 5 10 CM

No. 8495

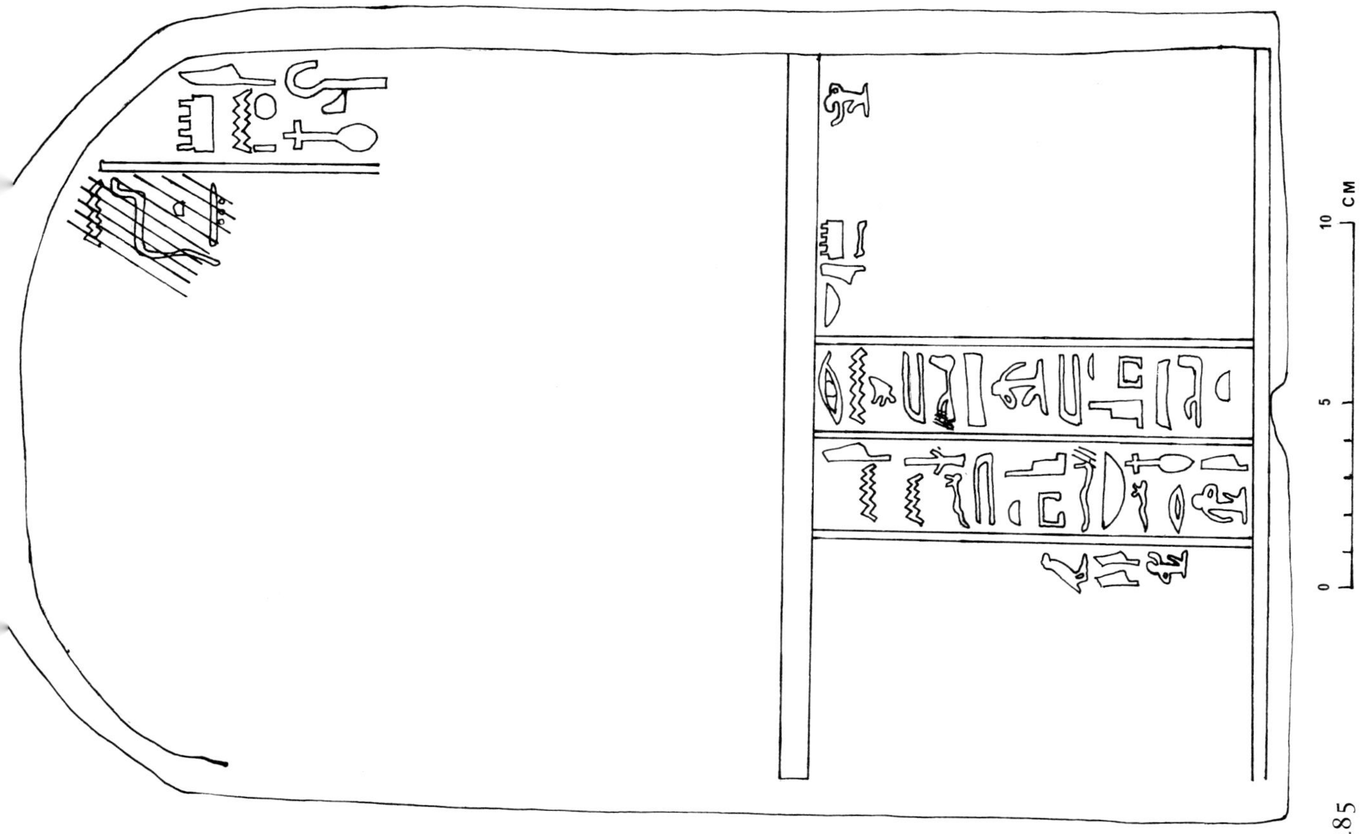

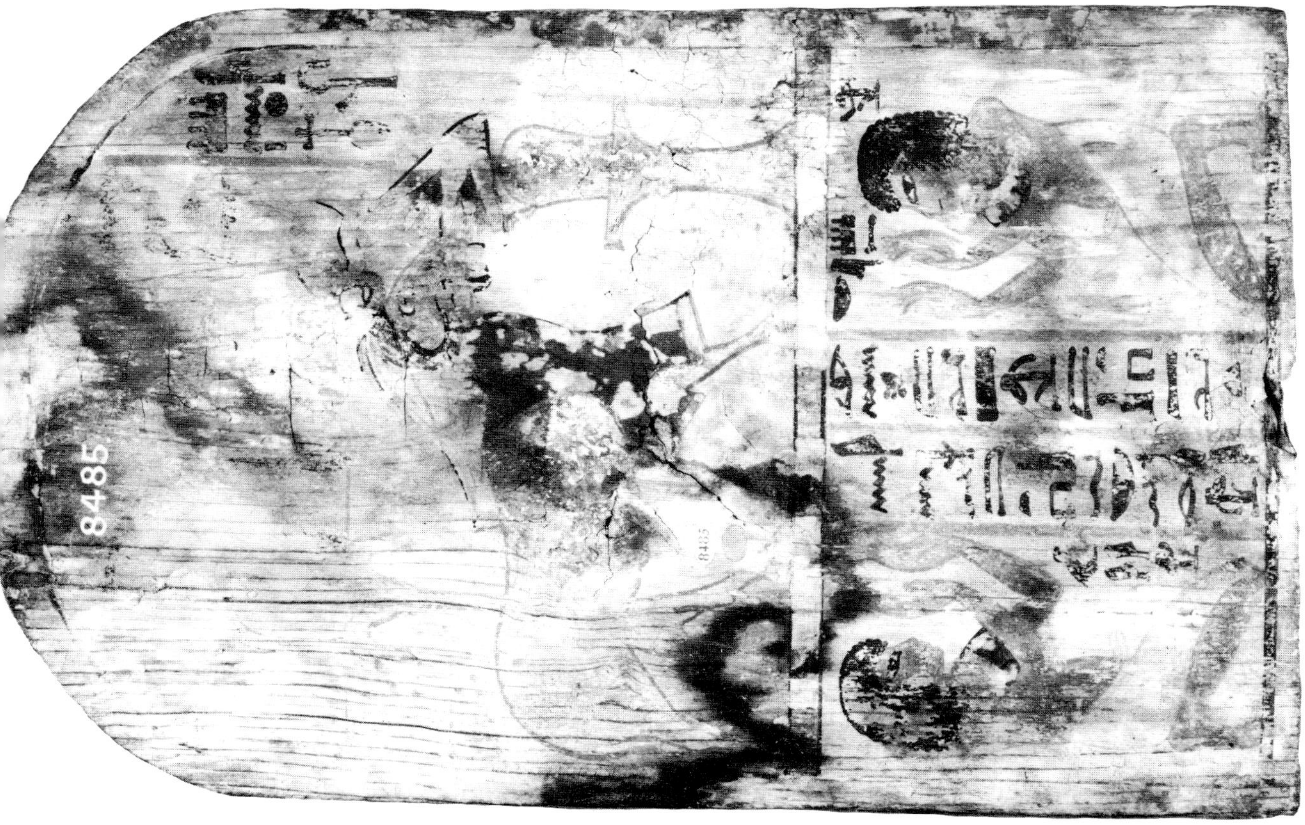

No. 8485

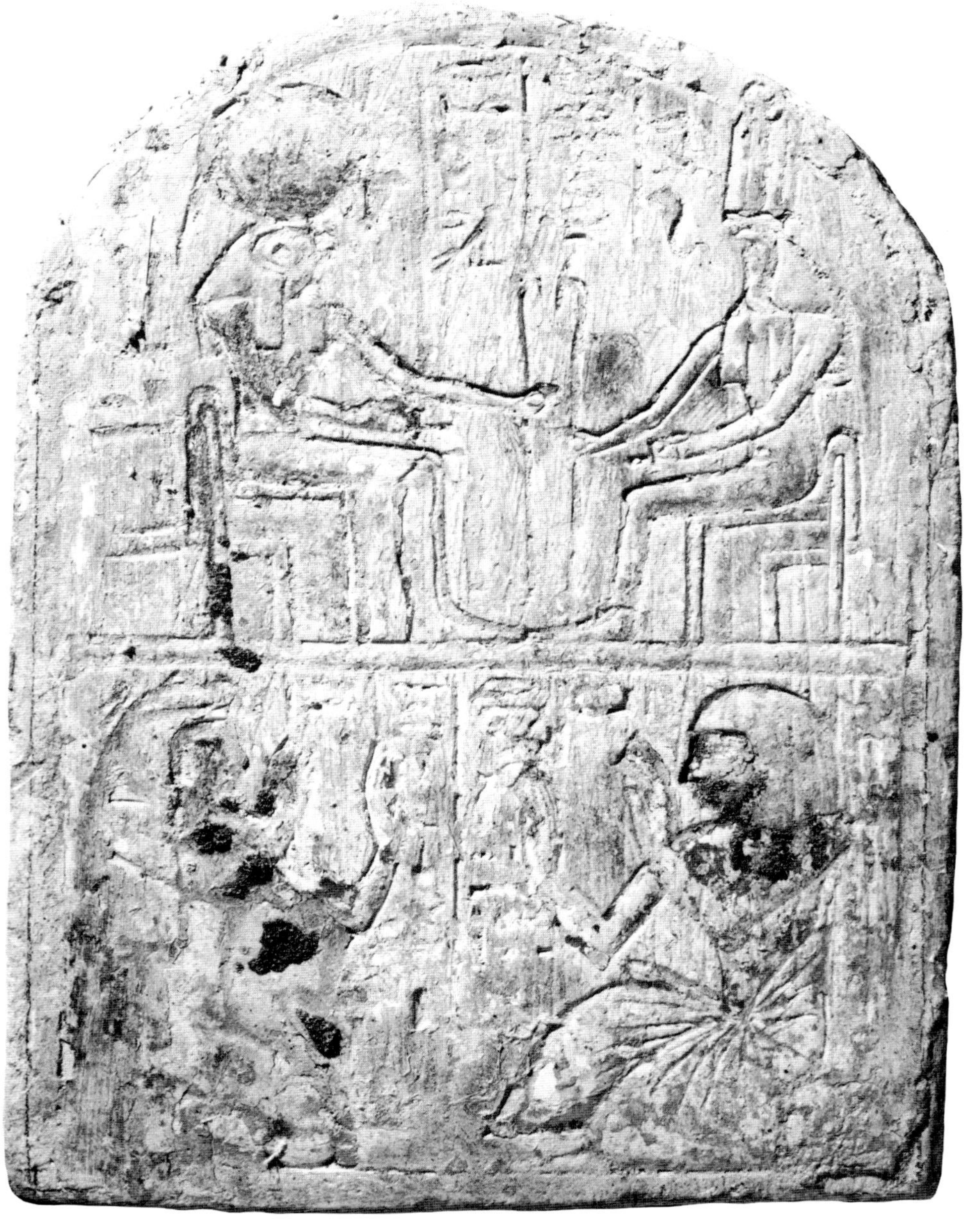

1. No. 8493

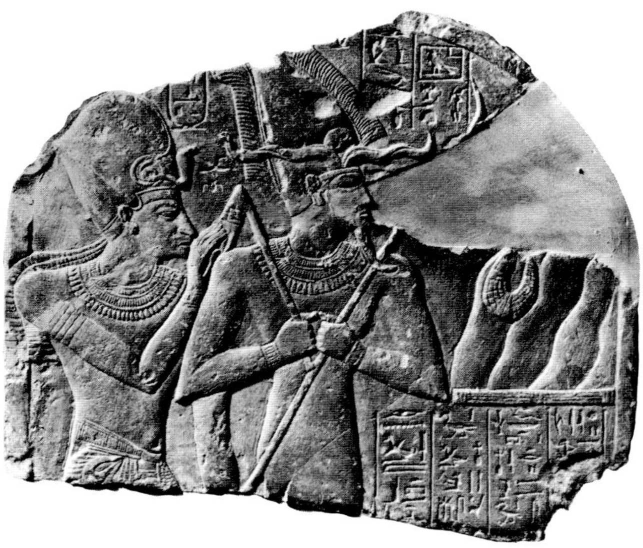

2. No. 815

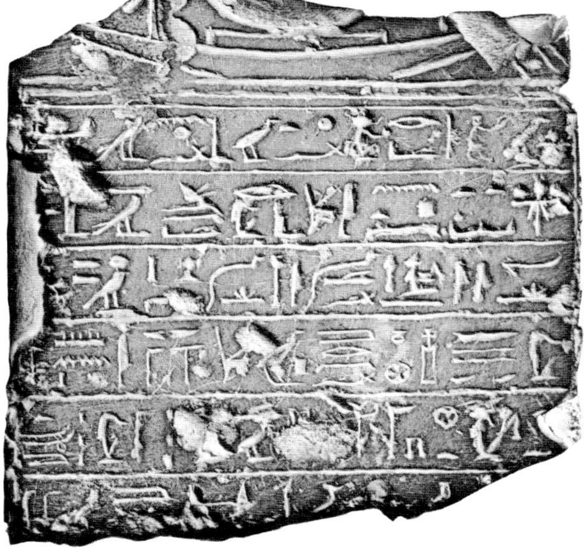

3. No. 942

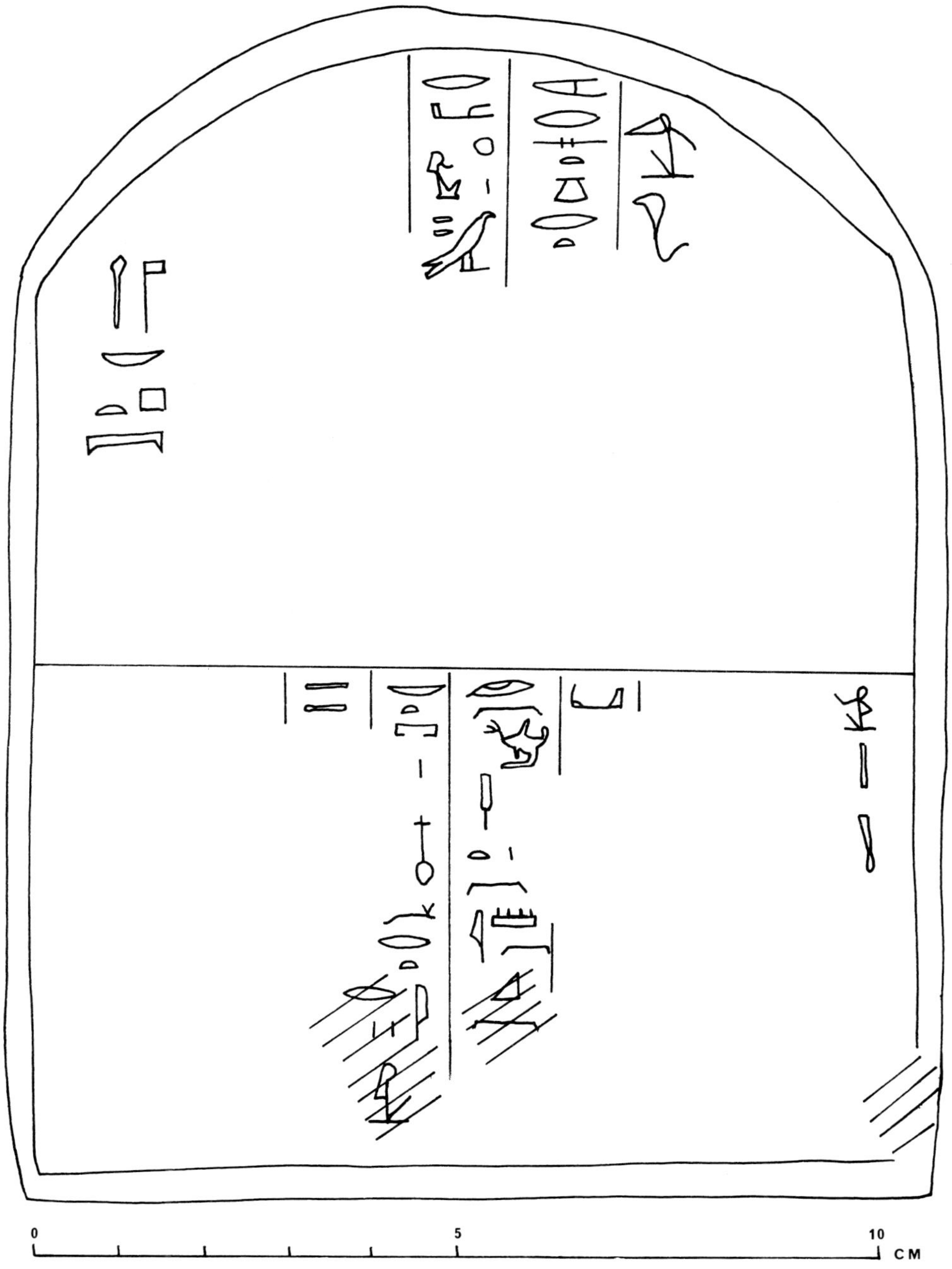

1. No. 8493

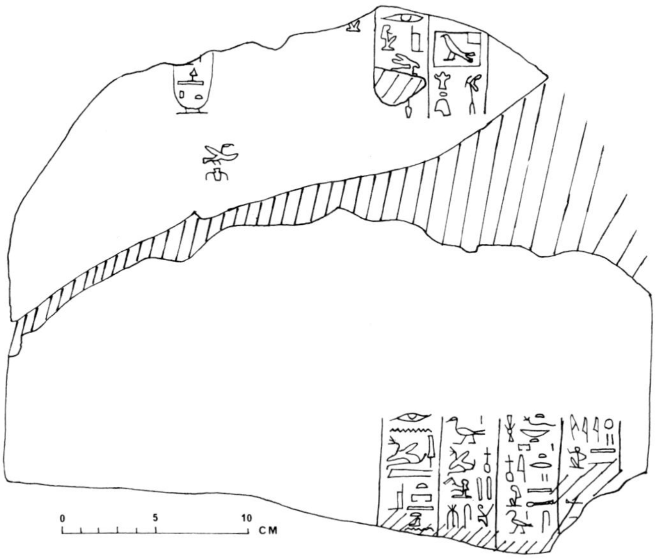

2. No. 815

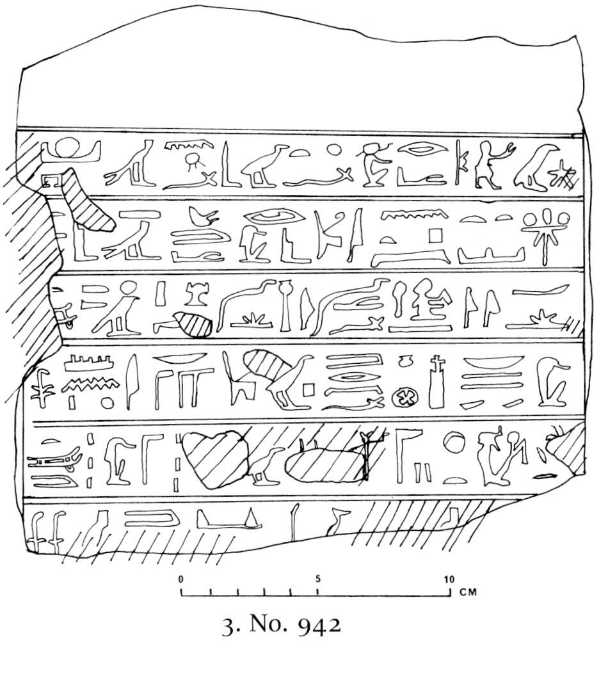

3. No. 942

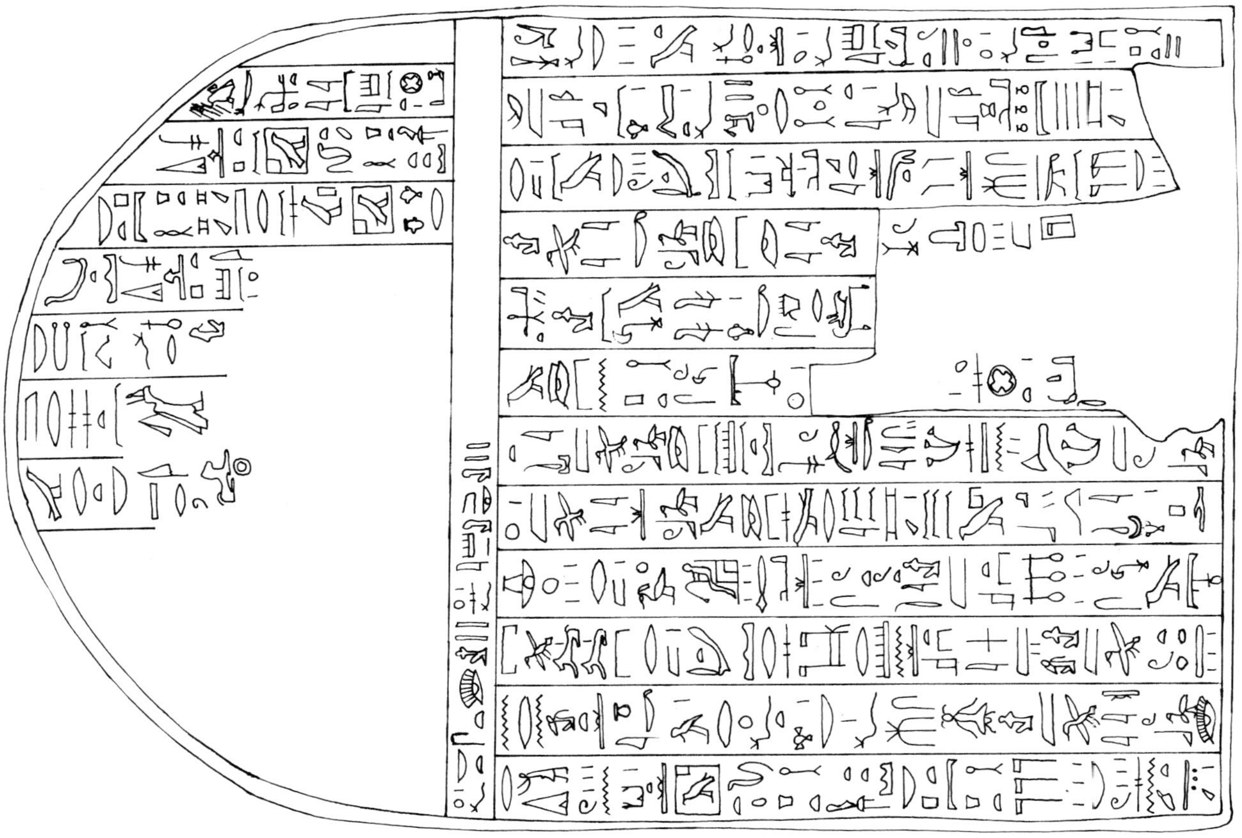

No. 278

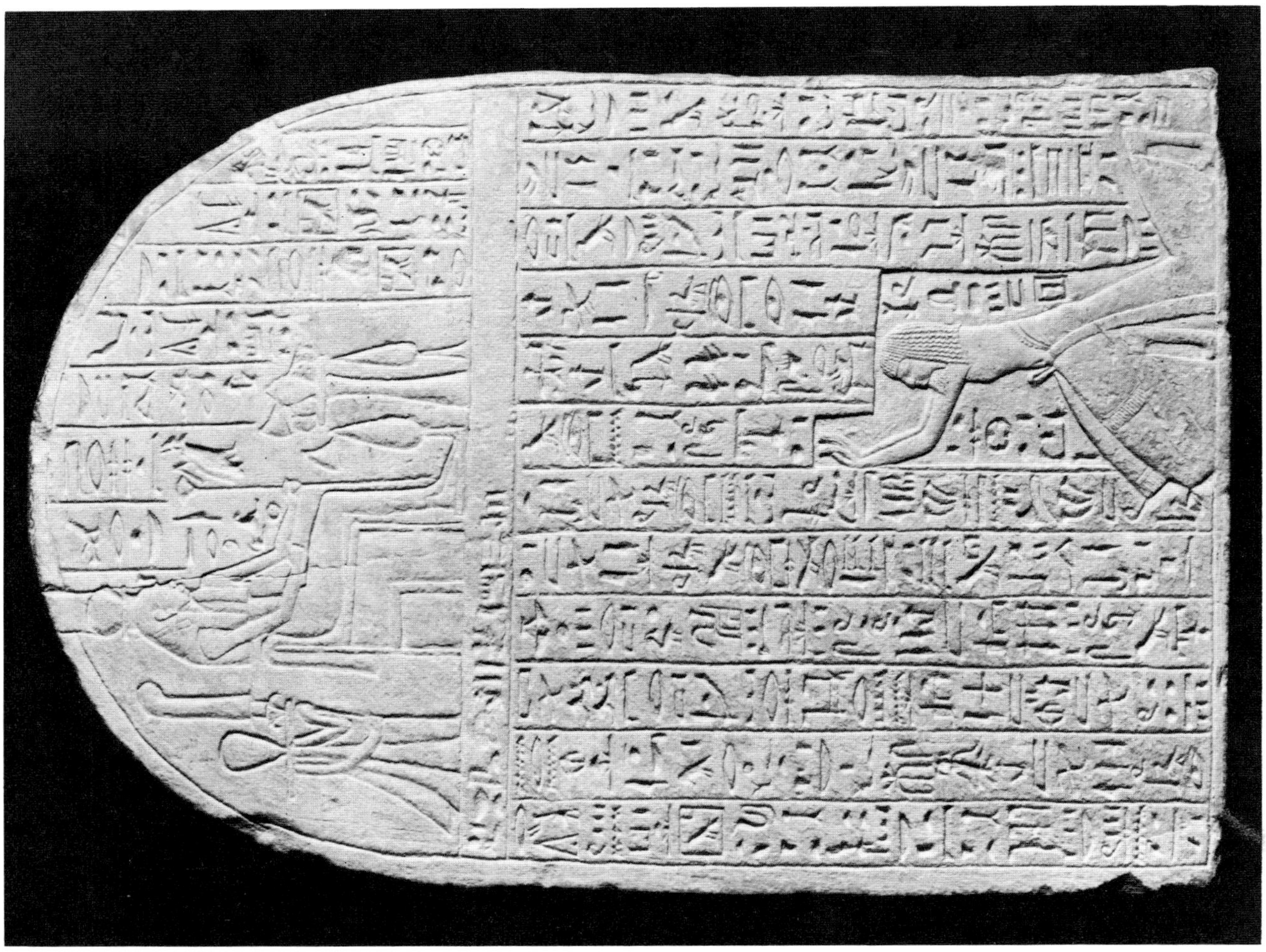

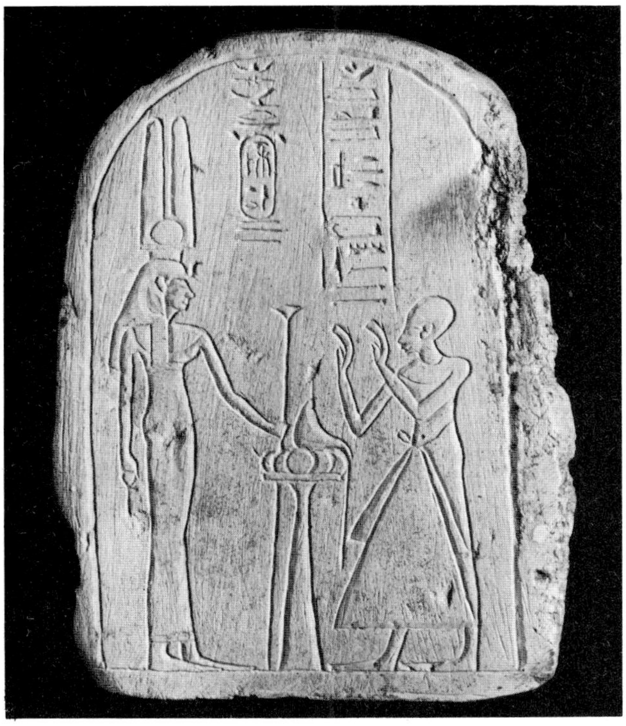

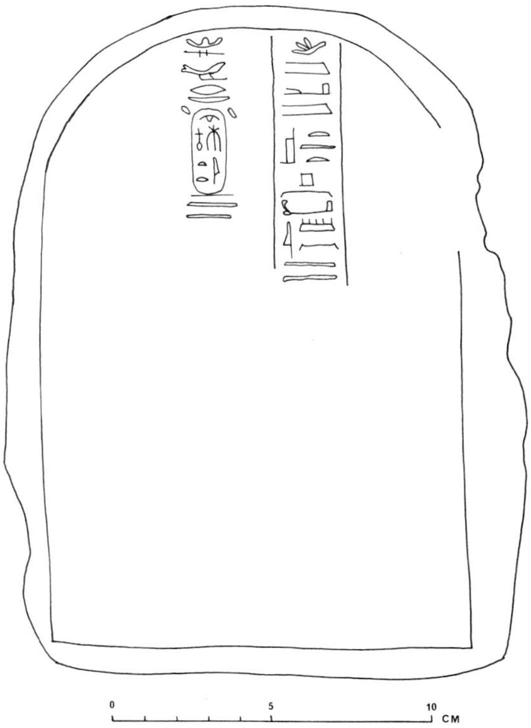

1. No. 916

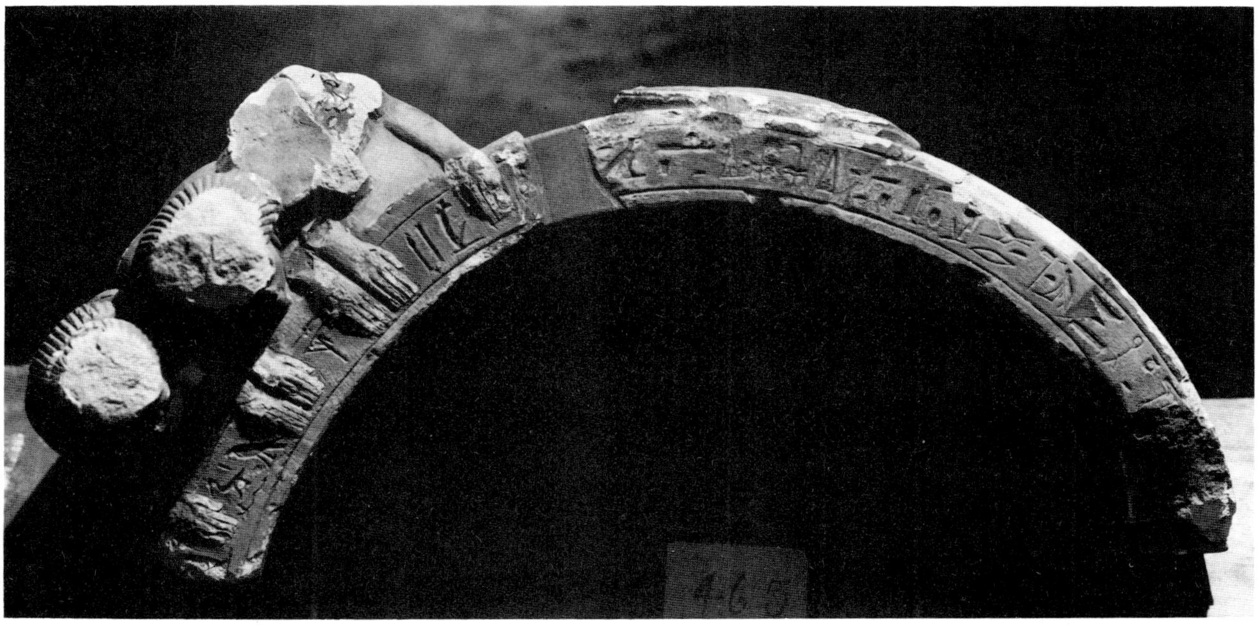

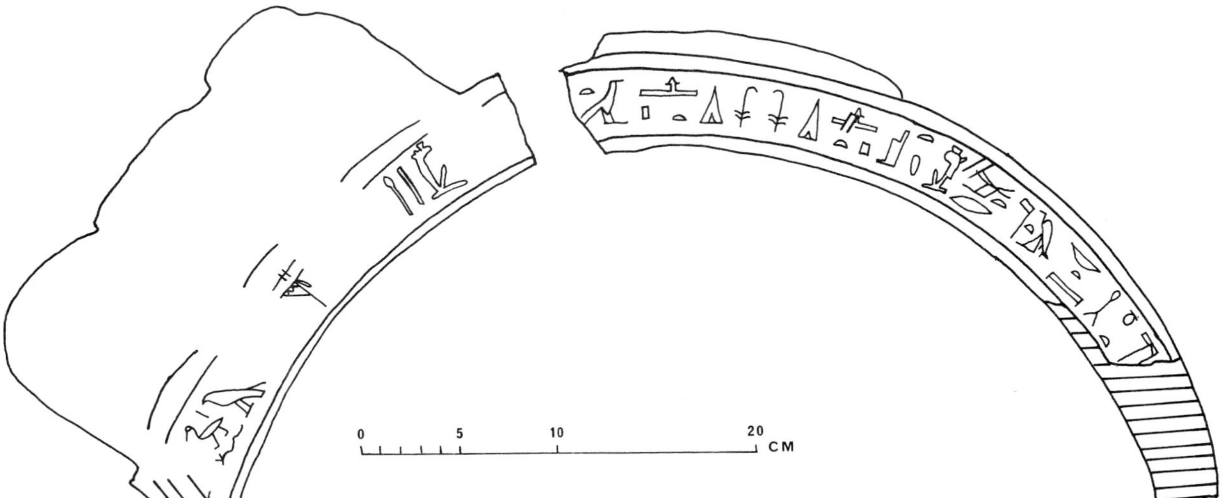

2. No. 465

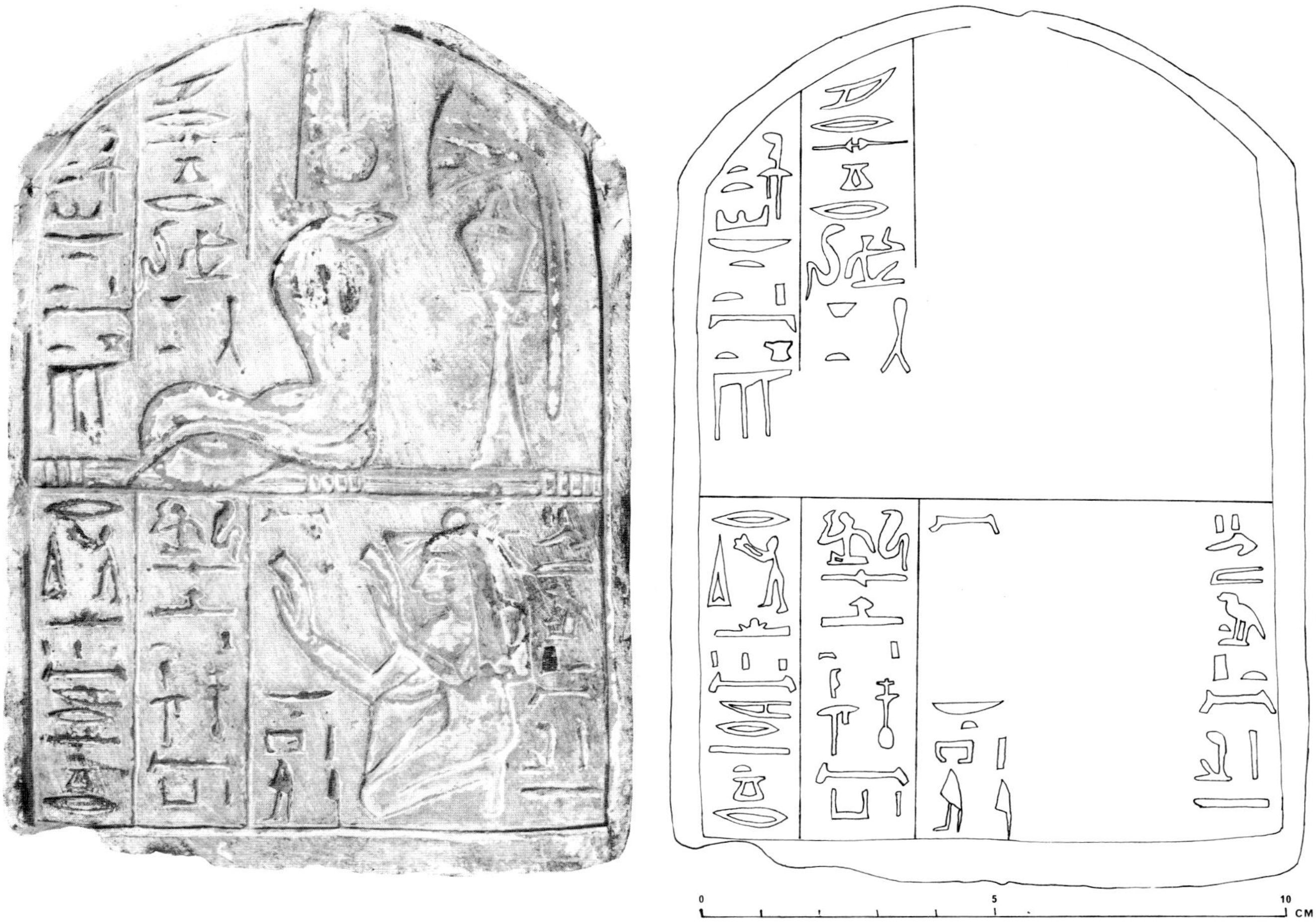

1. No. 8501

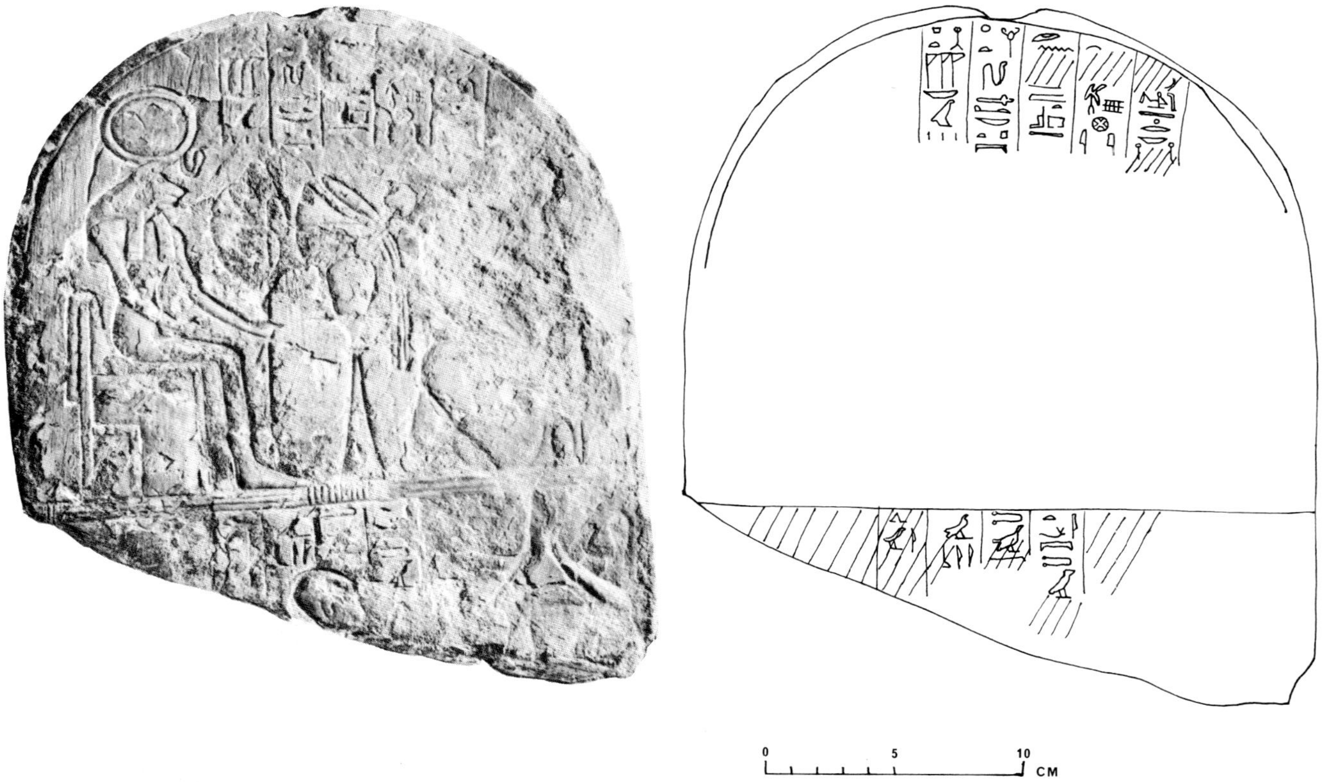

2. No. 810

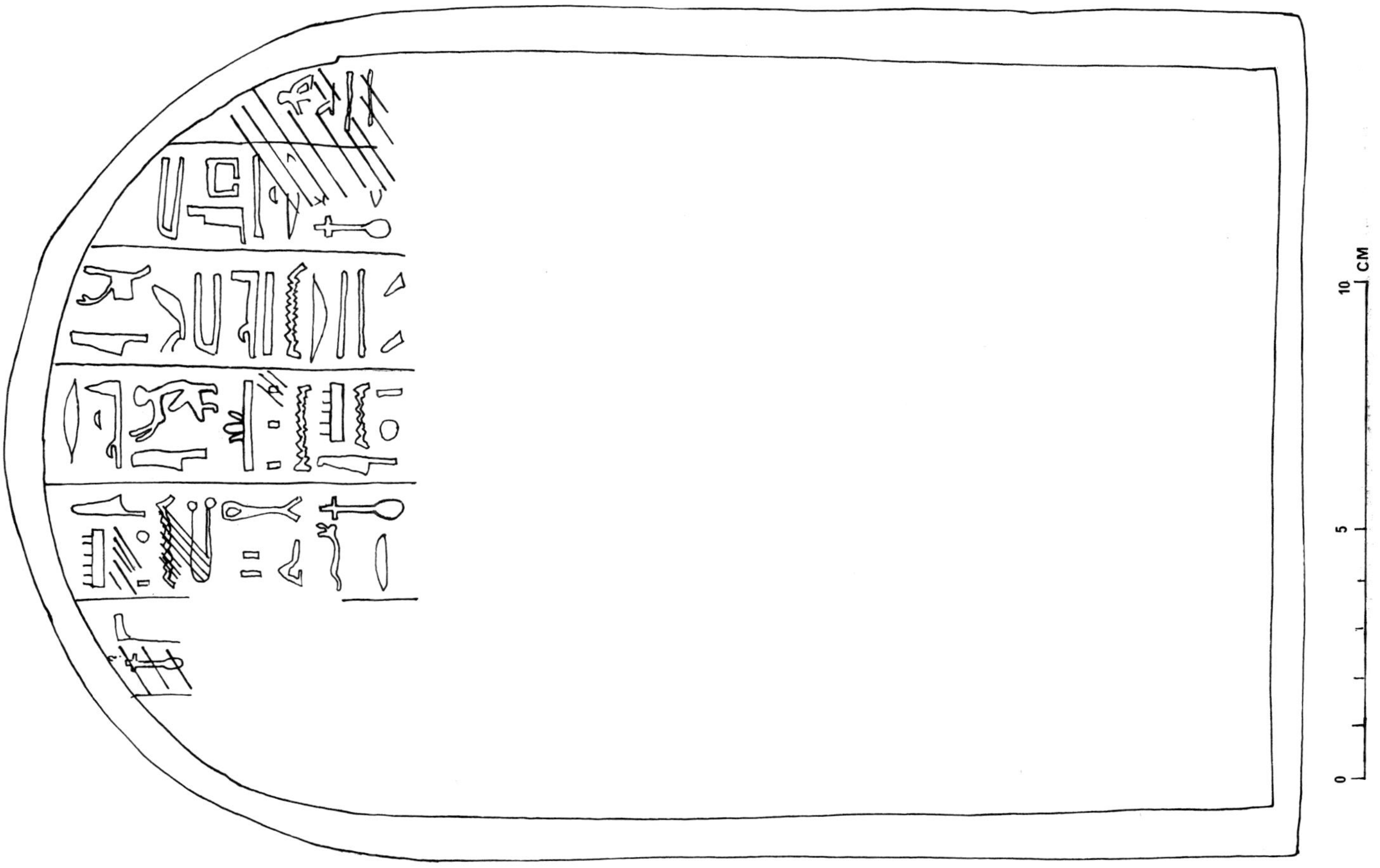

No. 65356

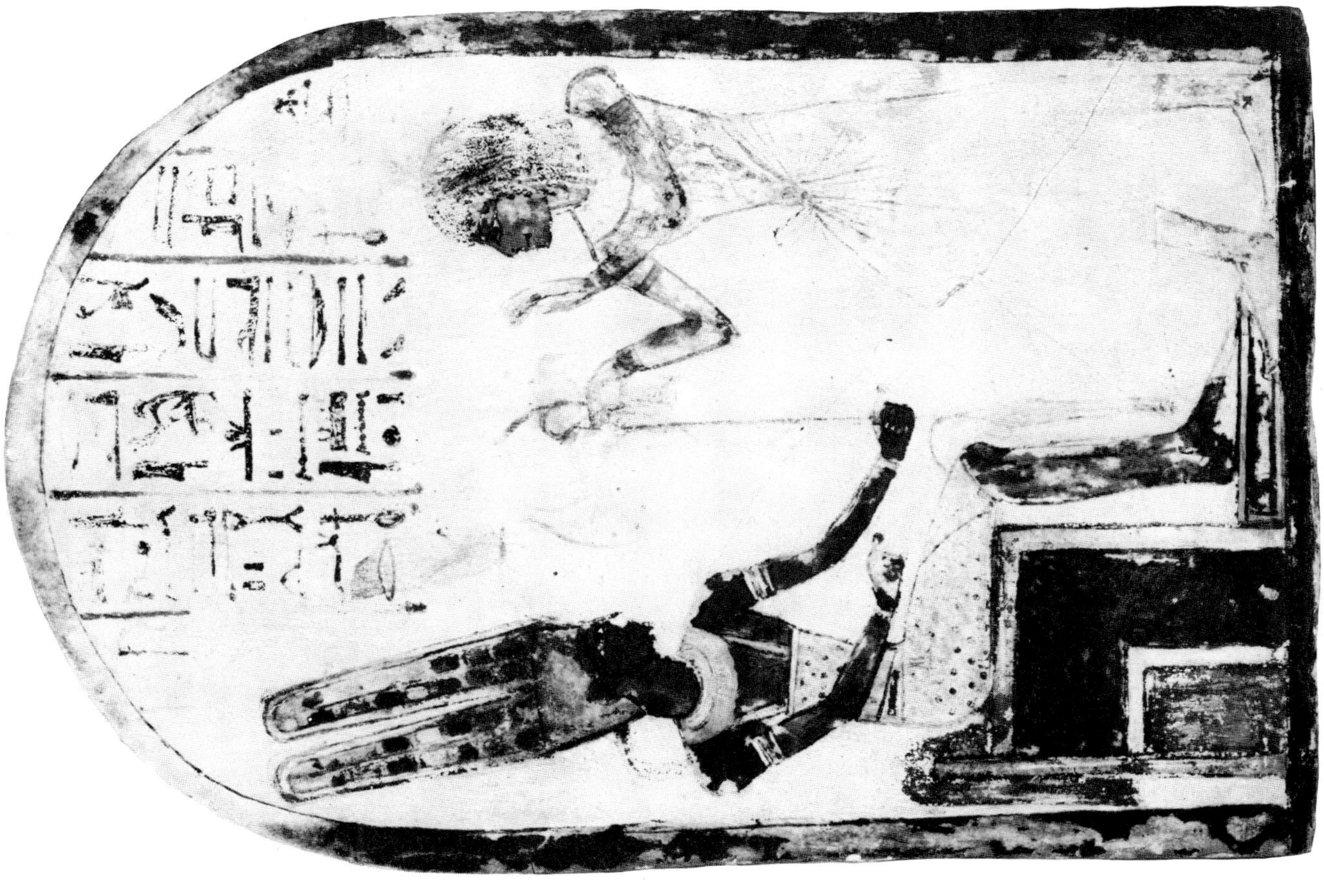

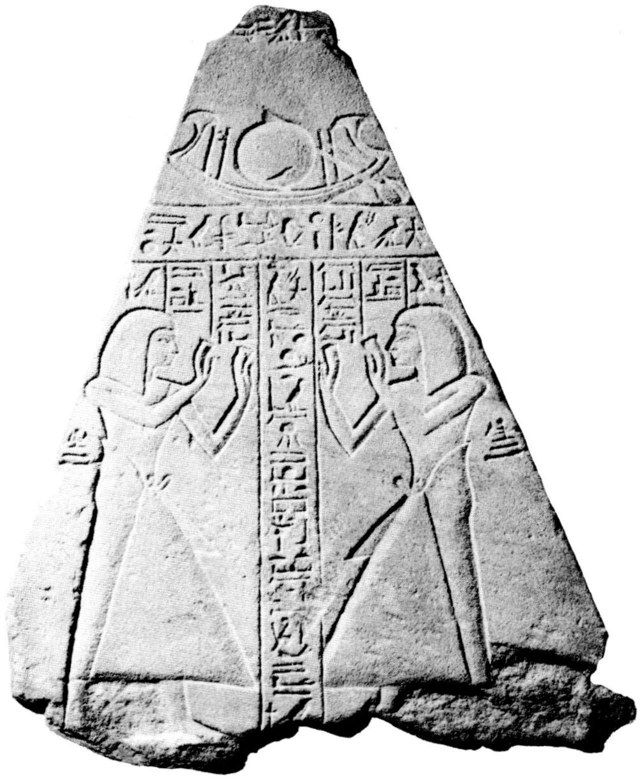

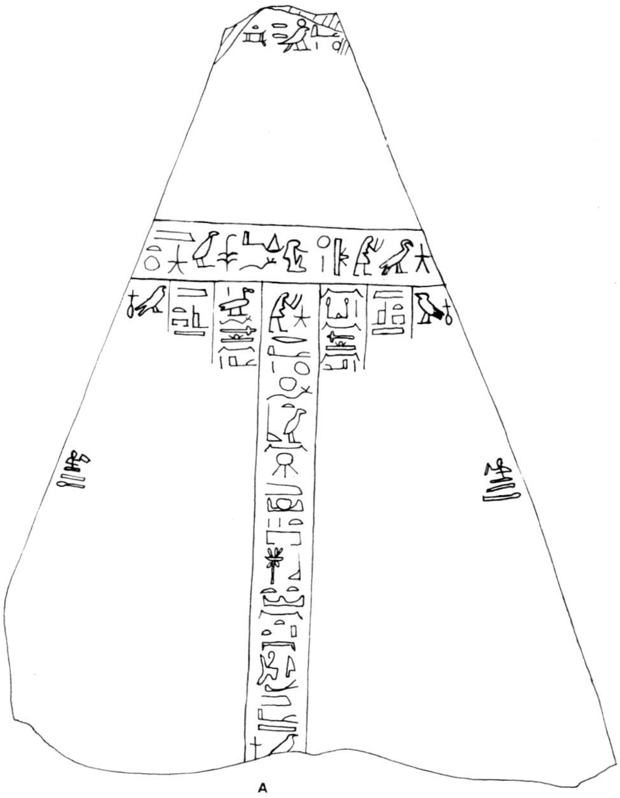

A

0 5 10 CM

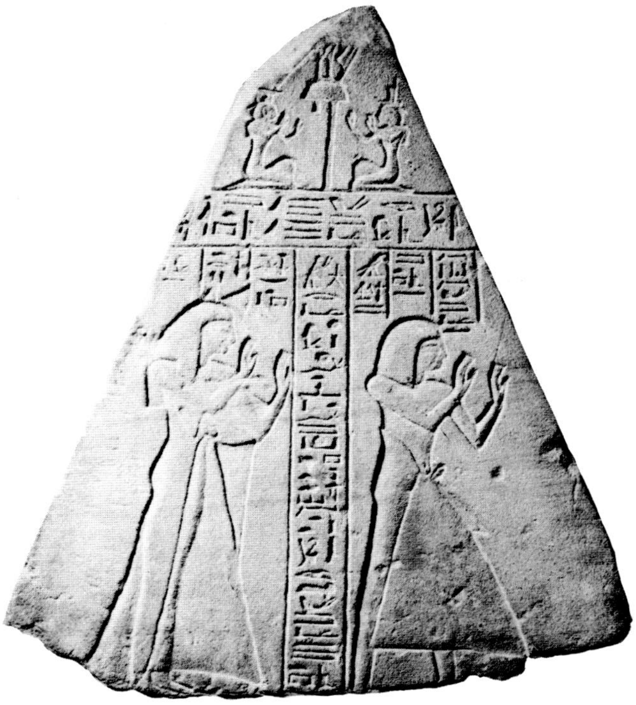

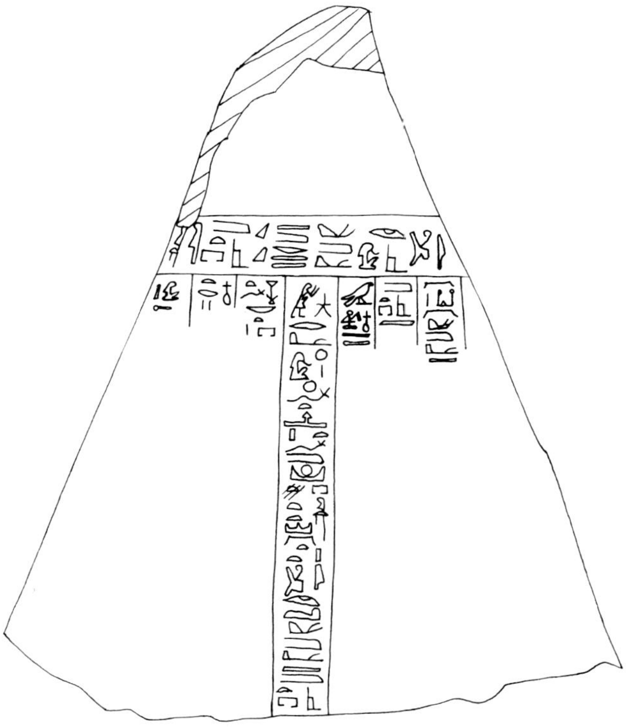

B

0 5 10 CM

No. 479

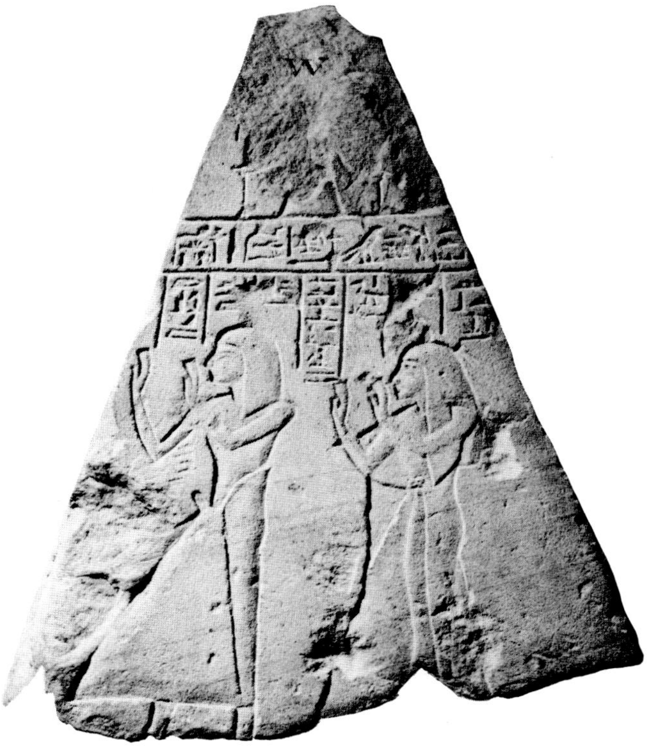

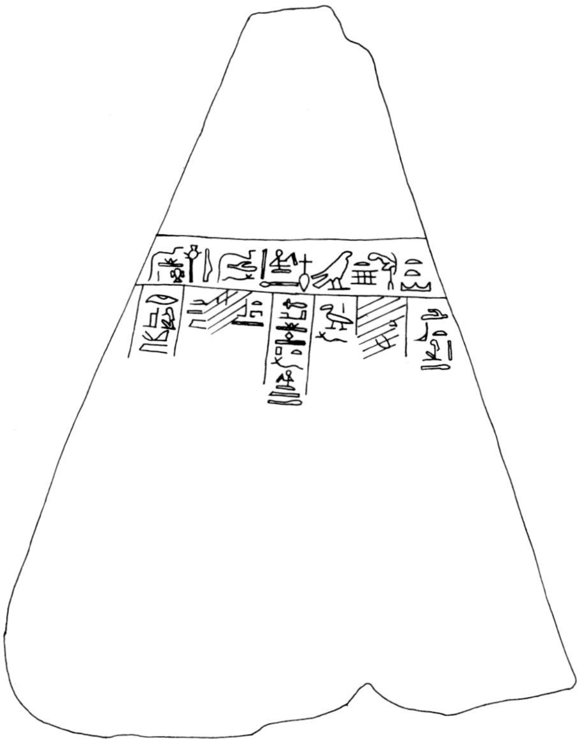

C

0 5 10 CM

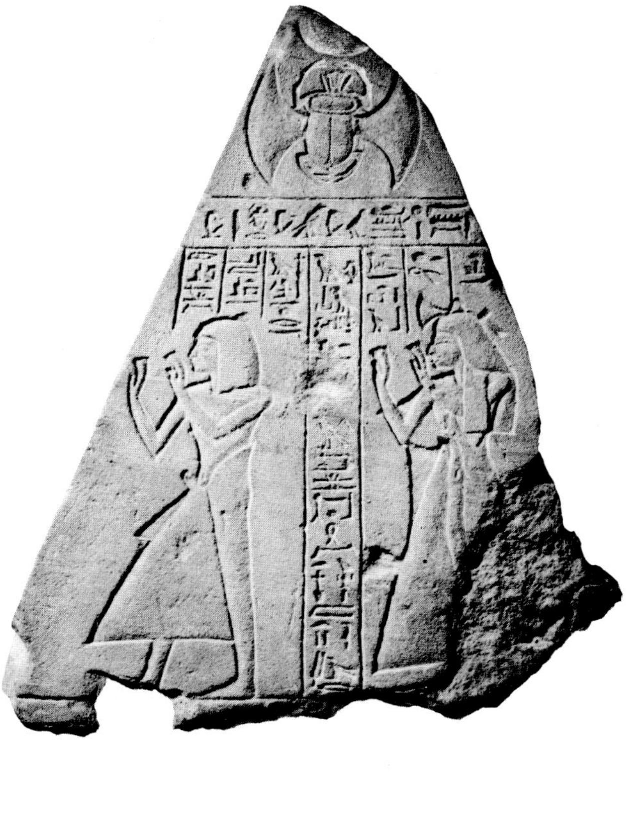

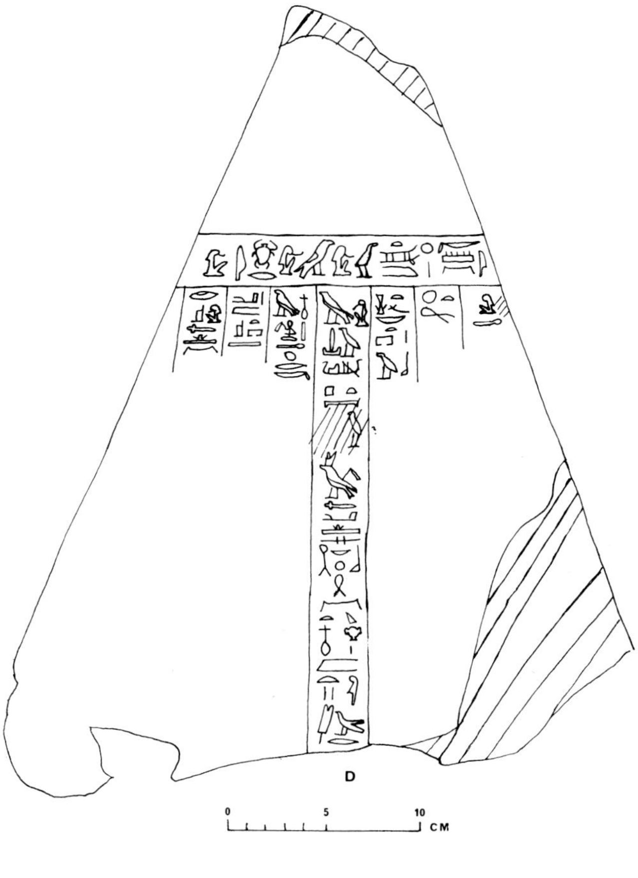

D

0 5 10 CM

No. 479

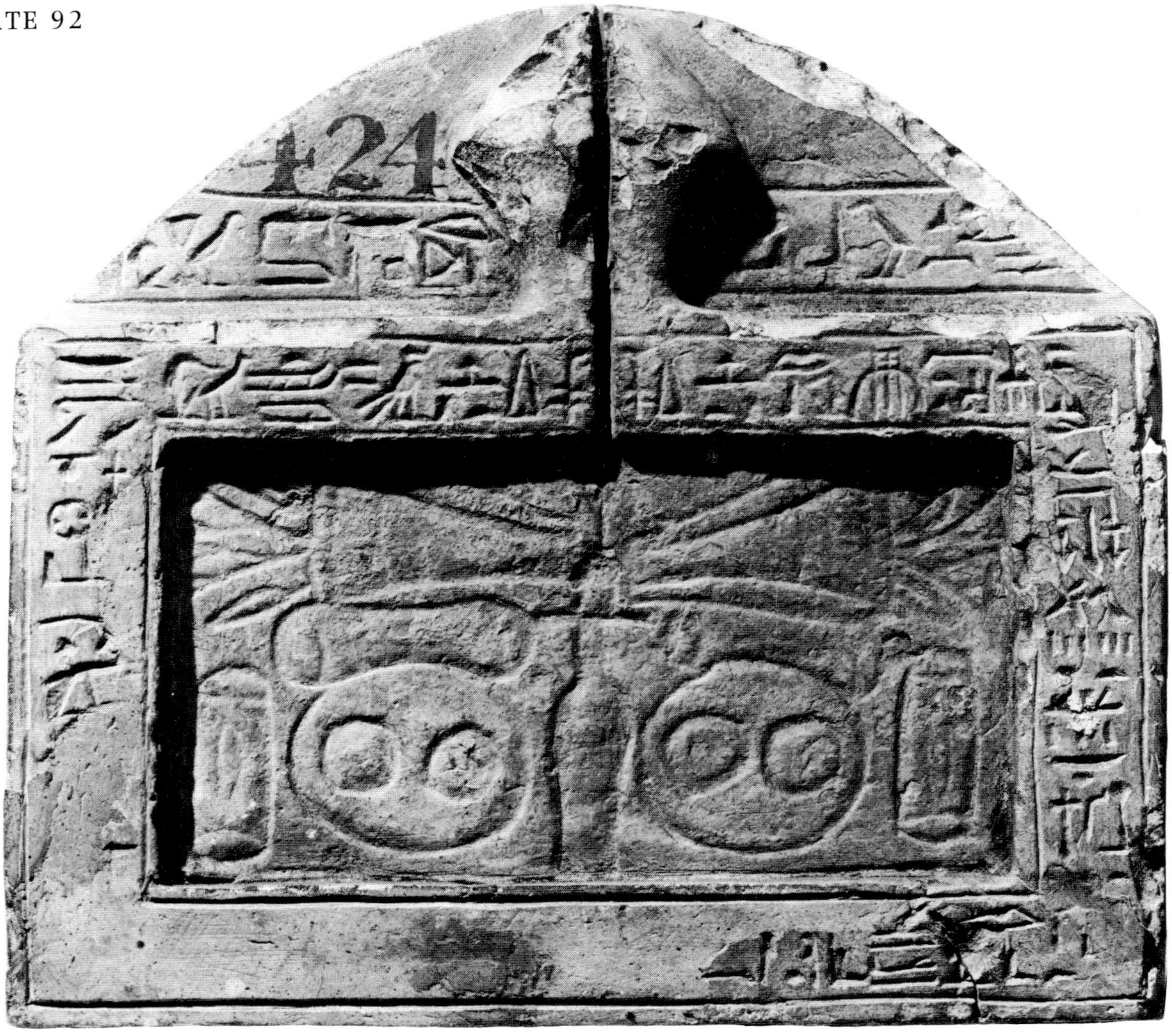

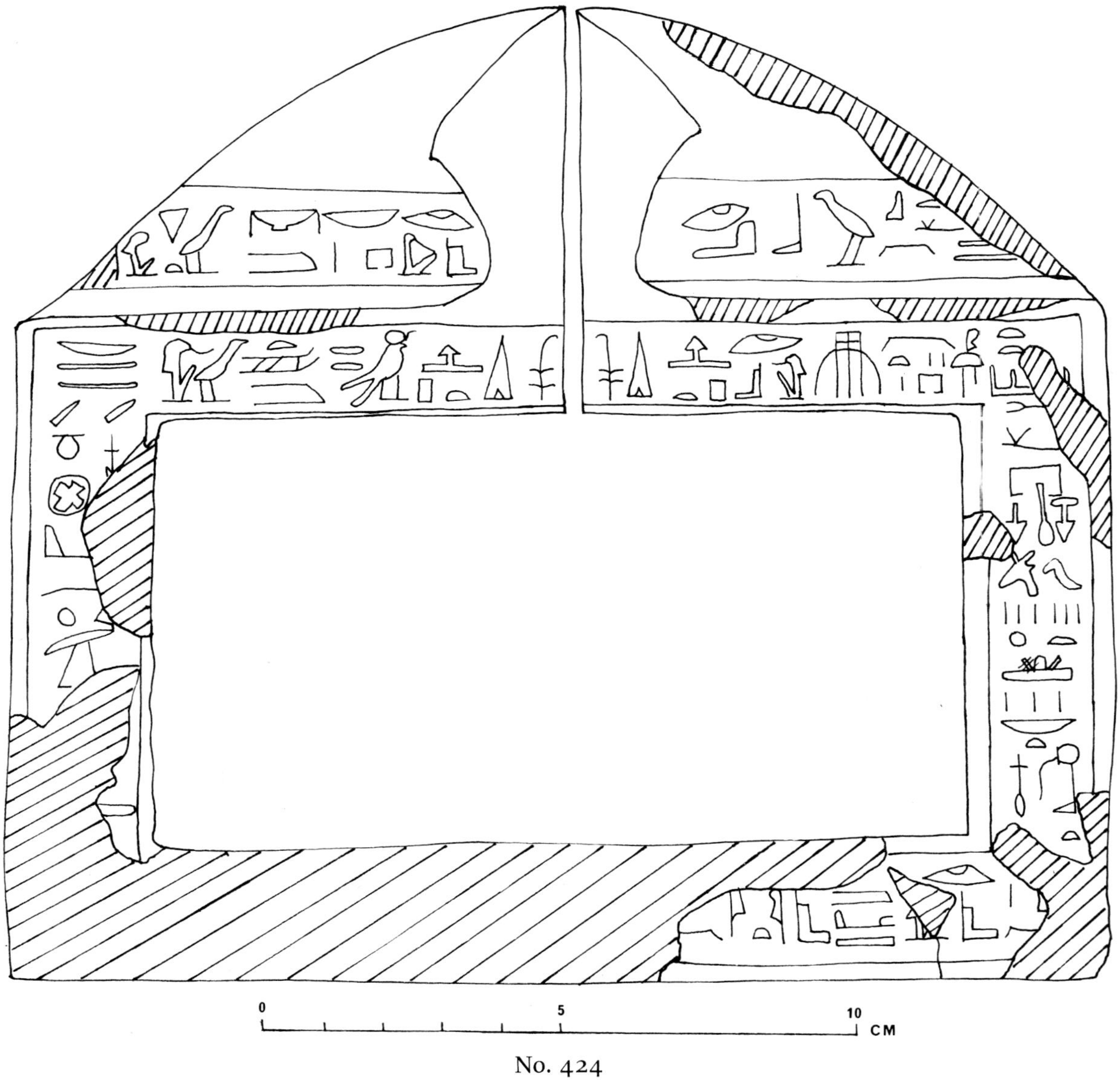

No. 424

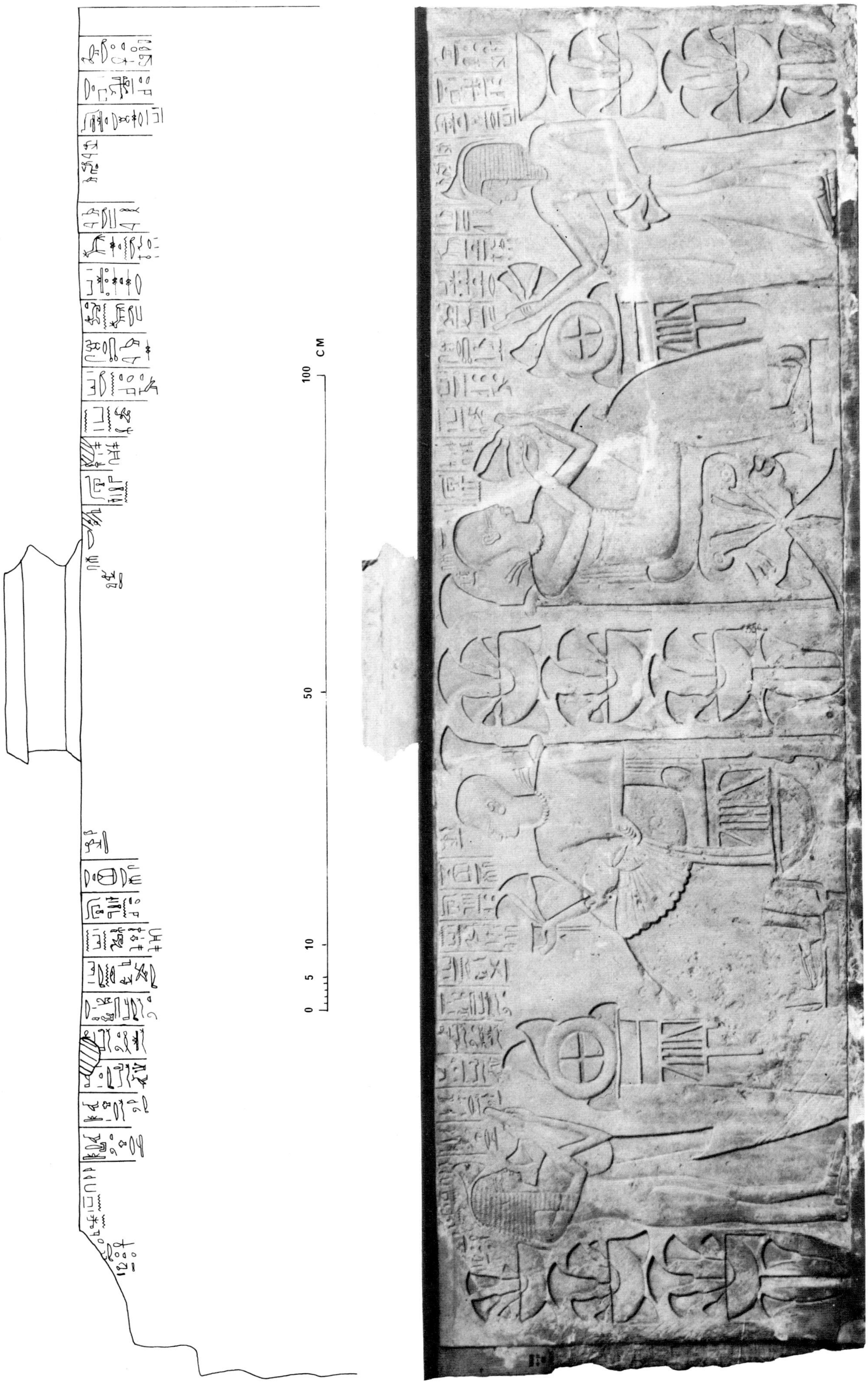

No. 1465

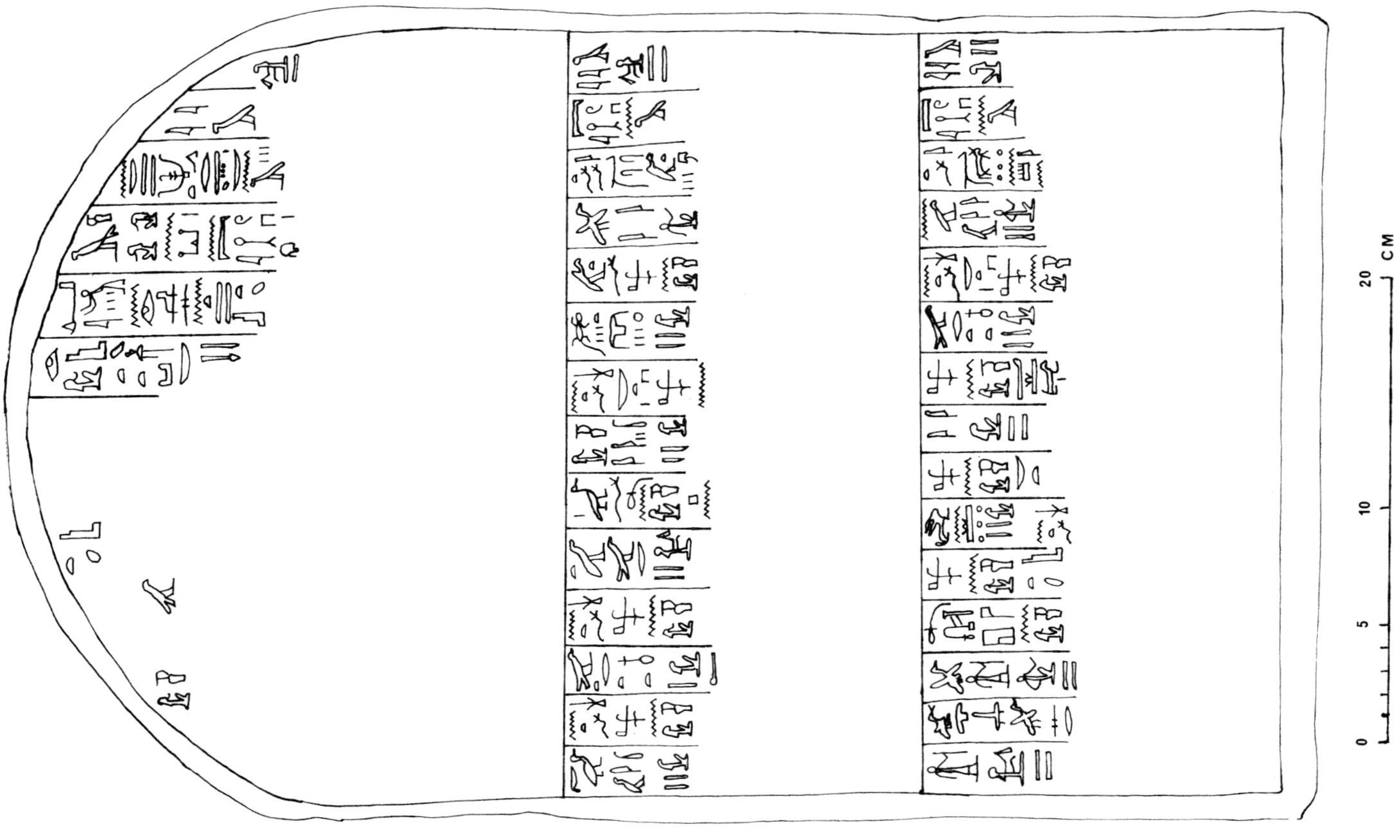

No. 795

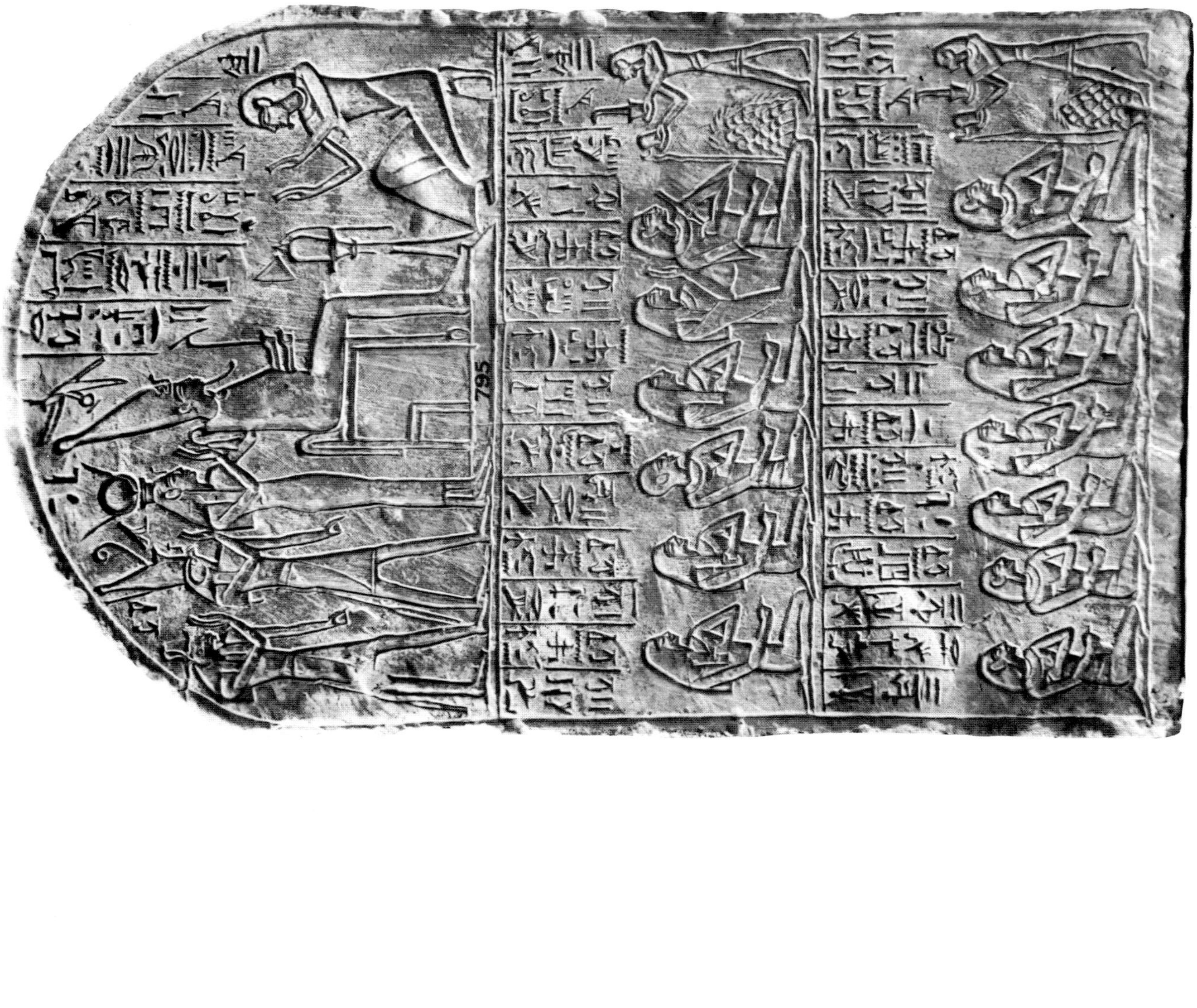

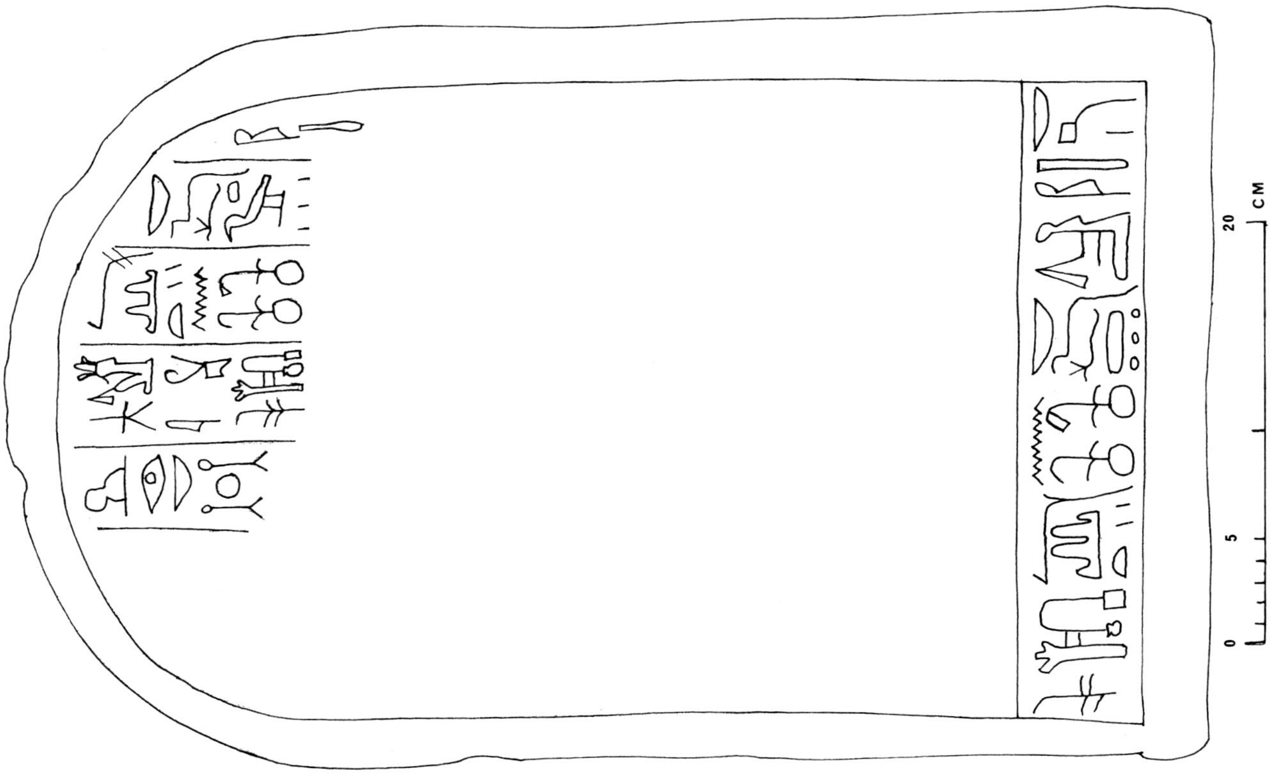

No. 793

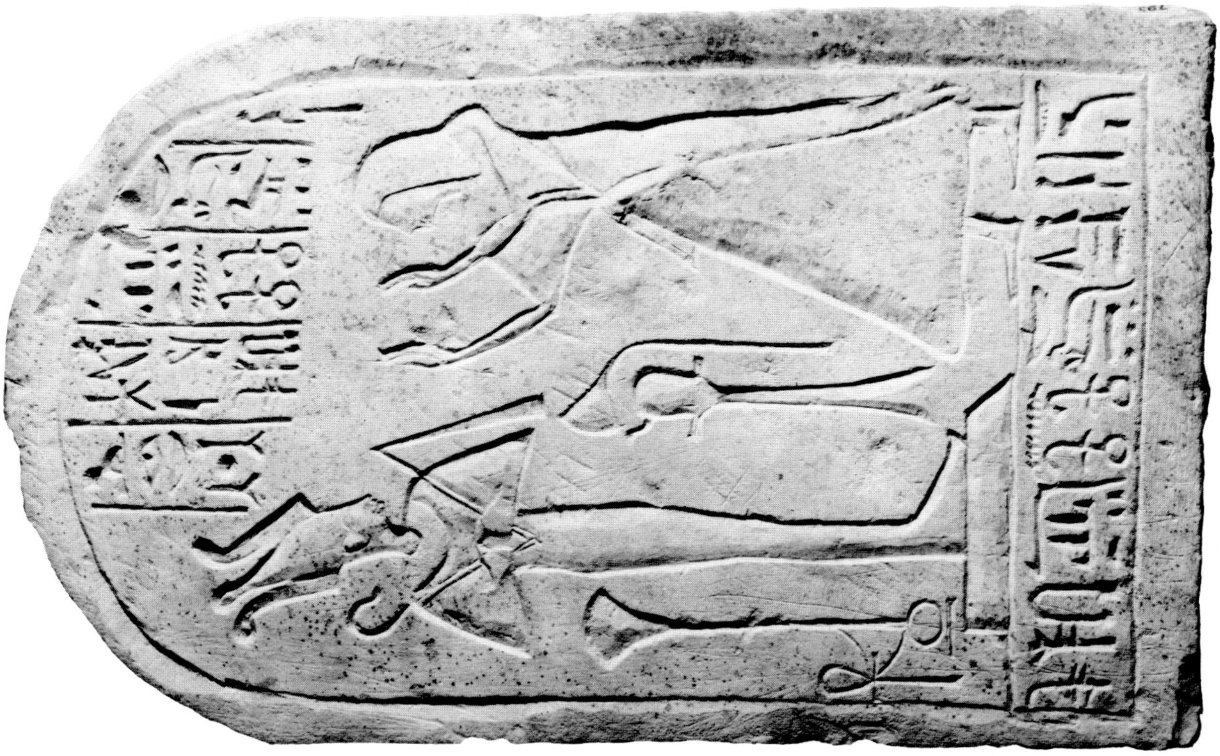

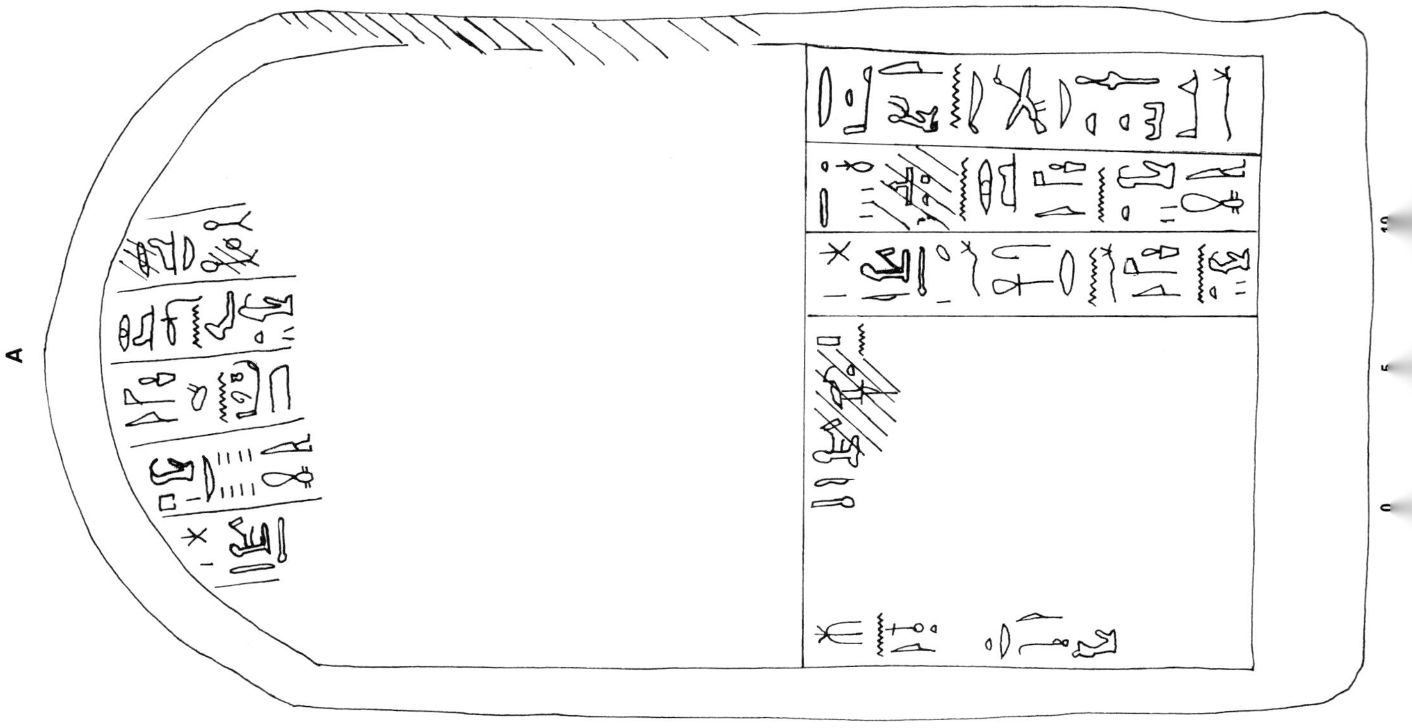

No. 1680

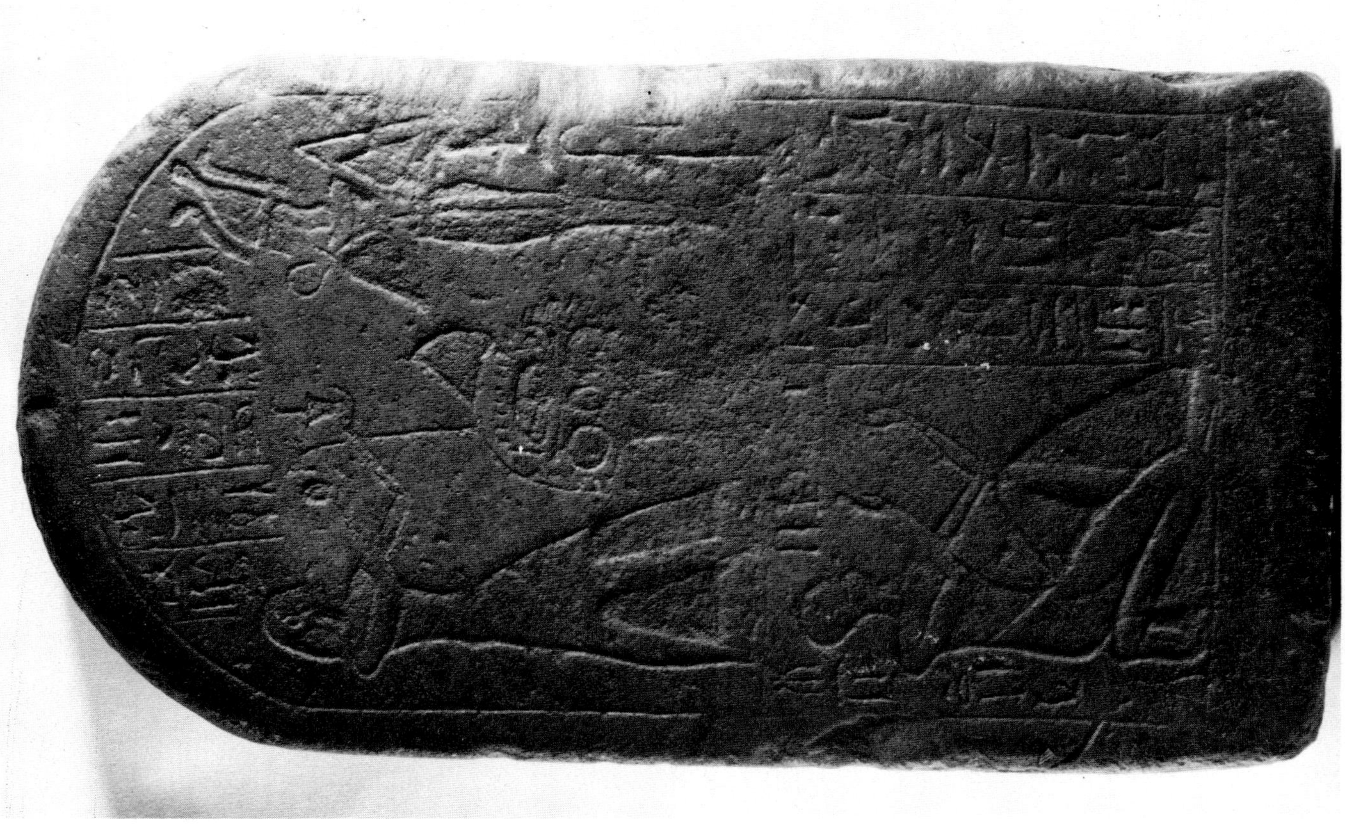

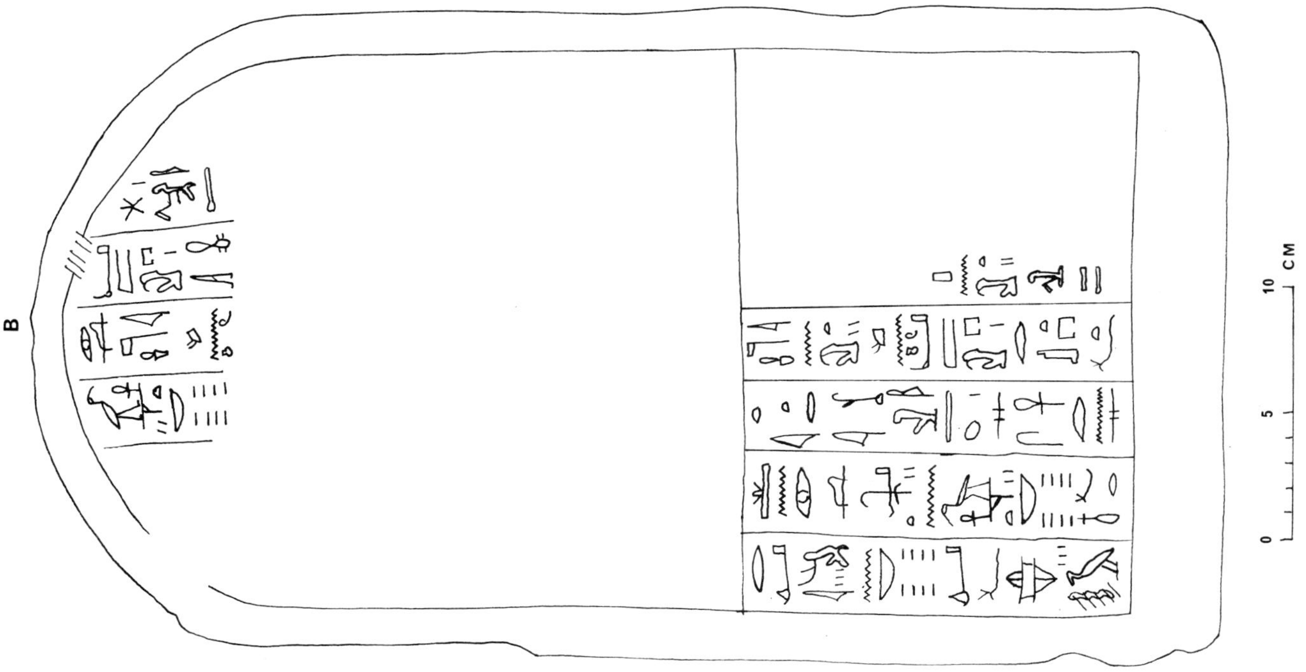

No. 1680

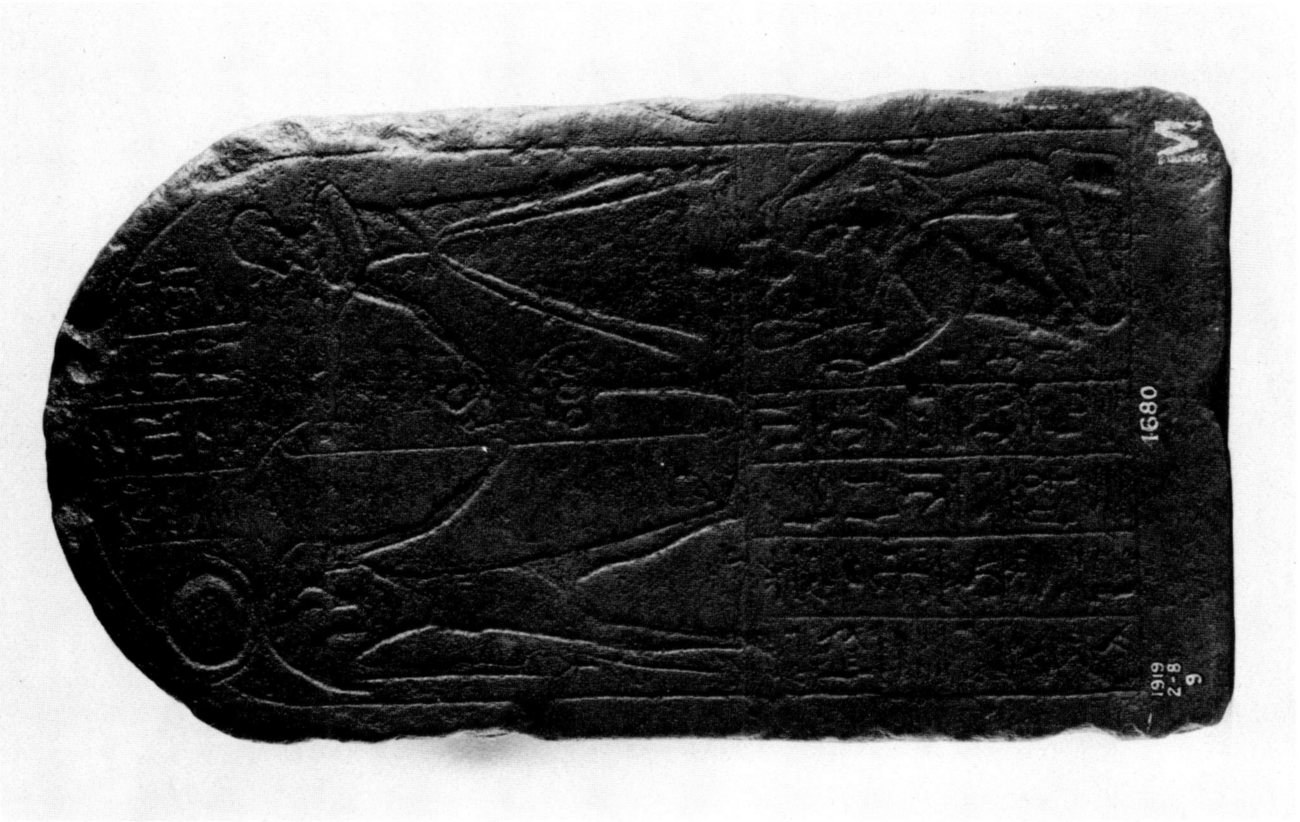

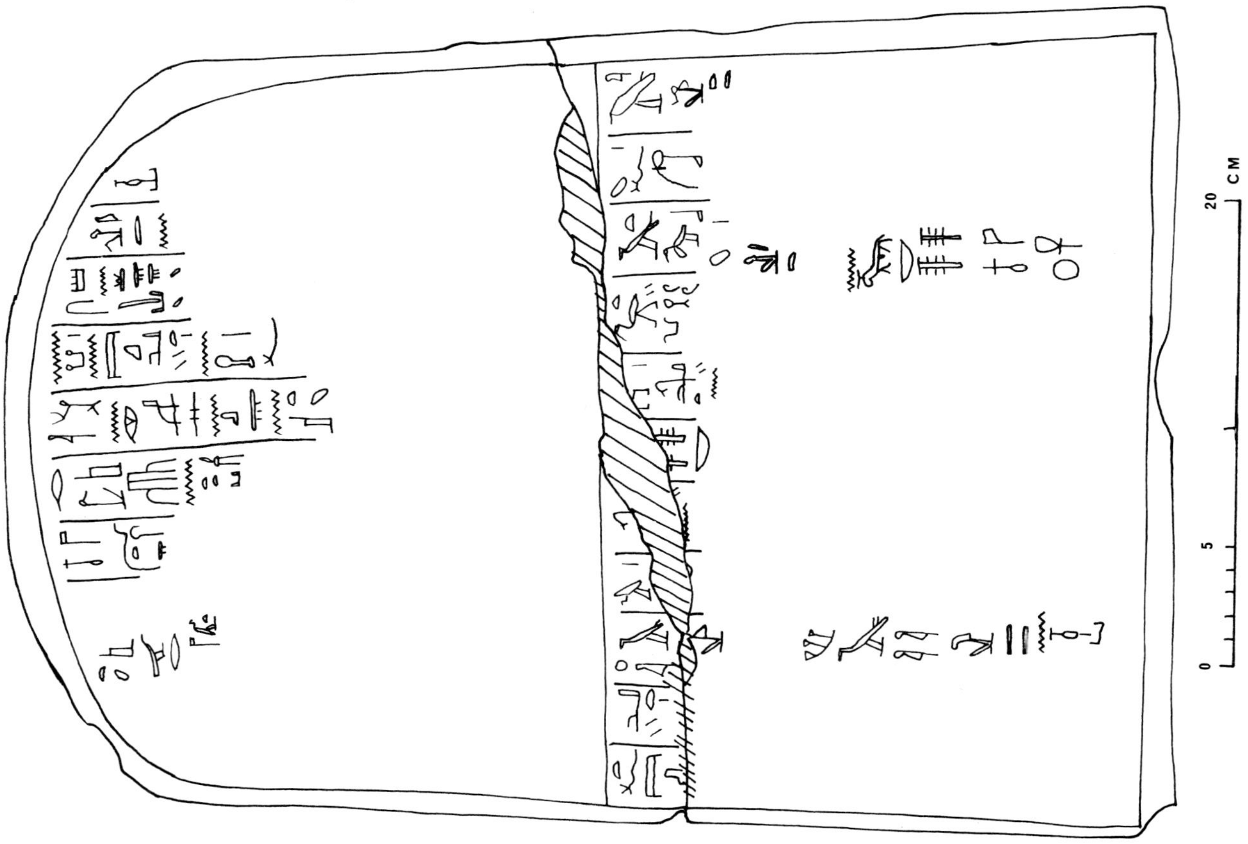

No. 312

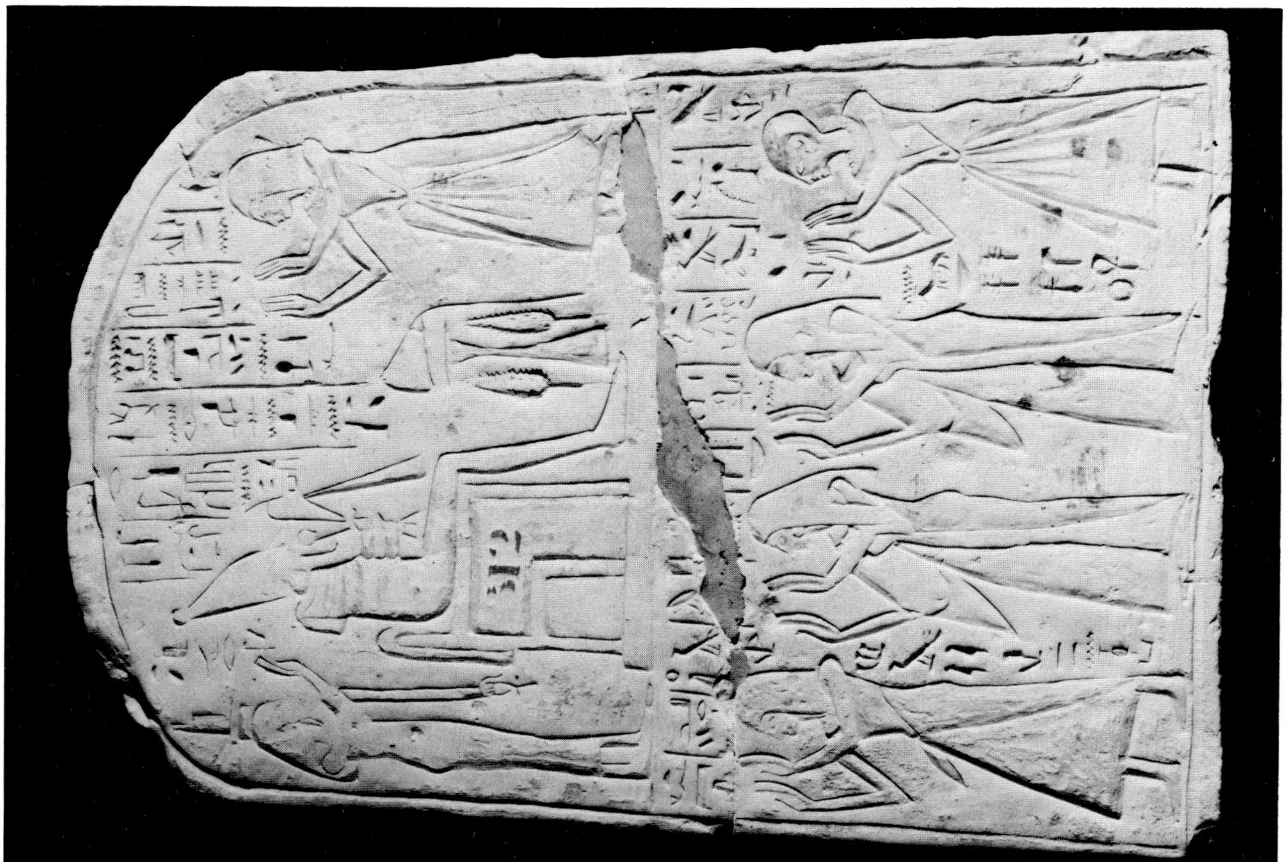

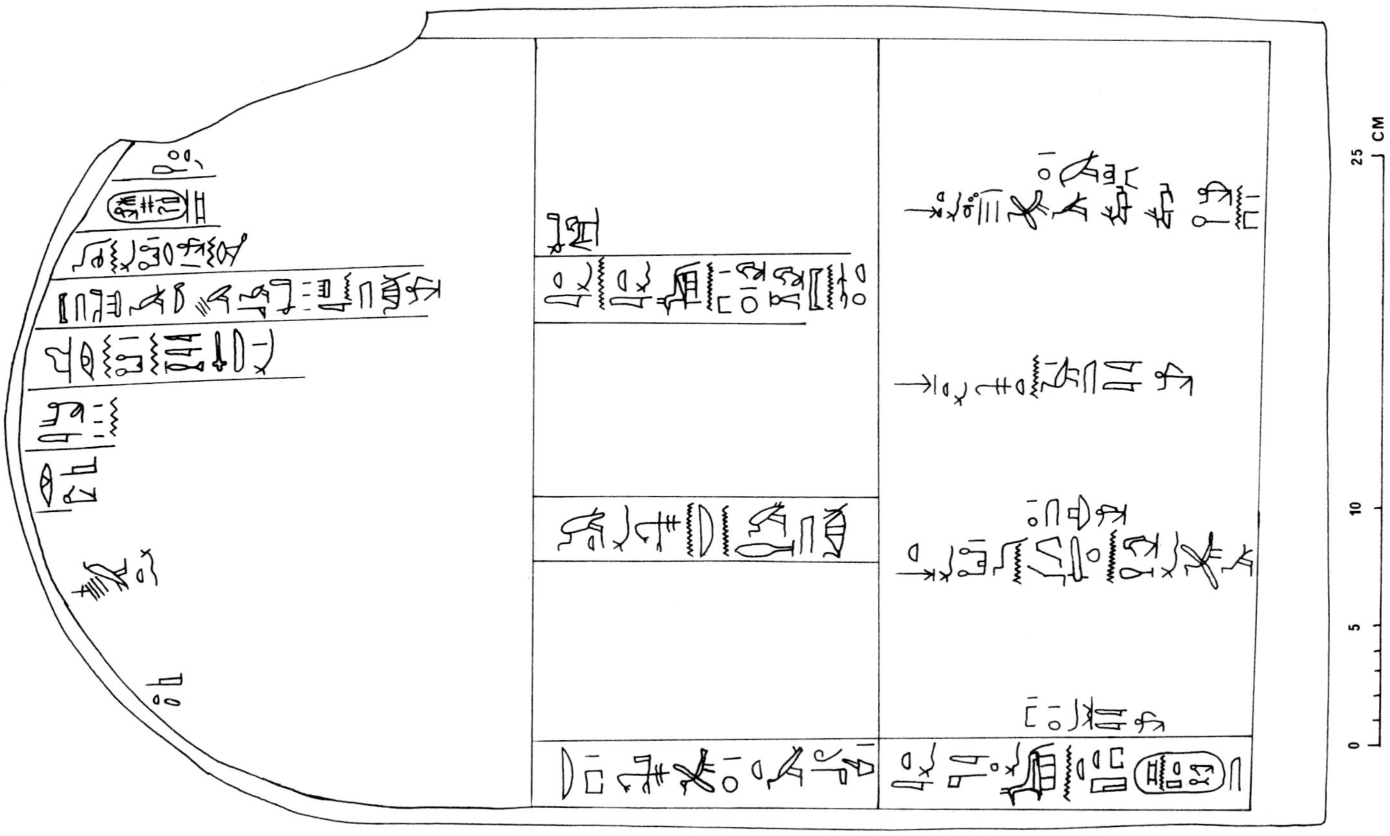

No. 1183

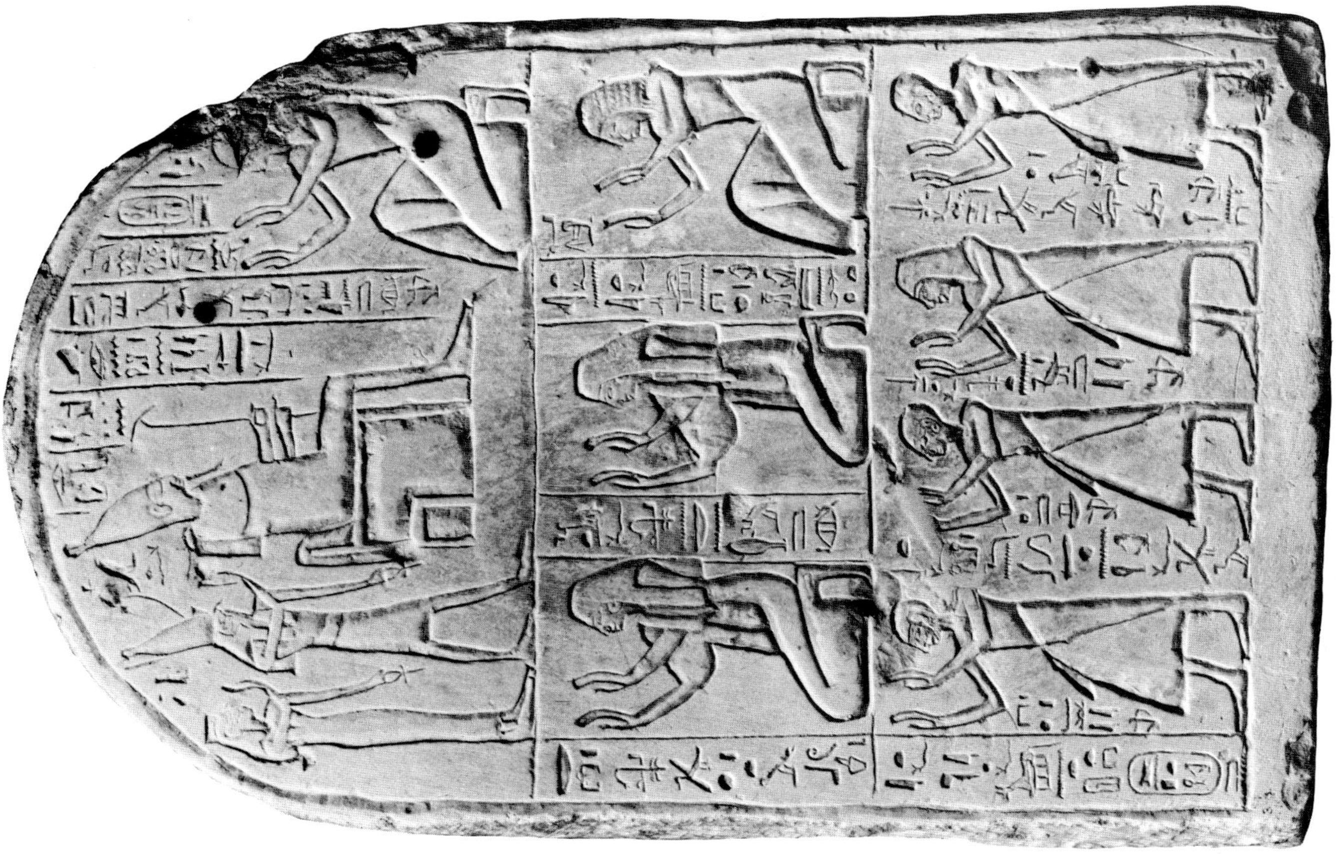

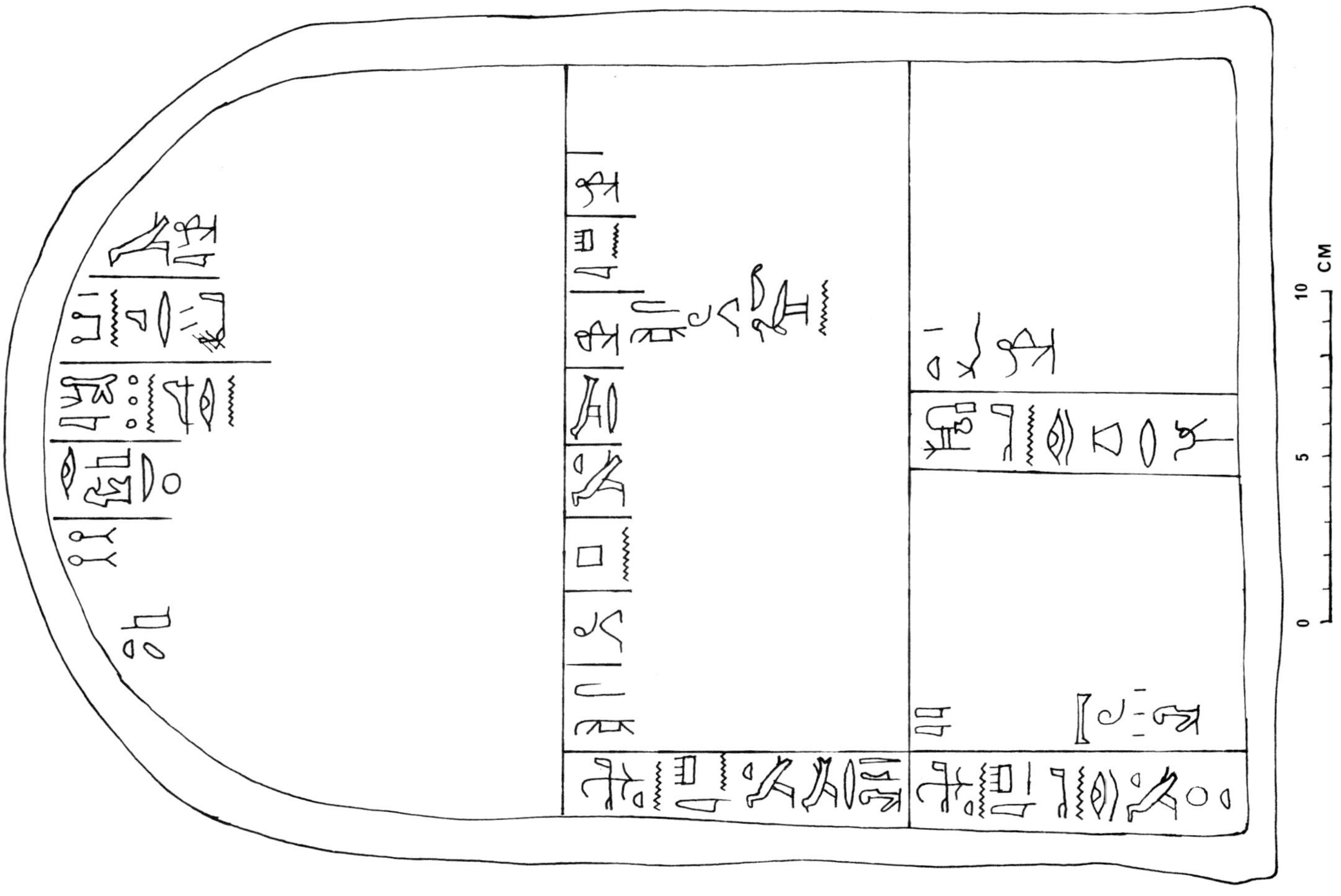

No. 327

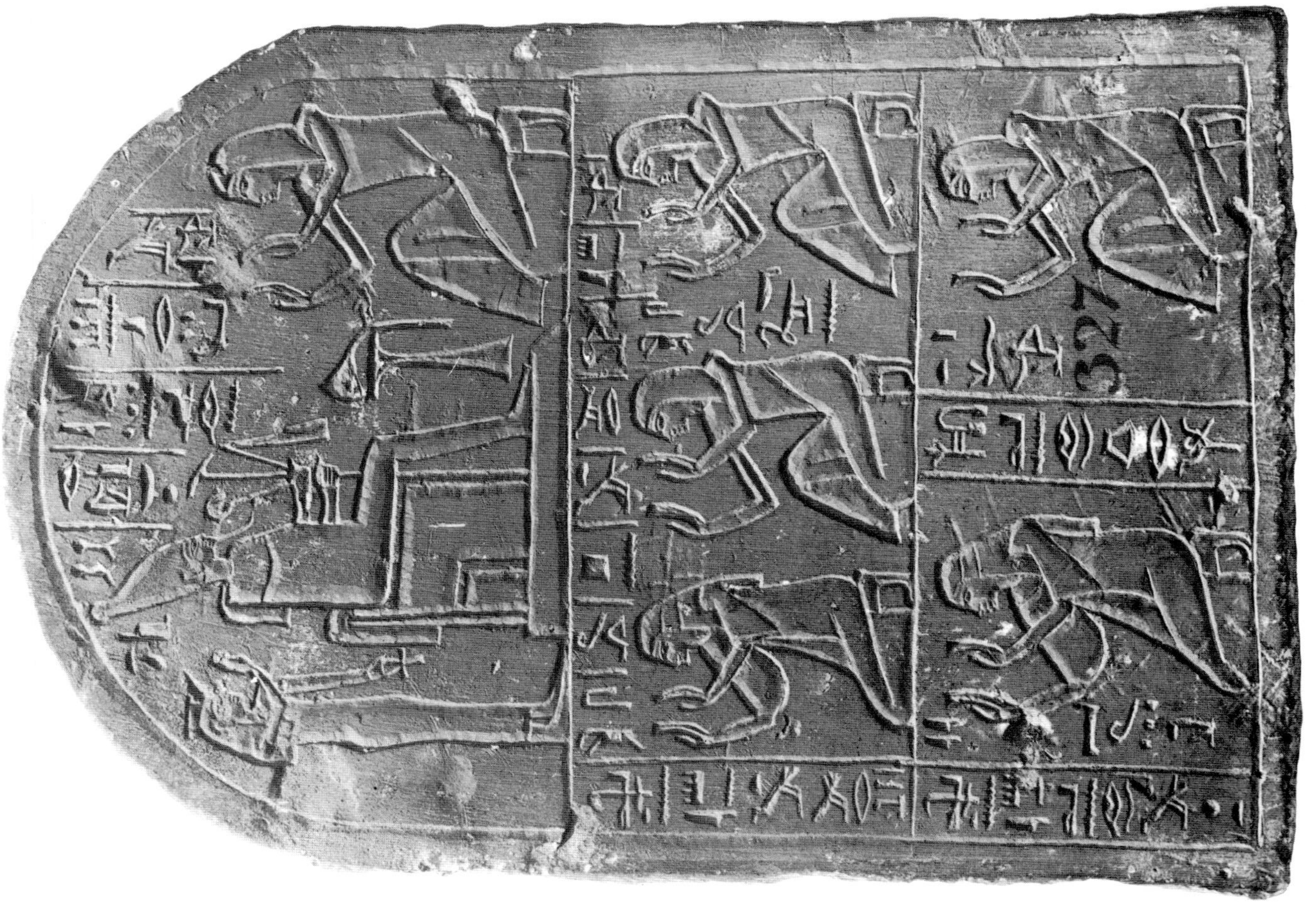